GUIDELINES FOR THE FUTURE

HUMAN
– and anti-human –
VALUES IN
CHILDREN'S BOOKS

A CONTENT RATING INSTRUMENT FOR
EDUCATORS AND CONCERNED PARENTS

Council on Interracial Books for Children

PREPARED BY THE
CIBC RACISM AND SEXISM
RESOURCE CENTER FOR EDUCATORS

Published by the
Racism and Sexism Resource Center for Educators
A Division of the
Council on Interracial Books for Children, Inc.
1841 Broadway, New York, N.Y. 10023

ACKNOWLEDGMENTS

Many people, for many years, have thought and written about criteria for judging children's books. This volume has built upon the contributions of Nancy Larrick, Isabelle Suhl, Albert V. Schwartz, Antonia Pérez and Rae Alexander. Special insights came from Betita Martinez. Essential to the project were Jean Carey Bond, Lyla Hoffman, Joyce Toney and Virginia Rice. And the Council reviewers: Joyce Arkhurst, Jose Armaz, Lydia Bassett, Rustin Basturni, Norman Bober, Donna Brown, Naomi Brown, Diane M. Burns, Jane Califf, Rochelle Chandler, Jimmie Durham, Clarice Erricsson, Adrian Felton, Carmen Figueroa, Liz Fong, Michiko Fromartz, Barbara Furukawa, Irma Garcia, Nikki Grimes, Lyla Hoffman, Marjorie Johnson, Ina King, Vickie Lawrence, Johann Lee, Donna Lippman, Elizabeth Martinez, Jacqueline Moniquette, Emily Moore, Betty Nyangoni, Sue Ribner, Judy Richardon, Lynne Rosenthal, Porfirio Sanchez, Albert V. Schwartz, Debria Smith, EdCelina Snowden, Carol Snyder, Patricia Spence, Dotty Starks, Gelvin Stevenson, Joyce Toney, Harry Wallace, Elizabeth Young, Taye Brooks Zerihoun.

And neither criteria nor a Council on Interracial Books for Children would have been possible without the original impetus of Stanley Faulkner, Franklin Folsom and Lillian Moore.

So we offer many thanks to these many people.

Beryle Banfield, President
Bradford Chambers, Director
Council on Interracial Books for Children, Inc.

iii

CONTENTS

(Continued)

v

INDEX

ABOUT THE GROUP

THAT PREPARED THIS VOLUME

The Council was founded in 1966 by writers, editors, illustrators, teachers and parents committed to affecting basic change in books and other media. Council programs are designed to promote learning materials that embody the principles of cultural pluralism. Council programs include:

The Interracial Books Bulletin *features critical analyses of racist and sexist stereotypes prevalent in children's books and learning materials.* It reviews new children's books and educational materials, publishes the findings of Council studies and research projects and recommends materials for combatting racism and sexism at home, in libraries and in the classroom.

Consciousness-raising conferences, workshops and university courses for parents, publishers and educational professionals. Resource specialists and scholars representing Black, Puerto Rican, Chicano, Asian American, Native American and women of all races focus on the stereotypes, distortions and omissions commonly found in children's trade and text books and on the development of new criteria for analyzing educational materials.

A *contest for third world writers* previously unpublished in the field of children's literature. The annual contest offers cash awards to encourage the publication of socially significant and bias-free books.

A *national resource and referral center*—the Racism and Sexism Resource Center for Educators. The Center collects, adapts and publishes books, pamphlets, lesson plans and teaching strategies to eliminate racism and sexism and to develop pluralism in education. The Center also provides consultants and conducts teacher training programs. A catalog listing all materials and services of the Resource Center will be sent on request.

Council on Interracial Books for Children
1841 Broadway, New York, N.Y. 10023

TERMINOLOGY

Language, reflecting society, is no more static nor sacred than is anything else in the political arena. In our racist and sexist society, our decisions about word usage are political decisions. When one uses the male pronoun to mean both sexes, one is making a political statement. The use of "Negro" or "Colored" today has clear political connotations. Both the words we use and the connotations those words imply are in constant state of change, as our society's consciousness of racism and sexism develop.

Words which sound "funny" to us one day, become comfortable in a short time if we are truly determined to rid our language and our society of sexism and racism. But the process must be constant. While this book was being printed we decided not to use "heroine" but to use "hero" for both sexes. This is because we—along with many feminist groups—believe that "feminine" noun endings have been historically used to connote something "lesser than" the same words with "male" suffixes. (But "heroine" still appears on many pages , which were set before our decision was made.)

This book always upper cases "Black" when it represents "African American." When "white" stands for "white American person" it is lower-cased. Should we speak of a particular group of white Americans, such as Polish Americans, we would, of course use the capital letter.

Other terms are still in a state of flux and this book represents confusion on designation of Native American as against "Indian" and "nation" or "people" as against "tribe.." Some of our Native American reviewers used the latter terms. However, most comments on the subject by Native Americans suggest that white people NOT use "Indian," "tribe" and a host of other such words.

In any case, using words as political weapons is a mind stretching exercise. We recommend it.

EVALUATING CONTENT

1. The Mirror and the Matrix

"Where are you coming from?" people ask these days, and it is a good beginning. We are coming, first of all, from some basic realities as perceived in our experience. Let us start with the fact that children's books are not merely a matter of text (which may be lively, entertaining and stirring, or not) plus pictures (which may be well-done or not). Children's books are not merely exciting, imaginative and full of good characters or the opposite. No; Hugh Lofting's modest Dr. Dolittle is actually a very political fellow and *Bright April,* by Marguerite De Angeli, sets forth an entire ideology in her quiet way. No writer is just a reporter, and artists put more on paper than their eyes see.

Most of us who work with children's books know this. We realize that such books do carry a message—a moral, a value or set of values—and that they mold minds. But how often do we stop to consider the source of those values? Do they come from the personal beliefs of the writer? Do they come from the publisher's mind? If so, then we must ask in the persistent way of children themselves: where do *their* values come from?

We propose, in this book, that those values are not simply individual, not creatures of a series of vacuums, but that they rise from the total society. In any given society, children's books generally reflect the needs of those who dominate that society. A major need is to maintain and fortify the structure of relations between dominators and dominated. The prevailing values are supportive of the existing structure; they are the dominator's values.

We further propose that children's books play an active part in maintaining that structure by molding future adults who will accept it.

1

Today, we see how such books can also mold human beings with counter-values that may help to restructure the society. Children's books are both mirror and matrix.

Stop right there, some will say; you are talking about brain-washing. It is only in totalitarian societies that books are *used* by a class of people to suit its purposes; in a democracy, books just reflect the interests of the majority. Sad to say, examination of thousands of children's books published in the United States over the years does not bear up this belief. The value-system that dominates in them is very white, very contemptuous of females except in traditional roles, and very oriented to the needs of the upper classes. It is very geared to individual achievement rather than community well-being. It is a value-system that can serve only to keep people of color, poor people, women and other dominated groups "in their place," because directly or indirectly it makes children—our future adults—think that this is the way things should be. So powerful is that system that authors can write *totally unaware* of its influence upon them. More often than not, they are unconscious tools of that system.

If all this seems shocking, let us stop to think: how often have we attended a wedding ceremony and never stopped to think about those words: "I now pronounce you man and wife." Why *man* and *wife*, which reduces the female to a person defined by her relation to another, while the male retains his independent identity? And how many of us speak of it being "a black day," without realizing that those words equate black with bad and thus help to perpetuate racism? There is a whole world of conditioning and control around us that most people have not even perceived. This is not to say that words in themselves can be the cause of sexism or racism; they only reflect those realities. But they are important, for they condition people—especially children—to accept the maintenance of sexism and racism.

The second place that we are "coming from" is that we have no desire to see children's books that would solely help the dominated get a bigger piece of the pie. We don't like the pie, period. We are not interested in seeing certain people win a place in the status quo, the present social structure; we are challenging the structure itself. Very often, for example, the study of "women's accomplishments" in history has a give-me-more-pie approach and fails to question the very definition of "accomplishments." We should not study merely the few women who have overcome sexist barriers, but examine the very standards that have excluded other women's actions from being considered "accomplishments."

There is one more important place that we are "coming from," and it is closely related to the previous points. We propose that most of what has been labelled *human nature* in our society really should be called "culturally conditioned behavior." The idea predominates that jealousy, possessiveness, competitiveness and war (between nations, peoples, classes and sexes) are inevitable because of this invisible, all-powerful force called "human nature." Yet actual experience, in the U.S. and other countries, shows that those human tendencies we consider immutable are in fact variable. Experiences here show the potential for change. So do reports of visitors to countries where children are cared for communally and constantly taught cooperation as a value (with the society as a whole also placing its highest value on collective rather than merely individual achievement).

If we did not believe that most "human nature" is in fact cultural conditioning, there would be little point in publishing this book. If we believed that human beings are doomed to continue crippling and destroying each other without end, there would be no point at all. But we do not; we firmly believe that when the cultural environment is changed, people will change. We reject that vision of the future which portrays human beings as oxen forever yoked to the painful weight of so-called "human nature." We reject it for the sake of our own lives and, above all, for the generations of children now and tomorrow.

We do not see this view of life as some impossible dream. History has shown that value-systems, like social systems, are not static. Human values change when society changes, and because society changes.

The last decade in the United States has seen strong pressures on the society to change, to become less oppressive for large groups of people. These pressures have, in turn, brought major upheavals in concepts about social relations. If many people now realize there is something wrong with "a black day" or "man and wife," it is because Black people and women, as groups, have strongly challenged the status quo and its values.

Concepts about race and sex relationships are presently the major areas of upheaval, but we have also seen other challenges. People— primarily young people—are questioning the dog-eat-dog, materialistic life style that prevails. We have seen factory workers and poor people of all colors, long suffering out-of-sight of the more privileged, now challenging the reason for that privilege. We have seen the aged speak out against the idea that "old" should be equated with forgotten, useless, half-witted. Developments in other countries have also inspired new insights, as more and more people have traveled and reported about societies where very different concepts prevail.

If we are honest with ourselves, we will admit that our whole structure of relations is rattling and creaking, as people of all types challenge its usefulness to humanity. The demand for a more humane structure and more humane values echoes across the land. Can those of us concerned with children and their books stand by, blind and deaf? We say no; let us listen to the challenge and re-examine those books.

For the mirror flashes with new images. The matrix trembles with change.

2. Goals and Targets

In an age of great and necessary upheaval, new educational materials—including children's books—must be developed. Failure to do so would be a betrayal of our children, for it would leave them stranded and lost in a changing world, unprepared to relate to that process of change. We propose that children's literature become a tool for the conscious promotion of human values that will help lead to greater human liberation. We are advocates of a society which will be free of racism, sexism, ageism, classism, materialism, elitism, and other negative values. We are advocates of a society in which all human beings have the true, not rhetorical, opportunity to realize their full human potential. We therefore frankly advocate books that will help achieve such a society and help prepare children for such a society.

We have named a number of "isms" as our targets; they form the criteria used in the evaluation of children's literature presented in this book. It is important to offer a definition of each, and some reasons why we see combatting each as necessary.

RACISM

Racism is the systematic oppression and exploitation of human beings on the basis of their belonging to a particular racial group or people. "Systematic" indicates that we must look at the status of the group as a whole, and not at those few individuals who may have climbed a "ladder of success" in the white society. The word "systematic" also connotes practices and policies which are pervasive, regardless of whether they are intentional or unintentional. Racism is different from individual prejudice because it requires the possession of genuine power in a society. It is often used by those with power to divide white from non-white. As the U.S. Civil Rights Commission stated in 1970, "Racism is any attitude, action or institutional structure which subordinates a person or group because of their color." Thus, racism is no accident, no problem of individual quirk. In other words, in the United States, racism is institutionalized and it is white. It is white because the institutions are controlled by white society. So racism is not merely prejudice, but prejudice plus power.

In saying this, we note that the concept of race or racial group is no longer considered scientific. The classification of human beings by races like caucasian, mongoloid, negroid, has long been rejected. However, ra*cism* is a fact, a reality, and the word will be used as long as the reality exists.

TERMINOLOGY DEFINED

A comment on terminology. Many "minority" people dislike that term, for various reasons including the subtle deprecation of being a "minority." The term "non-white" has racist implications that white is the norm by which all else is defined. Therefore, we will use, instead, the term "third world," in the spirit of the times and the new consciousness that we described earlier. Its exact meaning has sometimes been debated; here it simply refers to Black, Chicano, Puerto Rican, Native American and Asian American peoples.

In children's books, racism has many faces. In the days of Dr. Dolittle, it was overt to the point of being grotesque. Today, it may still be overt but is more often covert, and thereby a more complex problem. During the last ten years, there has been a growing awareness of racism in children's books as a result of the popular pressure mentioned earlier. This has led to the publication of many children's books which deal with race relations or with national minority groups. This is good in itself, but all too often these books have been written from a white perspective and are covertly racist. Many readers may at first be blinded by the superficial "good intentions" of an author. Reviewers may hail a new book as liberal, progressive, full of "brotherhood," when in fact it is as racist as ever but in ways that are less obvious (at least, to most reviewers, especially those who do not come from the racial group depicted in the book).

Racism in children's books runs from simple omission of third world peoples . . . to stereotypes . . . white paternalism . . . and a host of other problems. Some types of racist treatment apply to all groups, such as insensitivity to—or abuse of—their language. Some types are particular to only one group. For example, while Native Americans may be constantly portrayed as bloodthirsty savages, the problem for Asian

Americans is the stereotype of docility, lack of emotion.

In the work of the Council on Interracial Books for Children, we have studied these different forms. The Council's first major re-evaluation of a children's classic for racist content was done in 1967 by a librarian, Isabelle Suhl, who took on none less than Dr. Dolittle. She concluded that the beloved doctor was in fact the personification of the paternalistic, racist Great White Father Nobly Bearing the White Man's Burden. The consternation caused by this article was expressed in editorials across the nation. Even across the seas the London *Times* was appalled at this irreverence. Many more white people today can recognize racism because of heightened awareness in recent years. But there are more subtle versions of the Great White Father—or Mother— in contemporary children's books. *Josie's Handful of Quietness* by Nancy C. Smith (Abingdon Press, 1975) shows how a friendly white man "adopts" a Chicano migrant family and changes their lives so nicely for the better. The implication is that "non-whites" cannot do it alone; they would be lost without Great White Father. Many books about urban Black or Puerto Rican youth have a standard character, the kindly white social worker, teacher or parole officer, who saves the third world child from hopeless delinquency. This character is almost never Black or Puerto Rican.

OMISSION

We find so many different patterns of racism in children's books that only a few more can be mentioned here. There is, first, the book with no third world characters, or perhaps only one, when it would be natural to include them—as in almost any urban situation in this country. This is the racism of total omission; third worlders are not visible, or next-to-invisible, when in fact they are *there*. Such unjustifiable omission tends to support ethnocentricity in the white reader, as well as promote the idea that racial minorities are tolerable so long as they come only in small quantities (or not at all). For both white and third world readers, the message comes across unmistakably: WHITE IS THE NORM. Or, in the words of that little ditty from the streets: "If you're white, all right—if you're brown, get down—if you're black, get back."

Then there are children's books with mixed characters, or primarily third world characters. In general, the existence of racism in the characters' lives is not acknowledged; it would seem that racism just doesn't exist. Problems are purely personal. A racist act may take place, and no comment is made—which serves as implicit sanction of the act, leaving the young reader with the impression that it was correct. A third world character may be shown as distrustful of whites, angry, bitter—

but the book never explains where those feelings come from. For the reader, the characters are just people "with a chip on their shoulders."

By ignoring the reality of racism and its economic origins, such books are deceitful and do nothing to prepare children of any color for the society around them. They encourage confusion and self-hatred in the third world child. And they encourage white chauvinism and distortion of reality in the white child. Such books reflect an unwillingness to face the truth about U.S. society and about the responsibility of whites who hold power for racism. At most, racism becomes an unpleasant, minor detail, rather than a central pivot of this society which affects everyone living in it.

COLOR-BLIND

Lately, there has been an increasing number of books which attempt to deal directly with the problem of racism. Unfortunately, their perspective is almost always white-oriented. The white child learns to accept the Black as "just like me." *The Cay* by Theodore Taylor (Doubleday, 1969), which won a host of awards is a classic example of this. So is *Bright April,* another "favorite." In both, the Black person is finally accepted *by* whites. But what about a Black person's acceptance *of* the white? That is just automatically assumed. This aspect of the relationship has no importance; white is the norm, the standard that counts.

And on what basis has the Black been accepted? Always, it is on the basis of some version of that good old formula: be neat and clean, don't get bitter, patiently turn the other cheek, be intelligent, but don't forget "your place." That formula, in turn, rests on an ideology that is racist to the core. It blames the victims of racism for their long history of oppression. If it is up to the third world person to win "acceptance," then by implication they are defective until they prove themselves worthy of white approval. Also, that ideology includes what has been called "the Bootstrap Syndrome": or "Work yourself up the ladder of success. Others have." It is the concept that personal, individual virtue brings inevitable rewards, and that the problems one encounters by being Black will be resolved by the same economic system that has made Blackness a handicap. (In other words, that the oppressor out of sheer good will is going to free the oppressed, or the burglar return stolen goods out of compassion for those robbed.) Actual experience of this society simply does not bear out those beliefs. Personal virtue or strength may have worked for many white people but not for the vast majority of not white—not for any third world people *as a group.*

The whole formula is fraudulent, and to foist it on children is truly abusive. Unfortunately, many readers tend to love the "acceptance" book, because it leaves them all warm and tingly with feelings of "See, there doesn't have to be hate, does there?" But the problem is not simply hate, which of course nobody wants; it is racism, it is a *system.* Here again we see the unwillingness to come to grips with the truth about U.S. society and about white responsibility for racism. Racism will never be eliminated by denial of its existence, or by individual solutions instead of social solutions. The problem will not go away by simply saying "In the end, we're all the same."

Furthermore, that approach is insulting to other racial groups and their cultures, their histories, their languages. The peoples of the U.S. are not all the same, nor do they want to be.

LANGUAGE

Many children's books have been published lately that seem to approve of such differences and to view a multi-cultural society as desirable. Many of them have been good. But many include another entire set of problems. These include gestures to language differences; the author has the characters speaking English in what the author thinks are constructions of the character's mother tongue ("I go now"), or the author sprinkles the text with bits of the mother tongue which are full of error. Chicanos and Puerto Ricans speak broken Engleeesh and Native Americans "how" their way through life. The richness of Black English rarely comes across and any gestures white writers make toward its unique qualities usually end up making it sound inferior. Which is, of course, the final impression given by all those other gestures: inferiority.

Many other problems come to mind. Asian American children are constantly shown in stories where the highlight is the Lunar New Year celebration (it's "colorful"), when this makes as little sense to them as if most stories about white children focussed on a Fourth of July celebration. Often certain foods are used to make the third world characters seem authentic but in effect leaving the impression that this is all they eat (tortillas and beans, for example). Supposed cultural patterns are milked for authenticity to the point where one expects that every child in the U.S. must think, for example, that every Black family has a dominating mother and a weak father. All in all, when the existence of differences is portrayed as acceptable, those differences often appear in distorted form. They are caricatures, not portraits, and they can do grave damage to the reader.

Books that attempt to deal with the historical experiences of racial minorities also have their serious weaknesses. *The Slave Dancer* by Paula Fox (Bradbury, 1973) was apparently intended to show the horrors of slavery and the slave trade, but it is nevertheless filled with its own racism. The slaves have no individuality, no spirit, no brains, and are compared at one point to scrambling rats. The blame for slavery is placed primarily on Africans themselves—plus a few evil whites—while the U.S. system emerges generally blameless. *The Slave Dancer,* cited by the American Library Association as the "most distinguished" work of 1973, may show the horrors of the slave trade but it does so in such a way that no young reader would be left with respect for Black people. The book's main characters express hatred and disgust toward Blacks; there is *no* contradiction of their attitudes; so those are the emotions that stand.

The lack of individuality mentioned above pervades many of the children's books with third world characters. Stereotypes are one form of the problem; lack of individualized, realistic human characteristics is just as important. Asian Americans in particular have been the victims of both. They emerge either as Charlie Chan types, laundry-workers, cooks or very studious students (the stereotype), or, as in *The Five Chinese Brothers,* indistinguishable from one another with the same slant eyes, hair in pigtails, and nauseous yellow coloring (has anyone ever seen those yellows in reality?). One can almost hear the white artist complaining, "But they all look alike." Only to you, one must reply, only to you.

GOOD INTENTIONS IRRELEVANT

The source of all the problems described here is racism itself. Most of the books were not written by authors who are from the racial group represented, and who identify with their group. Furthermore, editors in publishing companies are mostly white. Four hundred years of racism on this continent have left book writing and publishing primarily in the hands of a white, college-educated elite. Four hundred years of racism have left an ethnocentric majority with little knowledge or under-standing of other peoples. No matter how good the intent of white authors and artists, they have rarely done a satisfactory job of depicting third world people.

And it is the final *product* that counts—not the intent. We must be concerned above all with the effects of a book on the children who read it. What happens to children from the racial group depicted, when they look in that mirror and see sameness, ugliness, dependency on whites, lack of resistance, acceptance only on the basis of an endless willingness to suffer? What happens when they see something they can never have—whiteness—embodied with superiority and desirability? What happens when they see a pretty world free of racism, which they know to be unreal? What happens when they see their own kind always "in trouble with the law'''? What happens when they see none of their own kind showing strength? What happens when they see their culture and language reduced to quaintness, at best, and more often to inferiority? We must ask, as loudly as possible: AFTER READING THE AVERAGE CHILDREN'S BOOK, WHAT CHILD WOULD WANT TO BE BLACK, CHICANO, PUERTO RICAN, ASIAN, INDIAN?

There is a similar list of questions for white children, and it also points to a pattern of harmful effects. What happens when white children look in that mirror and see only themselves, although the world itself is not thus? What happens when they see racism approved? What happens when they see minority people incapable of doing for themselves, desiring only to be accepted by persons unlike themselves? Does this prepare white children for reality? Does it enrich their lives and minds? Does it inspire the best human values, anger against injustice, a desire to unite with others in order to make this a healthy society? Or does it help breed another generation of white chauvinists?

LOOKING AHEAD

We know that we are asking a lot of children's books. We are asking that third world people be shown as fully human individuals—and at the same time, that their historical group experience be recognized and treated with honesty. We are asking that cultural differences be portrayed—and, at the same time, that those differences be non-stereotyped. We are asking that oppression and suffering be shown—and at the same time, that minority peoples be depicted not only as suffering but also as resisting.

We would even ask that books show the ways in which racism indirectly oppresses and exploits white people. Racism dehumanizes its advocates, although few may see it that way at first. Also, there are whites among the dominated of this society, whom the dominators keep in line by the use of racism—telling them to enjoy their superior place because at least *they* are white; not to join in common concerns with others who are not white.

It is a lot to ask, and it is very little. Thousands of racist children's books have done untold damage in a wide variety of ways. We have a responsibility to study each of these ways, and demand an end to all of them. It can be done; that has been proven. Some worthwhile children's books about third world peoples have been published. Some excellent books which increase white sensitivity and understanding have been written. To them, we give our unequivocal support. Many have strong points and some weaknesses; we distinguish between these. Many others have been published which might be called neutral. They do no particular harm. However, we question whether the correct word is "neutral." In the end, a failure to work for change actually supports the status quo. Books can strike a blow against racism. At this point in history, directly or indirectly, one serves either the racist past or a humanistic future.

SEXISM

Although there are similarities, the definition of sexism is more complex than that of racism because its *direct* victims can be found on "both sides"—meaning, both women and men. We see the primary victims of sexism as women because they are subordinated in an institutionalized way, as well as by cultural forces. The sexist oppression of men comes mainly, though not exclusively, from cultural forces.

We can therefore define sexism primarily as the systematic oppression and exploitation of human beings on the basis of their belonging to the female sex. Secondarily, we see sexism as the repression of people based on cultural definitions of femininity and masculinity, which prevents both sexes from realizing their full human potential. Briefly, sexism is any attitude, action or institutional structure which subordinates or limits a person on the basis of sex.

As with racism, the possession of power is key. Most real power in the United States lies in the hands of men (although certainly not all men). Men use that power to oppress and exploit women. But women *as a group* have no power base—no institutional control—from which to oppress and exploit men, either as a group or separately (although individual women may exploit individual men, like the rich woman her chauffeur).

WHO BENEFITS?

The subordination of women is as fundamental to U.S. society as is racism. Limiting women to the roles of housewife and mother serves basic economic purposes; for example, it provides vast amounts of unpaid labor that have been estimated as worth $8,285 a year per woman. Outside the home, unequal pay for equal work saves business billions of dollars every year (it is estimated that women earn 57 per cent of what men earn for similar work). If nursing were a high status occupation, most nurses would be well-paid men. But by making this "women's work," a lower salary is justified.

The image of women as an inferior group serves many purposes. Men of all colors can have someone to look down upon, to exploit, which pacifies and deflects their anger away from poverty, injustice and racism.

The conservation of life is generally viewed as a "feminine" (read, inferior) function. This places peace-keeping and environmental concerns on a scale below "masculine" war-making and profit-making. Definitions of supposed manhood and womanhood also interlock with the social structure. Masculinity is defined in terms of "toughness" and "rugged individuality," while femininity is equated with "weakness" and "easily influenced." This kind of "masculinity" often pervades our institutions and policies; it is not only Kissinger who has advocated "showing our manhood" in foreign policy (let's not act like women is the unspoken message).

Of course, the male is not seen as superior—not even as competent—in functions such as raising children or "home-making," delicate hand-work or demonstrating tenderness. The female may even be exalted in those roles. But this is hardly an asset. First of all, women are stereotyped as possessing supposedly *natural* excellence in those functions when it may not be natural at all to many women. Secondly, such functions are rarely if ever viewed as commanding the highest respect of the society: they are nice, even necessary, but taken for granted and hardly exciting. They demonstrate no special accomplishment, since they come "naturally." Men are the real doers.

SEXISM PLUS

These facts and attitudes have been widely exposed by the women's movement. Not so well understood is the role of sexism in the lives of poor and third world peoples. Women of those groups are, of course, not simply oppressed by sexism, but also by their class status and by racism as well. The most brutal forms of sexism—death by illegal abortion and unwanted sterilization—are most common among these women. Furthermore, if white women suffer the stereotypes mentioned above, Chicanas and Puerto Rican women suffer them doubly. Latin women in general are seen as super-passive, super-domestic and super-submissive to their men. Black women, on the other hand, are often seen as domineering, matriarchal figures. The strong Latino woman who has challenged the welfare office or a racist school system, the Black woman who has stood firmly in support of her husband—these are lost in a Moynihan-type blindness to reality. Racism and poverty have made sexism worse than ever for the third world woman.

Also not well understood are the ways in which sexism oppresses and limits options for males. There is the male who would rather be a dancer than a football player; who prefers a supportive rather than an aggressive role; who has so-called "feminine" qualities. The pressures put on males to be "real men" in order to avoid ridicule are enormous, and often lead to premature heart attacks and death.

How do children's books reflect all this, and what are they doing to correct it—or to sustain it?

FEMALE ROLES

As in the case of racial minorities, females are traditionally less present in children's books than males. (Since they comprise at least half the population, there is even less excuse.) The concept of white as the norm is matched by the concept of male as the center of attention and female as "the other one." In most books, females who are brave or aggressive or adventurous have been compared to males just as third world persons get compared—directly or indirectly—to whites. A female who accomplishes a difficult feat is described as remarkable; normally, the author implies, she is just a cheerleader for the male. Normally, it is the boy who saves the day and leads the way; it is the boy who knows the secret way of opening a locked door; it is the boy who calms down his emotional sister. The familiar face of paternalism looms again.

Sexist stereotypes prevail in children's books, and not even the animal world escapes. The rabbit family in *Nicky Goes to the Doctor* by Richard Scarry (Golden Books, 1974) has the same sexist role-playing that a human family might have. Mr. Bunny do housework? Forget it. Molly Patch's male animal friends cook for *her?* Never! (Ben Shecter, Harper & Row, 1975)

LANGUAGE

The language problem is perhaps even greater in the case of sexism than racism, because sexism has a longer history. If "blackness" is equated with badness in racist writing, womanhood simply disappears in sexist writing. "He," "man," "mankind" or "the average man"— supposedly representing both female and male—occurs constantly. There are dozens of words with built-in sexism which turn up in children's books, such as salesman, repairman, mailman, spokesman, manpower and brotherhood (with "ooh, it's a *lady* doctor" as counterpart). Women are constantly made into human baggage, as in "man and wife" or "Daddy took the family along to California." The assumption of femaleness or maleness according to role is still another example of sexist language: "Each citizen must pay *his* taxes" or "A good nurse cares about *her* patients' feelings."

Sexism has not resulted in many books with *no* female characters at all, but this is only because of another sexist concept. To leave out the mother would put the father in uncomfortable "female" roles (while a family without a father would have the woman assuming "male" responsibilities). Therefore two women—mom and sis—usually make it into children's books. But they might as well not be there because they only play roles: baking a pie, setting their hair, welcoming Daddy home from work. For these roles, females even have a uniform: the dress, and an apron over it for mother.

And what about those "girl stories"—meaning books in which the central character is female? Publishers claim that books about girls are less profitable because boys will not read them—while girls *will* read about boys. "Girl stories" are dull, it seems, which is of course inevitable so long as authors portray girls doing dull things. (The old publishing ratio, used by the industry for years, was three boy characters to one girl character.)

IMPROVEMENT

Lately there has been an increasing number of books with females doing more interesting things. There have even been anti-sexist books. In general, they have been somewhat better than their counterparts in the field of racial minorities. The reason appears to be that women often write children's books, ironically a function allowed them by sexism itself. (It is not a well-paying occupation.)

This is not to say that a woman cannot write a sexist book; many do. And many of the new stories are *semi*-sexist. In *Cissy's Texas Pride* by Edna Smith Makerney (Abingdon Press, 1975) the central character is an eleven-year-old girl who rides horses well and has great initiative. But her long-range goals are sexist (to get married and be "as pretty and sweet as her mother"). Her mother is the traditional commuter between kitchen and beauty salon. This is a pattern in many of the new "feminist" books, where young females are portrayed untraditionally but adults are not. It occurs again in Julia First's *Amy* (Prentice-Hall, 1975), where the main figure is again an active girl but the author, indirectly, glorifies a mother who bakes at least four cakes in the course of the book, while criticizing another woman who paints all day in a studio and doesn't prepare dinner on time.

We are not anti-homemaking or anti-housewife; let that be clear. We only oppose sexist attitudes toward those forms of work. We oppose the idea that housekeeping is the primary, correct and "natural" task of *all* women, and not of *any* men. Our concern is also the notion that housework has less value and importance than work outside the home. We do not oppose women doing housework in children's books so long as they do other things too; so long as men also do housework; and so long as the book does not telegraph a lower value for housework compared to other work.

Many anti-sexist books have been published lately about female historical figures from the suffrage movement and other struggles. They fill a giant gap and are much needed in the battle against sexism. Marjorie Drake's *A Question of Courage* and John Anthony Scott's excellent *Fanny Kemble's America* are two recent examples (both T.Y. Crowell). The first, however, occasionally points toward materialistic values and elitism. This is a common problem: the book that combats sexism but falls into another "ism"—often racism. In the very popular *The Matchlock Gun* by Walter D. Edmonds (Dodd, Mead, 1941) the "valiant" mother lures three "evil" Indians to their deaths with one blast of a gun. Unfortunately, we often find anti-sexist books which are racist and vice versa.

MALE ROLES

In some books, the story itself may help to combat sexist values. Sexism has labelled women as "emotional" and men as "rational," and this implies it's bad to get "emotional" or "all hung up with personal problems." By giving importance to feelings and to a humanistic resolution of conflicts, books can have an anti-sexist effect. Unfortunately, once again, they often contain other serious faults and tacitly support most white, middle class values.

Thus far, only a few new books have explored role-revision for males as well as females. Because of sexism, having boys do "girls things" is far more controversial than having girls do "boy things." Most of the new anti-sexist books have therefore concentrated on providing more positive, active images of girls. We see this as worthwhile, but the ways in which sexism oppresses the male ought to be dealt with more.

Most of the books which either have major female characters and/or confront sexism overtly have been written by white authors. No surprise then that the most neglected and stereotyped kinds of females have been women and girls from third world groups. A study made by the Council on Interracial Books for Children of 100 books about Puerto Ricans revealed not only the predictable racism but heavy sexism as well. With only a few, minor exceptions, the books mirror those super-traditional stereotypes described earlier. The girls play with dolls, rarely go outside the home alone, learn English and are generally "sweet." Mothers are grown-up versions of the same and fathers are supreme commanders. All this does not add up to the general Puerto Rican reality, nor does it do anything positive for Puerto Rican girls reading such books.

A 1976 Council study of 80 books about Asian Americans also shows sexism, racism and elitism in constant combination. The sweet passive females are all ultra genteel—as befits well-mannered stereotypic "Orientals."

Sexism in today's books is far from dead, despite the women's movement; Miss Goody-Goody minces on, with her hair tied in the same pink bow. Even in the current efforts to combat sexism, there is reason for serious dissatisfaction. Too often, books which are anti-sexist are still about the middle class, still ageist, and often stress competition. On the whole, the new feminist books still do not deal with changing society in any deep or meaningful way. We need books about girls who are not afraid of snakes, but we need more than that. Only the surface of sexism—its cultural form—has been seriously confronted. Its institutionalized foundations, and its links with other aspects of the society, remain untouched. This probably reflects the fact that the feminist movement itself has been dominated by white, upper-middle-class women. That is changing, and the change—like all others—should be reflected in children's books.

AGEISM

Ageism is the systematic subordination of human beings on the basis of their age, primarily old age. It is any action or attitude that demeans and/or ridicules old people, that limits the fulfillment of their human potential. Ageism is institutionalized and also cultural. Forced retirement, lack of adequate government programs to benefit the aged, relegation of the old to atrocious "rest homes"—these institutional abuses work hand in hand with the "Rocking Chair Syndrome" of attitudes toward the old as useless, unproductive nuisances.

Children's books contain a host of stereotypes reflecting that syndrome. In physical appearance, old people are constantly shown with bent bodies, blank faces, dressed in baggy and frumpy clothes, with canes or endlessly rocking in that chair. Old women are portrayed as sexless; old men as perhaps raunchy in speech but impotent in actuality.

The old hobble through children's books, loaded down with all sorts of infirmities: deafness, poor sight, forgetfulness. Their speech is "high-pitched" or "halting." Their manners and attitudes are rigid, stubborn, old-fashioned, annoying, interfering—and are often ridiculed. The elders are allowed a minimum of ideas, which they constantly repeat. Sometimes they are allowed to be "wise," but this supposed wisdom is usually given the form of a few truisms or clichés.

Some children's books do present old people as interesting, alive individuals with their own emotional complexity and the ability to interact with younger people as equals. But we still find far too many Grannies clucking "a stitch in time saves nine"; far too many Grandpas forgetting where they put their glasses; far too many old folks who "just can't understand this younger generation."

ANTI-YOUTH

Though we are defining ageism as oppression of old people, oppression because of age also applies to the young: "You're too young to understand"; "too young to vote"; "too young to go to the store alone." Intelligence and the ability to act responsibly are judged by the sole criterion of physical age, as in the case of old people.

It might at first seem that this form of put-down is not common in children's books, since they are written specifically to appeal to the young. But at a deeper level we see that most children's books are indirectly biased against the young. To say, as many have said, that children's books should not deal with controversial social issues is highly paternalistic. It demeans the young and their interests, their ability to comprehend, their concern with the world beyond their own immediate lives. Children of four and five are developing their self-concepts. They are looking in books to see how the world sees them. They are also exploring in books to see how they are to look at others, to see how concerned they should be about others. Their curiosity deserves respect. Just as the intellectual curiosity of an eleven-or twelve-year-old deserves respectful challenges rather than mushy pablum. Limiting the achievement of *any* child's full human potential is the most anti-human deed of all. It is the anti-human value that permits all the other anti-human values to prevail in children's books.

ELITISM, MATERIALISM and INDIVIDUALISM

One of the great myths of U.S. society has been that we have no class problem or class conflict. We have a democracy, and anybody who works hard enough can "make it" regardless of whether that person was born rich or poor, white or Black, male or female, etc. If some people do possess more than others, they earned it by working hard. Or they were lucky. But nobody is stuck in a "class."

That myth is being exploded in the minds of more and more people. Corporate corruption, compounded by political collusion, added to

Spiro Agnew, Watergate and CIA have turned many toward distrust of privilege. Failure of the "War Against Poverty" has shown that this country's large percentage of poor remain poor. And the small percentage of very rich remain a small percentage and remain very rich. The realization is growing that this nation really has an elite possessing tremendous power as well as wealth. Ours is, in fact, a class society as well as a society divided by race and sex status.

More and more people have also questioned the values that go with our society. Is the definition of success, status, or "a good life" defined primarily in terms of material possessions? Do a second car and a color TV, a golf club membership and a vacation in Europe really create superiority and self-worth? Should we, it has been asked, judge the moral fiber and intelligence of people by such standards? Or could it be that such criteria have been laid down by a system which must sell-sell-sell in order to survive?

ME-FIRST-ISM

Also in those years, people have seriously questioned the concept of achieving a "good life" for oneself—regardless of others and regardless of principles. They have questioned the concept that says: if you just work hard, be smarter than the next person, and don't mind stepping on others, you'll climb the ladder of success. From kindergarten to the grave, in school, in sports, on the job, everywhere we are told to *compete* with other human beings. The football coach stands in the locker-room, symbolizing a whole set of values as he exhorts: Get out there and WIN, WIN, WIN! Kill 'em if you have to, but WIN! Competitiveness is a cornerstone of any society ruled by an elite, or class that stays in power by pitting people against each other to acquire material possessions.

Competitiveness is an extreme form of another basic value in the society: individualism. Individualism is the cult of human separateness, the doctrine that each person is indeed "an island." It encourages a dog-eat-dog society, where "I'm looking out for number one" is the prevailing motto. Individual welfare, rather than the collective welfare, becomes the goal. It differs from individuality, which is simply the special personality qualities of each human being. No two people—or trees or animals or any living thing—are exactly alike; these differences are good; they *enrich* human relations and society. Individua*lity* is a reality; it cannot be denied and should not be discouraged. Individua*lism* is a philosophy of life; it has not always existed in every human society and should be discouraged as a highly negative force. Sometimes, of course, the line between the two can become blurred. Some so-called individuality is actually the result of negative conditioning, and anti-social. The key question must be: *does a particular quality in a person oppress others? Does it serve that person alone, or humanity as a whole?* Since our educational system, and our culture as a whole, encourage elitism, materialism and competitiveness (including individualism), it is inevitable that we find these values in children's books as well. Beginning with elitism, we see that "poor but honest" characters do appear occasionally but they are lost in the tide of middle and upper class people whose activities, life-style and problems usually have little relevance to those below them in that social structure. Factory and blue-collar workers, of *any* racial group, are the rarest of specimens. Families on welfare do turn up, but usually in books about Blacks.

STATUS

Manual labor is generally viewed as inferior to intellectual or professional work; the friendly mail carrier or garbage collector may appear, but books rarely bring out the fact that *their* kind of labor makes the society go around. If they do, it is usually in a paternalistic way. Children get the message, in obvious or subtle form: some people are better than others because they have supposedly "good" jobs, homes, clothing, taste, manners, speech.

Elitism often combines with materialism to produce atrocious results in children's books. One example is *Liliuokalani* by Mary Malone (Garrard, 1975). This biography of Hawaii's last, beloved queen shows how the U.S. took over the Hawaiian islands—bringing racism and private property, alcoholism and venereal disease—despite her opposition. Veiled by the author's superficial tributes to Hawaii's old customs and ways, and by the omission of important historical facts, there lies a clear endorsement of the belief that the U.S. has the *right* to rule other peoples in the name of material "progress." Progress (and profits) for some; subservience for others.

Children's books also set forth the concept that there are only individual problems in this society—no class problems. If you can save yourself, then all's right with the world. In *A Bicycle from Bridgetown* by Dawn C. Thomas (McGraw-Hill, 1975), a poor boy finds an old, lost bicycle and is rewarded for his honesty by the owner with a brand new one. This takes place in Barbados, of all places, where the poor but happy "natives" just watch the tourists come and go, fascinated by their clothes and other goodies. The author makes no comment on the brutal contrast between rich tourists and poor "natives," thus giving tacit support to the status quo. Seen through the author's eyes, it is material possessions—starting with the bicycle—that determine everyone's relationships, and the assumption is that those relations are as they should be. Edgar has a bicycle at the end of the book; thus we can forget about the rest of his class and his people. Perhaps they are all supposed to rise in the world by way of finding things lost by rich people and returning them. The author must want children to believe this is possible; we do not.

We realize that the intentions might be good—to encourage individual strength, self-reliance, honesty. Unfortunately, the actual results of such books is to encourage elitism, materialism, individualism. The reality of the society, as said above, is a division into social groups or classes which operates for the benefit of few and the harm of many. This must be changed, not endorsed. Such books serve as a matrix of lies and fraudulent solutions.

ESCAPISM and CONFORMISM

These two are siblings, and part of the same family as elitism, materialism, competitiveness.

Many children's books are escapist, for they encourage the reader to wait for luck, magic, or help from some rich or powerful person in order to solve problems. Dawn C. Thomas', *A Bicycle from Bridgetown* (McGraw-Hill, 1975) exemplifies this tendency, as do most fairy tales. They may postulate morality, as the prerequisite for that luck, magic or help, but this does not undo the basic escapism of such stories. One can be honest fifteen times over without it ever bringing a new bicycle; the solution offered is not really one's own initiative or morality but the entrance on the scene of that outside force.

In rejecting escapism, we do not propose an end to fantasy in children's books. Good fantasy can be a splendid stimulus to the imagination. But when a book encourages escape into the fantastic as a *substitute* for confronting reality, it does the reader no good at all. It discourages children from examining problems realistically and then acting. It makes children feel that they are helpless pawns in the game of life, rather than that they can indeed fight for their beliefs, their rights, and a better society for all.

DON'T MAKE WAVES

Conformism trails along behind escapism, implying that the best behavior is to leave the boat unrocked. *Marly the Kid* by Susan Pfeffer (Doubleday, 1975), a nice book in some ways, ends with the rebellious Marly choosing not to join a group of students who organized to participate in her challenge of the school system. She conforms, after all. (As a substitute, Marly decides to become the first overweight cheerleader at her school—an example of an individual, rather than a collective, action.)

Conformism discourages readers from questioning whether the "usual" way of doing things is best for all people concerned. It serves to prop up the status quo. In saying this, we do not advocate an end to norms as such, or to behavioral rules; we do not advocate a denial of all standards, a total absence of order—anarchy. We urge that existing norms be re-examined in the light of new consciousness and in the light of what is truly best for most people. We are, in fact, highly concerned with norms; the need is for new ones, *not* the elimination of norms. Non-conformism with the worst in this society should mean conformism with the best.

One of the quirks of our present society is that it attaches great value to both individualism and conformism—two apparent opposites. We propose that they do not in fact *function* as opposites. To be individualistic is, in fact, to conform—because individua*lism* is the norm. The society does not truly encourage individuality, only individualism; if it did, it would have made the fulfillment of individual potential a real possibility for everyone—whether male or female, white or non-white, rich or poor, young or old.

LITERARY and ARTISTIC QUALITY

At this point, our readers may cry for a halt to all the "isms" and demand some words about *quality* in children's books. After all, children deserve beautiful writing and art; they are values, too. Not only content, but also form, is important.

We could not agree more warmly, and we do evaluate books for form as well as content. We have found that good values can appear in a poorly written book; if so, they are largely self-defeating. It cannot be called a truly great book. We also find books that are stylistically admirable but have anti-human values which cause children harm and pain. With such books, one can hardly talk about their "beauty"; the inner ugliness of their racism or sexism, ageism or elitism, corrupts the very word itself. This type of book is especially venal because, by the very skill of its writing or pictures, it is likely to impress a child more. The more exciting, the more compelling, the more realistic it seems, the more damage it can do; its smooth surface masks its true nature all the more effectively.

There is no automatic correlation between good values and good writing, or bad values and bad writing. Nor is there contradiction between good values and good writing, bad values and bad writing. We seek both good values and good writing. Authors and artists who wish to combat anti-human values in children's books have a responsibility to offer the best quality in their work as well. If we have emphasized content more than form, it is because good form has always been in demand but good content has not. Stylistic values are already recognized; human values are not—*at this time*. And these are the times that concern us, in every aspect of this book.

It should be obvious by now that we frankly seek to impose our values on children's books—although they are not merely ours, but the creation of millions of people. To those who argue that it is not the business of children's books to be the vehicle of change, we answer with our opening statement: no writer is just a reporter. All books contain messages and by tolerating them, we are in effect endorsing those messages. This we cannot do—not when the message is racism or sexism, materialism or ageism, or any other anti-human value.

Books together with television, schools, comics, advertisements and, of course, adult behavior are the forces that socialize children, mold their ideas. These forces today are almost always sexist, elitist and materialist. They are often racist and ageist. Far from whimsical, those forces have roots in the society as a whole. To combat them requires a constant, difficult, uphill struggle. Along with many other people, we are committed to that struggle for a single reason: we care about the future of our children and of all children.

3. The Rating Instrument

In evaluating children's books utilizing 1975 as a sample year, our reviewers have used a specific checklist which follows this introduction. The main reason for using a checklist is that we realize some of our readers will be interested in *some* of our evaluations and unconcerned about others. With the checklist, a reader can see—at a glance—how a book has been rated in the category of racism, sexism, or whatever category is important to that reader.

The main section of the chart is headed "Values Checklist"; most of its terminology has already been defined here. However, we should explain the different between "anti" and "non," in relation to racist, sexist, etc. We found many books which, for example, were not sexist but could never be seen as contributing toward the elimination of sexism. An anti-sexist book would contribute in some way to the elimination of sexism; a sexist book contributes to the maintenance of sexist oppression; and a non-sexist book does neither.

We also considered that building "a positive image" (a term used in the checklist) for a female and/or third world reader is—in our present society—anti-sexist or anti-racist. It is also important for the white and/or male child to perceive those positive images. The reader will also find another value not previously mentioned: "Inspire action against social oppression." This is one step more than being anti-racist or anti-sexist. *Very* few books received a positive rating in that category, but it is the value that we wish to encourage most of all. We should also point out that, in the category of racism, "Omission" means that third world people could have logically been included in the book, but were not. "Commission" means racism overtly appeared in the book and will be detailed in the review. "N.A." (Not Applicable) would apply, for racism, to a story limited entirely to a single white family, or to a story set in an area where it is unlikely that any third world people would be present.

Naturally there are border-line cases in all the categories, and other complications. No checklist can provide for all the subtleties, all the hidden messages, *all* the qualities of a book. Reviewers, whether they work as individuals or in teams, must at some point rely on judgments and preferences which are uniquely their own. A subjective element will inevitably enter every analysis.

NIT-PICKING

Readers might think that our evaluations are nit-picking, that we get carried away by a few words or a single drawing, and judge a book to have anti-human values on the basis of what might seem to be minor details. Indeed, we *are* nit-picking, and with reason. Anti-human values can be very subtle, very hidden; they have been so long accepted and so pervasive in this society that authors who, for example, might sincerely believe themselves to be anti-racist and even intend to write an anti-racist book actually end up writing a racist one. We want to expose every form taken by anti-human values, every vestige. Authors, readers and reviewers should become truly aware of the harm done by those values. It is our hope that they will then be incensed enough to work to eliminate anti-human values thoroughly.

How did we decide which books to analyze here? Approximately 2,500 children's books have been published in the United States every year for the past twenty years. We asked publishers to send us all their books on minority and feminist themes, as well as books that dealt with social problems or concerns. We sifted through those which came, and eliminated many. However, *we do not know which books should have been sent but were not.* In an attempt to cover possible omissions, we also read most "Establishment" reviews and requested books they mentioned which seemed to fit our categories.

WHO REVIEWS?

In assigning reviews, we followed the policy of the Council on Interracial Books for Children that books about particular cultures must be examined by a person of that culture. Therefore we had Blacks review books about Blacks, Chicanos review books on Chicanos, etc. In addition, we asked *all* our reviewers to be alert to sexism, elitism, materialism and our other areas of concern. We often found reviewers who were sensitive to problems in some areas and not in others. This necessitated trying many reviewers and rejecting many reviews. The reviewers' perception of the many forms taken by anti-human values was *more* important to us than their writing skill. Finally, we should say that we made an effort to use the services of reviewers who have contact with children and who actively sought their reactions to books.

All of the criteria and analyses presented in this book rest upon our present understanding of ourselves and our society. Strengthening the self-image of a third world child, or of a girl, may not be of critical concern in a future society. But under present conditions it has a positive effect. So our criteria are not timeless, nor are our targets. They do suit today's situation, in which revised values are certainly blowing in the wind and the times are not only changing but profoundly revolutionary. We make no claim to eternal verities; if anything, we look forward to the day when a book like this will no longer be relevant.

May *Human Values in Children's Books* help to bring that day.

VALUES CHECKLIST

	ART	WORDS		ART	WORDS			ART	WORDS	N.A.
anti-Racist			non-Racist			Racist	omission			
							commission			
anti-Sexist			non-Sexist			Sexist				
anti-Elitist			non-Elitist			Elitist				
anti-Materialist			non-Materialist			Materialist				
anti-Individualist			non-Individualist			Individualist				
anti-Ageist			non-Ageist			Ageist				
anti-Conformist			non-Conformist			Conformist				
anti-Escapist			non-Escapist			Escapist				
Builds positive image of females/ minorities			Builds negative image of females/ minorities				Excellent	Good	Fair	Poor
Inspires action vs. oppression			Culturally authentic			Literary quality				
						Art quality				

N.A. stands for Not Applicable.

"Racist by omission" means that third world people could logically have been included but were not.

"Racist by commission" means that the words or the art were openly racist in some way which the book's analysis will detail.

"Non" before a negative value means that the book's impact was neutral in that regard.

"Anti" before a negative value means that the book made some positive impact.

"Inspires action against oppression" means that the book not only describes injustice but in some way encourages readers to act against injustice.

Note: The Checklist will always *follow* the analysis of the book.

THE ANALYSES —1

Pre-School and Early Years

BECKY AND THE BEAR
by Dorothy Van Woerkom
illustrated by Margot Tomes
G. P. Putnam's Sons
$4.69, 45 pages, grades 1-3

This true story about an eight-year-old colonial "pioneer" named Becky is a delight from beginning to end. It has adventure, humor, suspense and good sense, as well as several palatable morals.

Wanting to "be brave," Becky wishes she could go hunting like her father and brother Ned. In the course of one day's experience, she discovers that courage has many faces. When her father and brother come home to report "We hunted all day and caught nothing," Becky proudly displays the bear she caught—*without a gun*. How she did it is the nub of the story, and it's a lot of fun.

In addition to its general wholesomeness, *Becky* promotes positive values in several areas. *Work:* The house needed by Becky's family is not simply given, it must be built. Family members clear the ground, cut down the wood and get the job done. Food must be grown and the animals who provide milk and eggs or pull the plow must be fed and cared for. *People:* When a neighbor is ill, Becky's grandmother goes to help. It is a matter of course that she will do so and that Becky will understand. *Women:* Although Becky and her grandmother share the work of keeping the floor clean, getting oil for the lamps, taking care of the pigs and preparing dinner, their tasks are not regarded as less important than those of Ned and Becky's father. There is a division of responsibility and a mutual dependence among the family members. Also Becky's father and brother laugh and enjoy her clever entrapment of a bear rather than feeling put down, even though they had hunted all day with a gun and failed. *Nature:* People, animals and the earth are shown as interdependent. What happens to one, affects all. ("With so little rain in the spring, here is not much food in the forest. Many animals have gone over the mountain in search for food.") Becky's father and brother will have to trudge far into the forest to find bear.

A fine complement to the story are the pen-and-ink and watercolor illustrations, which depict a lovely countryside, a Becky full of character, and a bear whose facial expressions lend humor to his fate.

The preface contains the book's only negative element: ". . .the people lived on wild berries and plants and on corn, which the Indians taught them to use." When will white writers stop differentiating between Native Americans, slaves, natives, etc. and "people"?

	ART	WORDS		ART	WORDS			ART	WORDS	N.A.
anti-Racist			non-Racist	✓	✓	Racist — omission / commission				
anti-Sexist		✓	non-Sexist	✓		Sexist				
anti-Elitist		✓	non-Elitist	✓		Elitist				
anti-Materialist		✓	non-Materialist	✓		Materialist				
anti-Individualist		✓	non-Individualist	✓		Individualist				
anti-Ageist	✓	✓	non-Ageist			Ageist				
anti-Conformist	✓	✓	non-Conformist			Conformist				
anti-Escapist	✓	✓	non-Escapist			Escapist				
Builds positive image of females/minorities			Builds negative image of females/minorities		✓		Excellent	Good	Fair	Poor
Inspires action vs. oppression			Culturally authentic			Literary quality		✓		
						Art quality		✓		

HENRIETTA, THE WILD WOMAN OF BORNEO
by Winifred Rosen
illustrated by Kay Chorao
Four Winds Press
$5.50, unpaged, grades p.s.-2

Everyone in Henrietta's family picks on her. She is not neat, ladylike or pretty like her older sister, Evelyn. Her hair is brown and bushy, she wears braces and loves to play in comfortable, casual clothes. Mother calls her daughter "the wild woman of Borneo" because of Henrietta's unconcern about such matters as hair-combing and room-straightening.

Fed up with her parents' criticisms and Evelyn's air of superiority, Henrietta decides to resolve her problems by going to Borneo, where she can ride horses like other "wild women" and be free from criticism. She packs herself into a crate and Evelyn sends her off. When the crate is opened, Henrietta emerges to find her family standing around. Disappointed, she throws a tantrum. The family responds by assuring her she is loved, and Henrietta realizes they are accepting her for what she is.

Unlike her manipulative older sister, Henrietta emerges as an active, sensitive young person who is the victim of negative parental expectations. Continually called a "wild woman," she begins to live up to the name.

While the book's theme is a valid one, the message that girls should be accepted as they are instead of prodded to fit a sexist stereotype has limited value as presented. (The presentation is particularly marred by the author's stiff and awkward writing style—although the outstanding illustrations are beautiful and humorous.) Nor does Henrietta's escapist "solution" to her problems offer a wholly satisfactory model to young children for confronting their difficulties realistically.

But by far the worst aspect of this book is its title. It perpetuates the stereotype of non-white people as "primitive," less-than-human savages whose legitimate "differentness" is necessarily distasteful. (Borneo is, after all, a *real* place.) Such racism is inexcusable.

	ART	WORDS		ART	WORDS		ART	WORDS	N.A.
anti-Racist			non-Racist	✓		Racist — omission / commission		✓	
anti-Sexist	✓		non-Sexist		✓	Sexist			
anti-Elitist			non-Elitist	✓	✓	Elitist			
anti-Materialist			non-Materialist	✓	✓	Materialist			
anti-Individualist			non-Individualist	✓	✓	Individualist			
anti-Ageist			non-Ageist			Ageist			✓
anti-Conformist	✓	✓	non-Conformist			Conformist			
anti-Escapist			non-Escapist	✓		Escapist		✓	
Builds positive image of females/minorities			Builds negative image of females/minorities	✓		Excellent	Good	Fair	Poor
Inspires action vs. oppression			Culturally authentic			Literary quality — Fair ✓			
						Art quality — Excellent ✓			

I'M GOING TO RUN AWAY!
by Jean Thompson
illustrated by Bill Myers
Abingdon Press
$4.95, unpaged, grades p.s.-3

One morning during which many things have gone wrong, little Jimmy gets very frustrated and decides to run away. His search for a new home is unsuccessful because no one on his block needs a little boy. At the end of the day, he is back on his own doorstep and is welcomed warmly by his parents.

Jimmy's family lives comfortably in a middle-class neighborhood. Is the neighborhood integrated or not? The illustrations depicting neighbor Ginger (Ginger is Jimmy's second best friend; Steve is his best) and her four brothers and sisters would be clearly Black to Black people and to some adults of all races. But white children might not recognize them as such. Why the lack of clarity? And why did the author give the "Black" family many more children than any of the white families?

In one illustration a girl is watching two boys play ball while another girl stands by and a baby girl stares out of a crib. In the only other illustration depicting a girl, we find her clutching a doll and sticking her tongue out at Jimmy. Mother and all other adult women cook, clean house and serve meals.

At a point Jimmy speaks to "old Mr. MacArthur" who is grouchy, hard of hearing and misinterprets everything Jimmy says. "I'm Jimmy," Jimmy said. "Sure you're busy," said Mr. MacArthur. This ageism is supposed to be funny.

Although a sense of security is conveyed through the parents' warm reunion with their prodigal offspring, nowhere are alternatives to running away suggested. This escapist solution, along with the instances of sexism, ageism, and poor illustrations of non-white children, make this book unacceptable.

	ART	WORDS		ART	WORDS			ART	WORDS	N.A.
anti-Racist			non-Racist		✓	Racist — omission / commission		✓	✓	
anti-Sexist			non-Sexist			Sexist		✓	✓	
anti-Elitist			non-Elitist	✓	✓	Elitist				
anti-Materialist			non-Materialist	✓	✓	Materialist				
anti-Individualist			non-Individualist	✓		Individualist			✓	
anti-Ageist			non-Ageist	✓		Ageist			✓	
anti-Conformist			non-Conformist			Conformist				
anti-Escapist			non-Escapist	✓		Escapist			✓	
Builds positive image of females/ minorities			Builds negative image of females minorities		✓		Excellent	Good	Fair	Poor
Inspires action vs. oppression			Culturally authentic			Literary quality			✓	
						Art quality		✓		

A GUN IS NOT A TOY
by Beverly Breton
illustrated by same
Stop & Grow Book Nook
$1.50, 20 pages, grades 1-3

In spite of this book's numerous faults, it will have been worth the effort if it inspires a commercial publisher to do a really good book about the ev:' ° the "bang-bang, you're dead" game.

With no pretensions to artistic or literary style, *A Gun I: : A Toy* describes Phillip, an ordinary little boy who likes school and hi: .1er and is thrilled to learn that Police Officer Young is coming to talk to ...5 class. The officer's "a gun-is-not-a-toy" message gets a mixed reception. Phillip, however, returns home and decides to throw away his own toy guns. Although his two best school friends continue to play "cops and robbers," Phillip now refuses to join in—even with imaginary guns. In a flush of maturity, he gives up his old friends and makes a new one—Sally (she had persuaded her own younger brother to discard his gun, too).

What goes awry? The female role models are an impatient older sister, a mother on kitchen duty, a female teacher, Sally in a pretty dress. The grey shading used in the illustrations to identify one child (and Officer Young) as Black is an aesthetic disaster. The use of a Black cop to deliver a pacifist-type anti-gun message to an integrated class of youngsters raises several questions with which the book never deals. The central theme—that guns are dangerous playthings—is handled so inaptly that the book would hardly raise the consciousness of the gun-toting young fellows I know.

One nice touch deserves note: Phillip's soul searching before he reaches his *big* decision, shows respect on the part of the author for children's feelings and mental processes. But while Ms. Breton's good intentions are praiseworthy, a better-conceived work than hers is needed to encourage relations among children that are free of macho gun-play.

The Stop & Grow Book Nook is located at Wild Lake Interfaith Center, Columbia, Md. 21044

	ART	WORDS		ART	WORDS		ART	WORDS	N.A.
anti-Racist			non-Racist	✓	✓	Racist — omission / commission			
anti-Sexist			non-Sexist			Sexist	✓	✓	
anti-Elitist			non-Elitist	✓	✓	Elitist			
anti-Materialist			non-Materialist	✓	✓	Materialist			
anti-Individualist		✓	non-Individualist	✓		Individualist			
anti-Ageist			non-Ageist			Ageist			✓
anti-Conformist			non-Conformist	✓	✓	Conformist			
anti-Escapist		✓	non-Escapist			Escapist			

							Excellent	Good	Fair	Poor
Builds positive image of females/minorities			Builds negative image of females/minorities			Literary quality				✓
Inspires action vs. oppression			Culturally authentic			Art quality				✓

JENNIE JENKINS
by Mark Taylor
illustrated by Glen Rounds
Little, Brown
$4.95, 44 pages, grades p.s.-3

This nasty little book stereotypes and makes fun of country people. The term "hillbillies" is not used, but Appalachian people are the butt of this sick joke.

Jennie is the youngest member of her family. Her oldest brother fiddles, three older sisters husband-hunt, mother and father scream at one another. According to brother Zeph, Jennie is ". . . the only gal I know who can plow and hoe and help with hayin', dig 'taters, milk a cow, chop wood, hitch a team, and ride Contraption" (Contraption is an ornery horse).

What does our heroine think about ordinary women-folk like her sisters? "They aren't good for much. Primpin' themselves and makin' dreamy eyes at menfolk is all they know how to do."

While the family and townfolk are planning what to wear to the big Nettel Bottom Ball, Jennie decides she will not attend such a foolish event. Angry at her family for insisting that she go, Jennie decides to play cruel and dangerous "jokes" on each of her sisters' beaus as a way of getting out of going to the ball. Each joke backfires and results in the suitors asking the sisters to marry them. Jennie, enraged, asks Brute Smith, the local "man's man," to escort her to the ball. "Brute Smith was the strongest, richest, handsomest young man in all the county. . . . All the girls dreamed about him." Naturally, this dreamboat and our little Jennie win first prize in a jig dancing contest.

Human frailties are the source of humor in this ugly story. Being female—especially a freaky, "tomboy," female, like Jennie—is a gas. The black and white cartoon-style illustrations underscore the book's negativism. Author and illustrator are both male.

	ART	WORDS		ART	WORDS		ART	WORDS	N.A.
anti-Racist			non-Racist	✓	✓	Racist — omission / commission			
anti-Sexist			non-Sexist			Sexist	✓	✓	
anti-Elitist			non-Elitist			Elitist	✓	✓	
anti-Materialist			non-Materialist	✓		Materialist		✓	
anti-Individualist			non-Individualist	✓		Individualist		✓	
anti-Ageist			non-Ageist	✓	✓	Ageist			
anti-Conformist	✓	✓	non-Conformist			Conformist			
anti-Escapist			non-Escapist	✓	✓	Escapist			
Builds positive image of females/minorities			Builds negative image of females minorities		✓		Excellent	Good	Fair	Poor
Inspires action vs. oppression			Culturally authentic			Literary quality		✓		
						Art quality			✓	

MANDY'S GRANDMOTHER
by Liesel M. Skorpen
illustrated by Martha Alexander
Dial Press
$4.95, 28 pages, grades p.s.-3

Mandy's Grandmother explores the relationship between Mandy (a jean-wearing, pony-riding preschooler), her mother (a frantic, ultra-domestic type) and her grandmother (a grey-hair-in-a-bun knitter), who is paying her very first visit to Mandy's home.

Grandmother and granddaughter do not meet each other's expectations, but their loneliness and need for affection happily result in mutual acceptance. Grandmother becomes more appreciative of Mandy the way she is, and the two come to enjoy one another's company—Mandy learning to knit and Grand-mother learning to whistle.

While the warm age-youth relationship depicted here is a welcome plus, and the style of the writing and illustrations reinforce this ambience, they do not quite offset the chill of one more image of a super housewife—Mandy's mother.

	ART	WORDS		ART	WORDS		ART	WORDS	N.A.
anti-Racist			non-Racist			Racist — omission / commission			✓
anti-Sexist			non-Sexist			Sexist	✓	✓	
anti-Elitist			non-Elitist	✓	✓	Elitist			
anti-Materialist			non-Materialist	✓	✓	Materialist			
anti-Individualist			non-Individualist	✓	✓	Individualist			
anti-Ageist			non-Ageist	✓	✓	Ageist			
anti-Conformist			non-Conformist	✓	✓	Conformist			
anti-Escapist			non-Escapist	✓	✓	Escapist			
Builds positive image of females/minorities			Builds negative image of females/minorities				Excellent	Good	Fair	Poor
Inspires action vs. oppression			Culturally authentic			Literary quality		✓		
						Art quality		✓		

ME AND NEESIE
by Eloise Greenfield
illustrated by Moneta Barnett
Thomas Y. Crowell
$5.50, unpaged, grades p.s-4

A familiar situation—the relationship between an only child and her imaginary friend—is depicted in this picture book. Janell's alter ego, Neesie, is a happy-go-lucky free spirit who defies all parental authority in an amusing and delightful way. When Aunt Bea, an older person, arrives to visit the family, Janell is asked by her mother to refrain from her make-believe play. But Neesie, being irrepressible, intrudes herself upon the scene, creating a delicate situation for all. Aunt Bea proves more understanding than Janell's parents.

When Janell's first day at school leads to the formation of new and real friendships, she returns home to find that Neesie has mysteriously disappeared—the need for her existence having faded away. (Parents who read this book to their children should be prepared to explain Neesie's disappearance and Janell's final adjustment to her absence.)

This story about a Black family has a very warm texture. Janell's mother and father are portrayed as being sensitive and sympathetic regarding their daughter's growing pains. Moneta Barnett's illustrations are lively and expressive. There are so few good stories written about young Black children that this book is especially welcome for its portrayal of a warm family relationship.

	ART	WORDS		ART	WORDS			ART	WORDS	N.A.
anti-Racist	✓	✓	non-Racist			Racist	omission			
							commission			
anti-Sexist			non-Sexist	✓	✓	Sexist				
anti-Elitist			non-Elitist	✓	✓	Elitist				
anti-Materialist			non-Materialist	✓	✓	Materialist				
anti-Individualist			non-Individualist	✓	✓	Individualist				
anti-Ageist	✓	✓	non-Ageist			Ageist				
anti-Conformist			non-Conformist	✓	✓	Conformist				
anti-Escapist			non-Escapist	✓	✓	Escapist				
Builds positive image of females/minorities	✓	✓	Builds negative image of females/minorities				Excellent	Good	Fair	Poor
Inspires action vs. oppression			Culturally authentic	✓	✓	Literary quality	✓			
						Art quality		✓		

MOLLY PATCH AND HER ANIMAL FRIENDS
by Ben Shecter
illustrated by same
Harper & Row
$5.50, 59 pages, grades p.s.-2

This seemingly inoffensive, sweet-little-girl-book proves that an incredible amount of sexism can be injected into a simple story described on the book jacket as being "filled with gentle affection." When Molly Patch moves to the country to escape "city noises" and unfriendly faces (who might they be?), plenty of friendly faces soon begin to appear. Enter Raccoon, Mole, Bear, Mouse, Porcupine, Toad, Snake, Crow, Rabbit, and Cat—*all* males. Goose and Chicken are the only female friendly faces, and their frequent, foolish squabbles suggest that their friendliness does not extend to each other.

What does Molly do to win her friends love? She nurses, feeds and hugs them. In addition, Molly grows flowers, cleans up after parties, cooks soup, tea, toast, jam and jellies, pies and pastries, cookies, fudge and cereal. She also gardens and usually wears a hat and an apron.

The consciousness of author-artist Ben Shecter could do with a little raising.

	ART	WORDS		ART	WORDS		ART	WORDS	N.A.
anti-Racist			non-Racist			Racist omission / commission			✓
anti-Sexist			non-Sexist			Sexist	✓	✓	
anti-Elitist			non-Elitist	✓	✓	Elitist			
anti-Materialist			non-Materialist	✓	✓	Materialist			
anti-Individualist			non-Individualist	✓	✓	Individualist			
anti-Ageist			non-Ageist			Ageist			✓
anti-Conformist			non-Conformist			Conformist	✓	✓	
anti-Escapist			non-Escapist			Escapist	✓	✓	
Builds positive image of females/ minorities			Builds negative image of females/ minorities	✓	✓		Excellent	Good	Fair	Poor
Inspires action vs. oppression			Culturally authentic			Literary quality		✓	
						Art quality			✓

THE QUEEN WHO COULDN'T BAKE GINGERBREAD: AN ADAPTATION OF A GERMAN FOLK TALE
by Dorothy Van Woerkom
illustrated by Paul Galdone
Alfred A. Knopf
$5.50, 32 pages, grades p.s.-3

This up-dated version of an old fairy tale concerns King Pilaf of Mulligatawny who desires a beautiful and wise wife who can also bake perfect gingerbread, and Princess Calliope of Tintinnabulum who wants a husband who is handsome, kind and can also play a slide trombone.

The fact is, both are homely and neither one can perform the desired feats. However, the king is kind and the princess is wise, and they decide to build their marriage on this foundation. But time's passage finds them blaming each other for their respective inabilities to cook and play music. A marital fight, estrangement and reconsideration of the issues lead to a resolution: *He* will learn to bake perfect gingerbread and *she* will learn to play the slide trombone. Both live happily ever after.

This picture book is entertaining and fun for its twist ending. It also provides a good lesson: You should not put on others a role expectation that is your thing, not theirs. Unfortunately, this feminist twist takes place within a framework that reflects the age-old assumptions of universal heterosexuality and marriage, an all-white cast, and a royal state in which the citizens' happiness depends upon the good moods of their king and queen. Do we still need to read about a king who, for all his "kindness," orders around his servants who obey his every whim without question? Pretty much the same old German fairy tale.

The colorful illustrations put down people who are not beautiful.

	ART	WORDS		ART	WORDS			ART	WORDS	N.A.
anti-Racist			non-Racist			Racist	omission / commission			✓
anti-Sexist			non-Sexist	✓		Sexist			✓	
anti-Elitist			non-Elitist			Elitist		✓	✓	
anti-Materialist			non-Materialist	✓	✓	Materialist				
anti-Individualist			non-Individualist	✓	✓	Individualist				
anti-Ageist			non-Ageist	✓	✓	Ageist				
anti-Conformist	✓	✓	non-Conformist			Conformist				
anti-Escapist			non-Escapist	✓	✓	Escapist				

Builds positive image of females/minorities			Builds negative image of females/minorities				Excellent	Good	Fair	Poor
						Literary quality		✓		
Inspires action vs. oppression			Culturally authentic			Art quality		✓		

THE JONESES
by Corinne Ramage
illustrated by same
J. B. Lippincott
$4.95, 36 pages, grades 1-3

To fully enjoy this picture book fantasy, the reader must be prepared to accept it on its own terms. The Joneses, says the book jacket, are "just like any other family with thirty-one children." Mother drives a submarine and Father stays home to care for the army of offspring, one of whom is an adopted dragon brought home by Mother from one of her adventures at sea.

There is only one line of text in the entire book: "Have a good day, dear husband," says Mother, without a trace of malice in her expression. Wearing an apron, Father waves good-bye. Through a bevy of funny, minutely-detailed pen and ink drawings, we follow the vagaries of this strange household as Father serves breakfast, peels vegetables, does the laundry and presides over the mayhem, while Mother does her Jacques Yves Cousteau thing.

Suddenly, all hell breaks loose. The sub is attacked by a larger-than-"Jaws" sea monster. The cartoon frame depicting the household simultaneously opens up, causing several children to fall into the sea below, and THEN—it's *anybody's* guess what's going to happen!

The bus which brings Mother home from work is on schedule. As she arrives with the rescued children and the adopted dragon-child, Father and the rest of the brood are posted in the doorway—and in the garden, and at the window and in a treetop—to welcome them back. Supper, story-and-bedtime follow so the Joneses can recuperate for the next day's activity.

Trying to keep up with these Joneses will be fun for all ages. Children will have a good time pouring over the intricate line drawings to follow the action and making up their own embellishments for the plot.

	ART	WORDS		ART	WORDS			ART	WORDS	N.A.
anti-Racist			non-Racist			Racist — omission / commission				✓
anti-Sexist	✓		non-Sexist			Sexist				
anti-Elitist			non-Elitist	✓		Elitist				
anti-Materialist			non-Materialist	✓		Materialist				
anti-Individualist			non-Individualist	✓		Individualist				
anti-Ageist			non-Ageist			Ageist				✓
anti-Conformist	✓		non-Conformist			Conformist				
anti-Escapist			non-Escapist	✓		Escapist				
Builds positive image of (females) minorities	✓		Builds negative image of females/ minorities				Excellent	Good	Fair	Poor
Inspires action vs. oppression			Culturally authentic			Literary quality				
						Art quality	✓			

MICHAEL
by Liesel Moak Skorpen
illustrated by Joan Sandin
Harper & Row
$5.95, 40 pages, grades p.s.-2

Michael, a farm boy of about five, is afraid of thunder. Scolded by his father for leaving toys around, he stomps outdoors to sulk. There he finds a lost baby rabbit which, in order to survive, must be bottle-fed around the clock. When the rabbit gets hungry during a thunderstorm, Michael must overcome his fear. Braving the lightning and thunder out of affection for his new charge, Michael discovers that his father has overcome his anger and is feeding the bunny. Happy ending.

What distinguishes this little book from hundreds like it are the illustrations. They are warm, humorous and very, very wet during the storm. Another plus is that two illustrations show a nurturing father, once feeding baby and once feeding bunny.

	ART	WORDS		ART	WORDS			ART	WORDS	N.A.
anti-Racist			non-Racist			Racist — omission / commission				✓
anti-Sexist			non-Sexist	✓	✓	Sexist				
anti-Elitist			non-Elitist	✓	✓	Elitist				
anti-Materialist			non-Materialist	✓	✓	Materialist				
anti-Individualist			non-Individualist	✓	✓	Individualist				
anti-Ageist			non-Ageist			Ageist				✓
anti-Conformist			non-Conformist	✓	✓	Conformist				
anti-Escapist			non-Escapist	✓	✓	Escapist				
Builds positive image of females/ minorities			Builds negative image of females/ minorities				Excellent	Good	Fair	Poor
Inspires action vs. oppression			Culturally authentic			Literary quality			✓	
						Art quality		✓		

MORRIS AND HIS BRAVE LION
by Helen Spelman Rogers
illustrated by Glo Coalson
McGraw-Hill
$5.95, 48 pages, grades p.s.-3

How a four-year-old learns to live with his parents' divorce is the subject of *Morris and His Brave Lion.* On the day Morris' father goes away, he leaves a huge box for Morris that contains a toy lion, just like the one he had seen in the zoo the day before. His dad tells Morris that the lion is brave and strong. In the days and months that follow, the toy lion is a silent but constant reminder to Morris to be brave and strong. Although he receives many gifts and letters from him, Morris misses his father very much. For his fifth birthday, he thinks of a way to bring his father back to see him.

The author's tender and straightforward handling of the divorce issue, without condescension, shows depth and understanding of children's needs as well as a basic respect for human feelings. Ms. Rogers depicts a warm relationship between Morris and his mother, punctuated by humorous moments and frank discussions of what divorce is and why his parents cannot live together anymore. The mother also tries to help Morris understand that reality involves times of sadness as well as of joy. Human feelings are treated as being more important than property in that Morris' unhappiness is not allayed by his father's gift. Neither Morris nor his mother is portrayed as bitter or self-centered. In fact, the mother encourages Morris to consider his father's feelings.

The only criticism is the author's emphasis on strength and courage in males. The zoo lion is automatically a male. Yet Morris' father's "strong and brave" image is superficial and stiff. He tells Morris "your mother has a problem," as if divorce results from only one partner's "problem." He evades Morris' questions by promising to "explain it all some other time," then cops out completely by leaving.

By contrast, the mother is multi-dimensional and strong. She tells Morris it is all right to cry and still be brave, and she answers his questions about divorce thoughtfully. At the end, Morris realizes "she knows what it means to be brave." The sensitive text and warm illustrations make this a very good book.

	ART	WORDS		ART	WORDS			ART	WORDS	N.A.
anti-Racist			non-Racist	✓	✓	Racist	omission commission			
anti-Sexist	✓	✓	non-Sexist			Sexist				
anti-Elitist			non-Elitist	✓	✓	Elitist				
anti-Materialist		✓	non-Materialist	✓		Materialist				
anti-Individualist			non-Individualist	✓	✓	Individualist				
anti-Ageist			non-Ageist			Ageist				✓
anti-Conformist			non-Conformist	✓	✓	Conformist				
anti-Escapist		✓	non-Escapist	✓		Escapist				

				Excellent	Good	Fair	Poor
Builds positive image of females/minorities			Builds negative image of females/minorities				
Inspires action vs. oppression			Culturally authentic	Literary quality	✓		
				Art quality ✓			

PIERO VENTURA'S BOOK OF CITIES
by Piero Ventura
illustrated by same
Random House
$4.95, 52 pages, grades p.s.-4

The author/illustrator responsible for this book tells us that in re-creating scenes from cities he has visited, he was seeking to "combine the special elements and colorful impressions that made each city a unique experience. While he succeeds in fulfilling his own aims, he fails to fulfill the publisher's promise of showing "how people live, work, travel and have fun in cities around the world."

The contrast between the text and drawings is curious. Although the drawings are the focus of the book, it is the text which has the greatest strengths—good description, sound observations, good detail and liveliness. In the drawings, charming and colorful though they are, Ventura fails to capture the very quality of the cities which makes them cities. Indeed, the *reality* of a city seems to have been lost in the process of abstracting those "unique and special elements" from their surroundings.

The whole emphasis, in drawing after drawing, seems to be on fairy-tale qualities. A garden in Kyoto, St. Basil's Cathedral in Moscow, the Spanish Steps in Rome—each of these subjects looks like a ballet set prettily drawn, centered in a large white space. But the *feel* of the city—the busy streets, the pace, the crowds, the constant activity, and—above all—the glorious variety of the city's population—is largely missing. All right, if one wants to show a certain homogeneity in Copenhagen, fine. But in London's Hyde Park?! In New York's Central Park?! In Washington, D.C.?! In Rome, all of the 200-odd people so painstakingly drawn look as if they were born of the same mother and father. Thank God for Hong Kong, Baghdad and Tokyo!

The most successful blend of text and illustration is in the section on *Transportation*. Here, one gets the feel of a traffic jam in London; of the complexity of New York's subway system with its maze of stairs, exits, tracks, escalators; of the freeway in Los Angeles (although, again, abstracted from its surroundings, it looks more like New York's little old Major Deegan).

The chapters on *Work* and on *Fun* are well written and include scenes full of detail that will absorb children for hours on end. Hamburg, with its lakes, rivers, canals and railroad, is a fascinating harbor and wonderfully executed. There are also good scenes of the Baghdad markets, Stockholm's Fire Department, Venice's gondolas filled with vegetables, a wrestling exhibit in Tokyo and an exciting production of *Aida* at the La Scala Opera.

The *Au Printemps* store in Paris, however, seems strangely bare and sterile. And although it "sells everything from neckties to sailboats," only one woman—a mother with her young son—is shown among a sea of French*men* in the sports department. *Women* are depicted buying clothes (mutilating each other at a sales counter), perfume, wines and *Paris Match*. Voila! La liberation des femmes.

Mr. Ventura has a sense of humor, a gifted palette and is an enthusiastic and skilled observer. Since this is the first in a projected series of journeys, it will be interesting to see what happens when he travels again. I would like to see the "unique impressions" a unique city like Nairobi would make on Mr. Ventura.

	ART	WORDS		ART	WORDS			ART	WORDS	N.A.
anti-Racist			non-Racist	✓	✓	Racist	omission			
							commission			
anti-Sexist			non-Sexist			Sexist		✓	✓	
anti-Elitist			non-Elitist	✓	✓	Elitist				
anti-Materialist			non-Materialist	✓	✓	Materialist				
anti-Individualist			non-Individualist	✓	✓	Individualist				
anti-Ageist			non-Ageist	✓	✓	Ageist				
anti-Conformist			non-Conformist	✓	✓	Conformist				
anti-Escapist			non-Escapist	✓	✓	Escapist				
Builds positive image of females/minorities			Builds negative image of (females) minorities	✓			Excellent	Good	Fair	Poor
Inspires action vs. oppression			Culturally authentic			Literary quality	✓			
						Art quality	✓			

ROTTEN KIDPHABETS
by Robert Tallon
illustrated by same
Holt, Rinehart & Winston
$6.95, unpaged, grades p.s.-2

This expensive, anti-human book encourages laughing at, or making fun of, people.

The author is evenly disposed to the rottenness and ugliness of children of both sexes. He maintains this undiscriminatory pattern up to the letter "Z," giving us a nasty male "A" ("Awful Albert") matched by an ugly female "B" ("Bad Beulah"). And so on through the letters. But he goofs at "Z," leaving his alphabet of horrors with 14 males to 12 females. That is a small blessing in this not-nice, un-funny book. This is a form of "humor" which distorts our humanity.

The illustrations are fully in keeping with the hatefulness of the text.

	ART	WORDS		ART	WORDS			ART	WORDS	N.A.
anti-Racist			non-Racist	✓	✓	Racist	omission			
							commission			
anti-Sexist			non-Sexist	✓	✓	Sexist				
anti-Elitist			non-Elitist	✓	✓	Elitist				
anti-Materialist			non-Materialist	✓	✓	Materialist				
anti-Individualist			non-Individualist	✓		Individualist			✓	
anti-Ageist			non-Ageist			Ageist				✓
anti-Conformist			non-Conformist	✓	✓	Conformist				
anti-Escapist			non-Escapist	✓	✓	Escapist				
Builds positive image of females/minorities			Builds negative image of females/minorities				Excellent	Good	Fair	Poor
Inspires action vs. oppression			Culturally authentic			Literary quality				✓
						Art quality			✓	

BETSY'S BABY BROTHER
by Gunilla Wolde
illustrated by same
Random House
$1.95, unpaged, grades p.s.-1

Translated from the Swedish, this simple picture book explores a young child's mixed emotions about having an infant in the family. Sometimes she wishes she could give him away and be alone to enjoy her mother's affections. What the baby's needs are and how they are met is fully explained. In this apparently single-parent family, Betsy eventually learns to share responsibility for the baby with her mother.

Though short, this book offers several innovations in the literature of sibling rivalry. Author Gunilla Wolde notes Betsy's jealousy without judging it, allowing the little girl her anger and go-away-baby fantasy. At the same time, Betsy's sense of self-worth is reinforced. The cartoon-like illustrations include a breast-feeding scene, the baby's soiled diaper, and a glimpse of his penis. All of these subjects are presented in the most natural way without sensationalism. The baby, too, is described realistically: annoying, as well as cuddly and sweet.

	ART	WORDS		ART	WORDS			ART	WORDS	N.A.
anti-Racist			non-Racist			Racist	omission			✓
							commission			
anti-Sexist			non-Sexist	✓	✓	Sexist				
anti-Elitist			non-Elitist	✓	✓	Elitist				
anti-Materialist			non-Materialist	✓	✓	Materialist				
anti-Individualist			non-Individualist	✓	✓	Individualist				
anti-Ageist			non-Ageist			Ageist				✓
anti-Conformist			non-Conformist	✓	✓	Conformist				
anti-Escapist			non-Escapist	✓	✓	Escapist				
Builds positive image of females/minorities			Builds negative image of females/minorities				Excellent	Good	Fair	Poor
Inspires action vs. oppression			Culturally authentic			Literary quality		✓		
						Art quality		✓		

GLUE FINGERS
by Matt Christopher
illustrated by Jim Venable
Little, Brown
$4.50, unpaged, grades 1-3

Billy Joe, youngest of four brothers, stutters. Despite his skill as a "glue fingers" football player, he refuses to join the football team for fear the other boys will make fun of him. Finally deciding to play, but vowing never to speak a word, Billy Joe discovers that silence is impractical and begins to speak—stutter and all. No one makes fun of him, mainly because he also wins the game for his team with some spectacular plays.

Moral? Perhaps the author means to say that a handicap is okay so long as one is a super-something. But what if one does not happen to be a super-something? In that case, one must look for a better book.

Books which purport to deal with a problem but violate their subject by fudging on the salient issues are, at best, a rip-off. They also do a disservice to the many people who have one sort of handicap or another. They are an insult to the intelligence of all children.

The art work in *Glue Fingers* is as poor as the writing. The one female pictured among all the drawings of football helmets and padded shoulders is Billy Joe's mother. She is announcing that dinner is ready and, yes, there is an apron around her waist.

	ART	WORDS		ART	WORDS		ART	WORDS	N.A.
anti-Racist			non-Racist	✓	✓	Racist omission / commission			
anti-Sexist			non-Sexist			Sexist	✓	✓	
anti-Elitist			non-Elitist	✓	✓	Elitist			
anti-Materialist			non-Materialist	✓	✓	Materialist			
anti-Individualist			non-Individualist	✓	✓	Individualist			
anti-Ageist			non-Ageist			Ageist			✓
anti-Conformist			non-Conformist	✓		Conformist		✓	
anti-Escapist			non-Escapist	✓		Escapist		✓	
Builds positive image of females/ minorities			Builds negative image of females/ minorities				Excellent	Good	Fair	Poor
Inspires action vs. oppression			Culturally authentic			Literary quality				✓
						Art quality			✓	

FEELINGS: INSIDE YOU AND OUTLOUD TOO
by Barbara Kay Polland
photos by Craig DeRoy
Celestial Arts
$4.95, 64 pages, grades p.s.-3

This photographic exploration of love, fear, pain, frustration, closeness, and other feelings, encourages honest interaction between people. Unfortunately, poor choices in the photography and inconsistency in format and language subvert the author's intent.

Often, the emotions being depicted in the full-page photographs are unclear and require the boldly printed text to clarify them. Many of the photos must also be studied closely for important details: An anti-sexist photo of a man crying is puzzling until one notices the letter he is holding. In a few cases, an important subject in the background is not noticed at first glance.

The general format, plus the use of such early childhood terms as "icky," "crummy," "soooo special" and "yucky," suggest a pre-school or primary grade audience. However, the inclusion of a full-page review in the middle of the book, photographs of older children and occasional complex phrasing make the book too confusing and misleading for the very young. For example, the page on feeling "Close" shows and describes a child being left out of a play situation by two other "close" youngsters—inferring that being close hurts someone else.

Most ethnic groups are represented in the illustrations, but some depictions could be interpreted as racist. An Hispanic male carrying suitcases downstairs with a sad child watching his departure implies the stereotype of a father leaving home. A photograph of a classroom with a Black girl passing a note under the table to a Puerto Rican girl suggests the stereotype of minority children not concentrating in school. The fact that the teacher is Black is a positive, but secondary, image.

Sexism, too, is not totally absent. While it is good to see a father in a nurturing role, as shown in the "Fear" study, the picture suggests that only girls are fearful. The nude photo of a female toddler admiring her body in a mirror would be more appreciated if male nudity were also depicted. And in a supermarket scene, only women are shown with their children.

The author deserves points for stressing positive human values. For example, the "Jealousy" page offers helpful hints on what to do when you feel jealous—stop and think of the very special nice *qualities* that *you* have.

But, although they are promised, explanations as to the "why" of certain feelings are not given. An adult reading partner would be needed to supply this dimension.

	ART	WORDS		ART	WORDS		ART	WORDS	N.A.
anti-Racist			non-Racist		✓	Racist — omission / commission	✓		
anti-Sexist			non-Sexist	✓	✓	Sexist			
anti-Elitist			non-Elitist	✓	✓	Elitist			
anti-Materialist			non-Materialist	✓	✓	Materialist			
anti-Individualist			non-Individualist	✓	✓	Individualist			
anti-Ageist			non-Ageist	✓	✓	Ageist			
anti-Conformist	✓	✓	non-Conformist			Conformist			
anti-Escapist		✓	non-Escapist	✓		Escapist			
Builds positive image of females/ minorities			Builds negative image of females/ minorities				Excellent	Good	Fair	Poor
Inspires action vs. oppression			Culturally authentic			Literary quality			✓	
						Art quality			✓	

JUST MOMMA AND ME
by Christine Engla
illustrated by same
Lollipop Power
$2.00, 36 pages, grades p.s.-2

This pleasantly written, nicely illustrated story, told from the point of view of a girl who is jealously possessive of her mother, has a few unusual twists.

Regina, who appears to be five or six-ish, is the adopted daughter of a single mother—although that fact may well escape young readers or listeners. Regina and Momma share some very happy times together, just the two of them. Then, one day, Karl moves in. Regina resents his presence, and when Momma becomes pregnant and tells her,"We'll have a new person in our family," Regina does not welcome the news. But when Momma goes to the hospital, Karl proves to be loving. Regina then switches from cherishing "Just Momma and me," to "Just Karl and me and Momma."

The neighbor-baby-sitter-friend is Black. Karl is bearded. Momma is an artist. Both story and illustrations are warm and loving.

However, the feminists at Lollipop Power might reconsider one of the illustrations, should they ever reprint this little book. Regina and Momma are shown leaving a Loew's movie theatre whose marquee features *Pippi Long-stockings*. Although that film is not racist, the book is, and publicizing the film helps to promote the book. *Just Momma and Me* can be obtained from Lollipop Power, Inc., P.O. Box 1171, Chapel Hill, N.C. 27514.

	ART	WORDS		ART	WORDS			ART	WORDS	N.A.
anti-Racist			non-Racist	✓	✓	Racist	omission			
							commission			
anti-Sexist	✓	✓	non-Sexist			Sexist				
anti-Elitist			non-Elitist	✓	✓	Elitist				
anti-Materialist			non-Materialist	✓	✓	Materialist				
anti-Individualist			non-Individualist	✓	✓	Individualist				
anti-Ageist			non-Ageist			Ageist				✓
anti-Conformist	✓	✓	non-Conformist			Conformist				
anti-Escapist			non-Escapist	✓	✓	Escapist				
Builds positive image of females/minorities		✓	Builds negative image of females/minorities				Excellent	Good	Fair	Poor
Inspires action vs. oppression			Culturally authentic			Literary quality		✓		
						Art quality		✓		

THE MAGGIE B.
by Irene Haas
illustrated by same
Atheneum
$7.95, unpaged, grades p.s.-3

More than anything else, little Margaret Barnstable longs to have a ship "to sail for a day, alone and free, with someone nice for company." In her fantasy, the wish is fulfilled. Unfortunately, while the author is obviously enamored of the fantasy, Margaret could not be less "alone" or "free." There on the good ship "Maggie B." Margaret's "nice company" is her baby brother, whom she mothers (happily) throughout the journey. Instead of being free to enjoy the wind, air, space, and exercise that a sailing trip would offer, Margaret creates for herself a cosy, warm, confined world more reminiscent of a home than a ship. Clad in a dress, she spends an inordinate amount of time in the cabin washing dishes, cleaning the kitchen and preparing elaborate meals for herself and the baby. When the chores are out of the way, she sits on deck surrounded by a womb-like garden-farm that all but hides her view of the sea and paints a picture of baby. She survives a storm by dropping anchor and stowing gear, then goes below to be secure and warm and cook some more. The lullabye she sings makes the point succinctly:

Oh the sailor's life is bold and free

His home is on the rolling sea.

Y'heave ho, my *lads,* to come sail with me. (emphasis added)

What a shame that such beautiful illustrations are spent on creating a claustrophobic, "feminine" existence. To take a potentially adventuresome experience and turn it in upon itself is really quite perverse and certainly detrimental to the full growth of young girls in an already restrictive culture.

	ART	WORDS		ART	WORDS			ART	WORDS	N.A.
anti-Racist			non-Racist			Racist	omission / commission			✓
anti-Sexist			non-Sexist			Sexist		✓	✓	
anti-Elitist			non-Elitist	✓	✓	Elitist				
anti-Materialist			non-Materialist	✓	✓	Materialist				
anti-Individualist			non-Individualist	✓	✓	Individualist				
anti-Ageist			non-Ageist			Ageist				✓
anti-Conformist			non-Conformist	✓	✓	Conformist				
anti-Escapist			non-Escapist			Escapist		✓	✓	
Builds positive image of females/ minorities			Builds negative image of females/ minorities				Excellent	Good	Fair	Poor
Inspires action vs. oppression			Culturally authentic			Literary quality		✓		
						Art quality	✓			

THE WINTER WEDDING
by Robert Welber
illustrated by Deborah Ray
Pantheon
$4.95, unpaged, grades p.s.-2

This delightfully written picture book follows Joshua and Jenny through a school year of warmth and trust. Seasonal changes parallel the development of their friendship. They tumble together through the autumn leaves. Under the quiet guidance of their male teacher, they plant seeds with their classmates. One senses their gentle concern for one another throughout, and as an expression of this they agree to be "married." The snow will let them know when it's time to build their home together. And they will know it's time for their spring party when their seeds sprout.

This is a good non-sexist children's book in several ways. Most refreshing is the depiction of an equitable relationship between a little girl and boy. Children of both sexes are shown holding dolls, as well as building with wooden planks. Mention is made of boy-girl "sleep-overs" (which adults should be prepared to discuss). The illustrations are replete with active little girls, and when any sulking is to be done, it is Joshua who sulks. Jenny is every bit as assertive as Joshua. The one exception to these non-stereotyped roles is an illustration which shows Jenny watching as two boys play with trucks and blocks.

A male teacher in the children's apparently kindergarten class is a welcome innovation. His few but supportive responses to the children make him a rare character and a good role model.

The book deals realistically with problems encountered in friendship. Sharing and physical warmth are emphasized as opposed to those values usually fostered in this individualistic society.

The illustrations focus colorfully on the characters as sensitive beings against a subtly sketched background. Joshua is clearly illustrated as a white boy, while Jenny may or may not be Asian American. This lack of clarity is the one flaw in an otherwise pleasant book.

	ART	WORDS		ART	WORDS			ART	WORDS	N.A.
anti-Racist			non-Racist	✓	✓	Racist omission / commission				
anti-Sexist	✓	✓	non-Sexist			Sexist				
anti-Elitist			non-Elitist	✓	✓	Elitist				
anti-Materialist			non-Materialist	✓	✓	Materialist				
anti-Individualist			non-Individualist	✓	✓	Individualist				
anti-Ageist			non-Ageist			Ageist				✓
anti-Conformist	✓	✓	non-Conformist			Conformist				
anti-Escapist			non-Escapist	✓	✓	Escapist				
Builds positive image of females/ minorities		✓	Builds negative image of females/ minorities				Excellent	Good	Fair	Poor
Inspires action vs. oppression			Culturally authentic			Literary quality		✓		
						Art quality			✓	

I AM ADOPTED
by Susan Lapsley
illustrated by Michael Charlton
Bradbury Press
$4.95, unpaged, grades p.s.-1

Four-year-old Charles and his two-year-old sister were adopted when they "were little." "Adopted means belonging," explains Charles to his sibling. Published in England in 1974, this is a warm and pleasant little book. However, the illustrations, in their depiction of the "perfect" home and "perfect" family (pretty blond mother, business-suited father, smiling gray-haired grandmother, spotted dog, older-brother-nice-to-little-sister), are too reminiscent of Dick, Jane and Spot.

	ART	WORDS		ART	WORDS			ART	WORDS	N.A.
anti-Racist			non-Racist			Racist omission / commission				✓
anti-Sexist			non-Sexist	✓	✓	Sexist				
anti-Elitist			non-Elitist	✓	✓	Elitist				
anti-Materialist			non-Materialist	✓	✓	Materialist				
anti-Individualist			non-Individualist	✓	✓	Individualist				
anti-Ageist			non-Ageist			Ageist				
anti-Conformist			non-Conformist	✓	✓	Conformist				
anti-Escapist			non-Escapist	✓	✓	Escapist				
Builds positive image of females/ minorities			Builds negative image of females/ minorities				Excellent	Good	Fair	Poor
Inspires action vs. oppression			Culturally authentic			Literary quality			✓	
						Art quality		✓		

THE DAY AFTER CHRISTMAS
by Alice Bach
illustrated by Mary Chalmers
Harper & Row
$4.95, 29 pages, grades p.s.-2

Emily, a spoiled upper-middle-class second grader finds the day after Christmas depressingly ordinary. Down in the mouth, she behaves unpleasantly toward family and friends without being reprimanded. Eventually, she cheers up enough to play with her expensive new doll house and even resigns herself to not wearing the new party dress she received from Grandma. (Her brother received a truck.) Mother, wearing an apron, tries to cajole Emily into eating breakfast on ordinary, every-day dishes. (Father is away at work.)

Nowhere in this boring, sex-role stereotyped story does a parent or friend appear to discuss feelings or comment on behavior. Post-Christmas depressions are presented as the usual run of things, as is the assumption that new toys will eventually cheer up a child. Imagine the effect of this story on some less privileged children.

The art work is dull, though not offensive.

	ART	WORDS		ART	WORDS			ART	WORDS	N.A.
anti-Racist			non-Racist			Racist	omission / commission			✓
anti-Sexist			non-Sexist			Sexist		✓	✓	
anti-Elitist			non-Elitist	✓	✓	Elitist				
anti-Materialist			non-Materialist			Materialist		✓	✓	
anti-Individualist			non-Individualist	✓		Individualist			✓	
anti-Ageist			non-Ageist			Ageist				✓
anti-Conformist			non-Conformist	✓		Conformist			✓	
anti-Escapist			non-Escapist	✓	✓	Escapist				
Builds positive image of females/minorities			Builds negative image of females/minorities		✓					
Inspires action vs. oppression			Culturally authentic							

	Excellent	Good	Fair	Poor
Literary quality			✓	
Art quality			✓	

THE TERRIBLE THING THAT HAPPENED AT OUR HOUSE
by Marge Blaine
illustrated by John C. Wallner
Parents' Magazine Press
$4.95, 32 pages, grades p.s.-3

The terrible thing that happens to the straggly-haired main character of this picture book is that her mother changes from a "real mother" (homebound, available, calm) into a science teacher (her profession before marriage). As a result, the household is disrupted. The children must dress themselves, eat lunch at school, etc., and the harassed mother has less time and tolerance for the girl and her little brothers.

Distraught at this turn of events, she finally explodes: "No one cares anymore in this house, no one listens. No one helps you. No one even passes the milk when you need it." As a result, the parents *do* listen, and the family begins to make some adjustments. Unfortunately, the idea that the mother's return to work is a "terrible thing" is not really challenged.

The book's lessons are good ones: Family life is not always easy, but through the cooperative efforts of all parties workable arrangements can often be found. Secondly, readers are encouraged to make themselves heard and demand their rights as human beings.

Best of all are the illustrations by John C. Wallner, often from a child's eye-level view. There are lots of things close to the ground, like shoes and legs, and many absorbing little details.

	ART	WORDS		ART	WORDS			ART	WORDS	N.A.
anti-Racist			non-Racist			Racist	omission			✓
							commission			
anti-Sexist	✓	✓	non-Sexist			Sexist				
anti-Elitist			non-Elitist	✓	✓	Elitist				
anti-Materialist			non-Materialist	✓	✓	Materialist				
anti-Individualist			non-Individualist	✓	✓	Individualist				
anti-Ageist			non-Ageist			Ageist				✓
anti-Conformist	✓	✓	non-Conformist			Conformist				
anti-Escapist			non-Escapist	✓	✓	Escapist				

Builds positive image of females/minorities			Builds negative image of females/minorities				Excellent	Good	Fair	Poor
Inspires action vs. oppression			Culturally authentic			Literary quality		✓		
						Art quality	✓			

A LITTLE LION
by Christine Westerberg
illustrated by same
Prentice-Hall
$4.95, unpaged, grades p.s.-2

Little Jessie wants to play "explorer" with her older brother and his friends. They grudgingly agree, providing she will act the part of the lion whom they will scheme to trap for a zoo. Jessie is sent off to wait in the "jungle," where she busily practices her roar. She succeeds in surprising and frightening the older children and twice escapes their elaborate lion traps. Having thus passed muster, she is invited to play with them again the next day.

The pattern of older children who do not want to be bothered with younger siblings is an all-too-familiar one in children's books, as well as in real life. However, since many cultures do not feature such behavior patterns, we have a choice—as parents, teachers, writers or editors—to encourage kinder and more considerate behavior. A book in which a younger child does not have to outwit or outdo older children to win acceptance would be refreshing.

A Little Lion would be a pleasant little book but for one shortcoming. Jessie's brother's friend is Black. On the dedication page the Black child is illustrated standing in tall, "jungly" grass holding a large red umbrella. Later on he is shown with a bundle on his head following two white children in a safari-like procession. These shades of Little Black Sambo, though not repeated throughout, taint the book for this reviewer.

	ART	WORDS		ART	WORDS			ART	WORDS	N.A.
anti-Racist			non-Racist		✓	Racist	omission			
							commission	✓		
anti-Sexist			non-Sexist	✓	✓	Sexist				
anti-Elitist			non-Elitist	✓	✓	Elitist				
anti-Materialist			non-Materialist	✓	✓	Materialist				
anti-Individualist			non-Individualist	✓	✓	Individualist				
anti-Ageist			non-Ageist			Ageist				✓
anti-Conformist			non-Conformist	✓	✓	Conformist				
anti-Escapist			non-Escapist	✓	✓	Escapist				
Builds positive image of females/ minorities			Builds negative image of females/ minorities				Excellent	Good	Fair	Poor
Inspires action vs. oppression			Culturally authentic			Literary quality		✓		
						Art quality			✓	

THE MAN OF THE HOUSE
by Joan Fassler
illustrated by Peter Landa
Human Science Press
$5.95, unpaged, grades p.s.-3

Four-year-old David decides to serve as protector of his household while his father is away on a four-day business trip. Each night, David advises his mother that if she needs protection from monsters that might want to drag her away, she should call and he will fend them off with his magic weapons. When his father returns, David relinquishes his protector role for his former little boy status—although part of him is sad to do so.

This picture book reinforces sexist role expectations and escapist solutions to fantasized problems. How realistic or fair is it to encourage a four-year-old child to protect an adult woman, just because that child is a boy? Conversely, the implication that a female is completely defenseless in the absence of a male is insulting. Illustrations which depict David's mother as timid and passive compound the offense.

Since the monsters are totally fantastic, they can only be handled with correspondingly fantastic weapons, three of which—flame thrower, sword and gun—are obviously phallic. It is indeed insidious, first, to place such a heavy responsibility on a little boy and then to imply he cannot handle the situation without the assistance of extremely violent weapons. Lastly, the ease with which David disposes of the scary-looking monsters reeks of chauvinism (male, that is).

The Man of the House is part of a series on "Psychologically relevant themes . . . conceived and written by a child psychologist and approved by a panel of experts. . . ." The book purports to represent "a mentally healthy approach to help young children cope with behavioral problems at the age when anxieties about these situations occur." The cure is deadlier than the disease!

	ART	WORDS		ART	WORDS			ART	WORDS	N.A.
anti-Racist			non-Racist			Racist	omission / commission			✓
anti-Sexist			non-Sexist			Sexist		✓	✓	
anti-Elitist			non-Elitist	✓	✓	Elitist				
anti-Materialist			non-Materialist	✓	✓	Materialist				
anti-Individualist			non-Individualist	✓	✓	Individualist				
anti-Ageist			non-Ageist			Ageist				✓
anti-Conformist			non-Conformist	✓	✓	Conformist				
anti-Escapist			non-Escapist			Escapist		✓	✓	

	ART	WORDS		ART	WORDS		Excellent	Good	Fair	Poor
Builds positive image of females/ minorities			Builds negative image of (females) minorities	✓	✓	Literary quality			✓	
Inspires action vs. oppression			Culturally authentic			Art quality		✓		

CIRCUS CANNONBALL
by Judy Varga
illustrations by same
William Morrow
$5.95, 30 pages, grades p.s.-3

Nobody knows better than Mrs. Morelli, a bored circus housewife, that life under the Big Top is supposed to be full of excitement and adventure. Her search for meaning and self-fulfillment is the story of *Circus Cannonball.*

Two themes run concurrently through *Circus Cannonball* that could be detrimental to developing healthy attitudes towards women and work. First, the portrayal of women is stereotyped and sexist (all the more disturbing since the author is a woman). Housewives are terribly put down. Being a housewife is depicted as worthless and synonymous with boredom. Expectations for women are very low. They are not expected to lead interesting lives or to have identities of their own. Mrs. Morelli's daughter Lola "lived a life of excitement and adventure," but what does Lola do? She gets "sawed in half in her fancy new costumes." Even when Mrs. Morelli finds her ideal career, she is an assistant to the Great Morelli. Implicit here is the concept that the best a woman can do is to become a good assistant.

Even more damaging is the unrealistic and elitist concept of work. Rather than acknowledging that every type of work is important, Ms. Varga places value only on certain kinds of jobs. In Mrs. Morelli's eyes, "riding an elephant in the grand parade would be exciting and adventurous, scrubbing and dressing them was not." Glamorous, clean jobs are better than those behind the scenes or dirty physical ones. What makes a job exciting and special for Mrs. Morelli is hearing "the cheering of the crowd." Mrs. Morelli is actually seeking recognition and appreciation. She takes the individualistic road. She gets her "big break" and becomes a star. The final irony is that the work involved in preparing the cannon is "less complicated than making her spaghetti sauce." (An ethnic stereotype.)

The circus performers and audience are shown as all white. Although *Circus Cannonball* is colorfully illustrated and attempts to deal with important issues of work and women in an entertaining way, it falls far short of its goals—unless the author's goals were to encourage elitism, individualism and sexism.

	ART	WORDS		ART	WORDS		ART	WORDS	N.A.
anti-Racist			non-Racist		✓	Racist — omission / commission	✓		
anti-Sexist			non-Sexist			Sexist	✓	✓	
anti-Elitist			non-Elitist	✓	✓	Elitist	✓		
anti-Materialist			non-Materialist	✓	✓	Materialist			
anti-Individualist			non-Individualist	✓		Individualist		✓	
anti-Ageist			non-Ageist			Ageist			✓
anti-Conformist			non-Conformist	✓	✓	Conformist			
anti-Escapist			non-Escapist	✓	✓	Escapist	✓		

			Excellent	Good	Fair	Poor
Builds positive image of females/ minorities	Builds negative image of females/ minorities					
Inspires action vs. oppression	Culturally authentic	Literary quality		✓		
		Art quality		✓		

OIL: THE BURIED TREASURE
by Roma Gans
illustrated by Giulio Maestro
Thomas Y. Crowell
$4.50, 32 pages, grades 1-3

A volume in the Let's-Read-And-Find-Out science book series, *Oil: The Buried Treasure* is well-conceived and interesting both in text and illustrations. But it is equally interesting in its failure to illuminate the "treasure" aspect of oil—which we, as adults, know to be the rip-off profits of the oil industry. Also omitted is any reference ot the ecological effects of oil spills or pollution. Nary a word is said about the over-consumption of energy by some nations and under-consumption by others, nor about oil's effects on world economy, economic growth, political power or relations between nations.

An author who could so successfully simplify history and the production methods and uses of oil surely possesses the skills to have covered some of the above. Perhaps she, or the publisher, feels that young people are not able to deal with controversy and/or unpleasant realities.

Given the nature of our society, some pieces of information are presented in ways that reinforce racism. "Most oil is deep underground, but once in a while it has been found in pools on the surface. That's where the Indians found it long ago. The oil was thick, black and sticky. Some Indians used it to waterproof their canoes and paint their faces." The full-page illustration that accompanies this passage shows a fierce-looking, be-feathered Indian, smeared with the "thick, black and sticky" substance.

Sexism taints other comments. "The man at the gas station lifts the hood of your father's car." That's a double whammy, followed by, "Your mother may cook with corn oil or peanut oil."

Overall, this book is not without value, but its negative features dilute its general quality.

	ART	WORDS		ART	WORDS			ART	WORDS	N.A.
anti-Racist			non-Racist			Racist	omission			
							commission	✓	✓	
anti-Sexist			non-Sexist			Sexist		✓	✓	
anti-Elitist			non-Elitist	✓	✓	Elitist				
anti-Materialist			non-Materialist	✓		Materialist			✓	
anti-Individualist			non-Individualist	✓	✓	Individualist				
anti-Ageist			non-Ageist			Ageist				✓
anti-Conformist			non-Conformist	✓	✓	Conformist				
anti-Escapist			non-Escapist	✓	✓	Escapist				
Builds positive image of females/ minorities			Builds negative image of (females) (minorities)		✓		Excellent	Good	Fair	Poor
Inspires action vs. oppression			Culturally authentic			Literary quality		✓		
						Art quality		✓		

MY BROTHER FINE WITH ME

by Lucille Clifton
illustrated by Moneta Barnett
Holt, Rinehart & Winston
$5.50, unpaged, grades p.s.-3

Johnetta's misfortune can be summed up in one word: Baggy. Before her brother Baggy was born, life was fine. Wouldn't it be great if he weren't around? When Baggy decides to run away, Johnetta is delighted and encourages him to pack before their parents come home from work. After Baggy leaves, a disconcerting quiet permeates the house, and Johnetta feels his absence acutely. However, Baggy soon returns, at which time the children discover their mutual love and need for one another.

On the surface, *My Brother Fine With Me* is a typical sibling rivalry story with a happy ending. It is so appealing that one hesitates to find fault. However, as one pieces together the visual and written messages, some disturbing elements emerge.

First of all, Johnetta is depicted as a miniature housewife. A broom and dustpan appear in three of the pictures, the door keys dangle conspicuously from Johnetta's neck in almost every picture, and before Baggy departs she says, "Somebody have to stay here, see after the house while mama and daddy at work." Throughout the summer, Johnetta is responsible for taking care of herself and Baggy during the day. While this is an accurate representation of the role of an older child in a family of working parents, sexist roles are being reinforced—particularly when the characterizations of Johnetta and Baggy are compared. Baggy sees himself as a Black warrior. Rationalizing his fear of running away, he says, "Seem to me, a warrior better stay at home and take care of his family." Johnetta is pleased with this statement. Once more children will conclude that the male is the protector and the female, the one to be protected.

Also disturbing is the seeming lack of family unity as well as Johnetta's preoccupation with her own needs. The beauty of the book lies in excellent illustrations and in Clifton's keen talent for capturing the flavor of Black children's speech.

	ART	WORDS		ART	WORDS			ART	WORDS	N.A.
anti-Racist	✓	✓	non-Racist			Racist	omission			
							commission			
anti-Sexist			non-Sexist			Sexist		✓	✓	
anti-Elitist			non-Elitist	✓	✓	Elitist				
anti-Materialist			non-Materialist	✓	✓	Materialist				
anti-Individualist			non-Individualist	✓		Individualist			✓	
anti-Ageist			non-Ageist			Ageist				✓
anti-Conformist			non-Conformist	✓	✓	Conformist				
anti-Escapist			non-Escapist	✓		Escapist			✓	
Builds positive image of females/minorities			Builds negative image of females/minorities				Excellent	Good	Fair	Poor
Inspires action vs. oppression			Culturally authentic			Literary quality	✓			
						Art quality	✓			

THE DEVIL DID IT
by Susan Jeschke
illustrated by same
Holt, Rinehart & Winston
$5.95, 28 pages, grades p.s.-3

Nana is first introduced to the devil by her mother, who blames him for putting tangles in Nana's hair. That night, Nana meets the devil face to face, so to speak. He teases her, sleeps in her bed and generally makes life miserable for her. Although the devil is real to Nana, her parents refuse to take him seriously. Only Nana's grandma shows any understanding about the devil and tries to help Nana overcome her fantasy. In the end, Nana drives the devil away by treating him so nicely that he can't stand it. "You don't respect me," he exclaims.

Whether the devil is real or not is not this book's primary concern. What is most important is Nana's warm relationship with her grandmother. Grandma does not talk down to, or baby, Nana, nor does she accuse her of "making up" stories. Instead, she encourages Nana to confront her devil problem maturely.

Nana's devil symbolizes the many fears young children have which are often instilled by well-meaning parents. Instead of giving realistic answers to their children's questions, they tell "cute" stories, thus planting the seeds of fantasy and fear in impressionable young minds.

The author handles her subject well. The contrasting of Grandma's sensitive approach to Nana's fear with the parents' unenlightened one is instructive, as is Nana's besting of the culprit (not without some pain and inconvenience). The sexist assumption that the Devil (like God) is a "he" ("it" would have been more appropriate) is one of the book's two minor flaws. The second has to do with the art work. While it is excellent on the whole, Nana and Grandma (who wears a mandarin-collared robe) have decidedly Asian features, while Mother and Dad do not. And at one point, Nana tells the devil, "We are just alike." Why these ambiguities?

These factors aside, *The Devil Did It* is positive, entertaining reading which encourages healthy attitudes about one's fears and towards older people.

	ART	WORDS		ART	WORDS			ART	WORDS	N.A.
anti-Racist			non-Racist	✓	✓	Racist	omission			
							commission			
anti-Sexist			non-Sexist	✓	✓	Sexist				
anti-Elitist			non-Elitist	✓	✓	Elitist				
anti-Materialist			non-Materialist	✓	✓	Materialist				
anti-Individualist			non-Individualist	✓	✓	Individualist				
anti-Ageist	✓	✓	non-Ageist		✓	Ageist				
anti-Conformist			non-Conformist	✓	✓	Conformist				
anti-Escapist			non-Escapist	✓	✓	Escapist				
Builds positive image of females/ minorities			Builds negative image of females/ minorities				Excellent	Good	Fair	Poor
Inspires action vs. oppression			Culturally authentic			Literary quality		✓		
						Art quality		✓		

I LOVE MY MOTHER
by Paul Zindel
illustrated by John Melo
Harper & Row
$5.95, unpaged, grades p.s.-2

This book's magnificent full color illustrations depicting the moods and day dreams of a little boy will have enduring interest. Mother is sometimes stern and firm ("She says, 'Absolutely not!' when I want to drive the car."), but she is always comforting and understanding. On the last page, the words seem to suggest that Father is away and "he misses me too," but the shadowy figure in the illustration may infer to adults that he is dead. Wherever Father is, both children and adults should enjoy the pictures, the young storyteller and his very nice mother.

	ART	WORDS		ART	WORDS			ART	WORDS	N.A.
anti-Racist			non-Racist			Racist	omission			✓
							commission			
anti-Sexist	✓	✓	non-Sexist			Sexist				
anti-Elitist			non-Elitist	✓	✓	Elitist				
anti-Materialist			non-Materialist	✓	✓	Materialist				
anti-Individualist			non-Individualist	✓	✓	Individualist				
anti-Ageist			non-Ageist			Ageist				✓
anti-Conformist			non-Conformist	✓	✓	Conformist				
anti-Escapist			non-Escapist	✓	✓	Escapist				
Builds positive image of females/ minorities	✓	✓	Builds negative image of females/ minorities				Excellent	Good	Fair	Poor
Inspires action vs. oppression			Culturally authentic			Literary quality	✓			
						Art quality	✓			

SUPER SAM AND THE SALAD GARDEN
by Patty Wolcott
illustrated by Marc Tolon Brown
Addison-Wesley
$3.95, unpaged, grades p.s.-1

A Black girl and white boy plant "a salad" in their backyard. Other children, of all colors, climb the back fence and deliberately "wreck" the garden. Then the original pair build a dog house for great, big "Super Sam" and post the dog as a guard near the replanted garden. When the "wreckers" return, Sam attacks and they flee. Later, all of the group happily share the salad which has grown.

One of a series of *Read-By-Myself Books With 10 Word Texts*, this startling book manages to be anti-racist, anti-sexist *and* anti-social in only ten words. For children just learning to read, the idea of using ten words over and over may be logical, but the decision to introduce the word "wreck"—which is not spelled phonetically—as a first word to youngsters can be seriously questioned. "Wreck. Wreck. Wreck the salad garden."

The depiction of a dog attacking children will contribute to some children's fears. Having an integrated group of children and active girls who wantonly "wreck" for no apparent reason is anti-social. The waste of excellent art work in this awful little book raises questions about the publisher's judgment.

	ART	WORDS		ART	WORDS			ART	WORDS	N.A.
anti-Racist	✓		non-Racist			Racist omission / commission			✓	
anti-Sexist	✓		non-Sexist			Sexist				✓
anti-Elitist			non-Elitist	✓	✓	Elitist				
anti-Materialist			non-Materialist	✓	✓	Materialist				
anti-Individualist			non-Individualist	✓	✓	Individualist				
anti-Ageist			non-Ageist			Ageist				✓
anti-Conformist			non-Conformist	✓	✓	Conformist				
anti-Escapist			non-Escapist	✓	✓	Escapist				
Builds positive image of females/minorities			Builds negative image of females/minorities				Excellent	Good	Fair	Poor
Inspires action vs. oppression			Culturally authentic			Literary quality				✓
						Art quality	✓			

KEVIN'S GRANDMA
by Barbara Williams
illustrated by Kay Chorao
E. P. Dutton
$5.50, 28 pages, grades p.s.-2

In *Kevin's Grandma*, a book which promises much but delivers a negative message in the end, two grandmothers, both white and seemingly wealthy, present a striking contrast.

Our hopes rise steadily as the tale (told by two little boys about their grandmothers) unfolds with great charm and humor. The "traditional" grandma, on every other page, is shown driving a station wagon, bringing presents, buying new toys, making popcorn or playing bridge. Kevin's grandma, on the facing pages, rides a Honda motorcycle, practices yoga and karate, buys pizza at midnight and sky-dives. Great illustrations accompany all this action.

Do we finally have a positive anti-ageist and anti-sexist statement which celebrates the grooviness of *all* kinds of grandmas? No. Our hopes turn to disappointment as the final pages mock the credibility of Kevin's descriptions, which seem to be just tall tales told to top his friend's. The book's message to young readers supports conformity and clearly says that women—especially older women—are ridiculous if they step out of conventional roles.

	ART	WORDS		ART	WORDS			ART	WORDS	N.A.
anti-Racist			non-Racist		✓	Racist	omission	✓		
							commission			
anti-Sexist			non-Sexist			Sexist		✓	✓	
anti-Elitist			non-Elitist			Elitist		✓	✓	
anti-Materialist			non-Materialist			Materialist		✓	✓	
anti-Individualist	✓	✓	non-Individualist			Individualist				
anti-Ageist			non-Ageist			Ageist		✓	✓	
anti-Conformist			non-Conformist			Conformist		✓	✓	
anti-Escapist			non-Escapist	✓	✓	Escapist				

	ART	WORDS		ART	WORDS		Excellent	Good	Fair	Poor
Builds positive image of females/ minorities			Builds negative image of (females) minorities	✓	✓					
						Literary quality		✓		
Inspires action vs. oppression			Culturally authentic			Art quality	✓			

NICHOLAS
by Ginny Cowles
illustrated by Clement Hurd
Seabury Press
$6.95, unpaged, grades p.s.-2

Do we really need another undistinguished "teeny, tiny" person tale? Learning from the book jacket that the author is the mother of six children and a pilot who has flown all over the world in a single-engine plane, a reader expects something less mundane and dull. But we are presented with itty, bitty Nicholas, member of a large, happy farm family, leaving home because his size is not normal. As his worried mother sees it, "Nicholas is a very fine boy, but how will he ever manage in this world, being so small?"

For some reason, the author does not deal with this sensible question but, instead, moves Nicholas all the way into the family mailbox near the road. The box turns over in a snowstorm, and—would you believe—this mishap leads to Nicholas' discovery of a teeny, tiny bride with whom to live happily ever after in the cozy mailbox.

In our society where people are, or should be, concerned with making males who are smaller than "normal" feel adequate and accepted, stories like this one do great harm. Such stories also encourage children to believe that the physically "abnormal" should find their own way and their own partners outside of the mainstream. Add to these regrettable messages the ridiculous formal wedding scene with its "happily ever after" overtones, and readers are left with many of the same negative messages contained in many a "classic" fairy tale.

As for the illustrations, they manage to be as inoffensive as possible.

	ART	WORDS		ART	WORDS			ART	WORDS	N.A.
anti-Racist			non-Racist			Racist omission / commission				✓
anti-Sexist			non-Sexist			Sexist		✓	✓	
anti-Elitist			non-Elitist	✓	✓	Elitist				
anti-Materialist			non-Materialist	✓	✓	Materialist				
anti-Individualist			non-Individualist	✓	✓	Individualist				
anti-Ageist			non-Ageist			Ageist				✓
anti-Conformist			non-Conformist			Conformist		✓	✓	
anti-Escapist			non-Escapist			Escapist		✓	✓	
Builds positive image of females/ minorities			Builds negative image of females/ minorities				Excellent	Good	Fair	Poor
Inspires action vs. oppression			Culturally authentic			Literary quality				✓
						Art quality			✓	

THE KING WHO COULD NOT SLEEP
by Benjamin Elkin
illustrated by Victoria Chess
Parents Magazine Press
$4.95, unpaged, grades p.s.-3

All possible and impossible measures are taken to quiet the kingdom so that insomniac King Karl can get some sleep—but to no avail. Finally, a lullabye does the trick as we learn, on the last page, that King Karl is an infant. His singing nursemaid is a female as are one mother and one train passenger. All other folk are male, all workers are work*men* and all royal council members are council*men*. If sexist stories about sleepless kings are one's cup of tea, the humor and off-beat illustrations in this book will be appealing.

	ART	WORDS		ART	WORDS			ART	WORDS	N.A.
anti-Racist			non-Racist			Racist omission / commission				✓
anti-Sexist			non-Sexist			Sexist		✓	✓	
anti-Elitist			non-Elitist	✓		Elitist				✓
anti-Materialist			non-Materialist	✓	✓	Materialist				
anti-Individualist			non-Individualist	✓	✓	Individualist				
anti-Ageist			non-Ageist	✓	✓	Ageist				
anti-Conformist			non-Conformist	✓	✓	Conformist				
anti-Escapist			non-Escapist	✓	✓	Escapist				
Builds positive image of females/ minorities			Builds negative image of females/ minorities				Excellent	Good	Fair	Poor
Inspires action vs. oppression			Culturally authentic			Literary quality		✓		
						Art quality		✓		

HOORAY FOR ME

by Remy Charlip and Lillian Moore
illustrated by Vera B. Williams
Parents' Magazine Press
$4.95, unpaged, grades p.s.-2

No story here. Just,

> "Knock-knock."
>
> "Who is it?"
>
> "Me."
>
> "Who's me?"
>
> "I am me."
>
> "I am me, too."
>
> "Oh."

As dozens of people echo "Me, too," they begin to call out relationships, one to another, so that everyone's identity links them in many ways to many others. This is a warm, witty, social and enjoyable romp for young and old. Children appear in all colors and fathers (of all colors) are nurturing. Stepfathers, too.

The marvelous watercolor illustrations echo the celebration of life and human interdependence. *Every* day-care center, kindergarten and home should have this book.

	ART	WORDS		ART	WORDS		ART	WORDS	N.A.
anti-Racist	✓	✓	non-Racist			Racist omission / commission			
anti-Sexist	✓	✓	non-Sexist			Sexist			
anti-Elitist	✓		non-Elitist		✓✓	Elitist			
anti-Materialist	✓		non-Materialist	✓	✓	Materialist			
anti-Individualist	✓		non-Individualist		✓	Individualist			
anti-Ageist			non-Ageist	✓	✓	Ageist			
anti-Conformist	✓	✓	non-Conformist			Conformist			
anti-Escapist			non-Escapist	✓	✓	Escapist			
Builds positive image of females/minorities	✓	✓	Builds negative image of females/minorities				Excellent	Good	Fair	Poor
Inspires action vs. oppression			Culturally authentic			Literary quality ✓ / Art quality ✓			

I CLIMB MOUNTAINS

by Barbara Taylor
illustrated by Barbara Yacono
Canadian Women's Educational Press
$3.00, 26 pages, grades p.s.-3

This I-can-do-anything-better-than-you story is a lively invention that features a sustained and crescendoing counterpoint of imaginative bragging, defiant skepticism and steady realism. A wonderful ending tops it off, with the world made better for the interplay of its three youthful "voices."

Peter challenges Annie: "I can do lots of things you can't do . . . I can jump fences, and dig tunnels . . . and climb high trees. . . ." Annie retorts: *I* climb mountains. I scale peaks whose tips tickle the sun. I leap waterfalls whose sprays dampen the stars. . . ." "You're nuts," scoffs Peter, but Lucy says: "That's great! What else can you do?" Annie continues enumerating her gifts, with Peter resisting and Lucy accepting.

Then the spotlight shifts to Lucy: "Annie's stories aren't silly," she snaps. "And neither am I. I can hide in dark closets and not cry. I can fix bicycles when the tires go flat. And . . . I can make radios! I bet you can't do that!"

The other two are stunned. But Annie recovers quickly: "Lucy builds radios so small a fly could snuggle under its wing . . . radios that sing in Japanese while someone in Africa hums along."

In the end, the voices come together in beautiful harmony. Lucy promises to demonstrate the building of a radio, Annie promises to accompany her with a scary story and Peter asks if he can help make the radio—admitting that he would also like to hear Annie's story.

The text of *I Climb Mountains* is a delight—short enough to be read every night for a month, and deep enough to bring forth some good thoughts before sleep sets in. The illustrations get mixed notices. They are good in their appropriate depiction of Annie, the poet, and Lucy, the realist, in overalls and sneakers just like Peter, the scoffer. However, Peter's resemblance to the other characters, *except* for his apparent Afro, leaves the reader to ponder his racial identity. An art style that keeps readers guessing in such matters is offensive.

I Climb Mountains can be obtained from the Canadian Women's Educational Press, Suite 305, 280 Bloor St. W., Toronto, Canada.

	ART	WORDS		ART	WORDS			ART	WORDS	N.A.
anti-Racist			non-Racist	✓	✓	Racist	omission / commission			
anti-Sexist	✓	✓	non-Sexist			Sexist				
anti-Elitist			non-Elitist	✓	✓	Elitist				
anti-Materialist			non-Materialist	✓	✓	Materialist				
anti-Individualist			non-Individualist	✓	✓	Individualist				
anti-Ageist			non-Ageist			Ageist				✓
anti-Conformist	✓	✓	non-Conformist			Conformist				
anti-Escapist			non-Escapist	✓	✓	Escapist				
Builds positive image of females/minorities		✓	Builds negative image of females/minorities					Excellent	Good	Fair	Poor
Inspires action vs. oppression			Culturally authentic			Literary quality		✓		
						Art quality			✓	

AMY AND THE CLOUD BASKET
by Ellen Pratt
illustrated by Lisa Russell
Lollipop Power
$2.00, 38 pages, grades p.s.-3

Enter, a pleasant fantasy tale set in the village of Pan: "High on a slope of a mountainous land/Soar the high spires of the village of Pan./The buildings are towers. Each house is a steeple./Such dwellings are perfect for those climbing people." Each morning, all of Pan's inhabitants over ten climb to cover the moon and uncover the sun. Evenings, they climb again to reverse the process. Those under ten are learning how to perform their future tasks.

Pan is an almost-perfect paradise. But since the book was published by a feminist publishing collective, life in Pan is predictably flawed: The roles of these happy people are strictly segregated by sex (although they are integrated as to race and age, and heroine Amy is Black). On Amy's tenth birthday, she announces her wish to have what the males have—a basket instead of a spoon, which is the female lot in Pan. Everyone is aghast but Amy is adamant, and since the sun must be uncovered quickly, they give in. Thereafter, Pan is not merely idyllic but supremely perfect.

A sweet book but young children are capable of understanding more about 1) the struggle which inevitably accompanies change, and 2) the hurt caused by oppression—whether that oppression is sexism or racism. Another flaw is the picturing of Pan's "before" and "after" as almost equally idyllic, which weakens the intended message. That is unfortunate, since here is an interesting attempt to combine fantasy with a real issue—social justice.

The illustrations are remarkable in their depiction of Black and white adults and children as truly integrated equals. Black figures are often in the foreground and seem to have leadership positions. The usual one-Black-face-in-the-crowd acknowledgment of multiculturalism, common to the art work in most children's books, is absent in *Amy and the Cloud Basket*.

	ART	WORDS		ART	WORDS		ART	WORDS	N.A.
anti-Racist	✓	✓	non-Racist			Racist omission / commission			
anti-Sexist	✓	✓	non-Sexist			Sexist			
anti-Elitist	✓	✓	non-Elitist			Elitist			
anti-Materialist			non-Materialist	✓	✓	Materialist			
anti-Individualist			non-Individualist	✓	✓	Individualist			
anti-Ageist			non-Ageist	✓	✓	Ageist			
anti-Conformist	✓	✓	non-Conformist			Conformist			
anti-Escapist			non-Escapist	✓	✓	Escapist			
Builds positive image of females/minorities	✓	✓	Builds negative image of females/minorities				Excellent	Good	Fair	Poor
Inspires action vs. oppression			Culturally authentic			Literary quality		✓		
						Art quality		✓		

DO YOU LOVE ME?
by Dick Gackenbach
illustrated by same
Seabury Press
$5.95, unpaged, grades p.s.-2

Six-year-old Walter lives on a small farm with his older sister and their parents. The story takes place about thirty years ago—the only apparent reason being to permit illustrations of old stoves, hairstyles and cars.

Walter is too young to help with chores or to walk the long distances which separate him from other children. For amusement, he keeps bugs and a turtle. When his efforts to capture a hummingbird result in the bird's death, he becomes distraught. Sister comforts him, explaining that birds and animals have their own needs and do not necessarily enjoy being captured, fondled or confined as pets. Turtle and bugs are then released by penitent Walter, and his understanding sister replaces them with a puppy who enjoys Walter's petting and love. All well and good.

The two-color drawings of homely faces and details of the period setting are fun. The two female characters, mother *and* sister, wear aprons and cook or sew. Father eats food that is served to him by the women, farms or sits reading the newspaper—all of which makes *Do You Love Me?* another wonderfully illustrated, sexist book.

	ART	WORDS		ART	WORDS			ART	WORDS	N.A.
anti-Racist			non-Racist			Racist — omission / commission				✓
anti-Sexist			non-Sexist			Sexist		✓	✓	
anti-Elitist			non-Elitist	✓	✓	Elitist				
anti-Materialist			non-Materialist	✓	✓	Materialist				
anti-Individualist			non-Individualist	✓	✓	Individualist				
anti-Ageist			non-Ageist			Ageist				✓
anti-Conformist			non-Conformist	✓	✓	Conformist				
anti-Escapist			non-Escapist	✓	✓	Escapist				
Builds positive image of females/ minorities			Builds negative image of (females) minorities		✓		Excellent	Good	Fair	Poor
Inspires action vs. oppression			Culturally authentic			Literary quality		✓		
						Art quality	✓			

THE QUITTING DEAL
by Tobi Tobias
illustrated by Trina Schart Hyman
Viking Press
$5.95, unpaged, grades p.s.-3

The Quitting Deal is a warm and lovely book about a middle class family whose members are attempting to help one another solve problems. Mother wants to stop smoking, and seven-year-old daughter wants to stop sucking her thumb. They try total abstinence and substitutes, but both methods fail. After a series of amusing failures, they decide upon a process of gradual withdrawal.

Readers learn from the father's inability to fully identify with either problem, despite his concern, that only victims of a habit can totally understand the nature of their plight. By underplaying her characters generational differences and depicting supportive relationships, the author reveals the universality of minor human frailties and, at the same time, shows the rewards to be reaped from shared efforts and mutual respect.

Marvelously funny illustrations depict an anti-conformist household—Mother wears dungarees and beads and breast-feeds the baby. This pleasant exploration of a real life situation should appeal to all ages.

	ART	WORDS		ART	WORDS		ART	WORDS	N.A.
anti-Racist			non-Racist			Racist — omission/commission			✓
anti-Sexist	✓	✓	non-Sexist			Sexist			
anti-Elitist			non-Elitist	✓	✓	Elitist			
anti-Materialist	✓		non-Materialist		✓	Materialist			
anti-Individualist	✓	✓	non-Individualist			Individualist			
anti-Ageist			non-Ageist			Ageist			✓
anti-Conformist	✓	✓	non-Conformist			Conformist			
anti-Escapist		✓	non-Escapist	✓		Escapist			
Builds positive image of females/minorities		✓	Builds negative image of females/minorities						
Inspires action vs. oppression			Culturally authentic						

	Excellent	Good	Fair	Poor
Literary quality		✓		
Art quality	✓			

AROUND AND AROUND LOVE
by Betty Miles
photographs
Alfred A. Knopf
$2.50, 42 pages, p.s.-3

Consisting of forty-two pages full of twice as many beautiful black-and-white photos, plus a minimal text, this book is a bargain at $2.50. Love—"When you feel it and know it, tell it and show it." Love—"It's hard to tell about, easy to show."

This is a warm, life-affirming little book. Love is shown as being valid all ways: Between people of all ages and all races; people who are friends, people who are parents, people who care about other people—and people who care about pet animals. What a happy book to have around the house! Children will want to look through it time and time again. It can also serve as a springboard for many child-adult discussions—or even as a preface to hugging.

	ART	WORDS		ART	WORDS		ART	WORDS	N.A.
anti-Racist	✓		non-Racist		✓	Racist — omission/commission			
anti-Sexist	✓		non-Sexist		✓	Sexist			
anti-Elitist	✓		non-Elitist		✓	Elitist			
anti-Materialist	✓		non-Materialist		✓	Materialist			
anti-Individualist	✓		non-Individualist		✓	Individualist			
anti-Ageist	✓		non-Ageist		✓	Ageist			
anti-Conformist	✓		non-Conformist		✓	Conformist			
anti-Escapist			non-Escapist	✓	✓	Escapist			
Builds positive image of females/minorities	✓		Builds negative image of females/minorities						
Inspires action vs. oppression			Culturally authentic						

	Excellent	Good	Fair	Poor
Literary quality	✓			
Art quality		✓		

GRANNY'S FISH STORY
by Phyllis LaFarge
illustrated by Gahan Wilson
Parents Magazine Press
$4.95, 35 pages, grades p.s.-2

Julie's grandmother invites her to sleep over and bring along a friend. Since Granny lives in a house in the woods, Julie chooses to bring Sarah who has never been to the country before. Grandmother's kidding references to "swamp halibut and bush mackerel," as they drive through the woods, create fears in Sarah which result in nightmares during that night's big thunderstorm. However, Granny's sensitivity, patience and understanding make everything turn out okay, and the visit is a success.

A pleasant image of an understanding and slightly unconventional grandmother make this a reassuring bedtime story for children who are rattled by nightmares and/or thunderstorms. Unfortunately, the cartoon-like illustrations detract from the warmth of the story and fail to add to its humor.

	ART	WORDS		ART	WORDS			ART	WORDS	N.A.
anti-Racist			non-Racist			Racist omission / commission				✓
anti-Sexist			non-Sexist	✓	✓	Sexist				
anti-Elitist			non-Elitist	✓	✓	Elitist				
anti-Materialist			non-Materialist	✓	✓	Materialist				
anti-Individualist			non-Individualist	✓	✓	Individualist				
anti-Ageist	✓	✓	non-Ageist			Ageist				
anti-Conformist			non-Conformist	✓	✓	Conformist				
anti-Escapist			non-Escapist	✓	✓	Escapist				
Builds positive image of females/minorities			Builds negative image of females/minorities				Excellent	Good	Fair	Poor
Inspires action vs. oppression			Culturally authentic			Literary quality		✓		
						Art quality				✓

ONE FROG TOO MANY
by Mercer and Marianna Mayer
illustrated by Mercer Mayer
Dial Press
$3.50, 28 pages, grades p.s.-2

One Frog Too Many is a beautifully illustrated, wordless book which has as its central theme the issue of jealousy and how group pressure is used to force the protagonist, Frog, to conform. One day, Boy receives a surprise package, out of which pops a baby frog—a new addition to the group of Boy, Dog, Turtle and Frog. Frog number one is not too happy about this newcomer, and the remainder of the book focuses on his hostility and the group's reaction to it.

Finally, the group punishes Frog by leaving him behind while they go out for a raft ride. In an act of defiance and desperation, Frog jumps on the raft and kicks Little Frog overboard. Failing to recover Little Frog, the group goes home heartbroken and fully contemptuous of Frog. Little Frog's sudden and unexplained reappearance and the subsequent truce that is reached between the two frogs is very unrealistic. The seriousness of the issues at hand—jealousy, insecurity and the group's punitive approach—are glossed over. Frog's ultimate "acceptance" of Little Frog is more an expression of guilt and submission to group pressure than of healthy adjustment.

The jacket cover summary of the story describes as "hilarious" Frog's efforts "to rid himself of this invader" and promises that "the story and its comical drawings will have young children laughing aloud through many readings." If the expression of human feelings (jealousy and fear in this case) in individualistic and destructive acts is something to be viewed as light entertainment for children, this reviewer seriously questions what kinds of people we adults are trying to mold.

	ART	WORDS		ART	WORDS			ART	WORDS	N.A.
anti-Racist			non-Racist			Racist omission / commission				✓
anti-Sexist			non-Sexist			Sexist				✓
anti-Elitist			non-Elitist	✓		Elitist				
anti-Materialist			non-Materialist	✓		Materialist				
anti-Individualist			non-Individualist			Individualist		✓		
anti-Ageist			non-Ageist			Ageist				✓
anti-Conformist			non-Conformist			Conformist		✓		
anti-Escapist			non-Escapist	✓		Escapist				
Builds positive image of females/minorities			Builds negative image of females/minorities				Excellent	Good	Fair	Poor
Inspires action vs. oppression			Culturally authentic			Literary quality				
						Art quality	✓			

THE BIRTHDAY VISITOR
by Yoshiko Uchida
illustrated by Charles Robinson
Charles Scribner's Sons
$5.95, unpaged, grades 1-3

Yoshiko Uchida's heroines are model children who possess common sense, self-confidence, humor and modesty.

Emi, the Japanese American heroine of *The Birthday Visitor* is such a child. She is unhappy because a Christian minister is coming from Japan to stay at her house on her birthday—which means that she cannot have a party with her friends. However, her parents plan a party in her honor with their guest and an old neighborhood couple. Of course, Emi is delighted and realizes that it is the best birthday she ever had (fortunately, the minister turns out to be a nice person). One wonders, however, why the parents did not plan a party with her friends on another day.

Orderliness and serenity permeate this book, and the conflict is calmly resolved. The story takes place in a never-never land of non-materialistic middle-class comfort and stability which would seem rare in America today.

Could one consider this other-worldliness, this peace and feeling of unity a typically Japanese characteristic? If so, is it possible within the American societal setting? Furthermore, although the traits themselves are positive ones, do they in fact perpetuate certain myths of cool, collected, unemotional "Orientals"? One can almost hear an adult, after reading this book to children, saying, "Aren't they a lovely family?"—which is practically the same as saying, "Asians in America have strong family units and don't have overwhelming problems."

Although the illustrations are attractive, a picture with the characters bowing to each other is in error. Women in Japan do not bow with their arms hanging straight at their sides.

	ART	WORDS		ART	WORDS			ART	WORDS	N.A.
anti-Racist	✓	✓	non-Racist			Racist — omission / commission				
anti-Sexist			non-Sexist	✓	✓	Sexist				
anti-Elitist			non-Elitist	✓	✓	Elitist				
anti-Materialist			non-Materialist	✓	✓	Materialist				
anti-Individualist			non-Individualist	✓		Individualist			✓	
anti-Ageist			non-Ageist	✓	✓	Ageist				
anti-Conformist			non-Conformist	✓		Conformist			✓	
anti-Escapist			non-Escapist	✓	✓	Escapist				
Builds positive image of females/minorities		✓	Builds negative image of females/minorities				Excellent	Good	Fair	Poor
Inspires action vs. oppression			Culturally authentic			Literary quality		✓		
						Art quality		✓		

NEW KID IN TOWN
by Charles Robinson
illustrated by same
Atheneum
$6.50, unpaged, grades 1-3

A little white boy moves into a new suburban neighborhood and encounters another boy his own age who invites him to play. In the course of their games, the new boy always gets the dirty end of the stick. He ends up being tied up, hosed down, bulldozed and then towed away like a wreck. When he runs home to mother to have his wounds attended to, they look out the window and see that the bully has fallen out of his wagon and is crying. *"You* wouldn't cry like that," says mother proudly, in the true spirit of that "real-boys-don't-cry" ethic.

That night the new boy dreams of his counter-attack, relishing gory scenes of revenge. On the following day, when he succeeds in foiling his nemesis' attempts to dominate, a fierce physical fight ensues. Afterwards, the boys entwine arms and become good friends.

The ugly messages in this book are more than just sexist. They also promote the ideas that fighting is *the* way for boys to prove themselves, violence is acceptable behavior and revenge is sweet. Why could not the new boy have cried when he was hurt and then decided to reject the bully's "friendship"?

It is difficult to warm up to illustrations which are part of an anti-human message.

	ART	WORDS		ART	WORDS			ART	WORDS	N.A.
anti-Racist			non-Racist			Racist	omission			✓
							commission			
anti-Sexist			non-Sexist	✓		Sexist			✓	
anti-Elitist			non-Elitist	✓	✓	Elitist				
anti-Materialist			non-Materialist	✓	✓	Materialist				
anti-Individualist			non-Individualist	✓		Individualist			✓	
anti-Ageist			non-Ageist	·		Ageist				✓
anti-Conformist			non-Conformist	✓		Conformist			✓	
anti-Escapist			non-Escapist	✓	✓	Escapist				
Builds positive image of females/ minorities			Builds negative image of females/ minorities				Excellent	Good	Fair	Poor
Inspires action vs. oppression			Culturally authentic			Literary quality			✓	
						Art quality			✓	

I'LL BE THE HORSE IF YOU'LL PLAY WITH ME
by Martha Alexander
illustrated by same
Dial Press
$4.95, 28 pages, grades p.s.-3

This expressive, simply illustrated book examines how children relate to and play with each other.

Little Bonnie seems to live in an all-boy world. Big brother Oliver will only play horse and wagon with her if she is the horse, and cops and robbers if she is the robber. Whenever her turn comes around to be the cop or wagon-driver, Oliver tires of the game and quits. Bonnie understands the nature of her predicament and the injustice that is being done to her but feels powerless to change the situation. Even her attempts to play with the cat and dog are frustrated by Oliver.

Then along comes little brother Scott. When Bonnie discovers he is big enough to pull the wagon, she turns the tables and has Scott be the horse while she rides the wagon.

Elitism, sexism and materialism pervade the sub-text of this oh-so-simple story. "Playing" actually amounts to imitating adult exploitation and manipulation behaviors. Being the top dog and calling the shots is promoted as a goal. Although the concept of taking turns and exchanging roles is mentioned, it is not as strongly encouraged as is being the hero and assigning the hard, unglamorous tasks to a victim.

On several occasions, material considerations are prerequisites for play. In one instance, Oliver tells Bonnie she can play with him *if* he can use her new crayons and paper. In another, Bonnie asks Oliver and David if they "want to play with my toys and me"—realizing that her toys are her greatest asset.

The book's sexist overtones are pronounced, especially in the end. Bonnie is constantly weak and passive, playing house with the cat while the boys build something. Moreover, the author fails to question why Bonnie is constantly manipulated. Instead, her overall message to young readers is "Turn the tables whenever you can." Bonnie's exploitation of Scott implies that all women should want is a piece of the action instead of fundamental changes to correct injustice. "Get ahead, girls," the author seems to be saying, "at the expense of whoever is vulnerable."

This book cannot be recommended unless it is used by adults to expose and discourage such negative play relationships.

	ART	WORDS		ART	WORDS			ART	WORDS	N.A.
anti-Racist			non-Racist			Racist — omission / commission				✓
anti-Sexist			non-Sexist			Sexist		✓	✓	
anti-Elitist			non-Elitist	✓	✓	Elitist				
anti-Materialist			non-Materialist	✓		Materialist			✓	
anti-Individualist			non-Individualist	✓		Individualist			✓	
anti-Ageist			non-Ageist			Ageist				✓
anti-Conformist			non-Conformist	✓		Conformist			✓	
anti-Escapist			non-Escapist	✓	✓	Escapist				
Builds positive image of females/ minorities			Builds negative image of ⟨females⟩ minorities		✓		Excellent	Good	Fair	Poor
Inspires action vs. oppression			Culturally authentic			Literary quality		✓		
						Art quality		✓		

WHEN LIGHT TURNS INTO NIGHT
by Crescent Dragonwagon
illustrated by Robert Andrew Parker
Harper & Row
$4.95, 32 pages, grades p.s.-3

Ellen spends twilight luxuriating in the fields surrounding her rural home, where she feels at one with the sights, sounds, and smells of the earth. As day becomes night, her mother's voice calling her to dinner blends with nature. She reenters the "peopleplace" (home) full of warm feelings that are different from the ones she experiences out of doors. The watercolor-over-pen-and-ink illustrations heighten the ethereal quality of this setting.

Ellen's traditional family is typical of rural white America. Mother (in an apron) prepares dinner and calls the family to table. On the other hand, Father washes Ellen's face and mention is made of a cake baked by her brother.

Ellen's romance with nature is not escapist. Rather, she uses her natural surroundings to get in touch with her feelings—which, however, are explored in isolation from any social interaction. Stereotypically, it is again the girl/woman, not a boy/man, whose main needs are shown as emotional. Although Ellen seems like an active, alive little girl, we never actually see her *do* anything more than run through the grass.

Another mixed blessing is the author's lyrical, child-like prose which contains sophisticated images that may prove confusing for the very young reader. One only hopes that as a "feminist"—the book jacket's description of the author—Ms. Dragonwagon will apply her interesting talents to more specifically feminist concerns in the future.

	ART	WORDS		ART	WORDS		ART	WORDS	N.A.
anti-Racist			non-Racist			Racist — omission / commission			✓
anti-Sexist			non-Sexist	✓	✓	Sexist			
anti-Elitist			non-Elitist	✓	✓	Elitist			
anti-Materialist			non-Materialist	✓	✓	Materialist			
anti-Individualist			non-Individualist	✓	✓	Individualist			
anti-Ageist			non-Ageist			Ageist			✓
anti-Conformist			non-Conformist	✓	✓	Conformist			
anti-Escapist			non-Escapist	✓	✓	Escapist			

							Excellent	Good	Fair	Poor
Builds positive image of females/minorities			Builds negative image of females/minorities			Literary quality			✓	
Inspires action vs. oppression			Culturally authentic			Art quality		✓		

THE MOON WALKER
by Paul Showers
illustrated by Susan Perl
Doubleday
$4.95, 47 pages, grades p.s.-3

If this book is any indication, outer space has replaced the stork as the deliverer of new life on earth. *The Moon Walker* is the story of a little girl who regards the birth of her brother as the "earth-landing" of a creature from another planet who must adjust to his new world, just as astronauts who travel to the moon must do.

The baby's first days in his new environment and the step-by-step process by which he learns to use the parts of his body (his "space suit") up to the toddling stage are sympathetically related by his sister. She observes his progress with wonder—from his being able to hold onto an object to knowing how to pick it up, from gurgling to talking. Mama takes it all in stride, guiding his development and not panicking when the baby loses his balance or staggers and falls. Daddy's comments, which a four-year-old might find amusing, may be a bit too much for adult out-loud readers. "He doesn't know how to work his telephone" replies Dad to sister when she comments, "I think he wants to talk to me." "He doesn't know how to turn off the water," he explains when she asks about the diapers.

The children's faces are genuinely engaging in the pages and pages of black and white drawings. On a rainy day children will want to color them (and parents will say firmly, "Coloring books are for coloring. This book is for reading"). They depict your "typical" species of earthling, whose members grow up in comfortable houses and sleep on downy pillows surrounded by flowers, foliage and a cat right out of *Alice in Wonderland*. "Christopher is learning how to live on earth" concludes the text. Yes, indeed he is—under optimum conditions that do not prevail in the majority of America's homes. To non-affluent youngsters, Christopher's surroundings might seem like being on the moon.

	ART	WORDS		ART	WORDS		ART	WORDS	N.A.
anti-Racist			non-Racist			Racist omission / commission			✓
anti-Sexist			non-Sexist	✓	✓	Sexist			
anti-Elitist			non-Elitist	✓	✓	Elitist			
anti-Materialist			non-Materialist		✓	Materialist	✓		
anti-Individualist			non-Individualist	✓	✓	Individualist			
anti-Ageist			non-Ageist			Ageist			✓
anti-Conformist			non-Conformist	✓	✓	Conformist			
anti-Escapist			non-Escapist	✓		Escapist		✓	
Builds positive image of females/minorities			Builds negative image of females/minorities				Excellent	Good	Fair	Poor
Inspires action vs. oppression			Culturally authentic			Literary quality		✓	
						Art quality	✓		

COULDN'T WE HAVE A TURTLE INSTEAD?
by Judith Vigna
illustrated by same
Albert Whitman
$3.75, unpaged, grades p.s.-1

"Couldn't we have a turtle instead?" asks Lizzie. Or a hamster, a puppy, a tiger, or bear? An elephant that would sleep on the stairs? These alternatives are proposed by Lizzie in response to her mother's announcement that she is going to have a baby. When it is explained that space for the baby will be provided in Lizzie's room by replacing the toy box with a crib, Lizzie has visions of the baby confiscating her possessions, and of "Baby" written in large letters on the bedroom door with "Lizzie" written beneath in tiny letters. Animals, Lizzie figures, would not take up as much space.

This is a stupid book because 1) it seems to have been written merely as a showcase for illustrations of unlikely animals in a child's room; 2) newborn babies are rarely placed in an older child's room until they are old enough to sleep through the night, and 3) the mother (ergo the author) does not take seriously children's fears of being replaced by new babies.

	ART	WORDS		ART	WORDS		ART	WORDS	N.A.
anti-Racist			non-Racist			Racist omission / commission			✓
anti-Sexist			non-Sexist	✓	✓	Sexist			
anti-Elitist			non-Elitist	✓	✓	Elitist			
anti-Materialist			non-Materialist	✓	✓	Materialist			
anti-Individualist			non-Individualist	✓		Individualist		✓	
anti-Ageist			non-Ageist			Ageist			✓
anti-Conformist			non-Conformist	✓	✓	Conformist			
anti-Escapist			non-Escapist	✓		Escapist		✓	
Builds positive image of females/minorities			Builds negative image of females/minorities				Excellent	Good	Fair	Poor
Inspires action vs. oppression			Culturally authentic			Literary quality			✓
						Art quality		✓	

NEW NEIGHBORS
by Ray Prather
illustrated by same
McGraw-Hill
$4.95, unpaged, grades p.s.-3

On his first day in a suburban neighborhood, Rickey—an ex-New York City boy—goes out to make friends but finds that none of the children will talk to him. Sulking, Rickey goes back inside and presently comes upon an idea to make himself more interesting to the children. Searching through his new house, he finds an assortment of old toys. He takes the loot outside and sets up a stand, which immediately attracts attention. The children come over to his yard to barter, conversation and laughter follow, and Rickey is accepted into the local "gang" of six- and seven-year-olds—the Penguins. At days end, all of the children and Rickey go off together as friends.

New Neighbors is a carefully integrated book in which most of the children (including Rickey) are Black. It is also an inoffensive book. Materialism is, of course, implied in the use of toy bartering as a means of intitiating friendship, and the children are staunch conformists to the point of having a special club walk. Sexism makes a brief appearance in the illustrations (the two girls wear dresses, while the boys wear jeans), but the drawings are culturally authentic. This book's main drawback is the flat prose in which it is written which leaves one with the impression that the author has had little exposure to children. Livelier books explore the adjustment of children to new environments.

	ART	WORDS		ART	WORDS		ART	WORDS	N.A.
anti-Racist			non-Racist	✓	✓	Racist — omission / commission			
anti-Sexist			non-Sexist	✓	✓	Sexist			
anti-Elitist			non-Elitist	✓	✓	Elitist			
anti-Materialist			non-Materialist	✓		Materialist		✓	
anti-Individualist			non-Individualist	✓	✓	Individualist			
anti-Ageist			non-Ageist			Ageist			✓
anti-Conformist			non-Conformist	✓	✓	Conformist			
anti-Escapist			non-Escapist	✓	✓	Escapist			

		Excellent	Good	Fair	Poor
Builds positive image of females/minorities	Builds negative image of females/minorities				
Inspires action vs. oppression	Culturally authentic	Literary quality		✓	
		Art quality			✓

ULTRA-VIOLET CATASTROPHE
by Margaret Mahy
illustrated by Brian Froud
Parents Magazine Press
$4.95, unpaged, grades p.s.-3

In an English countryside setting, little Sally—alias Horrible Stumper the tree pirate—grudgingly submits to the ordeal of being scrubbed, brushed and fancily dressed to visit super-fastidious Aunt Anne. "She doesn't like me even to breathe. She fusses and fusses all the time," complains Sally.

Upon arriving at Aunt Anne's, she is introduced to her Aunt's father, Great Uncle Magnus—a "very clean, scrubbed-and-scoured, washed-up-and-brushed-down little old man" who calls himself "Ultra-Violet Catastrophe." When the two are sent out to take a walk, Sally and Uncle Magnus find they both enjoy similar activities. After great fun and adventure, they are found—muddy, messy and happy—by a scolding Aunt Anne.

Although a reader might wish that the older women were not portrayed as inveterate cleaners, Mother does understand that messiness is less important than fun and friendship.

The illustrations are delightful, as is the prose, and everyone will love the two main characters.

	ART	WORDS		ART	WORDS			ART	WORDS	N.A.
anti-Racist			non-Racist			Racist omission / commission				✓
anti-Sexist			non-Sexist	✓	✓	Sexist				
anti-Elitist			non-Elitist	✓	✓	Elitist				
anti-Materialist			non-Materialist	✓	✓	Materialist				
anti-Individualist			non-Individualist	✓	✓	Individualist				
anti-Ageist	✓	✓	non-Ageist			Ageist				
anti-Conformist	✓	✓	non-Conformist			Conformist				
anti-Escapist			non-Escapist	✓	✓	Escapist				
Builds positive image of females/ minorities			Builds negative image of females/ minorities				Excellent	Good	Fair	Poor
Inspires action vs. oppression			Culturally authentic			Literary quality		✓		
						Art quality	✓			

MAKE A CIRCLE KEEP US IN: POEMS FOR A GOOD DAY
by Arnold Adoff
illustrated by Ronald Himler
Delacorte Press
$4.95, 30 pages, p.s.-2

The daily routine of a white family provides the subject matter for this book of poetry written from the point of view of the young daughter. Getting up on a cold, dark morning, eating lunch prepared by mother, being hugged by father and taking a bath are among the activities described.

The author's poetic style is unusual for a children's book. Words are often arranged in a visual design, divided in surprising places (cri es) or have some letters above and below the plane (m$_u$sht$_a$sh). Some words, like "broken" and "trip," are on a slant. This makes reading certain passages difficult, as the eye must move in uncustomary directions.

All of this seems to be aimed at making words look like what they mean. Letters in the word "broken" are split, "yells" and "loud" are larger than adjacent words and the final letters in "tall" get progressively larger. This is certainly an imaginative device, but one wonders how much it adds to the sentiments expressed.

Both mother and father express affection for their children in the illustrations and jointly care for them. In the two instances when family harmony is broken, father yells and mother gives a "smack" in a "sneak attack."

For a change, father, not mother, is on a diet, and daughter wants to be a lawyer, a singer and a track star. The grandparents, however, maintain traditional sex roles: Grandpa farms and Grandma cooks and knits while telling tales of "marching women long ago with flags/ and brave old songs." If this is a reference to the women's suffrage movement (rare in literature for young children) it deserved more explanation.

	ART	WORDS		ART	WORDS			ART	WORDS	N.A.
anti-Racist			non-Racist			Racist — omission / commission				✓
anti-Sexist			non-Sexist	✓	✓	Sexist				
anti-Elitist			non-Elitist	✓	✓	Elitist				
anti-Materialist			non-Materialist	✓	✓	Materialist				
anti-Individualist			non-Individualist	✓	✓	Individualist				
anti-Ageist			non-Ageist			Ageist				✓
anti-Conformist			non-Conformist	✓	✓	Conformist				
anti-Escapist			non-Escapist	✓	✓	Escapist				
Builds positive image of females/ minorities			Builds negative image of females/ minorities				Excellent	Good	Fair	Poor
Inspires action vs. oppression			Culturally authentic			Literary quality		✓		
						Art quality	✓			

AVERAGES
by Jane Jonas Srivastava
illustrated by Aliki Brandenburg
Thomas Y. Crowell
$4.50, 33 pages, grades p.s.-3

Averages is a math book for youngsters describing three kinds of averages—mode, median and arithmetic mean. An average is defined as "not the best, not the worst from a group, but somewhere in-between." Ms. Srivastava explains the uses of the averages well, citing examples from daily life experiences to which children will easily relate. Some of the discussion, however, may be too deep for six- or seven-year-olds.

Colorful illustrations depict a cross-section of racial groups, but the use of oversimplified drawings in which facial features are dots or lines should have been avoided. This style of "shorthand" drawing only serves to reinforce stereotypes, especially of Asian eyes being slits.

The author's discussions of "average" meals and "average" physical characteristics become somewhat vague in that she fails to account for ethnic and cultural differences. The assumption that all children eat cereal, toast, eggs, etc. for breakfast and sandwiches for lunch is an ethnocentric one, and references to "average" physical characteristics such as noses and hair can be dangerous. Two illustrations show white children saying, "my nose is average" and "my hair is curlier than average." What does this mean to a black, brown, yellow or red child? What is an "average" complexion?

Despite these shortcomings, the book is generally interesting and a good learning tool. Boys and girls are equally portrayed as active people (but the librarian is stereotypically a woman).

	ART	WORDS		ART	WORDS			ART	WORDS	N.A.
anti-Racist			non-Racist			Racist — omission / commission		✓	✓	
anti-Sexist			non-Sexist	✓	✓	Sexist				
anti-Elitist			non-Elitist	✓	✓	Elitist				
anti-Materialist			non-Materialist	✓	✓	Materialist				
anti-Individualist			non-Individualist	✓	✓	Individualist				
anti-Ageist			non-Ageist			Ageist				✓
anti-Conformist			non-Conformist	✓	✓	Conformist				
anti-Escapist			non-Escapist	✓	✓	Escapist				
Builds positive image of females/minorities			Builds negative image of females/minorities				Excellent	Good	Fair	Poor
Inspires action vs. oppression			Culturally authentic			Literary quality		✓		
						Art quality				✓

GRANDMA'S BEACH SURPRISE

by Ilka List
illustrated by Ruth Sanderson
G. P. Putnam's Sons
$4.97, unpaged, grades p.s.-3

Jessie is walking along the beach to Grandma's house with her dad. It's a very long walk, so when they discover that Dad left Grandma's birthday present home on the kitchen table, they decide to collect beach items as a substitute gift. As a student of marine biology, the author invests Father with more knowledge of the sea world than most parents would possess. Readers will pick up a lot of interesting information about shells, sand crabs, clams and other forms of sea life. Lovely illustrations in beiges, browns and blues, plus a lovely father/daughter relationship, combine to make this book an excellent selection for any child who sometimes visits the seashore or would like to.

	ART	WORDS		ART	WORDS			ART	WORDS	N.A.
anti-Racist			non-Racist			Racist — omission / commission				✓
anti-Sexist			non-Sexist	✓	✓	Sexist				
anti-Elitist			non-Elitist	✓	✓	Elitist				
anti-Materialist			non-Materialist	✓	✓	Materialist				
anti-Individualist			non-Individualist	✓	✓	Individualist				
anti-Ageist			non-Ageist	✓	✓	Ageist				
anti-Conformist			non-Conformist	✓	✓	Conformist				
anti-Escapist			non-Escapist	✓	✓	Escapist				
Builds positive image of females/minorities			Builds negative image of females/minorities				Excellent	Good	Fair	Poor
Inspires action vs. oppression			Culturally authentic			Literary quality		✓		
						Art quality	✓			

STRAWBERRY DRESS ESCAPE
by Crescent Dragonwagon
illustrated by Lillian Hoban
Charles Scribner's Sons
$6.95, 25 pages, grades p.s.-2

It is almost summer and school is hot and boring, so Emily—a little Black girl— leaves her integrated classroom and Black school teacher to frolic in an imaginary field. In the field, Emily flies to the side of Esmerald, a goat, and gets a drink of milk. She finds a basket of fruit under a tree and begins to eat. Nearby, a yellow and black snake turns into a jump rope. Emily picks it up and begins to jump. When the jumping makes her sleepy, she goes over to a big brass bed, removes her dress and shoes (which turn into pigeons) and goes to sleep.

Females, the character of Emily implies, are lightheaded hedonists to whom school, learning or working are anathema. They are also hopelessly materialistic (everything in the valley belongs to Emily), individualistic (Emily's pleasure comes before all else) and escapist (ah, to roam in an enchanted field)!

Emily's credibility as a Black child is nil and as a role model for any child, she is absurd. The author's writing style borders on the syrupy, and the illustrations are insulting. *Strawberry Dress Escape* is an uninspired fantasy.

	ART	WORDS		ART	WORDS			ART	WORDS	N.A.
anti-Racist			non-Racist			Racist	omission			
							commission	✓	✓	
anti-Sexist			non-Sexist			Sexist		✓	✓	
anti-Elitist			non-Elitist	✓	✓	Elitist				
anti-Materialist			non-Materialist	✓	✓	Materialist				
anti-Individualist			non-Individualist	✓		Individualist			✓	
anti-Ageist			non-Ageist			Ageist				✓
anti-Conformist			non-Conformist	✓	✓	Conformist				
anti-Escapist			non-Escapist			Escapist		✓	✓	
Builds positive image of females/minorities			Builds negative image of females/minorities	✓	✓		Excellent	Good	Fair	Poor
Inspires action vs. oppression			Culturally authentic			Literary quality			✓	
						Art quality				✓

ONCE WE WENT ON A PICNIC
by Aileen Fisher
illustrated by Tony Chen
Thomas Y. Crowell
$6.95, unpaged, grades p.s.-3

Once We Went on a Picnic is a beautifully illustrated story in verse about four city children who enjoy observing the natural wonders around them on their way to the park for a picnic. They become so enthralled with the bugs, bees and butterflies they encounter that by the time they reach the park they have already eaten most of their picnic lunch.

The style of Tony Chen's illustrations is so attractive and colorful that it is a shame their content and that of the story fall short of their quality. Some of the rhymes are stiff and contrived, and sexist imagery emerges in a picture of John, the only boy on the trip, cupping a cricket in his hands for the girls to see. Both words and illustrations imply that girls are squeamish about bugs while boys are adventurous and brave. Although the racial composition of the group is varied (two whites, one Asian, one Black), only the two white girls are shown doing things alone, even though it is written that Rhonda (the Black girl) is also active. Rhonda and John are seen only in group scenes. Due to the lack of visual-verbal coordination it is only through a process of elimination that the reader is able to determine which girl is Rhonda, and although John appears to be an Asian in some of the drawings, his identity is never completely clear.

Once We Went on a Picnic is, nevertheless, a lovely book which encourages young children to observe the nature around them, even in the city. A map at the end featuring animals and plants seen by the children on their excursion (as well as ones they did not see) is thought-provoking and unique.

	ART	WORDS		ART	WORDS			ART	WORDS	N.A.
anti-Racist			non-Racist	✓	✓	Racist	omission / commission			
anti-Sexist			non-Sexist			Sexist		✓	✓	
anti-Elitist			non-Elitist	✓	✓	Elitist				
anti-Materialist			non-Materialist	✓	✓	Materialist				
anti-Individualist			non-Individualist	✓	✓	Individualist				
anti-Ageist			non-Ageist			Ageist				✓
anti-Conformist			non-Conformist	✓	✓	Conformist				
anti-Escapist			non-Escapist	✓	✓	Escapist				
Builds positive image of females/ minorities			Builds negative image of females/ minorities					Excellent	Good	Fair	Poor
Inspires action vs. oppression			Culturally authentic			Literary quality				✓	
						Art quality		✓			

MONNIE HATES LYDIA
by Susan Pearson
illustrated by Diane Paterson
Dial Press
$5.50, unpaged, grades p.s.-3

For Lydia's birthday, younger sister Monnie and their father arrange a surprise party and bake a huge chocolate cake. The family seems to be motherless.

In this tale of sibling conflict, older sister Lydia constantly belittles Monnie while Monnie tries, over and over, to win some sign of approval. Finally, in utter anger and frustration, Monnie throws the birthday cake in Lydia's face. This causes Lydia to change her behavior.

Patiently and passively, Father encourages the girls to settle their own conflicts while supporting both equally. It this a wise position for an adult to take when one child is being extremely inconsiderate and causing pain to another child? One must also ask whether a book which encourages physical action before negotiation is the kind of guide parents need for their children. Another more basic problem is the book's inherent assumption that sibling rivalry is a fact of human nature, rather than a peculiarity of our particular culture.

The illustrations are superior to the story, and one of the birthday guests is Black—but in that vague, suntanned sort of way so common to current children's books.

	ART	WORDS		ART	WORDS			ART	WORDS	N.A.
anti-Racist			non-Racist	✓	✓	Racist	omission			
							commission			
anti-Sexist	✓	✓	non-Sexist			Sexist				
anti-Elitist			non-Elitist	✓	✓	Elitist				
anti-Materialist			non-Materialist	✓	✓	Materialist				
anti-Individualist			non-Individualist	✓		Individualist				✓
anti-Ageist			non-Ageist			Ageist				✓
anti-Conformist			non-Conformist	✓	✓	Conformist				
anti-Escapist			non-Escapist	✓	✓	Escapist				
Builds positive image of females/minorities			Builds negative image of females/minorities				Excellent	Good	Fair	Poor
Inspires action vs. oppression			Culturally authentic			Literary quality			✓	
						Art quality		✓		

THE LION IN THE BOX
by Marguerite De Angeli
illustrated by same
Doubleday
$4.95, 63 pages, grades 1-4

It's the turn of the century and New York City is the best-of-all-possible-worlds for the lead character of *The Lion In The Box*—a pretty, recently widowed, immigrant mother of five. Gaily and bravely, she faces a life in which dire poverty is almost fun, neighbors are cooperative, storekeepers are kind, and children are obedient, non-complaining, clean and neat. The oldest girl is eleven, followed by two younger sisters, one brother, and a toddler not yet two—a hearty brood whose dear Mama, despite cleaning offices every night and moonlighting at other jobs by day, is never—ever—irritable or complaining.

It is the night before Christmas and Mama has scrimped to buy some makeshift toys for the little ones. While she is away at work, the children are awakened by a delivery man arriving with a huge wooden crate. Terrified when he jokingly tells them there is a lion in the box, the children open it up to find dolls for the girls, a truck for the boy, a lace-trimmed blouse and feathered hat for Mama, and fruit and candy enough for a neighborhood party. Santa Claus turns out to be the wife of one of Mama's bosses, who met her once, was charmed, and decided to spend hundreds of dollars to make their Christmas a merry one.

The author, a former Newbery winner writing her twenty-fifth book at age eighty-six, tells us that this is a true story. But a true story should truly reflect life instead of sugar-coating the realities of poverty. There is not the slightest reference to the oppression of women who clean offices and who also have to care for children, cook, shop and clean. The message delivered to children is: "Santa, or fairy godmother, or a rich-boss's wife, will take care of everything *IF* you are good."

No child this reviewer knows would, or should, believe this boring pap. The illustrations, equally cloying and dull, do not correspond in detail to the text.

	ART	WORDS		ART	WORDS		ART	WORDS	N.A.
anti-Racist			non-Racist			Racist — omission / commission			✓
anti-Sexist			non-Sexist			Sexist	✓	✓	
anti-Elitist			non-Elitist	✓		Elitist		✓	
anti-Materialist			non-Materialist	✓		Materialist		✓	
anti-Individualist			non-Individualist	✓	✓	Individualist			
anti-Ageist			non-Ageist	✓	✓	Ageist			
anti-Conformist			non-Conformist	✓		Conformist		✓	
anti-Escapist			non-Escapist	✓		Escapist		✓	

							Excellent	Good	Fair	Poor
Builds positive image of females/ minorities			Builds negative image of females/ minorities							
Inspires action vs. oppression			Culturally authentic			Literary quality			✓	
						Art quality			✓	

FAT AND SKINNY
by Philip Balestrino
illustrated by Pam Makie
Thomas Y. Crowell
$4.50, 33 pages, grades p.s.-3

Fat and Skinny is a Let's-Read-And-Find-Out science book which attempts to explain why people are fat or skinny (or in between). It offers the novel explanation that fat is good because it keeps you warm and gives shape to the body. Discussed at length are calories, metabolism and exercise and a simple chart depicting food/calorie/exercise correlations graphically reinforces these relationships. (One double-scoop ice cream cone is equivalent in calories to seventeen raw five-inch-long carrots.)

In his introductory and concluding statements, the author tries to project a non-judgmental attitude towards fatness and skinny-ness. The book's seemingly scientific and objective approach is negated in the illustrations, which are both subtly sexist and anti-fat. Interestingly, most of the fat people in the book are female, with the two main characters being fat and skinny girls, while the in-between or average person is a boy. The implication here is 1) that only women are concerned about weight or shape problems, and 2) that men are the "norm." Furthermore, the author continually uses the male pronoun "he" even though the illustrations clearly show girls.

The book's anti-fat attitudes are even more insidious. In an illustration of four cheerleaders, only the fat girl is wearing pants; whereas the three skinnier girls have on short skirts—implying that fat legs are unattractive and should be hidden. Fatness is further stigmatized in the book's final image—that of a fat girl gazing unhappily at her almost empty plate while four books about dieting, calories and exercise stare her in the face (the skinny girl is always portrayed as happy). There are also several ageist illustrations of old women in rocking chairs, implying that old people cannot lead active lives. A positive aspect of the illustrations is that they show active boys and girls and include minorities. But the book's sexist and anti-fat projections pose serious problems.

	ART	WORDS		ART	WORDS			ART	WORDS	N.A.
anti-Racist			non-Racist	✓	✓	Racist	omission			
							commission			
anti-Sexist			non-Sexist			Sexist		✓	✓	
anti-Elitist			non-Elitist	✓	✓	Elitist				
anti-Materialist			non-Materialist	✓	✓	Materialist				
anti-Individualist			non-Individualist	✓	✓	Individualist				
anti-Ageist			non-Ageist			Ageist		✓	✓	
anti-Conformist			non-Conformist	✓	✓	Conformist				
anti-Escapist			non-Escapist	✓	✓	Escapist				
Builds positive image of females/minorities			Builds negative image of (females) minorities	✓			Excellent	Good	Fair	Poor
Inspires action vs. oppression			Culturally authentic			Literary quality			✓	
						Art quality				✓

THE GIRL WHO WOULD RATHER CLIMB TREES
by Miriam Schlein
illustrated by Judith Gwyn Brown
Harcourt, Brace, Jovanovich
$4.95, unpaged, grades p.s.-3

This nicely illustrated book is an amusing and sensitive account of one girl's experience with social pressure to conform to traditional sex role expectations.

Melissa is an active, independent girl about six years old, who likes cooking, reading, solving puzzles and tree-climbing. In fact, she is pretty much an all-around girl. One day, Melissa's mother, grandmother and mother's friend give her a doll and carriage to socialize her into more "feminine" pursuits. Melissa hates playing with dolls, finding a real baby like her cousin, Phillip, much more interesting. Finally, Melissa resolves her predicament: Explaining in a whisper to the grown-ups that the doll is sleeping, she leaves her room and goes outside to climb trees.

Fortunately, the author has spared readers the pretentiousness and self-righteousness often found in books about girls fighting to be themselves. Melissa's clever solution to her predicament indicates her ability to be considerate of others without compromising her own likes and dislikes.

This reviewer especially enjoyed the author's treatment of the doll issue. She clearly explains the difference between playing with a doll and playing with a real baby. Yet Melissa's preference for playing with real babies is handled in such a way as not to belittle children who do play with dolls.

The Girl Who Would Rather Climb Trees is an exciting book that contains subtly-executed, non-sexist, non-conformist, non-individualistic messages.

	ART	WORDS		ART	WORDS			ART	WORDS	N.A.
anti-Racist			non-Racist			Racist	omission			✓
							commission			
anti-Sexist	✓	✓	non-Sexist			Sexist				
anti-Elitist			non-Elitist	✓	✓	Elitist				
anti-Materialist			non-Materialist	✓	✓	Materialist				
anti-Individualist			non-Individualist	✓	✓	Individualist				
anti-Ageist			non-Ageist	✓	✓	Ageist				
anti-Conformist	✓	✓	non-Conformist			Conformist				
anti-Escapist			non-Escapist	✓	✓	Escapist				
Builds positive image of (females) minorities	✓	✓	Builds negative image of females/ minorities				Excellent	Good	Fair	Poor
						Literary quality		✓		
Inspires action vs. oppression			Culturally authentic			Art quality	✓			

SNORKEL
by George Flexer
illustrated by James Victorine
Prentice-Hall
$4.95, unpaged, grades p.s.-3

Here is another book in which Older Brother teases and puts down Kid Sister. The younger child finally earns respect by knowing the rules of water safety and being a good junior life saver. Although Christine (called Snorkel by her brother, much to her consternation) is unable to beat her brother in a swimming race, she *is* able to rescue him from the dangers of a water skiing accident caused by his neglect of safety rules.

On the positive side, this slight story is helpful for a girl's self-image, okay in its treatment of boy-girl relationships and instructive in its projection of water safety rules. In addition, the line drawings feature decidedly unpretty youngsters. On the negative side, Mother is only shown serving food while Father is active, and the motel guests are all white. And why must a younger sibling prove herself in some dramatic fashion in order for her older brother to treat her with respect?

	ART	WORDS		ART	WORDS			ART	WORDS	N.A.
anti-Racist			non-Racist		✓	Racist	omission	✓		
							commission			
anti-Sexist			non-Sexist	✓	✓	Sexist				
anti-Elitist			non-Elitist	✓	✓	Elitist				
anti-Materialist			non-Materialist	✓	✓	Materialist				
anti-Individualist			non-Individualist	✓	✓	Individualist				
anti-Ageist			non-Ageist			Ageist				✓
anti-Conformist			non-Conformist	✓	✓	Conformist				
anti-Escapist			non-Escapist	✓	✓	Escapist				
Builds positive image of females/ minorities			Builds negative image of females/ minorities				Excellent	Good	Fair	Poor
						Literary quality			✓	
Inspires action vs. oppression			Culturally authentic			Art quality		✓		

DOUBLE-DOG-DARE
by Ray Prather
illustrated by same
Macmillan
$4.95, 40 pages, grades p.s.-2

Part of a Ready-to-Read series, this is an amusing, attractively illustrated little story about two Black youngsters in a semi-rural setting. Eddie finds a quarter and, instead of "Halfers, Halfers," he decides to go with "Finders Keepers." Rudy resents his selfishness and wants to share some of the ice cream cone Eddie buys with his find. An argument ends with the cone falling to the street, but after a chase the boys end up as friends once again, swinging from a large tree. Crisis Number Two: A seemingly fierce bull dog sits growling at the base of the tree and the boys are afraid to descend. Presently, a little girl and her mother appear to claim their actually friendly pet, and the nice mother buys each boy an ice cream cone to thank them for helping locate their prodigal dog.

The only ridiculous thing about this book is its price—but when it comes to ridiculous prices, it has a lot of company.

	ART	WORDS		ART	WORDS			ART	WORDS	N.A.
anti-Racist	✓		non-Racist		✓	Racist	omission			
							commission			
anti-Sexist			non-Sexist	✓	✓	Sexist				
anti-Elitist			non-Elitist	✓	✓	Elitist				
anti-Materialist			non-Materialist	✓		Materialist			✓	
anti-Individualist			non-Individualist	✓		Individualist			✓	
anti-Ageist			non-Ageist			Ageist				✓
anti-Conformist			non-Conformist	✓	✓	Conformist				
anti-Escapist			non-Escapist	✓	✓	Escapist				
Builds positive image of females/minorities			Builds negative image of females/minorities				Excellent	Good	Fair	Poor
Inspires action vs. oppression			Culturally authentic			Literary quality		✓		
						Art quality	✓			

SOMETHING QUEER AT THE BALL PARK: A MYSTERY
by Elizabeth Levy
illustrated by Mordicai Gerstein
Delacorte Press
$5.95, 46 pages, grades 1-3

The "queer" thing that happens at the park is that Jill (about ten-years-old), has her lucky Rusty McGraw bat stolen by someone on her baseball team. Her best friend, Gwen, with the help of her detective kit and her funny basset hound, Fletcher, solves the mystery, and all three of them capture the culprit—a little boy who is jealous of Jill's batting ability.

The baseball team is sexually and racially integrated (although predominantly white and male), and the fact that girls are on the team is not at all an issue—for a pleasant change. It is just assumed that girls are good enough to be there. (It is somewhat unfortunate, though, that Jill doesn't play very well without the aid of the "lucky" bat.)

The illustrations are clever, perhaps sometimes too clever and over-complicated. But aside from this, I would recommend *Something Queer* as a non-sexist mystery story for children. Top girl athletes and smart girl detectives are certainly hard to find.

	ART	WORDS		ART	WORDS				ART	WORDS	N.A.
anti-Racist			non-Racist	✓	✓	Racist	omission				
							commission				
anti-Sexist	✓	✓	non-Sexist			Sexist					
anti-Elitist			non-Elitist	✓	✓	Elitist					
anti-Materialist			non-Materialist	✓	✓	Materialist					
anti-Individualist			non-Individualist	✓	✓	Individualist					
anti-Ageist			non-Ageist			Ageist					✓
anti-Conformist	✓	✓	non-Conformist			Conformist					
anti-Escapist			non-Escapist	✓	✓	Escapist					
Builds positive image of females/minorities		✓	Builds negative image of females/minorities					Excellent	Good	Fair	Poor
Inspires action vs. oppression			Culturally authentic			Literary quality			✓		
						Art quality			✓		

SEDNA: AN ESKIMO MYTH
by Beverly Brodsky McDermott
illustrated by same
Viking
$5.95, unpaged, p.s.-3

Sedna, powerful spirit of the ocean, was ignoring the Innuit people, so that they went hungry and became ill. Their man of power, the Angakok, listened to her, discovered what was wrong and helped the Innuit get back into a good relationship with Sedna. The people discovered then, and know until this very day, that you must never forget the spirits or bad things will happen.

This myth is told by a non-Indian, but it is told in a manner that keeps very much to the sense of the story and its spirit. It does not distort the Native American values expressed in the story, either.

Those values are: respecting this planet, treating it with good techniques of conservation, preserving the balance of nature—the only way people will have enough to eat and have the rest of their needs fulfilled. To study the world and see how humans fit into the whole of it, in the best way they can, is the only way to survive.

This is a valuable myth, deserving of preservation and attention by Indians and non-Indians alike. However, in times like these, we do not need to preserve myths like jelly in a jar. Native Americans know this well, and very seldom tell a story just to be talking or to be entertaining an audience. Only within the framework of life today can myths fulfill their purpose. This is the one mistake this author makes—to become enchanted with a story and to love it for its own sake. The Innuit people today are in just as bad a situation as were their ancient ancestors who began this myth. Their situation, today, should have been worked into the tale, for without it the myth is only half there.

It is plain to see that Ms. McDermott has great sympathy and understanding for the Innuit. Her drawings, which are clearly her own and yet full of a sense of the people she is drawing, were the main motivation for the book. However, although she is sympathetic in a positive way in her drawings and the way she relates the story, it boils down to the same thing as being romantically attracted to lovely beadwork or amazing dances and caring less about Native people starving to death or being shot. That is cultural anthropology, a bad concept to Native Americans.

	ART	WORDS		ART	WORDS			ART	WORDS	N.A.
anti-Racist			non-Racist	✓	✓	Racist	omission			
							commission			
anti-Sexist			non-Sexist	✓	✓	Sexist				
anti-Elitist			non-Elitist	✓	✓	Elitist				
anti-Materialist			non-Materialist	✓	✓	Materialist				
anti-Individualist			non-Individualist	✓	✓	Individualist				
anti-Ageist			non-Ageist	✓	✓	Ageist				
anti-Conformist			non-Conformist	✓	✓	Conformist				
anti-Escapist			non-Escapist			Escapist		✓	✓	
Builds positive image of females/minorities			Builds negative image of females/minorities				Excellent	Good	Fair	Poor
Inspires action vs. oppression			Culturally authentic	✓	✓	Literary quality	✓			
						Art quality	✓			

DOCTOR SHAWN
by Petronella Breinburg
illustrated by Errol Lloyd
Thomas Y. Crowell
$5.95, 25 pages, grades p.s.-2

This is the second book about a little boy named Shawn by the Black British writer and illustrator team of Petronella Breinburg and Errol Lloyd.

In the current book, Shawn is left at home on a Saturday with his sisters and their friend Robert. Shawn's mother has told the children to be quiet and to keep the house tidy while she is away. When Shawn's older sister suggests a game of hospital, it is Shawn's turn to be the doctor, and his elder sister's turn to be the nurse. The two other children—along with the cat—are the patients. Predictably, a great mess is made. But when Shawn's mother returns, instead of fussing, she smilingly serves lunch to the children.

This book is most welcome. The author presents a warm and loving Black family with a mother who understands that play and neatness do not always mix. And since many Black parents must leave their children home unattended for lack of babysitting money, requiring the children to develop self-reliance at an early age, it is refreshing to have a book which depicts that "problem" in a positive light.

Another good feature of the book is that both Shawn and his sister, in their conversation, express awareness of the fact that the roles of doctor and nurse have nothing to do with being male or female.

	ART	WORDS		ART	WORDS			ART	WORDS	N.A.
anti-Racist	✓	✓	non-Racist			Racist	omission			
							commission			
anti-Sexist			non-Sexist	✓	✓	Sexist				
anti-Elitist			non-Elitist	✓	✓	Elitist				
anti-Materialist			non-Materialist	✓	✓	Materialist				
anti-Individualist			non-Individualist	✓	✓	Individualist				
anti-Ageist			non-Ageist			Ageist				✓
anti-Conformist			non-Conformist	✓	✓	Conformist				
anti-Escapist			non-Escapist	✓	✓	Escapist				
Builds positive image of females/minorities	✓	✓	Builds negative image of females/minorities				Excellent	Good	Fair	Poor
Inspires action vs. oppression			Culturally authentic	✓		Literary quality		✓		
						Art quality	✓			

THE WINTER WIFE: AN ABENAKI FOLKTALE
by Anne Eliot Crompton
illustrated by Robert Andrew Parker
Little, Brown
$6.95, 47 pages, grades 1-3

A hunter alone in the woods for the winter gets very, very lonely. He wishes desperately for a companion, and the wish is father to the reality. Derived from an Abenaki folktale, this story is about a hunter who is down on his luck. One day he sees a moose but does not shoot her. His traps are from then on always full and a mysterious woman waits in the wigwam for him. He must not take any other wife, she warns him as he leaves in the spring. The hunter returns each winter to his wife. Soon they have three small children. Each spring he goes to his home village alone, a rich man. His good fortunes do not go unnoticed; soon the chief's daughter wants to marry him. He takes her for his summer wife.

Since he has not remained true to his vision, it changes from being his reality and disappears, taking their children. Once again a cow moose, this time with three young ones, the winter wife is then understood by the hunter to be the reality and the vision he wants. He forsakes his former life, changes into a moose and goes away with her.

This is a fairly recent version of an old tale, which is told not only by the Abenaki but also by the Sioux and many other Native Americans. Its relative recentness is shown by the emphasis on getting rich, which the hunter achieved by obtaining many animal skins that would make him wealthy. It is true that an Indian trapper who gets many skins can better provide for his family than one who gets few. But the Indian measure is in terms of caring for people, rather than in rewards of paper or metal coins. This is an example of non-Indian values which have been put into the story by its non-Indian author. (It is very hard to break out of one culture enough to explain another on its own terms.)

And that is not the most serious fault of the book. It is presented as a legend only, with no background of the life-situation of the people who told it. Native American people usually do not tell stories like this one just for the sake of telling stories. The tales make little sense if they are not put into the full perspective of all that is happening to the people who are hearing and telling them. So, although this is an authentic foktale, it is also accompanied by some very bad drawings. They look like the work of a thirty-five-year-old person pretending to draw like a child. The people they show are certainly not recognizably Indian. For a wigwam, a tipi is substituted—why? Did the illustrator not know the difference, or did his racism make him think it didn't matter?

This tale makes a mockery of the values of the Native American people it is meant to portray, and will contribute to no child's understanding.

	ART	WORDS		ART	WORDS			ART	WORDS	N.A.
anti-Racist			non-Racist		✓	Racist	omission / commission	✓		
anti-Sexist			non-Sexist	✓	✓	Sexist				
anti-Elitist			non-Elitist	✓	✓	Elitist				
anti-Materialist			non-Materialist	✓		Materialist				✓
anti-Individualist			non-Individualist	✓	✓	Individualist				
anti-Ageist			non-Ageist			Ageist				✓
anti-Conformist			non-Conformist	✓	✓	Conformist				
anti-Escapist			non-Escapist			Escapist		✓	✓	
Builds positive image of females/minorities			Builds negative image of females/minorities					Excellent	Good	Fair	Poor
Inspires action vs. oppression			Culturally authentic				Literary quality			✓	
							Art quality				✓

LET'S MAKE A DEAL
by Linda Glovach
illustrated by same
Prentice-Hall
$5.95, 48 pages, grades p.s.-3

Tom and Dewey are two little boys who have decided to be "best friends forever." Both boys appear to be seven-ish. They have built a tree house where they go every day, after school, and remain until dark. One day they pick up a stray puppy to share their tree home and their life of friendship. A crisis disturbs this idyll when Tom's family makes plans to move to New Orleans. Who shall keep the puppy? Both boys behave unselfishly; and Dewey, after a difficult decision and a minor adventure, ends up with the dog.

In this innocuous, sweet story it seems merely incidental that Dewey is Black and Tom is white. Since so few books cross racial friendships, some parents and teachers may welcome this one. The book is not sexist, elitist, individualist or ageist. I don't *think* it is racist. However. . . .

The author-illustrator does not mention a single *word* in the text about color. Her illustrations show two look-alike little boys, and the one with the curlier, darker hair and brown wash over his face is Dewey. Was this done consciously? Was the author aware that the facial features of the two boys are alike? Or that Dewey is a so-called "Black" name? Or that Dewey lives on the *north* side of town on *Lincoln* Street? He lives alone with his grandmother, named Brown, who tells *spooky* stories late at night. Tom lives on the south side of town with two parents and a sister. What subliminal message does all this give to children?

Another worrisome point arises because every day both boys seem to have plenty of money for soda pop, hamburgers, dog food, etc. They are so much on their own that each walks, alone, to opposite ends of town when they leave each other after dark; and Dewey can take two buses to reach an unknown part of an unknown city, New Orleans, without the help of anyone. In our eagerness to liberate children in the new literature, let us not go overboard and set unrealistic and unwise examples.

	ART	WORDS		ART	WORDS			ART	WORDS	N.A.
anti-Racist			non-Racist		✓	Racist	omission			
							commission	✓		
anti-Sexist			non-Sexist	✓	✓	Sexist				
anti-Elitist			non-Elitist	✓	✓	Elitist				
anti-Materialist			non-Materialist	✓	✓	Materialist				
anti-Individualist		✓	non-Individualist	✓		Individualist				
anti-Ageist			non-Ageist	✓	✓	Ageist				
anti-Conformist			non-Conformist	✓	✓	Conformist				
anti-Escapist			non-Escapist	✓		Escapist				✓

							Excellent	Good	Fair	Poor
Builds positive image of females/ minorities			Builds negative image of females/ minorities							
Inspires action vs. oppression			Culturally authentic			Literary quality			✓	
						Art quality				✓

THE ANALYSES −2

Middle Grades

LILIUOKALANI
by Mary Malone
illustrated by Cary
Garrard Press
$3.40, 80 pages, grades 2-5

Liliuokalani is a biography of Hawaii's beloved last queen. Totally committed to her people, Liliuokalani strongly championed Hawaiian values and lifestyles and believed that Hawaii should be governed by Hawaiians. The book recounts her childhood, her marriage to a British *haole* (Hawaiian for white person), her service to her people (in combatting smallpox, the ravages of a volcanic eruption, etc.) and her unsuccessful struggle for control of Hawaii against the powerful *haoles*. Defeated, Liliuokalani became a kind of monument—without real political power, but a strong cultural symbol for her people.

Ms. Malone's account of Hawaiian history is racist to the core. She writes from a biased, white American point of view, and although enough facts are presented to give some semblance of historical reality, her half-truths oversimplify and gloss over the injustices perpetrated against Hawaiians by the white invaders. For example, she writes: "the white man brought new ideas and ways of living. They also brought diseases . . . many Hawaiians died." Smallpox and measles are the diseases mentioned. Ms. Malone leaves out VD and alcoholism—the leading killers of Hawaiians. Later, she explains that Asians were recruited to work on the sugar and pineapple plantations because "there were not enough Hawaiians." How could the reader know that between 1776, when the first whites came to Hawaii, and 1840, the population of 400,000 Hawaiians was reduced to 100,000 by the new diseases—which is why there were not enough Hawaiians to work on the plantations?

The racism which dominates white-Hawaiian relations, and that was manifest in Liliuokalani's relations with her mother-in-law, is noted by the author as follows: "It took a long time for John's mother to accept Lydia." (Lydia was Liliuokalani's Christian name.) The inadequacy of this less-than-candid reference is compounded by an illustration depicting Liliuokalani as white-skinned even though, in fact, she was very dark. Missionaries are described as people who "had come to Hawaii to teach the people about Christian religion. They started schools." True enough. But the missionaries also helped destroy traditional Hawaiian culture and morality. The white missionary influence on the royal family is clear enough—both Liliuokalani and her sister married *haoles*. The author explains Liliuokalani's marriage by stating that Liliuokalani "knew the old customs and ways were as dear to John as they were to her."

The last straw comes, appropriately, on the last page: "As Queen, Liliuokalani tried to save the ancient Hawaiian way of life. Time and change worked against her . . . and now her story is part of America's heritage."

Here, Ms. Malone perpetuates the concepts that 1) America has a pre-ordained right to rule and that 2) change and progress are synonymous even though "change" may mean the annihilation and oppression of a whole people. Pushed aside by the profit motive, private property and the concept of original sin, the old ways of Hawaii become—in Ms. Malone's perspective—relics of the past, something to be admired "as part of America's heritage."

This book endorses materialism and exploitation and encourages racist and paternalistic attitudes about a non-white people and culture.

	ART	WORDS		ART	WORDS			ART	WORDS	N.A.
anti-Racist			non-Racist	✓		Racist — omission / commission			✓	
anti-Sexist			non-Sexist	✓	✓	Sexist				
anti-Elitist			non-Elitist	✓		Elitist			✓	
anti-Materialist			non-Materialist	✓	✓	Materialist				
anti-Individualist		✓	non-Individualist	✓		Individualist				
anti-Ageist			non-Ageist			Ageist				✓
anti-Conformist			non-Conformist	✓		Conformist			✓	
anti-Escapist			non-Escapist	✓		Escapist			✓	
Builds positive image of females/minorities			Builds negative image of females/minorities		✓		Excellent	Good	Fair	Poor
Inspires action vs. oppression			Culturally authentic			Literary quality		✓		
						Art quality			✓	

THE LEOPARD
by Cecil Bodker
translated by Gunnar Poulsen
Atheneum
$7.25, 186 pages, grades 4-7

There is more to *The Leopard* than its title would indicate. On one level, it is a gripping and suspenseful story about the occasionally exasperating adventures of a shepherd-boy,Tibeso, in a rural village in central Ethiopia. The story focuses on Tibeso's courageous fight for survival when his discovery "that a disguised blacksmith, not a leopard, is responsible for a great many missing cattle in the area" imperils his life.

But the book has another dimension. It depicts graphically and, except for a few minor details, authentically, life in a rural Ethiopian village and offers relevant social commentary along the way. Among other things, Bodker succinctly describes the economic and social roles of women. Likewise, the male chauvinism prevalent in the rural society is tersely depicted (this is a good topic for classroom discussion). In one episode Tibeso is forced, by tactical imperatives, to dress as a girl. He is mortified: "Never had he imagined that such a shame would come to him."

The Leopard is a book that all children, and many adults, would find enjoyable and informative. Bodker's style is clear, and her handling of suspense is surprisingly unobtrusive. As a Dane who spent three months in the region from which the book's setting is derived, she is to be commended for having captured so well the texture of life in that area.

	ART	WORDS		ART	WORDS			ART	WORDS	N.A.
anti-Racist			non-Racist			Racist omission / commission				
anti-Sexist			non-Sexist		✓	Sexist				
anti-Elitist			non-Elitist		✓	Elitist				
anti-Materialist			non-Materialist		✓	Materialist				
anti-Individualist			non-Individualist		✓	Individualist				
anti-Ageist ·			non-Ageist		✓	Ageist				
anti-Conformist			non-Conformist		✓	Conformist				
anti-Escapist			non-Escapist		✓	Escapist				
Builds positive image of females/ minorities		✓	Builds negative image of females/ minorities				Excellent	Good	Fair	Poor
Inspires action vs. oppression			Culturally authentic		✓	Literary quality		✓		
						Art quality				

SHOESHINE GIRL
by Clyde Robert Bulla
illustrated by Leigh Grant
Thomas Y. Crowell
$5.95, 84 pages, grades 3-7

In the course of a summer, an independent but obnoxious and self-centered, ten-year-old brat matures into an independent, likable and unselfish girl.

It happens like this: Sarah Ida, who is too difficult for her ill mother to cope with, and whose father is a traveling man, is packed off to spend the summer with Aunt Claudia. The incredible gall shown by Sarah Ida in her determination to always have her own way will intrigue young readers.

When an automobile accident injures the local shoeshine man, Sarah Ida decides to help by operating his stand while he is in the hospital. The gratification which comes from doing meaningful work and being useful to others, combined with patience and concern on the part of her aunt and new employer, lead to changes in Sarah Ida's outlook and values. Upon returning home, she plays a cooperative family role during her mother's illness.

Although the writing is somewhat pedestrian and the quality of the illustrations only average, this book's message is important for the many children in our society who feel alienated because they do not feel needed. The concepts that all work is worth doing well, and that real satisfaction comes from maintaining warm relationships with others, are projected in a positive fashion.

	ART	WORDS		ART	WORDS		ART	WORDS	N.A.
anti-Racist			non-Racist			Racist omission / commission			✓
anti-Sexist	✓	✓	non-Sexist			Sexist			
anti-Elitist		✓	non-Elitist	✓		Elitist			
anti-Materialist		✓	non-Materialist	✓		Materialist			
anti-Individualist		✓	non-Individualist	✓		Individualist			
anti-Ageist			non-Ageist			Ageist			✓
anti-Conformist	✓	✓	non-Conformist			Conformist			
anti-Escapist			non-Escapist	✓	✓	Escapist			
Builds positive image of females/minorities		✓	Builds negative image of females/minorities				Excellent	Good	Fair	Poor
Inspires action vs. oppression			Culturally authentic			Literary quality			✓	
						Art quality			✓	

WHO GOES THERE, LINCOLN?
by Dale Fife
illustrated by Paul Galdone
Coward, McCann & Geoghegan
$4.86, 63 pages, grades 3-5

Who Goes There, Lincoln? describes the search for a new clubhouse by Lincoln Farnum and his friends, Wilbur and Bunky. Their search leads ultimately to an old, deserted firehouse which is about to be torn down. Lincoln becomes particularly interested in the building when Mrs. Crauch, an elderly neighbor, recounts tales from her youth when the firehouse was an opera house.

After the police interrupt the boys' initiation rites for new club members and chase them out of the condemned firehouse, they return to prowl about in the hope of finding something of value that will insure the building's preservation. The discovery of an old diary, a secret panel and an underground tunnel reveals that the firehouse had once been a station on the Underground Railroad. (The Railroad is described in the book as "how *people* helped *slaves* escape to the North and to Canada." [emphasis added.] Aren't slaves people?) Because of the boys' discovery, plans are made to save the firehouse and turn it into a community center and historical site.

This book is non-racist in that no distinctions based on race are made between the characters. However, that presents its own problems. Were it not for shading in the bland and racially inaccurate illustrations, it would be impossible to tell Black characters from white. As it stands, one cannot even distinguish Black from Black. The boys are supposed to be friends, not relatives, yet they resemble identical twins in most of the racist illustrations.

Another minus is the use of the term "swagger," with its macho overtones, to describe the boys walking down the street. It is also unfortunate that the boys' desire to have the firehouse for their personal use is the main motivation of their efforts to save it.

But the most objectionable element of this book is its treatment of the elderly Mrs. Patch, "the very oldest person on Plum Street," is regarded as a "weirdo" by the boys, and her references to a railroad (that is, the Underground Railroad) are presented as near-ravings. Neighbor Crauch is portrayed as a fluttery old keeper of cats. These depictions, plus the boys' lack of respect for the two women, convey the message that to be old is to be senile and out of step.

	ART	WORDS		ART	WORDS		ART	WORDS	N.A.
anti-Racist			non-Racist		✓	Racist omission/commission	✓		
anti-Sexist			non-Sexist	✓		Sexist		✓	
anti-Elitist			non-Elitist	✓	✓	Elitist			
anti-Materialist			non-Materialist	✓	✓	Materialist			
anti-Individualist			non-Individualist	✓		Individualist		✓	
anti-Ageist			non-Ageist			Ageist	✓	✓	
anti-Conformist			non-Conformist	✓	✓	Conformist			
anti-Escapist			non-Escapist	✓	✓	Escapist			
Builds positive image of females/minorities			Builds negative image of females/minorities	✓	✓		Excellent	Good	Fair	Poor
Inspires action vs. oppression			Culturally authentic			Literary quality			✓	
						Art quality				✓

A BICYCLE FROM BRIDGETOWN
by Dawn C. Thomas
illustrated by Don Miller
McGraw-Hill
$5.72, 64 pages, grades 3-5

A Bicycle From Bridgetown is an honesty-pays-off morality tale set in Barbados. A poor boy's seemingly impossible dream of owning a bicycle comes true when he finds an old, apparently ownerless, bicycle. We learn, however, that Barbados has a cycling team, and the old bike is the "lucky charm" of the team's captain who had ordered a new bicycle when he thought his old favorite was lost. He is so happy to have the old one back that he presents the new bike to our young hero, Edgar.

In telling Edgar's story, the author also paints a picture of island life. We meet poor but happy "natives" who eagerly await the arrival of the next tourist boat. Edgar is obsessed with the foreigners' material possessions, yet never feels any resentment. Among his happiest memories are watching "the big folk at the airport as they flagged down cars to take them to big hotels." The occupants of the hotels, on the other hand, are interested in the islanders only in terms of shopping.

The author makes no reference to urban life in Bridgetown. Except for the owner of a bicycle shop, all islanders are occupied with fishing, selling, driving a bus or cab or waiting on tourists. The women cook, care for their children and sell or shop in the marketplace.

Not only is the author's background use of tourism not essential to the story, but given that it is used in an unquestioning way, tacit support of the status quo is implied. Although the book describes local, Black poverty and white tourist wealth, it does not do so in a way which might cause young readers to consider the justice of the situation. The bitter anger which most sensitive tourists feel themselves the objects of when traveling in the Caribbean never surfaces in this book.

The text's individualist and escapist overtones are equally disturbing. Are readers to deduce, from Edgar's success in securing his heart's desire, that good fortune comes to all honest, deserving children?

The black and white illustrations are more authentic than the story.

	ART	WORDS		ART	WORDS		ART	WORDS	N.A.
anti-Racist			non-Racist	✓	✓	Racist — omission / commission			
anti-Sexist			non-Sexist	✓	✓	Sexist			
anti-Elitist			non-Elitist	✓		Elitist			✓
anti-Materialist			non-Materialist	✓		Materialist			✓
anti-Individualist			non-Individualist	✓		Individualist			✓
anti-Ageist			non-Ageist			Ageist			✓
anti-Conformist			non-Conformist	✓	✓	Conformist			
anti-Escapist			non-Escapist	✓		Escapist		✓	
Builds positive image of females/minorities			Builds negative image of females/minorities				Excellent	Good	Fair	Poor
Inspires action vs. oppression			Culturally authentic			Literary quality			✓	
						Art quality	✓			

POTAWATOMI INDIAN SUMMER
by E. William Oldenburg
illustrated by Betty Beeby
William B. Eerdmans
$5.95, 134 pages, grades 5-7

Six white children, between five and eight years of age, are exploring a cave in a sand dune behind their homes on Lake Michigan. Since it is "Indian summer," and they are walking "Indian-file," one child looks "like a scout," a bush looks like "an Indian chief" and they are "creeping up on the bush . . . as if they themselves were Indians," it comes as no surprise that they fall through the sand and, thus, through time, emerging three hundred years ago when the Potawatomi inhabited the area. From here on the author mixes equal parts of routine Native American stereotypes, paternalistic "we-are-all-alike" racism, white-savior racism, and a considerable amount of misinformation about Native Americans. Add to the brew a dash of criticism of stereotypes plus a bit of magic, and we have a vile, racist fantasy.

It develops that the Potawatomi had a prophetic dreamer who had anticipated the children's visit. Moreover, the white children are conveniently blessed with the ability to speak the Native language. No sooner does a Potawatomi boy named Mogawasie befriend them, than a group of evil

Mohawks intrude upon the scene and capture the two youngest children. The motto of these Mohawks is "Huron blood is good to drink."

As if these distortions of Native American culture were not enough, the author blunders on. Attempting cuteness, he suggests that Indian kids are pretty much like white kids by giving Mogawasie a younger sister—Sandagawah. ("Can we call you Sandy? Sandagawah is kind of long.") "Sandy" and her brother quarrel and tease just as the white sisters and brothers do, and "Sandy" takes the white girls to play with her dolls and doll house—a tiny wigwam—while Mogawasie takes the boys fishing.

Although the "greatest fishermen" of the Potawatomi have long been trying to snare "Old Warrior Pike," a giant of an old fish, it takes the intervention and skill of a few white youngsters to expedite the big catch. The white boys also supply the brains and brawn necessary to elude a trap set by those evil Mohawks. When the Mohawk chieftain is defeated, he weeps, thus embarrassing his warriors who "were trying very hard not to look at their chieftain." Real men did not cry in those times either, says the author.

Stereotypes are lightly made fun of in this exchange: "Andy said, 'Do you think he would speak with a forked tongue?' 'With a what?' Darnotigo (the Mohawk was puzzled. 'Do you think he would lie?' Bridget translated. She realized that Darnotigo hadn't had a chance to hear Indians talking on television."

Magic makes an appearance in the form of a magical bow and arrow and a talking doll belonging to one of the white children which the Mohawks think is magic. "'I have a date tonight,' the talking doll told the Mohawk sentry. The Indian's eyes opened so wide that Jennifer thought they would pop right out of his head. She was afraid he might drop the doll before she could pull the string again, but, on the contrary, the sentry's hands seemed to be glued to the doll. He stood rigid, frozen by fear." (Here the author stirs some Stepin Fetchit-type Black stereotypes into his anti-Indian brew.)

Inaccurate information regarding Native culture can be found on almost every page. *Potawatomi Indian Summer* is an abomination.

	ART	WORDS		ART	WORDS			ART	WORDS	N.A.
anti-Racist			non-Racist			Racist — omission				
						— commission		✓	✓	
anti-Sexist			non-Sexist	✓		Sexist			✓	
anti-Elitist			non-Elitist	✓	✓	Elitist				
anti-Materialist			non-Materialist	✓	✓	Materialist				
anti-Individualist			non-Individualist	✓	✓	Individualist				
anti-Ageist			non-Ageist			Ageist			✓	✓
anti-Conformist			non-Conformist	✓		Conformist			✓	
anti-Escapist			non-Escapist	✓		Escapist			✓	
Builds positive image of females/ minorities			Builds negative image of females/ minorities		✓		Excellent	Good	Fair	Poor
Inspires action vs. oppression			Culturally authentic			Literary quality			✓	
						Art quality				✓

THUNDER AT GETTYSBURG

by Patricia Lee Gauch
illustrated by Stephen Gammell
Coward, McCann & Geoghegan
$5.95, 48 pages, grades 2-6

Based on an actual observer's account of the Battle of Gettysburg, this book vividly describes a fourteen-year-old girl's experiences and feelings during the three days she was accidentally engulfed by this historic and bloody event.

Fear, excitement, mud and gore are experienced by the young Gettysburg resident when she becomes involved in the struggle and is willingly pressed into service of the wounded and dying Union troops. Few Civil War accounts are written from a pro-Union viewpoint. Southern heroines dominated the books of past generations.

Historical accuracy (except for the total whiteness of all soldiers and residents), plus the simple, strong and beautiful prose, make this a worthy and enjoyable effort that will enrich a child's perceptions of history, women's work and 19th century warfare. The past truly comes alive, and the somber black and white drawings contribute to evoking the bleakness of the moment.

	ART	WORDS		ART	WORDS			ART	WORDS	N.A.
anti-Racist			non-Racist			Racist omission / commission		✓	✓	
anti-Sexist	✓	✓	non-Sexist			Sexist				
anti-Elitist			non-Elitist	✓	✓	Elitist				
anti-Materialist			non-Materialist	✓	✓	Materialist				
anti-Individualist		✓	non-Individualist	✓		Individualist				
anti-Ageist			non-Ageist	✓	✓	Ageist				
anti-Conformist			non-Conformist	✓	✓	Conformist				
anti-Escapist			non-Escapist	✓	✓	Escapist				
Builds positive image of females/ minorities		✓	Builds negative image of females/ minorities				Excellent	Good	Fair	Poor
Inspires action vs. oppression			Culturally authentic			Literary quality		✓		
						Art quality		✓		

PAUL ROBESON

by Eloise Greenfield
illustrated by George Ford
Thomas Y. Crowell
$4.50, 33 pages, grades 1-5

It is fortunate to have this significant book about the late, great Black artist and leader, Paul Robeson, for young readers. It documents his militant international struggle to end the oppression of Black and poor people.

The author notes the support and inspiration afforded the young Robeson by his family (particularly his widowed father and his brother, Reeve) in Princeton, New Jersey, which created a foundation for his achievement as a scholar (he graduated from Rutgers with highest honors), athlete, concert singer and actor. That support also contributed to the strength of conviction and purpose he was to manifest later in his activities as a political figure.

The book describes Robeson's use of his extraordinary singing talent to inform audiences around the world about the rich heritage of Black people, his outspokenness as a critic of oppression, and the persecution that befell him when he became a political activist.

George Ford's illustrations in acrylics and black-and-white wash capture well Robeson's strength and vivacity and blend excellently with the text.

This book is an excellent introduction to a man of universal stature.

	ART	WORDS		ART	WORDS			ART	WORDS	N.A.
anti-Racist	✓	✓	non-Racist			Racist omission / commission				
anti-Sexist			non-Sexist	✓	✓	Sexist				
anti-Elitist	✓	✓	non-Elitist			Elitist				
anti-Materialist	✓	✓	non-Materialist			Materialist				
anti-Individualist	✓	✓	non-Individualist			Individualist				
anti-Ageist	✓	✓	non-Ageist			Ageist				
anti-Conformist	✓	✓	non-Conformist			Conformist				
anti-Escapist	✓	✓	non-Escapist			Escapist				
Builds positive image of females/minorities		✓	Builds negative image of females/minorities				Excellent	Good	Fair	Poor
Inspires action vs. oppression	✓	✓	Culturally authentic			Literary quality	✓			
						Art quality	✓			

CISSY'S TEXAS PRIDE
by Edna Smith Makerney
illustrated by Margaret Leibold
Abingdon Press
$3.75, 80 pages, grades 3-6

When the Russell family's bean crop is destroyed by an early Texas frost, they are faced with the prospect of losing their farm unless they can quickly raise $4,000. Eleven-year-old Cissy's primary concern is saving her beloved horse, Texas Pride, from being sold to raise the necessary money. In this quiet, boring, 1950's-style tale, the white, church-going, hard-working family of three launches a series of money-making schemes. Of course, they succeed in raising just the right amount of money in the nick of time.

Aside from her ability to work tirelessly without complaint and to ride horses well, Cissy is a rather bland character. But a worse flaw is that the author and illustrator seem not to have heard of feminism. Although Cissy is energetic and capable, she aspires to getting married and being "as pretty and sweet as her mother" when she grows up. Meanwhile, her mother (shown as ultra-feminine in contrast to her super-masculine husband) is confined to kitchen and beauty-salon work, while the father—self appointed President of the Russell Family Company (his name)—is waited on by the two already overworked females.

The moral of the story, in true American fashion, is that through hard work one can make it—a faulty concept if ever there was one. The author would have been well advised to do the hard work required to give her book more depth, reality and excitement.

Illustrations, black and white, are good on horses, characterless on people.

	ART	WORDS		ART	WORDS		ART	WORDS	N.A.
anti-Racist			non-Racist			Racist omission/commission			✓
anti-Sexist			non-Sexist			Sexist	✓	✓	
anti-Elitist			non-Elitist	✓	✓	Elitist			
anti-Materialist			non-Materialist	✓	✓	Materialist			
anti-Individualist			non-Individualist	✓	✓	Individualist			
anti-Ageist			non-Ageist			Ageist			✓
anti-Conformist			non-Conformist	✓		Conformist		✓	
anti-Escapist			non-Escapist	✓	✓	Escapist			

					Excellent	Good	Fair	Poor
Builds positive image of females/minorities			Builds negative image of females/minorities					
Inspires action vs. oppression			Culturally authentic			Literary quality			✓
					Art quality			✓

MAGGIE MARMELSTEIN FOR PRESIDENT
by Marjorie Weinman Sharmat
illustrated by Ben Shecter
Harper & Row
$4.95, 122 pages, grades 3-6

Maggie Marmelstein decides to run for president of the sixth grade after Thad Smith turns down her offer to be his campaign manager. In the end, her efforts to win the office are undone when the whiz kid who had managed her campaign, is elected on a "write-in" ballot.

This is a silly, sexist, unrealistic piece of juvenile literature.

Although Maggie is said to have the best brain in the sixth grade, she never concerns herself with issues in her campaign for the presidency. Indeed, it becomes clear to everyone (including the reader) that revenge against Thad, on whom she has a crush, is Maggie's sole motivation for entering the race. The fact that Maggie is the last one to realize this makes her appear shallow.

Of the other females who play significant roles in the story, nothing favorable can be said. Maggie's best friend, Ellen, is pathetic. Totally lacking in imagination, she is, at best, a stooge whom Maggie regards as needing to be encouraged, looked after and treated gently.

Mrs. Marmelstein (no father is mentioned) is illustrated as plain and slightly overweight. She is characterized as overly attentive, homebound and always on call to cook for Maggie and her friends. Her cup fairly runs over with understanding and moral support, the author having succeeded in making her as simple and innocuous as the children.

Some of the silliest, least-liked students are boys—but so are the brightest and most popular. When Maggie becomes emotional during the pre-election debate and attacks Thad personally, he naturally remains cool and rational, winning even more admiration—including Maggie's. Noah too, eclipses Maggie when, through talent and cunning, he enlists enough support to win the election as a write-in candidate.

No reference is made to third world people in the book, and all of the illustrated characters are white. Considering that the story is set in an urban area, these omissions are unwarranted.

This silly book reinforces sexist stereotypes, emphasizes competition and individual achievement, and fails to address itself to any issues that are real or important to today's urban children.

The cartoon-like illustrations add nothing to this book.

	ART	WORDS		ART	WORDS			ART	WORDS	N.A.
anti-Racist			non-Racist			Racist	omission	✓	✓	
							commission			
anti-Sexist			non-Sexist			Sexist		✓	✓	
anti-Elitist			non-Elitist	✓		Elitist			✓	
anti-Materialist			non-Materialist	✓	✓	Materialist				
anti-Individualist			non-Individualist	✓		Individualist			✓	
anti-Ageist			non-Ageist			Ageist				✓
anti-Conformist			non-Conformist	✓		Conformist			✓	
anti-Escapist			non-Escapist	✓		Escapist			✓	
Builds positive image of females/minorities			Builds negative image of (females)/minorities		✓		Excellent	Good	Fair	Poor
Inspires action vs. oppression			Culturally authentic			Literary quality			✓	
						Art quality			✓	

THE HUNDRED PENNY BOX
by Sharon Bell Mathis
illustrated by Leo and Diane Dillon
Viking Press
$5.95, 47 pages, grades 2-5

The Hundred Penny Box is a thoughtful and sometimes touching story about a Black family trying to adjust to the presence of their one-hundred-year-old Aunt Dew. The father, an authoritarian figure who rarely appears in the story, has invited her to live with them in appreciation to Aunt Dew for having raised him when he was orphaned.

The mother, Ruth, has problems with Aunt Dew. She is uncomfortable around her and seems jealous of the close ties between her son, Michael, and Aunt Dew. Intentionally or not, Ruth tries to strip Aunt Dew of her identity by burning the small treasures the old woman has accumulated over the years. Throughout the story, she threatens to burn Aunt Dew's hundred penny box. The battered wooden box holds one penny for each year Aunt Dew has lived, and she has a story for every penny.

The threat to the box elicits protective feelings from Michael towards his aunt and a warm relationship develops between the two. Unfortunately, however, this relationship is very much dependent upon the mother's hostility.

Conflicts which arise in the book are never really resolved. The ending is ambiguous, with Michael lying peacefully next to his sleeping aunt. He sees the box through different eyes and decides that it is a bit scruffy. Does this mean he has come to agree with his mother's plan to throw the box away?

The strength of the book lies in Aunt Dew's brief but vivid accounts of her life and in her relationship with Michael. Its weakness lies in the unexplained hostility of the mother and the absence of the father.

The illustrations are warm and eloquent, carrying the theme of the hundred penny box throughout the story.

	ART	WORDS		ART	WORDS			ART	WORDS	N.A.
anti-Racist	✓	✓	non-Racist			Racist	omission / commission			
anti-Sexist			non-Sexist	✓		Sexist				✓
anti-Elitist			non-Elitist	✓	✓	Elitist				
anti-Materialist			non-Materialist	✓		Materialist				✓
anti-Individualist			non-Individualist	✓	✓	Individualist				
anti-Ageist			non-Ageist	✓	✓	Ageist				
anti-Conformist			non-Conformist	✓	✓	Conformist				
anti-Escapist			non-Escapist	✓	✓	Escapist				
Builds positive image of females/minorities			Builds negative image of females/minorities				Excellent	Good	Fair	Poor
Inspires action vs. oppression			Culturally authentic			Literary quality	✓			
						Art quality		✓		

A BOOK FOR JODAN
by Marcia Newfield
illustrated by Diane de Groat
Atheneum
$6.25, 48 pages, grades 3-6

A Book for Jodan is about marital separation and its effects on an only child, nine-year-old Jodan. The book attempts to reassure children (1) that they are not the cause of their parents' separation, (2) that just because parents do not love each other anymore does not mean they no longer love their children, and (3) that just because one parent lives away from the child does not imply lack of love from that parent (Jodan and her mother moved cross-country).

Both Jodan and her father feel the separation terribly ("I miss you, too, and sometimes I cry about it," says the father in a letter), and the story focuses on the father's tender out-reaching to assure his daughter that he still loves her. Just as he had once created her name "Jodan" from the names of his grandfather and her mother's because "it had a lot of love in it," he now puts together a touching "Book for Jodan" filled with old mementos, jokes, advice, songs, etc. to comfort her when she misses him. The scrapbook segment comprises the best fourteen pages of the story.

Sex-role stereotyping is consciously but subtly attacked throughout, and Jodan, described as "graceful yet strong," builds bookcases with her mother, cooks pancakes with her father and alternately plays shortstop and dresses up in old gowns in the attic.

Excluded, unfortunately, is any discussion of why Jodan automatically moves with her mother, especially in light of her close relationship with her father. Also omitted is any mention of Jodan's friends, school, neighborhood, and the pain unquestionably involved in leaving these, too.

The black and white illustrations, plus photographs, add to the warmth of this very nice story.

	ART	WORDS		ART	WORDS			ART	WORDS	N.A.
anti-Racist			non-Racist			Racist	omission			✓
							commission			
anti-Sexist	✓	✓	non-Sexist			Sexist				
anti-Elitist			non-Elitist	✓	✓	Elitist				
anti-Materialist			non-Materialist	✓	✓	Materialist				
anti-Individualist			non-Individualist	✓	✓	Individualist				
anti-Ageist			non-Ageist			Ageist				✓
anti-Conformist	✓	✓	non-Conformist			Conformist				
anti-Escapist			non-Escapist	✓	✓	Escapist				
Builds positive image of females/minorities	✓	✓	Builds negative image of females/minorities				Excellent	Good	Fair	Poor
Inspires action vs. oppression			Culturally authentic			Literary quality		✓		
						Art quality		✓		

CATCH A DANCING STAR
by Carol H. Behrman
illustrated by Judy King Rieniets
Dillon Press
$5.95, 94 pages, grades 5-9

This story begins with Madame Sophie, the dancing teacher, announcing a contest for the selection of two young dancers to compete with students from other dance schools. The winners will be able to dance with a professional ballet troupe. Ellen Stone knows that she is one of the best students in Madame Sophie's class, but Fran Greene is catching up fast because she practices every day. Ellen is in a quandary. She wants to win the contest but does not want to give up other activities—art-editing the school magazine, parties, cheerleading. She tries to fit daily practice into her schedule but realizes she cannot do everything.

A week before the competition, Ellen sprains her ankle. Later when triumphant Fran comes to visit her, Ellen realizes that even had she not hurt herself Fran would have been selected. Fran has the single-mindedness and dedication necessary to become a professional ballerina. Ellen, on the other hand, is not ready to make a full commitment to the dance.

Catch A Dancing Star offers a realistic account of the many sacrifices a dancing career entails, and the author's impassioned defense of male dancers is moving. However, the portrayal of sex roles and expectations leaves much to be desired. The images of graceful, delicate women and strong, intense men, with which European ballet forms are associated, spill into the non-ballet segments of the book. What results are phrases like "a man isn't beautiful . . . a man is handsome" or "little Amy looks adorable and doll-like all dressed in pink." In addition, Ellen's mother is illustrated wearing an apron, and girls are described as emotional and lacking in direction.

Also unfortunate is the depiction of Fran as dull, odd, and out-of-it because she is serious and intense about ballet. Ellen chooses popularity and well-roundedness over dedication, the hidden message being that "normal" teenagers (especially girls) are too young to be serious and disciplined. They should be casual, fun-loving and confused, in keeping with the traditional myths about teenage behavior.

Another drawback is the book's reinforcement of the "competition first, friendship last" creed. Ellen's obsession with beating Fran is so intense that it eclipses her love for ballet. Moreover, the internal conflict from whence this obsession springs is never resolved. Instead, a cop-out device—the sprained ankle—is used to settle matters which cry out for more realistic and instructive handling.

One final note: Racism is implied in the description of Giselle as a "white" ballet, and in the black and white illustrations which reinforce, by their omission of third world faces, the concept that ballet is for whites only.

	ART	WORDS		ART	WORDS			ART	WORDS	N.A.
anti-Racist			non-Racist			Racist	omission	✓	✓	
							commission			
anti-Sexist			non-Sexist	✓		Sexist				✓
anti-Elitist			non-Elitist	✓		Elitist			✓	
anti-Materialist			non-Materialist	✓	✓	Materialist				
anti-Individualist			non-Individualist	✓		Individualist			✓	
anti-Ageist			non-Ageist			Ageist				✓
anti-Conformist			non-Conformist	✓		Conformist			✓	
anti-Escapist			non-Escapist	✓		Escapist			✓	
Builds positive image of females/minorities			Builds negative image of (females) minorities		✓			Excellent	Good	Fair	Poor
Inspires action vs. oppression			Culturally authentic			Literary quality			✓		
						Art quality				✓	

FOUR WOMEN OF COURAGE
edited by Bennett Wayne
photographs
Garrard Press
$4.48, 167 pages, grades 3-4

Here is a classic "woman's book"—a chronicle of the self-sacrificing, altruistic, tireless work of three women who spent their lives serving the sick, mentally ill and handicapped peoples of the world. The women are Dorothea Dix, an angel of mercy "crusader for mental hospitals"; Linda Richards, "the first American trained nurse"; and Helen Keller, the well-known blind and deaf scholar. For a little spice and excitement, the more contemporary Jacqueline Cochran, aviator, is thrown in—although at one time she too had been a nurse. The story goes that she took up flying so as to finance the expansion of her cosmetics business, the profits from which would enable her to help the poor and the sick.

These days, when women are striving to be regarded as other than service workers or to have service work upgraded and recognized as valuable, it is hard to accept a book such as this; yet had it been properly written, the lives of these undoubtedly courageous women could probably serve as outstanding models for us today. Unfortunately, the various authors portray their subjects as being insipid and unreal. They seem to succeed against what must have been enormous odds by asking, pleading, conning, having teas and petitioning Congress. There must have been more to their struggles than this, and the essence of their pioneering lives is missing—as are some important facts. For example, why no mention of the fact that Helen Keller was a well-known Socialist?

Although each chapter is written by a different man or woman, the writing is remarkably similar in its over-long, boring, chronological presentation of repetitive and trivial information. (Some of the old photographs, however, are quite interesting.) All of the writers seem impressed with how many presidents, kings or other "important people" their subjects had lunch with, and how much money they did or did not have. The constant references to "helping the poor" make the women appear unpleasantly patronizing.

	ART	WORDS		ART	WORDS			ART	WORDS	N.A.
anti-Racist			non-Racist			Racist	omission / commission			✓
anti-Sexist			non-Sexist	✓		Sexist			✓	
anti-Elitist			non-Elitist	✓		Elitist			✓	
anti-Materialist			non-Materialist	✓		Materialist			✓	
anti-Individualist			non-Individualist	✓	✓	Individualist				
anti-Ageist			non-Ageist	✓	✓	Ageist				
anti-Conformist		✓	non-Conformist	✓		Conformist				
anti-Escapist		✓	non-Escapist	✓		Escapist				
Builds positive image of females/minorities			Builds negative image of females/minorities				Excellent	Good	Fair	Poor
Inspires action vs. oppression			Culturally authentic			Literary quality				✓
						Art quality		✓		

PATRICK DES JARLAIT: THE STORY OF AN AMERICAN INDIAN ARTIST
as told to Neva Williams
illustrated by paintings
Lerner Publications
$5.95, 57 pages, grades 3-5

In this short autobiography, Patrick Des Jarlait (1921-1972) tells of his childhood on the Red Lake Indian Reservation in Minnesota and of becoming the most widely known Chippewa artist. His descriptions of traditional woodland Indian life are accurate and vivid. However, the book is curiously dispassionate, even detached, in its account of Des Jarlait's own life. His experiences on the reservation, at Indian boarding schools and as art supervisor in a Japanese internment camp during World War II are touched on only lightly and at times seem to be products of a "selective" memory. Any negative experiences he might have had as a struggling Indian artist have been so down-played as to go virtually unreported.

Only twice is any sort of racial oppression mentioned. At boarding school, assimilation is encouraged: "We were not allowed to speak to each other in Chippewa, or to participate in activities related to our heritage. . . ." At the internment camp, Des Jarlait felt sympathy for the Japanese "because they had been placed in a situation similar to that of my own people." At no time is responsibility for these policies fixed or a solution discussed.

Des Jarlait's artwork has been reproduced, but the size (two pictures per page) is too small to show much of the fine detail that is so characteristic of his style. Nevertheless, these plates lend a visual accompaniment to the traditional Chippewa activities described in the first part of the book. In keeping with the spirit of Chippewa society, the paintings depict community cooperation rather than individual culture roles.

	ART	WORDS		ART	WORDS			ART	WORDS	N.A.
anti-Racist			non-Racist	✓	✓	Racist	omission	•		
							commission			
anti-Sexist			non-Sexist	✓	✓	Sexist				
anti-Elitist			non-Elitist	✓	✓	Elitist				
anti-Materialist			non-Materialist	✓	✓	Materialist				
anti-Individualist			non-Individualist	✓	✓	Individualist				
anti-Ageist			non-Ageist			Ageist				✓
anti-Conformist			non-Conformist	✓	✓	Conformist				
anti-Escapist			non-Escapist	✓	✓	Escapist				
Builds positive image of females/minorities	✓	✓	Builds negative image of females/minorities				Excellent	Good	Fair	Poor
Inspires action vs. oppression			Culturally authentic			Literary quality		✓		
						Art quality	✓			

NOT JUST SUGAR AND SPICE
by Janet Sheffield
William Morrow
$5.95, 189 pages, grades 4-6

Eleven-year-old Lani is trying (though not very hard) to adjust to a new life in California following her parents' divorce. She is unhappy about almost everything—her new friends, her mother's boyfriend (whom she calls "Beast"), the dumpy two-story house with the violet door—and lets everyone know it. In her misery, Lani idealizes her father and their family's past life in Connecticut. When she finds out that her father is coming to San Francisco on a business trip, she runs away to see him, hoping he will take her back East. When her father tells her she must stick it out in California, she is sorely disappointed.

Then Mom gets sick and enters the hospital. Unhappy with the housekeeper who has been hired in her mother's absence, Lani convinces Beast to let her take care of the house and of her little brother, Luther. Through doing the housework, Lani comes to appreciate what her mother does for the family.

Very few of the human relationships depicted in *Not Just Sugar and Spice* are open or up front. Lani's mother lies to her ex-husband. Lani constantly lies to her friends. Her father tries to sneak into San Francisco on business without seeing his children. Name-calling is not infrequent, and conversations between characters are often hostile and vicious.

Better books are available than this chronicle of a girl who is not made of "sugar, spice and everything nice."

	ART	WORDS		ART	WORDS		ART	WORDS	N.A.
anti-Racist			non-Racist			Racist omission / commission			✓
anti-Sexist			non-Sexist			Sexist	✓		
anti-Elitist			non-Elitist			Elitist	✓		
anti-Materialist			non-Materialist			Materialist	✓		
anti-Individualist			non-Individualist			Individualist	✓		
anti-Ageist			non-Ageist			Ageist			✓
anti Conformist			non-Conformist			Conformist	✓		
anti-Escapist			non-Escapist			Escapist	✓		

	ART	WORDS		ART	WORDS		Excellent	Good	Fair	Poor
Builds positive image of females/minorities			Builds negative image of (females) minorities		✓					
Inspires action vs. oppression			Culturally authentic			Literary quality			✓	
						Art quality				

JOSIE'S HANDFUL OF QUIETNESS
by Nancy Covert Smith
illustrated by Ati Forberg
Abingdon Press
$4.95, 143 pages, grades 3-7

The racism implicit in this book is difficult to pinpoint. In fact, racism is denounced in the book. The overt stereotype of Mexicans or Chicanos as dishonest and lazy is absent, and there is even some exposure of the greed of the white landowners and their exploitation of farmworkers. But this story about an elderly white man who "befriends" a family of Mexican migrant farmworkers and ends up providing them with all the good things in life is paternalistic to an outrageous degree. One kindly white man can change everything, the book seems to suggest.

Each member of Josie's family is a stock character: the patient, hard-working, long-suffering mother; the taciturn father who beats his wife out of deep frustration; the honest, bright young daughter who wants to get ahead in her modest little way. These are not necessarily negative stereotypes, but they are stereotypes nevertheless.

Sexism also appears: "Like all mothers, they began the conversation with talk of their children" (this is somewhat countered by the fact that Josie has quite a bit of initiative, is fearless and engages in a physical fight with another girl).

The use of Spanish is paternalistic and racist. The author clearly got her

Spanish straight from a dictionary and makes some hilarious errors *(partido* for a party of social type). Furthermore, the author has the characters speak English in Spanish constructions—"I go. Already supper is late for the baby"—one of the grossest forms of literary racism to be found.

A positive feature of the book is that it places great emphasis on the value of love between friends and family members, on love of the land for its own sake, on trust, on healthy anger—in short, on the value of human qualities over high social status. It is also non-ageist in that the old man who is Josie's best friend is realistically portrayed as having dreams and needs.

However, in addition to subtle racism, elitism is reinforced by the plot (a superior, non-racist white man saves an above-average Mexican family), and competitiveness between individuals is sanctioned.

Highly stylized black and white renderings add a pleasant touch to the printed pages.

	ART	WORDS		ART	WORDS		ART	WORDS	N.A.
anti-Racist			non-Racist	✓		Racist omission / commission			✓
anti-Sexist			non-Sexist	✓		Sexist			✓
anti-Elitist		✓	non-Elitist	✓		Elitist			
anti-Materialist			non-Materialist	✓	✓	Materialist			
anti-Individualist			non-Individualist	✓		Individualist			✓
anti-Ageist		✓	non-Ageist	✓		Ageist			
anti-Conformist			non-Conformist	✓	✓	Conformist			
anti-Escapist			non-Escapist	✓		Escapist			✓
Builds positive image of females/ minorities			Builds negative image of females/ minorities		✓				
Inspires action vs. oppression			Culturally authentic						

	Excellent	Good	Fair	Poor
Literary quality			✓	
Art quality		✓		

MALCOLM X: BLACK AND PROUD
by Florence M. White
illustrated by Victor Mays
Garrard Press
$3.58, 93 pages, grades 4-6

I guess we should all be happy that Malcolm X was included in the *American All* series. But unfortunately, he has been cramped into the rigid structure of the series in such a way that the book fails to capture the essence of his greatness.

In attempting to make the book easy to read, the author oversimplifies her characters' thoughts and words. She misses the opportunity to give depth to and clarify the relationship between the problems Malcolm faced personally and the broader issues of U.S. oppression and racism.

The author implies that as a prison inmate Malcolm accepted the anti-white philosophy of the Black Muslims because of his own experience with individual whites—a simplistic and inaccurate formulation. She fails to reveal the more complex but truer reality—that is, the fusion Malcolm evolved between his personal experience and the political and historical understanding he developed in prison. He entered prison totally involved with his own existence but left with a total commitment to the liberation of Black people, willing to sacrifice all material benefits for the goal of Black freedom.

The author also glosses over the women in Malcolm's life. His mother and later his wife were left with children when their husbands had to leave home. They lived in constant danger and showed tremendous strength throughout. One is particularly disturbed when the author describes Betty X, a full-grown woman, as a "tall dark girl with brown friendly eyes."

The book devotes too much space to the rift between Malcolm X and Elijah Muhammed, especially since so much of this issue is controversial and unclear. There was also no need to attempt to "place blame." The book does not do justice to Malcolm X.

The green and white illustrations are superb. Photographs of Malcolm are also used.

	ART	WORDS		ART	WORDS			ART	WORDS	N.A.
anti-Racist	✓	✓	non-Racist			Racist	omission			
							commission			
anti-Sexist			non-Sexist	✓		Sexist			✓	
anti-Elitist			non-Elitist	✓	✓	Elitist				
anti-Materialist		✓	non-Materialist	✓		Materialist				
anti-Individualist	✓	✓	non-Individualist			Individualist				
anti-Ageist			non-Ageist			Ageist				✓
anti-Conformist		✓	non-Conformist	✓		Conformist				
anti-Escapist	✓	✓	non-Escapist			Escapist				
Builds positive image of females/minorities		✓	Builds negative image of females/minorities				Excellent	Good	Fair	Poor
Inspires action vs. oppression		✓	Culturally authentic			Literary quality			✓	
						Art quality	✓			

PLEASE DON'T SAY HELLO
by Phyllis Gold
photographs by Carl Baker
Human Science Press
$6.95, 47 pages, grades 3-6

This is a touching story about an autistic youth who, encouraged by his unusual family and friends, is helped to break out of his shell. When Eddie Mason's family first moves to Westmore Drive, the neighborhood children label Eddie's aloof and perplexing behavior as strange. The Masons' efforts in encouraging the children to talk to Eddie are often frustrated by Eddie's inability to share his world with them. But through the family's patience the youngsters learn to accept him as their friend and begin to understand his unique condition, as well as his off-beat intelligence.

The value of commitment is strongly supported in this work. Readers come away from the story with a feeling of hope for Eddie and for children like him. The author does an excellent job of challenging the stigmatization of autistic children and making their behavior intelligible to "normal" youngsters. However, it must be noted that Mrs. Mason's efforts on behalf of her son are aided by an income sufficient to afford private school and a home with swimming pool and barbecue to attract the neighborhood's all-white children.

Although Eddie's father is shown once playing ball with Eddie, his role in Eddie's life is not clearly defined and appears secondary to Mrs. Mason's. The other female models in the story are teachers at Eddie's special school. (It is true that most teachers of young children are currently women, but to continue to portray only women in such roles reinforces the sexual stereotypes.)

A competent writing style, plus a nice selection of photographs, make *Please Don't Say Hello* a warm, serious, informative and useful book.

	ART	WORDS		ART	WORDS			ART	WORDS	N.A.
anti-Racist			non-Racist		✓	Racist — omission / commission		✓		
anti-Sexist			non-Sexist	✓	✓	Sexist				
anti-Elitist			non-Elitist	✓		Elitist			✓	
anti-Materialist			non-Materialist	✓	✓	Materialist				
anti-Individualist			non-Individualist	✓	✓	Individualist				
anti-Ageist			non-Ageist			Ageist				✓
anti-Conformist		✓	non-Conformist	✓		Conformist				
anti-Escapist	✓		non-Escapist	✓		Escapist				

Builds positive image of females/minorities			Builds negative image of females/minorities					Excellent	Good	Fair	Poor
Inspires action vs. oppression			Culturally authentic			Literary quality			✓		
						Art quality			✓		

THE HOUSE ON PENDLETON BLOCK
by Ann Waldron
illustrated by Sonia Lisker
Hastings House
$5.95, 151 pages, grades 4-7

Soon after the Ransom family moves into their rented Texas mansion, twelve-year-old Chrissie begins exploring the once fashionable house. Rummaging through the many valuable mementos and furniture stored in the attic, she becomes interested in the mansion's deceased millionaire owner, Alberta Hamilton. Chrissie begins compiling bits of information about the woman, the better to understand what kind of person she had been. Her inquiries bring her into contact with an assortment of greedy neighbors, and she discovers that a collection of paintings—Rothkos, Klees, Pollocks—are missing from the estate.

As a mystery novel about a resourceful young girl, the book is entertaining.

Although young readers may end up critical of the greedy and materialistic characters who want to get their hands on some of the mansion's valuables, no criticism of the "nice" mystery woman, the late Alberta Hamilton, is implied. The right of a very rich individual to acquire and store a vast amount of beautiful art possessions for personal pleasure is never questioned.

Very little in this book relates to the lives or interests of most young people.

The black and white, pen and ink illustrations are not essential to the story.

	ART	WORDS		ART	WORDS			ART	WORDS	N.A.
anti-Racist			non-Racist	✓	✓	Racist — omission / commission				
anti-Sexist			non-Sexist	✓	✓	Sexist				✓
anti-Elitist			non-Elitist	✓		Elitist		✓		
anti-Materialist			non-Materialist	✓		Materialist		✓		
anti-Individualist			non-Individualist	✓		Individualist		✓		
anti-Ageist			non-Ageist	✓	✓	Ageist				
anti-Conformist			non-Conformist	✓	✓	Conformist				
anti-Escapist			non-Escapist	✓	✓	Escapist				
Builds positive image of females/ minorities			Builds negative image of females/ minorities				Excellent	Good	Fair	Poor
Inspires action vs. oppression			Culturally authentic			Literary quality		✓		
						Art quality			✓	

AMY
by Julia First
Prentice-Hall
$5.95, 84 pages, grades 4-6

Amy portrays a sixth grader struggling in the competitive atmosphere of a white American suburb. The heroine is insecure because she is poor at math and jealous because the pretty and bright new girl next door might steal her friend Eddie. But most of all, she is consumed with hatred for Donald Randall, a smart-alecky classmate who always thinks he's right and is a racist to boot. His racism offends Amy's supposedly strong, liberal feelings.

The resolution of these problems is highly unsatisfactory and often confusing. Amy launches a one-girl campaign to "change the system"—her objective is to make math non-compulsory. But strong social pressure (in the form of an unwritten rule which says a person cannot be class vice president and flunk math at the same time) forces her to knuckle under. Says Amy, "I got the strange feeling that I had to do something the way I was expected for a change." A conformist is born.

The jealousy issue is never really resolved, and Amy ultimately apologizes to her arch enemy, Donald (this reader cannot imagine why, since he is indeed obnoxious and very racist). Amy asks herself the question: "Am I really that carried away about changing the world? Maybe I could just set aside one day of the week for the cause. . . ."

Mass distrust, jealousy and competitiveness dominate the atmosphere of this book, yet the author never seriously questions these phenomena. A contrived attempt to handle a racial issue comes off as being racist instead. Donald insults a Black girl who then socks him in the jaw. Amy's mother (a positive figure in the book) thinks the girl "overreacted," and the Black child apologizes more than once. Donald never does.

The author's anti-feminist bias also seeps through now and then. Amy criticizes her friend's mother who paints in a studio all day but forgets to defrost the TV dinners on time, whereas *her* mother cooks everything from scratch and bakes at least four cakes during the course of the book.

	ART	WORDS		ART	WORDS		ART	WORDS	N.A.
anti-Racist			non-Racist			Racist — omission / commission		✓	
anti-Sexist			non-Sexist			Sexist		✓	
anti-Elitist			non-Elitist			Elitist		✓	
anti-Materialist			non-Materialist	✓		Materialist			
anti-Individualist			non-Individualist			Individualist		✓	
anti-Ageist			non-Ageist			Ageist			✓
anti-Conformist			non-Conformist			Conformist		✓	
anti-Escapist			non-Escapist	✓		Escapist			
Builds positive image of females/minorities			Builds negative image of (females)/minorities		✓		Excellent	Good	Fair	Poor
Inspires action vs. oppression			Culturally authentic			Literary quality				✓
						Art quality				

WHERE WAS PATRICK HENRY ON THE 29TH OF MAY?

by Jean Fritz
illustrated by Margot Tomes
Coward, McCann & Geoghegan
$5.95, 48 pages, grades 3-5

In a lighthearted and humorous vein, this story describes the childhood, adulthood and old age of Patrick Henry. The author uses Henry's birthday—the 29th of May—as a focal point for summing up the different stages of his life.

The book's cheerful style is engaging. It is unfortunate, however, that the author studiously avoids any mention of the seamier sides of life in Virginia.

Early in the book we are told that Henry praised freedom all his life. Strange then, the following sentence about Henry's marriage to Sarah Shelton: "As a wedding present, Sarah's father gave them six slaves and 300 acres · of land. . . ." This is the first and last mention of slavery in the book! Nowhere is there any discussion of the evils of slavery or even of the important role slaves played in the development of the Virginia economy. In fact, Henry gets all the credit for farming his new estate: "For three years he went through the business of planting, cultivating, leafing, worming and curing tobacco, and then his house burned down and he gave up the farm."

Patrick Henry became one of the largest landowners and slaveholders in Virginia. The contradiction between his cry for freedom and liberty during the Revolutionary War, and his holding of large numbers of Black people in bondage, is never pointed out. Also ignored is the fact that as a shareholder in the Ohio Company, he was an active speculator in land, particularly in West Virginia. Can anyone honestly profess a belief in life, liberty and the pursuit of happiness and yet be actively involved in stealing Native American territory?

The art work is pleasant and amusing but, like the text, does not accurately reflect the racial composition of Virginia. Everyone is white! There is not even the usual isolated picture of slaves working on a plantation.

Children do not need the distorted and racist view of history presented in this book.

	ART	WORDS		ART	WORDS			ART	WORDS	N.A.
anti-Racist			non-Racist			Racist	omission	✓	✓	
							commission			
anti-Sexist			non-Sexist	✓	✓	Sexist				
anti-Elitist			non-Elitist			Elitist		✓	✓	
anti-Materialist			non-Materialist	✓		Materialist			✓	
anti-Individualist			non-Individualist	✓		Individualist			✓	
anti-Ageist			non-Ageist			Ageist				✓
anti-Conformist			non-Conformist	✓	✓	Conformist				
anti-Escapist			non-Escapist	✓	✓	Escapist				
Builds positive image of females/minorities			Builds negative image of females/minorities					Excellent	Good	Fair	Poor
Inspires action vs. oppression			Culturally authentic			Literary quality			✓		
						Art quality			✓		

DORRIE'S BOOK
by Marilyn Sachs
illustrated by Anne Sachs
Doubleday
$4.95, 136 pages, grades 5-7

Eleven-year-old Dorrie is the spoiled only child of lovely, ideal parents (Dad looks like Robert Redford) with whom she shares cozy dinners in a spacious apartment overlooking San Francisco. But into each life some rain must fall. At the ripe old age of thirty-eight, Mom gets pregnant. Dorrie prepares for a new brother, not wanting a sister to compete with, but Mom comes home with triplets—two boys and a girl.

The care of the triplets demands so much time and energy that Dorrie rarely gets to be alone with her parents. Moreover, the family moves into a run-down Victorian house which Dorrie hates. She also hates her new next door neighbor, Genevieve, who is a bully. Gradually, Genevieve and her brother become attached to Dorrie's family. When it is discovered that their mother has abandoned them, Dorrie's folks take them in. All parties manage to adjust to these new circumstances—except Dorrie, who prefers to whine and be miserable. Finally, in response to her mom's advice, she develops an interest in one of the family members and all turns out well.

Dorrie's Book has an imaginative structure. It takes the form of an autobiography written by Dorrie as an English class assignment, in lieu of reading *King Arthur*. Ms. Sach's style is often witty with the funniest element being the 'whodunit' ending Dorrie invents to bring her story to a happy conclusion. Ms. Sachs is to be commended for her clever use of humor as a means of achieving realism.

But unfortunately, *Dorrie's Book* has limited interest with its focus on a 'precocious'' brat whose only problems in life are being fat and losing her "only child" status. The book also promotes self-serving and individualistic values. The permissiveness of Dorrie's parents encourages her many negative behaviors. She is a selfish, competitive, status-conscious, materialistic, name-dropper, whose belated interest in her foster brother, Harold, falls short of redeeming her or the book.

Sexism emerges in the author's description of the triplets. The baby girl is dressed in pink, the boys are in blue and the three are called "fraternal" (non-identical) even though one is a girl.

The illustrations—line drawings executed by the author's college-age daughter—are too contrived to be believable as Dorrie's own work, and add little to the book.

	ART	WORDS		ART	WORDS		ART	WORDS	N.A.
anti-Racist			non-Racist			Racist omission / commission			✓
anti-Sexist			non-Sexist	✓		Sexist			
anti-Elitist			non-Elitist	✓		Elitist	✓		
anti-Materialist			non-Materialist	✓		Materialist	✓		
anti-Individualist			non-Individualist	✓		Individualist	✓		
anti-Ageist			non-Ageist			Ageist			✓
anti-Conformist			non-Conformist	✓		Conformist	✓		
anti-Escapist			non-Escapist	✓	✓	Escapist			

							Excellent	Good	Fair	Poor
Builds positive image of females/minorities			Builds negative image of females/minorities							
Inspires action vs. oppression			Culturally authentic			Literary quality		✓		
						Art quality				✓

LAST NIGHT I SAW ANDROMEDA
by Charlotte Anker
illustrated by Ingrid Fetz
Henry Z. Walck
$5.95, 126 pages, grades 5-8

Buy this marvelous book if you want youngsters to read an anti-sexist, anti-racist, pro-people, warm, funny, exciting story which also painlessly imparts information about fossils, snakes, astronomy and white profiteering on Black land.

The author's first book is about eleven-year-old Jenny Berger who decides to collect fossils to gain the love of her scientist father. Jenny's parents are divorced, and she worries that her father will stop his weekly visits because he often seems bored with her company. Toby Terrell, a Black boy, moves next door and helps with fossil collecting while teaching Jenny about his hobby —snakes. The two share adventures that are accompanied by emotional and intellectual growth. At one point they meet an old, poor Black farmer who chases them off of his property with a gun. The old man's life experiences have taught him that Black people are cheated and stolen from. Toby helps turn this into an important learning experience for Jenny.

The middle-class parents, both Black and white, are intelligent and caring.

Both mothers respect children and are not fazed by mud, snakes or departures from conformity. Jenny is finally assured that her father loves her, even if they do not communicate all of the time.

Though the author gives us a traditional, very-happy-ending preceded by the obligatory narrow-escape-from-death episode, we nevertheless warmly welcome her entrance into the field of writing for juveniles.

Black and white illustrations are as respectful of children as is the text.

	ART	WORDS		ART	WORDS		ART	WORDS	N.A.
anti-Racist	✓	✓	non-Racist			Racist — omission / commission			
anti-Sexist	✓	✓	non-Sexist			Sexist			
anti-Elitist		✓	non-Elitist	✓		Elitist			
anti-Materialist			non-Materialist	✓	✓	Materialist			
anti-Individualist			non-Individualist	✓	✓	Individualist			
anti-Ageist		✓	non-Ageist			Ageist	✓		
anti-Conformist	✓	✓	non-Conformist			Conformist			
anti-Escapist		✓	non-Escapist	✓		Escapist			
Builds positive image of females/minorities	✓	✓	Builds negative image of females/minorities				Excellent	Good	Fair	Poor
Inspires action vs. oppression			Culturally authentic			Literary quality		✓		
						Art quality		✓		

SONG OF THE TREES
by Mildred D. Taylor
illustrated by Jerry Pinkney
Dial Press
$4.95, 48 pages, grades 2-5

When the author was growing up in Ohio, her father told her about his own childhood in rural Mississippi during the Depression. *Song of the Trees* is based on one of his stories. Ms. Taylor has retold the story from the point of view of eight-year-old Cassie who lives with her mother, grandmother and brothers.

Cassie's father is away in Louisiana, laying railroad ties to earn money. Her mother and grandmother ("Big Mama") struggle to feed the children, who sense something of the family's hardship without really understanding it.

The Taylors own land on which beautiful trees grow. Cassie loves the trees and is convinced they "sing" to her. One day, Mr. Andersen (a white man) discovers he can make a sizable profit on lumber by leveling the ancient trees. Soon a work crew comes, and the beloved trees begin to fall. The confrontation which follows symbolizes much of the history of Black struggle. Its components—economic defenselessness, Black bravery in the face of white power, the forced assumption of adult responsibility by children, and the children's fears—speak volumes. Furthermore, the author's handling of these factors encourages readers to struggle against their own and/or others' oppression—a most rare and welcome quality in children's books.

Delicately shaded black and white illustrations complement the text, show character and individuality, and contribute to making this and enjoyable and meaningful story for young readers. (The book was a 1974 winner in the Council on Interracial Books for Children's contest for new minority writers.)

	ART	WORDS		ART	WORDS			ART	WORDS	N.A.
anti-Racist	✓	✓	non-Racist			Racist — omission / commission				
anti-Sexist	✓	✓	non-Sexist			Sexist				
anti-Elitist	✓	✓	non-Elitist			Elitist				
anti-Materialist	✓	✓	non-Materialist			Materialist				
anti-Individualist	✓	✓	non-Individualist			Individualist				
anti-Ageist	✓	✓	non-Ageist			Ageist				
anti-Conformist	✓	✓	non-Conformist			Conformist				
anti-Escapist	✓	✓	non-Escapist			Escapist				
Builds positive image of females/minorities	✓	✓	Builds negative image of females/minorities				Excellent	Good	Fair	Poor
Inspires action vs. oppression	✓	✓	Culturally authentic	✓	✓	Literary quality	✓			
						Art quality	✓			

JACOB TWO-TWO MEETS THE HOODED FANG
by Mordecai Richler
illustrated by Fritz Wegner
Alfred A. Knopf
$5.50, 84 pages, grades 3-7

I was rooting for this book before I started to read it in the hope that it might serve as a bridge between youngsters of different age groups. Few publishers print stories about six-year-olds for readers who are eight to twelve.

Alas, despite the fact that the author's real-life family of five children is just like the family in the book, the book is a failure. The story revolves around six-year-old Jacob, called Jacob Two-Two because "I am two plus two plus two years old. I have two ears and two eyes and two arms and two feet and two shoes. I also have two sisters and two brothers. I am the littlest. Nobody hears me the first time. They only pay attention if I say things two times." So far, so good. (My six-year-old listener was enthralled. My twelve-year-old listener was amused.)

Jacob is constantly being teased for repeating all of his words twice. When a policeman joins in the teasing, Jacob becomes terrified and runs away. Presently, he falls asleep and dreams of children's prisons and monster men, of daring rescues and escapes. When he is found, everyone is feeling repentant about the way they have treated him.

Wherein lies the book's failure? The plot is too complicated for six- or eight-year-olds, some parts are a bit too sophisticated for twelve-year-olds, and the endless repetition of double responses which make Jacob "cute" become irritating for older readers. Like many of the words, the black and white line drawings are too sophisticated for a six-year-old child's dreams.

Actually, I lost enthusiasm for this book early on. The second paragraph in Chapter One says, "His two older brothers, and *even his two older sisters,* could ride two-wheel bicycles, . . ." (italics added). By the time I reached the page where Mom is preparing dinner while Dad reads a newspaper on the couch, my listeners and I were unanimous in suspecting it was going to be a "Thumbs down—Thumbs down" book. It might be said that these instances of sexism are somewhat countered by the equal participation of Jacob's sister in the big prison rescue (a scene in Jacob's dream), but the depiction of that event has other problems. The rescuers, dressed in capes like superpeople, call themselves "the intrepid Shapiro and the fearless O'Toole." This is offensive as humor.

Jacob Two-Two's shortcomings notwithstanding, I seriously hope publishers and authors will produce more books about younger children for older children. The insights children often have about those a few years younger can foster the development of greater self-knowledge, patience and sympathy for others.

	ART	WORDS		ART	WORDS			ART	WORDS	N.A.
anti-Racist			non-Racist			Racist omission / commission				✓
anti-Sexist			non-Sexist	✓	✓	Sexist				
anti-Elitist			non-Elitist	✓	✓	Elitist				
anti-Materialist			non-Materialist	✓	✓	Materialist				
anti-Individualist			non-Individualist	✓	✓	Individualist				
anti-Ageist			non-Ageist	✓	✓	Ageist				
anti-Conformist			non-Conformist	✓	✓	Conformist				
anti-Escapist			non-Escapist			Escapist		✓	✓	

Builds positive image of females/minorities			Builds negative image of females/minorities				Excellent	Good	Fair	Poor
Inspires action vs. oppression			Culturally authentic			Literary quality		✓		
						Art quality		✓		

ARTHUR MITCHELL
by Tobi Tobias
illustrated by Carole Byard
Thomas Y. Crowell
$4.50, 32 pages, grades 3-5

This book is an easy-to-read biography of the dancer Arthur Mitchell. His childhood in Harlem is shown as having been filled with the love and warmth of a strong Black family. The eventual desertion of the family by Mitchell's father is depicted as the result of his unsuccessful struggle to support his family with dignity. In spite of economic hardship, the family nurtured young Mitchell and prepared him to overcome the many obstacles he was to encounter.

Arthur Mitchell dreamed of combining his concepts of style and rhythm with classical dance forms. He was aware of the tremendous prejudice against Blacks in the field of classical ballet but resisted the suggestion that he study, instead, modern dance, a field in which Blacks had found acceptance. At the peak of his career, Arthur Mitchell's goal of personal success expanded and became a dream for a school that would train other Black youngsters for careers in ballet. The same qualities that enabled him to become a top star in the New York City Ballet came into play in the founding and development of the Dance Theater of Harlem. The book confronts racism and describes an individual who struggles—but for his people.

The author's occasional use of the male pronoun to mean both sexes is a demerit. But this is a minor flaw in a well-written, often moving, really good book. The illustrations by Carole Byard communicate the joy and movement, as well as the beauty, of the dancer's world.

	ART	WORDS		ART	WORDS		ART	WORDS	N.A.
anti-Racist	✓	✓	non-Racist			Racist — omission / commission			
anti-Sexist			non-Sexist	✓	✓	Sexist			
anti-Elitist		✓	non-Elitist	✓		Elitist			
anti-Materialist		✓	non-Materialist	✓		Materialist			
anti-Individualist		✓	non-Individualist	✓		Individualist			
anti-Ageist			non-Ageist			Ageist			✓
anti-Conformist	✓	✓	non-Conformist			Conformist			
anti-Escapist		✓	non-Escapist	✓		Escapist			
Builds positive image of females/minorities		✓	Builds negative image of females/minorities				Excellent	Good	Fair	Poor
Inspires action vs. oppression		✓	Culturally authentic		✓	Literary quality / Art quality			

GEORGE WASHINGTON CARVER
by Peter Towne
illustrated by Elzia Moon
Thomas Y. Crowell
$4.50, 33 pages, grades 4-6

George Washington Carver is the newest entry in the well-thought-of Crowell Biography series. It is the story of the Black scientist, who in addition to teaching at Tuskegee Institute, developed hundreds of by-products from the peanut and sweet potato. But anyone concerned about racism in children's literature would do well to avoid this book, which is the type often purchased for school and classroom libraries.

It should no longer be possible to speak about slavery in a casual tone. To evade slavery's moral dimensions while purporting to tell the story of a Black man born into slavery is unacceptable. At the outset, the author writes:

> For a long time some white people in America had been buying and selling black people. The black people were called slaves. They were used like work animals. Moses Carver thought it was wrong to own slaves the way he owned his plow horse. But his wife wanted help with the housework. So for $700 Mr. Carver bought Mary. (Mary was Dr. Carver's mother.)

The Civil War is called "a terrible war in America." It is explained away with, "People from the south of the country were fighting hard for the right to keep their slaves. The northern people said that was wrong."

The illustrations support the racism of the text. The Blacks all look alike, and they are well dressed and healthy looking (even while toiling in the cotton fields). A slave family being auctioned off seems remarkably calm and content.

Carver's disregard of material rewards, his struggle to overcome the evils of oppression and his success as a scientist are factors which, presented in the proper context, could serve as positive images for the third world child. It is unfortunate that a book about Carver has the effect of perpetuating racism.

	ART	WORDS		ART	WORDS			ART	WORDS	N.A.
anti-Racist			non-Racist			Racist	omission			
							commission	✓	✓	
anti-Sexist			non-Sexist	✓	✓	Sexist				
anti-Elitist			non-Elitist	✓	✓	Elitist				
anti-Materialist	✓	✓	non-Materialist			Materialist				
anti-Individualist		✓	non-Individualist	✓		Individualist				
anti-Ageist			non-Ageist			Ageist				✓
anti-Conformist		✓	non-Conformist	✓		Conformist				
anti-Escapist		✓	non-Escapist	✓		Escapist				
Builds positive image of females/minorities			Builds negative image of females/minorities	✓	✓		Excellent	Good	Fair	Poor
						Literary quality			✓	
Inspires action vs. oppression			Culturally authentic			Art quality			✓	

CHLORIS AND THE FREAKS
by Kin Platt
Bradbury Press
$6.95, 217 pages, grades 5-7

This disquieting and very cynical book leaves the reader with the certainty that lasting love relationships are impossible, and that women are the chief cause of their failure. The message is unfortunate, for Kin Platt writes well and interjects some gems of wisdom and humor on a subject of import to many children.

Set in a white, middle class environment, the book concerns the attempt of twelve-year-old Jenny Carpenter to sort out the truth about her parents' divorce of several years back, her father's subsequent suicide, and her mother's current and troubled marriage to Fidel Mancha—a sixty-year-old Mexican American sculptor.

Jenny is inhibited and confused in her judgment by the limitations of her age, and by the bizarre opinions of her fourteen-year-old sister, Chloris, who believes most people are freaks—especially Mancha. Blaming her mother for her father's suicide, Chloris claims to have been directed by her father's spirit to destroy her mother's current marriage. Jenny, on the other hand, in her need for security and out of love for Mancha (presented as the ultimate in a loving and wise human being) hopes the marriage will last. She conscientiously reads daily horoscopes and fortune cookie messages, discusses "relationships" with her friend Cathy (whose parents are getting divorced) and has dialogues with her alcoholic science teacher (whose wife is leaving him), with her grandmother and with Mancha.

The story is quite interesting (although a little too long to be so plotless) until the shocking end when, unbelievably, the mother divorces Mancha because she feels neglected by him. Given Mancha's positive qualities, the mother can only appear a selfish, uncaring villain by contrast (as do the other wives in this story). This, plus the author's retraction of the one and only "Girl's Lib" action of the book, leaves no doubt that Kin Platt has it in for women.

At story's end, Mancha has been abandoned, Jenny and Cathy are depressed, Chloris is as evil as ever, and there is no apparent hope for the future. This book should not be given to any child, especially one who has experienced divorce first-hand or is upset by the topic. A far better book, similar in treatment and subject matter but more positive in its resolution, is Judy Blume's *It's Not the End of the World.*

	ART	WORDS		ART	WORDS			ART	WORDS	N.A.
anti-Racist		✓	non-Racist			Racist	omission / commission			
anti-Sexist			non-Sexist			Sexist			✓	
anti-Elitist		✓	non-Elitist		✓	Elitist				
anti-Materialist		✓	non-Materialist			Materialist				
anti-Individualist			non-Individualist		✓	Individualist				
anti-Ageist			non-Ageist			Ageist				✓
anti-Conformist			non-Conformist		✓	Conformist				
anti-Escapist		✓	non-Escapist			Escapist				
Builds positive image of females/ minorities		✓	Builds negative image of females/ minorities					Excellent	Good	Fair	Poor
Inspires action vs. oppression			Culturally authentic			Literary quality			✓		
						Art quality					

OLD MOTHER WITCH
by Carol Garrick
illustrated by Donald Garrick
Seabury Press
$5.95, 29 pages, grades 3-5

It is Halloween, and David and his friends are going trick-or-treating. Stopping in front of old Mrs. Oliver's house, David scribbles the phrase "Old Mother Witch" (with an accompanying drawing) on the sidewalk. Other friends join David's group along the way. After a while, the children become bored and tired and head back to David's house for hot chocolate. As they pass Mrs. Oliver's, David's friends dare him to ring her bell. Goaded, David runs onto her porch and trips over "something" in the dark. The "something" turns out to be Mrs. Oliver. He runs home and his parents notify the authorities, who take Mrs. Oliver (the victim of a heart attack) to the hospital. When Mrs. Oliver returns from the hospital weeks later, she goes to David's house to leave a bag of cookies in a gesture of thanks.

Old Mother Witch is a well-conceived book, written in a style that respects the intelligence of children. The accompanying art work is also good. Although it is neutral on many other issues, it reinforces conformism and ageism. David conforms to the behavior of his peers by harassing and jeering Mrs. Oliver at their urging, and the children view Mrs. Oliver as an "old witch" mainly because she is old. Nonetheless, read under the supervision of a teacher or parent, *Old Mother Witch* could be a positive learning tool.

	ART	WORDS		ART	WORDS			ART	WORDS	N.A.
anti-Racist			non-Racist		✓	Racist	omission	✓		
							commission			
anti-Sexist			non-Sexist	✓	✓	Sexist				
anti-Elitist			non-Elitist	✓	✓	Elitist				
anti-Materialist			non-Materialist	✓	✓	Materialist				
anti-Individualist			non-Individualist	✓	✓	Individualist				
anti-Ageist			non-Ageist	✓		Ageist			✓	
anti-Conformist			non-Conformist	✓	✓	Conformist				
anti-Escapist			non-Escapist	✓	✓	Escapist				
Builds positive image of females/ minorities			Builds negative image of females/ minorities				Excellent	Good	Fair	Poor
						Literary quality		✓		
Inspires action vs. oppression			Culturally authentic			Art quality		✓		

BLOOD IN THE SNOW
by Marlene Fanta Shyer
illustrated by Maggie Kaufman Smith
Houghton Mifflin
$5.95, 124 pages, grades 3-7

Well-written and well-illustrated, *Blood in the Snow* has a double message, both components of which are needed in juvenile literature: 1) Trapping and killing animals for their fashionable pelts, in ways which cause great pain and suffering to those animals, should cease; 2) Boys need not play a "he-man, toughie" role in order to be brave and loved.

Warm-hearted, poetic Max Murphy, a bitter disappointment to his father because he is "more enamored of a flute than a gun," is pitted against Crow Hintz, a cold-blooded and merciless bully, in a duel that is angel's wing against cloven hoof all the way. At the end, each is excactly what he was in the beginning—Max remains sweet Max who never, ever, will hunt or shoot; Crow remains Crow, unredeemed and unexplained.

Small, amusing details are used by the author as vehicles for insight, but she at times distorts significant events by assuming the reader's agreement about things which require further explanation. What is the young reader to make of Crow, "a sort of mini-gorilla who should be in a cage instead of going to school?" Why is he so monstrous and brutal to humans and animals alike?

It is unfortunate, too, that sensitivity is depicted as being synonymous with physical weakness. And why did the author, in attempting to promote respect for male tenderness, feel the need to create a monster like Crow and a father who behaves like an army drill sergeant? Youngsters today need to have the complexities of human behavior exposed and clarified, not caricatured.

In the end, Max himself gets caught in the web of cruelty when he is forced to shoot a trapped fox to spare it further pain. But when his father, in an uncharacteristic burst of understanding, says, "You have to listen to your own music. Go ahead. Save the fox. Maybe you're not like every other boy," he is not actually retracting his desire that Max be "as rugged as one of the trees in the forest, with a bark so tough you could endure anything." Rather, he is resigning himself to the fact that Max will have to follow his own nature, hopefully without bleeding too much in the process.

A comment on the women in the story. Max is befriended and sustained by a female school-crossing guard named Bernice (a well-drawn character), and there is a moving vignette which describes Crow's life-worn mother. But Max's own mother, who goes to school "to study the Middle Ages," evidences the emergence in recent books of a whole new genre of independent mothers whose "independence" is mainly characterized by a zombie-like unawareness of what is happening to their children, except in the most dire crises. Why?

	ART	WORDS		ART	WORDS		ART	WORDS	N.A.
anti-Racist			non-Racist		✓	Racist omission / commission			
anti-Sexist			non-Sexist		✓	Sexist			
anti-Elitist			non-Elitist		✓	Elitist			
anti-Materialist			non-Materialist		✓	Materialist			
anti-Individualist			non-Individualist		✓	Individualist			
anti-Ageist			non-Ageist			Ageist			✓
anti-Conformist	✓		non-Conformist			Conformist			
anti-Escapist			non-Escapist		✓	Escapist			
Builds positive image of females/ minorities			Builds negative image of females/ minorities				Excellent	Good	Fair	Poor
Inspires action vs. oppression			Culturally authentic			Literary quality		✓		
						Art quality		✓		

MAN AND MATERIALS: OIL
by Ian Ridpath
photographs
Addison-Wesley
$3.95, 32 pages, grades 4-up

This little book is part of the Man (sic) and Materials series.

The highly technical text, with its lifeless vocabulary, is not well-suited to fourth grade level, and there are other problems as well. Although the possibility "that oil will run out at some time" is mentioned, no hint is given as to who decides how supplies are used or shared. Nor does the author cite the need for developing other forms of energy, whether or not they turn out to be profitable. The only mention of the oil industry's profit orientation implies total acceptance. On the book's last page the author writes: "The growing demand for oil is making it worthwhile to work these less rich sources."

Any child capable of absorbing the technical information in *Man and Materials: Oil* deserves some exploration of the ethical, economic and environmental debates that are currently raging over the misuse of this natural resource. Since Esso, Gulf and Shell found it "worthwhile" to contribute photos for use in the book, perhaps the publisher did not find it "worthwhile" to question some of these companies' activities.

Of the thirty-three humans illustrated, thirty-three are male.

	ART	WORDS		ART	WORDS			ART	WORDS	N.A.
anti-Racist			non-Racist			Racist — omission / commission				✓
anti-Sexist			non-Sexist		✓	Sexist		✓		
anti-Elitist			non-Elitist			Elitist				✓
anti-Materialist			non-Materialist			Materialist		✓	✓	
anti-Individualist			non-Individualist			Individualist				✓
anti-Ageist			non-Ageist			Ageist				✓
anti-Conformist			non-Conformist			Conformist			✓	
anti-Escapist			non-Escapist			Escapist				✓
Builds positive image of females/minorities			Builds negative image of females/minorities				Excellent	Good	Fair	Poor
Inspires action vs. oppression			Culturally authentic			Literary quality				✓
						Art quality	✓			

THE TELLTALE SUMMER OF TINA C.
by Lila Perl
Seabury Press
$6.95, 160 pages, grades 4-8

Here is yet another book about adolescents and divorce. Thirteen-year-old Tina Carstairs and her nine-year-old brother, Arthur, have been living in a New York suburb with their rich, materialistic grandmother and lack luster father for the four years since their artist mother left home. When mother moves to New York City, Tina and Arthur are packed off to spend a summer with her and her new husband, Peter—a likable person who enjoys cooking and entertaining his stepchildren.

Tina, with her adolescent insecurities, is the focus of the book. She feels tall and awkward, her hair is never "right" and her nose twitches when she is nervous. She organizes a Saturday club whose members are other sad, self-negating souls. Many of the girls are also the children of divorced and/or remarried parents.

A bundle of middle class stereotypes and unrealistic characters burden this slow moving novel. The adult women comprise a sorry lot: an unpleasant materialistic grandmother, a blonde man-hunting schemer, helpless divorcees who need male assistance in financial matters and who are nervous, sick and dependent. Marriage seems to be a "must" for all of these women.

This pattern is further extended when Tina meets a knowledgeable, handsome young man while visiting in the city, who manages to solve all of her "problems." Although the author seems to basically disapprove of conformity and acquisitiveness she, nevertheless, inundates readers with swimming pools and tennis clubs. That endless quest for teenage female perfection is also prevalent in the constant sampling of new kinds of make-up, shampoos and perfumes. The author might have revealed, through these preoccupations, the poor self-image that is foisted on females who feel incapable of living up to impossible ideals of beauty. But instead, they merely blend into the book's general dullness. The author's intended message, that "when you're thinking of someone else you don't have nearly so much time to worry about yourself," is totally lost in a maze of characters who do nothing but worry about themselves and avoid confronting reality.

	ART	WORDS		ART	WORDS			ART	WORDS	N.A.
anti-Racist			non-Racist			Racist	omission			✓
							commission			
anti-Sexist			non-Sexist			Sexist			✓	
anti-Elitist			non-Elitist		✓	Elitist				
anti-Materialist			non-Materialist			Materialist				✓
anti-Individualist			non-Individualist			Individualist			✓	
anti-Ageist			non-Ageist			Ageist			✓	
anti-Conformist			non-Conformist			Conformist			✓	
anti-Escapist			non-Escapist			Escapist			✓	
Builds positive image of females/minorities			Builds negative image of females/minorities				Excellent	Good	Fair	Poor
Inspires action vs. oppression			Culturally authentic			Literary quality			✓	
						Art quality				

SUMMER AT HIGH KINGDOM
by Louise Dickinson Rich
Franklin Watts
$6.95, 112 pages, grades 5-9

In this highly unbelievable tale, one summer's visit by a hippie commune fosters dramatic changes in thirteen-year-old Dana Chadwick, his Maine farm family and their community. Clashes in values and lifestyles between two groups of middle-class whites are the meat of the story. By the time the young hippies depart in November, the conventional townsfolk have become more open, generous and mature, less provincial, materialistic and rigid. As the hippie van heads for parts unknown, the reader is left to pray they will shed some of their light in other selected spots—for example, Washington, D.C.

Stereotyped sex roles and behaviors characterize young and old alike. In soliciting pickers for his bean crop, a farmer refuses to allow his wife to assist in the picking. Prejudices of various kinds wind their way through the story as the townspeople blame the newcomers for certain happenings, intimidate their family members into shunning "them" and threaten to chase "them" out of town. Ironically, the young people whose dress and lifestyles elicit criticism, epitomize the self-sustaining, hard-work ethic to which rural people subscribe. They differ only in their occasional penchant for enjoying life and nature. Ultimately, the commune members must prove themselves to be super-honest and super-skilled in order to be gradually accepted by the townspeople.

One of the book's pivotal characters—Dana's grandfather—is strong, open-minded and wise. Owing to his particular life experience, his perspectives are broad and his judgment sharp. He is presented as a valued family member, not an "old coot," and it is he who makes the first overtures to the hippies and becomes their "guru." But in the final analysis, it is merely the commune's assistance in picking the bean crop which dissipates the prejudice against them.

	ART	WORDS		ART	WORDS			ART	WORDS	N.A.
anti-Racist			non-Racist		✓	Racist omission / commission				
anti-Sexist			non-Sexist			Sexist			✓	
anti-Elitist			non-Elitist		✓	Elitist				
anti-Materialist			non-Materialist		✓	Materialist				
anti-Individualist			non-Individualist			Individualist				✓
anti-Ageist		✓	non-Ageist			Ageist				
anti-Conformist			non-Conformist		✓	Conformist				
anti-Escapist			non-Escapist			Escapist				✓
Builds positive image of females/minorities			Builds negative image of females/minorities				Excellent	Good	Fair	Poor
Inspires action vs. oppression			Culturally authentic			Literary quality			✓	
						Art quality				

LET'S HEAR IT FOR AMERICA!
by Bennett Wayne
photographs
Garrard Press
$4.48, 168 pages, grades 3-4

Let's Hear It For America might as well have been written in 1915. A *Target* book, it is a compilation of short, "snappy" (the publisher's word) selections about the symbols, songs and celebrations of our past.

It is the second *Target* book this reviewer has seen which effectively obliterates the Black presence in American culture and history although room is found for a "snappy" selection on "Confederate flags which rippled bravely over the ranks of Southern soldiers." Moreover, for all of his book's interesting detail, author Wayne has not the foggiest understanding of the *essence* of symbols, songs or celebrations.

On the Flag: From the many early flags of the settlers to the flag of the Union, to the War of 1812 and the banner raised at Iwo Jima, the author is consistent in reporting the changes that occurred in the flag's evolution without citing the forces to which these changes were related. Arbitrary evaluations of flag symbolism are made: "To the French the sight of the Stars and Stripes was more important than the soldiers." Events are blandly recreated: The flag-raising at Iwo Jima refers only to the photographer, not to the Native American G.I. who held the flag or to his death a few years later from neglect and despair over unemployment. Photos which have had wide exposure elsewhere are re-used here—what child has not seen Neal Armstrong planting the flag on the moon a hundred times? A better choice would have been the shot of Matthew Henson at the North Pole with Perry.

On Songs: *Dixie* is cited but not *Mine Eyes Have Seen the Glory;* God Bless

America, but not James Weldon Johnson's song for the Civil War's Black flag-bearers—*She's Been in Many a Fix Since '76.*

On Symbols and Celebrations: When the French people, led by Laboulaye who was a member of the Anti-Slavery Society, financed the construction of the Statue of Liberty in honor of Benjamin Franklin and Lafayette, four years elapsed before money was raised for the pedestal and land was set aside for the statue's installation. While waiting for a home, the statue's head was exhibited at the World's Fair in Paris and the hand and torch were shown at the Centennial in Philadelphia. Erection of this symbol of hope grew more urgent each day for the world kept changing and moving further away from the ideals for which it stood. The sculptor finally crated the statue and simply informed the U.S. that it was coming. When its plight was made known, dimes and quarters came rolling in, especially from the people of New York City. On the day of the unveiling the band played—YES! "DIXIE"!!! Instead of levelling with readers regarding the contradictions of our complex nation as revealed in this slice of past history, the author concludes the statue's story with:

"What a marvelous land! Standing close together on the sidewalks were Germans, Swedes, Frenchmen and Italians, Russian and Englishmen! To each one, the Statue of Liberty would say: America is opportunity. America gives you a chance to work, to live where you wish."

An all white cast of thousands!

	ART	WORDS		ART	WQRDS			ART	WORDS	N.A.
anti-Racist			non-Racist			Racist	omission / commission	✓	✓	
anti-Sexist			non-Sexist	✓	✓	Sexist				
anti-Elitist			non-Elitist		✓	Elitist		✓		
anti-Materialist			non-Materialist			Materialist		✓	✓	
anti-Individualist			non-Individualist	✓	✓	Individualist				
anti-Ageist			non-Ageist	✓	✓	Ageist				
anti-Conformist			non-Conformist	✓		Conformist			✓	
anti-Escapist			non-Escapist			Escapist				
Builds positive image of females/ minorities			Builds negative image of females/ minorities		✓		Excellent	Good	Fair	Poor
Inspires action vs. oppression			Culturally authentic			Literary quality			✓	
						Art quality				✓

THREE FOOLS AND A HORSE
by Betty Baker
illustrated by Glen Rounds
Macmillan
$6.95, 62 pages, grades 3-up

The Foolish People were an imaginary group invented by the Apaches as an object of humor. *Three Fools and a Horse* chronicles the misadventures of three of the Foolish People of Two Dog Mountain—Little Fool, Fat Fool and Fool About. The trio decide they must have one of the horses of the "flat land men" (Plains Indians) in order to be "big men, the biggest men of the Foolish People."

Little Fool challenges one of the flat land men to a horse race (Little Fool has no horse). Surprisingly, he wins the race and the horse. Unexpected consequences follow from the Fools' attempt to ride horseback.

Native American folk stories should be told by Native Americans, not appropriated from "folklore and anthropology magazines" and then vulgarized by whites. Ms. Baker has no business writing about the Foolish People if their stories are going to be, as they have been in this book, "combined, slightly changed and much elaborated. . . ." The Apache's Foolish People stories are entertaining in their own context, and their misrepresentation here is unethical and racist. Both the Fools (portrayed as ugly and self-seeking) and the Plains Indians (equally ugly and ridiculous) are maligned. The flat land people are differentiated in looks from the Fools only by the addition of leggings, braids, feathers and hook noses.

Though the author claims these stories taught moral lessons to Apache children her book strongly reinforces the "heap dumb Injun" stereotype.

	ART	WORDS		ART	WORDS			ART	WORDS	N.A.
anti-Racist			non-Racist			Racist — omission				
						Racist — commission		✓	✓	
anti-Sexist			non-Sexist			Sexist				✓
anti-Elitist			non-Elitist	✓	✓	Elitist				
anti-Materialist			non-Materialist	✓	✓	Materialist				
anti-Individualist			non-Individualist	✓	✓	Individualist				
anti-Ageist			non-Ageist			Ageist				✓
anti-Conformist			non-Conformist	✓	✓	Conformist				
anti-Escapist			non-Escapist	✓	✓	Escapist				
Builds positive image of females/minorities			Builds negative image of females/minorities	✓	✓		Excellent	Good	Fair	Poor
Inspires action vs. oppression			Culturally authentic			Literary quality			✓	
						Art quality				✓

SOUP AND ME
by Robert Newton Peck
illustrated by Charles Lilly
Alfred A. Knopf
$4.95, 115 pages, grades 3-6

In *Soup and Me* Robert Newton Peck recreates some of the childhood adventures he shared with his best friend, Soup, in their small Vermont home town. Sadly, none of the exploits described are really interesting or funny. In fact, they are corny and trite.

In most of these inconsequential escapades stereotyped characterizations figure prominently. Except for name changes, the same "stiff school marm type" appears in each story. Miss Kelly and Miss Boland, a teacher and school nurse respectively, are depicted as old-fashioned and old-maidish. The reader is given no more information about characters Norma Jean Bissell and Janice Riker than that the former is "cute" (in the eyes of Rob) and the latter is unattractive and a menace.

In addition to these dashes of ageism and sexism, the book also has a touch of racism. References to "screaming savages," "stupid savages," and "cannibals" made by the boys in response to a radio program are offensive.

A book of this type has nothing to offer except some very pleasant charcoal illustrations.

	ART	WORDS		ART	WORDS			ART	WORDS	N.A.
anti-Racist			non-Racist	✓		Racist	omission			
							commission			✓
anti-Sexist			non-Sexist	✓		Sexist				✓
anti-Elitist			non-Elitist	✓	✓	Elitist				
anti-Materialist			non-Materialist	✓	✓	Materialist				
anti-Individualist			non-Individualist	✓	✓	Individualist				
anti-Ageist			non-Ageist			Ageist				✓
anti-Conformist			non-Conformist	✓	✓	Conformist				
anti-Escapist			non-Escapist	✓	✓	Escapist				
Builds positive image of females/ minorities			Builds negative image of females/ minorities		✓		Excellent	Good	Fair	Poor
Inspires action vs. oppression			Culturally authentic			Literary quality			✓	
						Art quality		✓		

TO LIVE A LIE
by Anne Alexander
illustrated by Velma Ilsley
Atheneum
$6.95, 165 pages, grades 4-6

In the wake of her parents' divorce, eleven-year-old Jennifer moves to a new town with her father and younger brother and sister. As Jennifer sees it, her mother is to blame for all of her troubles, so she decides to tell her new friends that Mom is dead instead of explaining why Mom does not live with her. One lie leads to another, and soon Jennifer finds herself trapped in an elaborate web of lies which keep her from being closer to her friends and from doing the things she wants to do.

To Live A Lie is based on the sexist premise that women are mothers first, and that a mother should keep her children "no matter what." Mothers' points of view in this matter are not presented. Other sexist values about women's work include Dad's advice that Jennifer choose something useful for an elective like typing, sewing or cooking. In general, girls are treated harshly by the author. They are either hateful "bitches" like Rose, or walking dictionaries like Becca. Other girls just giggle a lot.

Jennifer's image as a female is weak as well. She is deeply insecure, cannot stand to be laughed at or teased and is generally so self-absorbed that she ignores her younger siblings' insecurities and fears until it is too late. In addition to these highly individualistic traits, she is escapist in her penchant for lying and blaming someone else for her difficulties.

The book includes one racist remark about a Chinese girl being the only student in Spanish class who knows why she wants to take Spanish. This perpetuates the so-called "positive" stereotype that all Asians are excellent students. The poorly executed illustrations look scrawly.

	ART	WORDS		ART	WORDS			ART	WORDS	N.A.
anti-Racist			non-Racist	✓		Racist — omission				
						Racist — commission			✓	
anti-Sexist			non-Sexist	✓		Sexist			✓	
anti-Elitist			non-Elitist	✓	✓	Elitist				
anti-Materialist			non-Materialist	✓	✓	Materialist				
anti-Individualist			non-Individualist	✓		Individualist			✓	
anti-Ageist			non-Ageist			Ageist				✓
anti-Conformist			non-Conformist	✓		Conformist			✓	
anti-Escapist			non-Escapist	✓		Escapist			✓	
Builds positive image of females/minorities			Builds negative image of females/minorities				Excellent	Good	Fair	Poor
Inspires action vs. oppression			Culturally authentic			Literary quality	✓			
						Art quality				✓

HE AND SHE
by S. Carl Hirsch
illustrated by William Steinel
J. B. Lippincott
$7.95, 156 pages, grades 5-8

Here is a thought-provoking book which challenges all preconceived ideas of what is "natural" behavior and what parallels exist between animals and people. It is fascinating to read and should prove to be an exciting teaching tool.

The author invites readers into the laboratories of such familiar scientists as Charles Darwin, Konrad Lorenz and Margaret Mead, as well as the less familiar Jean Henri Fabre, Nikolaas Tinbergen and others, as they observe and ponder behavioral mysteries.

The glaring omission (always, always the same one!) of third world contributions to the behavioral sciences is most regrettable, especially since present-day knowledge has drawn upon the experience of African, Asian and Native American civilizations. In excluding third world scientists, the book perpetuates a racist situation wherein third world peoples are the observed but not the observers.

Focusing on male and female behavior, both animal and human, *He and She* introduces the reader to male birds who sit on and hatch eggs, females who work while males loaf, birds who are docile worm eaters in one environment and aggressive nut-gatherers in another, females who use males as food for their children, etc. Much of the information presented jolts our preconceptions about sexual behavior, as well as challenging readers to consider the disparities between our stereotyped assumptions about nature and nature's actual functioning.

Readers will no doubt be impressed by the commitment of Fabre who sought to discover the secrets of life without a microscope, tools, or a lab—but with the help of children. After years of struggle, he was dismissed from his job and evicted from his house because he opened his lectures to women. Yet despite his respect for women, we learn that this great scientist was so imprisoned by the morality of his time that he was indignant at the "monstrous" sex habits of the wasp.

The pen, ink and watercolor illustrations are finely wrought with good detail.

	ART	WORDS		ART	WORDS		ART	WORDS	N.A.
anti-Racist			non-Racist	✓		Racist omission / commission			✓
anti-Sexist		✓	non-Sexist	✓		Sexist			
anti-Elitist		✓	non-Elitist	✓		Elitist			
anti-Materialist		✓	non-Materialist	✓		Materialist			
anti-Individualist		✓	non-Individualist	✓		Individualist			
anti-Ageist		✓	non-Ageist	✓		Ageist			
anti-Conformist		✓	non-Conformist	✓		Conformist			
anti-Escapist		✓	non-Escapist	✓		Escapist			
Builds positive image of females/minorities			Builds negative image of females/minorities				Excellent	Good	Fair	Poor
Inspires action vs. oppression			Culturally authentic			Literary quality		✓		
						Art quality		✓		

DANNY, THE CHAMPION OF THE WORLD
by Roald Dahl
illustrated by Jill Bennett
Alfred A. Knopf
$5.95, 196 pages, grades 3-8

Here is sentimental, escapist humor at its delicious best. Since mother died "suddenly" when Danny was four months old, "Father washed me and changed my diapers and did all the millions of other things a mother normally does for her child. That is not an easy task for a man, especially when he has to earn his living at the same time by repairing automobile engines and serving customers with gasoline."

Despite this sexist opening, the tale of Danny and his father is hilarious fun. Danny's pop is warm, imaginative and totally devoted to his son in a totally unrealistic way. Father tells great stories, builds marvelous toys, never leaves his son's side and teaches him how to take an automobile engine apart and put it together before he starts attending school.

Danny is shocked, one night, to learn that this pluperfect father loves to poach pheasants. But stealing birds from nasty, rich oafs turns out to be the most respectable "sport" in this small English town. (Can killing any birds or animals truly be called a sport?) And Danny turns out to be the most imaginative and effective poacher of all times. (Even though most of the pheasants he drugs end up flying away.)

The pen and ink line drawings are part of the fun.

Children will adore this idyllic parent-child relationship. They will adore the bravery and zaniness of Danny and Dad and can probably expect to soon see it on the wide screen as a "G" film with Fred MacMurray playing the father. If you are not turned on by this warm and joyous brand of escapism, then,—bah! humbug! don't buy this book.

	ART	WORDS		ART	WORDS		ART	WORDS	N.A.
anti-Racist			non-Racist			Racist omission / commission			✓
anti-Sexist			non-Sexist			Sexist	✓	✓	
anti-Elitist	✓	✓	non-Elitist			Elitist			
anti-Materialist	✓	✓	non-Materialist			Materialist			
anti-Individualist			non-Individualist	✓	✓	Individualist			
anti-Ageist		✓	non-Ageist	✓		Ageist			
anti-Conformist		✓	non-Conformist	✓		Conformist			
anti-Escapist			non-Escapist	✓		Escapist		✓	
Builds positive image of females/minorities			Builds negative image of females/minorities				Excellent	Good	Fair	Poor
Inspires action vs. oppression			Culturally authentic			Literary quality	✓			
						Art quality		✓		

INDIAN PAINTBRUSH
by Edna Walker Chandler
illustrated by Lee Fitzgerald-Smith
Albert Whitman
$4.25, 128 pages, grades 4-7

Maria Lopez is the daughter of a Sioux mother and a Chicano father. As the story opens, the family has returned to live in Sand Plum, on the Sioux reservation, with Maria's grandparents following the death of Maria's father.

Spanish-speaking Maria feels out of place and rejected by the Sioux children who ridicule her speech. Enter Miss Jean Brave, a young Sioux schoolteacher who grew up in Sand Plum. She teaches the children in Sioux, Spanish and English, combining knowledge and respect of both Native American and Chicano cultures. All the children, including Maria, are motivated to attend school and learn. When all seems to be working well, Maria discovers that Miss Brave is considering moving on to a new area. Recalling a story about Indian Paintbrush flowers, she tries to procure some in order to use their magic to convince her teacher to remain.

Indian Paintbrush presents some details of changing traditional Indian life and has some exciting highlights, but the plot is weak and the writing and art are uninspired. Maria's problems are nearly always solved by a male friend. Miss Brave is described as "pretty as a princess." There are other weaknesses. The author mentions—without comment—that the owners of the town's only store and only gas station are both white. She tells us—without comment—that Maria's father was killed in a copper mine "accident" and Maria's mother received no compensation and had to wash clothes for the "rich mineowners'" wives to earn some money. She reports that Maria's older brother works on a dam which he believes will bring "progress" for Indians. We are told that many Indians oppose this dam but no explanation of their viewpoint appears in the book. These flaws are considerable; however, a book in which a positive role in motivating third world children is played by a minority teacher—instead of the usual white teacher—is heartily welcome.

	ART	WORDS		ART	WORDS		ART	WORDS	N.A.
anti-Racist			non-Racist	✓	✓	Racist omission / commission			
anti-Sexist			non-Sexist	✓		Sexist			✓
anti-Elitist			non-Elitist	✓	✓	Elitist			
anti-Materialist			non-Materialist	✓	✓	Materialist			
anti-Individualist			non-Individualist	✓	✓	Individualist			
anti-Ageist			non-Ageist	✓	✓	Ageist			
anti-Conformist			non-Conformist	✓		Conformist			✓
anti-Escapist			non-Escapist	✓	✓	Escapist			
Builds positive image of females/minorities			Builds negative image of females/minorities				Excellent	Good	Fair	Poor
Inspires action vs. oppression			Culturally authentic			Literary quality				✓
						Art quality			✓	

WAITING FOR MAMA
by Marietta Moskin
illustrated by Richard Lebenson
Coward, McCann & Geoghegan
$5.95, 91 pages, grades 4-6

Becky, Rachel, Jake and their father anxiously await the arrival in America of Mama and baby Leah. The year is 1903 and, in the family's Russian homeland, the Czar's troops—who "didn't like Jews"—are burning villages and killing Jews. Mama and baby had been left behind two years before because the baby was ill when the family boarded the boat in Europe. "America does not want sick immigrants," the ship's captain had said, wanting to turn the entire family back. But Mama had bravely sent them ahead and stayed behind until they could save money to send for her.

The poverty, child labor and sweatshop working conditions of immigrant ghetto life are accurately portrayed here. Since the older children must be wage earners along with their parents and cannot go to school, only the younger girl (who is spared the burden of work) learns English. The family's life is confined to the ghetto where everyone speaks Yiddish, and they only venture beyond when the time comes to meet Mama. According to the author, this was a time when they were entering the "real America." "I have an American daughter," says Mama with great pride upon her arrival in the promised land.

Despite her good descriptions of Jewish immigrant life, the author does not offer young readers insight into Russian or American anti-semitism of that period or into the exploitation of labor which undergirded America's turn-of-the-century industrial growth. We meet Papa's foreman but not Papa's boss. Although the author quite rightly depicts sex roles within the context of the era, her female characters are resourceful, even as seamstresses.

It is important for Jewish children to learn of the hardships their grandparents encountered and for all children to learn of American immigrant travails. This book can be used to stimulate many discussions about prejudice and labor struggles, and about the many different kinds of people who form the ranks of "real Americans." The touching illustrations add to understanding of the period.

	ART	WORDS		ART	WORDS		ART	WORDS	N.A.
anti-Racist			non-Racist			Racist omission/commission			✓
anti-Sexist			non-Sexist	✓	✓	Sexist			
anti-Elitist			non-Elitist	✓	✓	Elitist			
anti-Materialist			non-Materialist	✓	✓	Materialist			
anti-Individualist			non-Individualist	✓	✓	Individualist			
anti-Ageist			non-Ageist			Ageist			✓
anti-Conformist			non-Conformist	✓	✓	Conformist			
anti-Escapist		✓	non-Escapist	✓		Escapist			
Builds positive image of females/minorities			Builds negative image of females/minorities				Excellent	Good Fair Poor	
Inspires action vs. oppression			Culturally authentic			Literary quality / Art quality		Good ✓ / Excellent ✓	

AN ESKIMO BIRTHDAY
by Tom D. Robinson
illustrated by Glo Coalson
Dodd, Mead
$5.25, 39 pages, grades 2-5

Eeka is a young Innuit (Eskimo) fifth-grader who wants a fur ruff for her birthday to go with the velveteen parka her mother has made for her. But the trapping season has been poor and her father barely makes it back through an Alaskan blizzard in time for her birthday feast. The only thing that mars Eeka's perfect day is the absence of fur trimming on the beautiful but lifeless-looking parka. It is a love of beauty, not materialism or pretentiousness, which promotes her desire for the fur.

The author has delightfully and believably interwoven traditional and modern elements in his description of Eeka's hometown and of her special day. (An "Author's Note" tells us that "Point Hope is both the old and the new—young and growing, ancient and solid. There are some old people who speak very little English and who wear tennis shoes, and young people who speak very little Eskimo and wear caribou mukluks.") The warmth and kindness within Eeka's home are neatly contrasted with the harsh cold outside. And a cooperative spirit marks her family's relationships, as well as those of the townspeople.

Gently amusing and executed with warm feelings for the people depicted, the drawings add a dimension of immediacy to the story in their detail—Eeka's grandfather stripping baleen (whalebone) to make baskets and telling stories when Eeka returns from school, her father returning from the hunt with caribou in the sled behind his snowmobile.

Eeka's emotions of anticipation, disappointment, embarrassment and elation are understandable and prompt the reader's identification with her. Congratulations are due the author and illustrator for creating a charming and worthwhile book.

	ART	WORDS		ART	WORDS		ART	WORDS	N.A.
anti-Racist	✓	✓	non-Racist			Racist omission / commission			
anti-Sexist			non-Sexist	✓	✓	Sexist			
anti-Elitist	✓	✓	non-Elitist			Elitist			
anti-Materialist			non-Materialist	✓	✓	Materialist			
anti-Individualist			non-Individualist	✓	✓	Individualist			
anti-Ageist	✓	✓	non-Ageist			Ageist			
anti-Conformist			non-Conformist	✓	✓	Conformist			
anti-Escapist			non-Escapist	✓	✓	Escapist			
Builds positive image of females/minorities	✓	✓	Builds negative image of females/minorities				Excellent	Good	Fair	Poor
Inspires action vs. oppression			Culturally authentic			Literary quality: Good ✓ — Art quality: Excellent ✓			

HEROINES OF SEVENTY-SIX
by Elizabeth Anticaglia
illustrated by same
Walker
$5.83, 109 pages, grades 3-6

The author does not take sides regarding the revolution of 1776, nor does she clarify any of the vital issues of the British-American conflict. Her interest in the "heroines" seems to derive solely from the fact of their being women. Hence, the endurance of a Hessian captain's wife is equated with the courage of a Molly Pitcher; a spy for the British and a spy for Benjamin Franklin are treated with equal admiration.

The book also inadvertently provokes thinking about the relationship of Native Americans to the Revolutionary War. Two of the "heroines" were defending their homes against Indian raids; another was Molly Brant, a Mohawk who, with her brother, Joseph, persuaded most of the Iroquois to remain on the side of the British. Although the book airs the Native American viewpoint to some extent, it also reinforces the "murderous savage" stereotype.

Among the book's most interesting stories are those of the legendary Molly Pitcher; Mary Hays McCauley, cannoneer and gunner at the battle of Fort Monmouth, New Jersey, who carried wounded soldiers on her shoulders on a day when sixty Redcoats died from heat prostration, and Phillis Wheatley, Black poet and ex-slave who became a famous scholar and correspondent of George Washington (for whom she wrote a poem, using the word *Columbia* for the first time to mean America). It must be noted, however, that Wheatley's story is told in a paternalistic, racist manner. Also related is the story of Nancy Hart, mother of eight children, who dared to sneak behind British lines disguised as a demented old man and walked out with important information for the Revolutionary Army. When some British troops whom she held at gun point in her house offered to pay her for their release, she replied, "I live in my home with honor. You need your money, for you have no honor."

The scant illustrations are insignificant.

Ms. Anticaglia would do well to study the three-volume history of the period written by Mercy Otis Warren which not only documents the revolution's occurrence but discusses *how* and *why* the American colonies fought for freedom from British rule.

	ART	WORDS		ART	WORDS		ART	WORDS	N.A.
anti-Racist			non-Racist	✓		Racist — omission / commission			✓
anti-Sexist		✓	non-Sexist	✓		Sexist			
anti-Elitist			non-Elitist	✓		Elitist			
anti-Materialist		✓	non-Materialist	✓		Materialist			
anti-Individualist			non-Individualist	✓	✓	Individualist			
anti-Ageist			non-Ageist	✓	✓	Ageist			
anti-Conformist		✓	non-Conformist	✓		Conformist			
anti-Escapist			non-Escapist	✓	✓	Escapist			
Builds positive image of females/minorities		✓	Builds negative image of females/minorities				Excellent	Good	Fair	Poor
Inspires action vs. oppression			Culturally authentic			Literary quality		✓	
						Art quality			✓

ADVENTURES OF B. J. THE AMATEUR DETECTIVE
by Toni Sortor
illustrated by Allan Eitzen
Abingdon Press
$3.50, 94 pages, grades 3-6

When the only department store in the small town of Ellington is hit by a rash of shoplifting, eleven-ear-old B. J. (short for Betty Jane) helps her detective mother solve the case. An independent young girl, B.J. follows up leads despite her mother's warnings to keep out of trouble. Even the newly hired live-in babysitter, Mrs. Pierpont, cannot restrain her from wandering into danger. The shoplifters are revealed to be some of B.J.'s schoolmates. Sammy, Mrs. Pierpont's sullen eleven-year-old son, regarded as one of the supects by B.J., turns out to be an ally and an aide in her adventures.

Adventures of B.J. The Amateur Detective is the story of an energetic young girl with a probing and witty mind. Her precociousness has two aspects: On the positive side, it is refreshing to read about an active and irrepressible girl who makes plans and pursues them, takes risks and seeks answers. On the negative side, B.J.'s energy and enthusiasm are portrayed as something quite unusual and almost deviant.

Since the author does not clearly portray B.J.'s energy and curiosity as being a good or bad thing, young readers are apt to be confused. Girls who might otherwise be inclined to identify with B.J. or use her as a role model may see her active nature as being not quite legitimate.

A male shoplifter gives orders to the female shoplifters and commands their compliance with a jerk of the head. When B.J. asks Sammy if he is hiding from her, he replies, "That's silly, I don't hide from anyone, especially a girl."

Sue Niles, a fat girl who is used as a focus for humor is shown grunting as she heaves herself upstairs, stuffing her face in the cafeteria, and being pushed around by other girls. At one point, B.J. thinks to herself ". . .who would ever trust Sue with a secret? Maybe that's not fair—you're not supposed to judge a person by looks are you? But in her case it's hard not to. Sue is a compulsive eater and it shows." Now what could be the logical connection between obesity and untrustworthiness? The author should not have let such cruelty pass for humor.

One final point: It turns out that Mrs. Pierpont's husband has been arrested by B.J.'s grandfather and given a two-year sentence. Having hired Mrs. Pierpont to babysit out of compassion, B.J.'s mother is characterized as nothing short of a missionary or savior. And while Sammy resents this compassion in the belief that his father had been framed, B.J. asserts "you don't go to jail for nothing." By the end of the book, it appears that Sammy has been partially persuaded of this "truth." This is a thoroughly middle class and elitist theme. Third world and poor people know that one can indeed end up in jail for nothing and that the law is neither always on their side nor always just. It is doubtful that the book holds much relevance for these two groups and is, in addition, rather naive and insulting.

	ART	WORDS		ART	WORDS			ART	WORDS	N.A.
anti-Racist			non-Racist			Racist	omission / commission	✓	✓	
anti-Sexist			non-Sexist	✓		Sexist				✓
anti-Elitist			non-Elitist	✓		Elitist				✓
anti-Materialist			non-Materialist	✓	✓	Materialist				
anti-Individualist			non-Individualist	✓	✓	Individualist				
anti-Ageist			non-Ageist	✓	✓	Ageist				
anti-Conformist			non-Conformist	✓		Conformist				
anti-Escapist			non-Escapist	✓	✓	Escapist				
Builds positive image of females/ minorities			Builds negative image of females/ minorities				Excellent	Good	Fair	Poor
Inspires action vs. oppression			Culturally authentic			Literary quality			✓	
						Art quality				✓

RICH AND FAMOUS
by James Lincoln Collier
Four Winds Press
$5.95, 155 pages, grades 5-9

A sequel to the author's *The Teddy Bear Habit, Rich and Famous* is one of those very white middle class books which purport to spoof dreams of becoming "rich and famous." But it only succeeds in reinforcing the values and mores at which it takes feeble swipes.

After singing for six seconds on a TV program, thirteen-year-old George Stables is approached by a two-bit press agent, Woody, who promises him fame, fortune and national billing as "The Boy Next Door."

George's dad is unmoved by Woody's vision (Mom is dead). When Dad goes honeymooning in Paris for a month, George is sent to live in upstate New York with his Uncle Ned. Prodigious lies told to Uncle, Aunt, cousins and Dad (by mail) permit George to keep traveling into New York City to advance his career and get into trouble. A complex plot results in George's inadvertent exposure of a record company manager's moonlight drug dealings. And so it happens that George becomes famous, if not rich, as the headlines read: "Young Singer Outwits Dope Mobster."

Chock full of "in" dialogue, some of which is very funny but much of which is tedious, this escapist adventure strongly reinforces the belief in making "a million bucks" by any means possible. Sexism, too, is well-represented in the characters of Aunt Cynthia and Denise (Dad's fiancee), who "believes in Women's Lib" but seeks to persuade a reluctant Dad to marry her because "I'm not getting younger." Even an unstereotypical description of a woman has a sexist ring: "It doesn't turn you on about drugs too much when you see people like that—especially some woman nodding out on a bench with her bare feet all filthy and her hair messed up."

The villainous big-time-drug-dealer is a cripple who conceals a spring-triggered sword in one of his crutches. Ho-ho-ho.

	ART	WORDS		ART	WORDS			ART	WORDS	N.A.
anti-Racist			non-Racist			Racist omission / commission			✓	
anti-Sexist			non-Sexist			Sexist			✓	
anti-Elitist			non-Elitist	✓		Elitist				
anti-Materialist			non-Materialist			Materialist			✓	
anti-Individualist			non-Individualist			Individualist			✓	
anti-Ageist			non-Ageist			Ageist				✓
anti-Conformist			non-Conformist	✓		Conformist				
anti-Escapist			non-Escapist			Escapist			✓	
Builds positive image of females/ minorities			Builds negative image of females/ minorities				Excellent	Good	Fair	Poor
Inspires action vs. oppression			Culturally authentic			Literary quality		✓		
						Art quality				

NANCY WARD, CHEROKEE
by Harold W. Felton
Dodd, Mead
$4.95, 86 pages, grades 3-6

This book tells the story of Nanye'hi, known to Euro-American historians as Nancy Ward. She was a Ghigau or "Beloved Woman" of the Cherokee Nation during the rapid encroachment of Euro-Americans on Cherokee land (the mid 1700's through the War of 1812). Although she won her status in battle with the Creeks, Nanye'hi continually favored peace with the settlers and nonalignment during the Revolutionary War (the Cherokees sided with the British). At one point, she gave many of her own cattle to feed hungry U.S. soldiers who were attacking the Cherokees. Yet before her death she argued against relinquishing additional land. She died before the forced removal of the Cherokee Nation from their lands, the event called the Trail Where They Cried Blood (often mistranslated as the Trail of Tears).

This is a very biased book which presents Cherokees as either "good" or "bad"—i.e., those who helped Euro-Americans versus those who fought them; those who wanted peace even at the price of much land versus the "hotheads" who wanted war. It is a very moralistic, preachy book that expresses a simplistic concept of good and evil. The men in the illustrations all wear scalp locks, and Nanye'hi's white swan wing is described as "powerful medicine" rather than as a symbol of earned authority. (Is the Christian cross "powerful medicine?")

	ART	WORDS		ART	WORDS			ART	WORDS	N.A.
anti-Racist			non-Racist			Racist omission / commission				✓
anti-Sexist			non-Sexist	✓		Sexist				
anti-Elitist			non-Elitist	✓		Elitist				
anti-Materialist			non-Materialist	✓		Materialist				
anti-Individualist			non-Individualist	✓		Individualist				
anti-Ageist			non-Ageist	✓		Ageist				
anti-Conformist			non-Conformist			Conformist		✓		
anti-Escapist			non-Escapist	✓		Escapist				
Builds positive image of females/minorities			Builds negative image of females/minorities					Excellent	Good	Fair	Poor
Inspires action vs. oppression			Culturally authentic			Literary quality		✓		
						Art quality				

WHEN THE SAD ONE COMES TO STAY
by Florence Parry Heide
J.B. Lippincott
$4.95, 74 pages, grades 5-8

Sara and her ambitious mother, Sally, live in a fashionable urban neighborhood where Sara is learning to reject the simple ways of her past for the cultivated and stylish existence Sally has worked so hard to make possible.

Not having completely mastered this new lifestyle, and not fully understanding her mother's admonishment to "meet the right kind of girls . . . who will do you some good," Sara befriends an old, simple, and wistful woman named Maisie Best who encourages her to remember and savor the good times of her poorer days. Maisie has been deserted by her own striving-to-be-middle-class children just as Sara has deserted her own loving father. Caught between two sets of class values, Sara gives in to the pressure to conform and opts for her mother's "refined" world, betraying Maisie's friendship.

To dramatize the shallowness of elite lifestyles, Ms. Heide juxtaposes them with a romanticized formulation of the lives of so-called simple folk. Sara's and her mother's former life of relative poverty is depicted as having been carefree—full of dancing, singing, blowing bubbles, and needing only "potatoes, eggs, and each other." No mention is made of the hardship of living with few possessions, of having little money and meager provisions, of ugly confrontations between family members who tend to take out their anger over unfulfilled needs on each other. The author implies that one should be satisfied and thankful for what one has no matter how little or how plain—in other words, accept one's lot in life.

This message is conveyed largely through the characterization of Maisie, a lonely woman whose son has apparently married a social climber. She lives on old memories and rituals: sets two places instead of one at mealtime and knits booties for a grandchild she has never seen and who is a grown woman by now. By creating the fantasy of having friends or of expecting guests, Maisie escapes from the reality of her condition. Instead of living on past memories and depending on one fragile relationship (with Sara) to sustain her, she could be out making new friends and getting involved in activities. Ms. Heide does not point this out, but rather confuses what is truly beautiful about Maisie—her sensitivity and kindness—with her eccentric, cookie jar wisdom, and total acceptance of her limited life. Moreover, the portrayal of Maisie as ineffectual and vaguely senile is disturbingly ageist!

	ART	WORDS		ART	WORDS			ART	WORDS	N.A.
anti-Racist			non-Racist		✓	Racist — omission / commission				
anti-Sexist			non-Sexist			Sexist			✓	
anti-Elitist			non-Elitist			Elitist			✓	
anti-Materialist			non-Materialist			Materialist			✓	
anti-Individualist			non-Individualist			Individualist			✓	
anti-Ageist			non-Ageist			Ageist			✓	
anti-Conformist			non-Conformist			Conformist			✓	
anti-Escapist			non-Escapist		✓	Escapist				
Builds positive image of females/minorities			Builds negative image of (females)/minorities		✓		Excellent	Good	Fair	Poor
Inspires action vs. oppression			Culturally authentic			Literary quality		✓		
						Art quality				

AMBER WELLINGTON, DAREDEVIL
by Dianne Glaser
illustrated by Marvin Glaser
Walker
$5.95, 116 pages, grades 3-7

For her initiation as the only girl member of the Daredevils' club, Amber Wellington has to steal a barbecued ham from Ol' Larnie's Smokehouse. Ol' Larnie catches her in the act and assigns the Daredevils the task of cleaning up the junk in his back yard as penance for the attempted theft. The balance of the book describes the children's discovery of several hundred dollars in Ol' Larnie's tool shed, Larnie's death, the appearance of a stranger claiming to be Larnie's nephew, the sudden disappearance of the money, and the youngsters' eventual solving of the mystery.

As a mystery thriller, *Amber Wellington, Daredevil* is exciting reading. The intricate, well fashioned plot moves quickly and Mr. Glaser's black and white illustrations add a dimension to the story. Unfortunately, the text is filled with stereotypes about females and Blacks. One of the Black characters, Alta May, is portrayed as a loyal, Aunt Jemima-type cook and housekeeper; Clee, the nine-year-old Black member of the Daredevils, is the club "chicken" who is afraid of the dark. Amber's mother, who is "always good and kind," perpetuates the idolize-but-don't-touch image of Southern white womanhood so long a staple of racist/sexist ideology. Amber's grandmother, who is afraid of growing old, is constantly worried about her appearance and easily fooled by a young man's flattery. Girls always giggle when they get together, and even Amber "squeals" about Ol' Larnie's money—much to the boys' displeasure.

The author's most subtle sexism emerges towards the end when a boy does all of the detective work and is primarily responsible for solving the mystery—to which Amber responds with admiration for his inquisitive mind and bravery. Once again, the implication that women can only find their identity through men, as accomplices or as assistants, comes through loud and clear.

Theism is plugged in a scene in which Amber and a friend find themselves locked in a church. Amber prays hard and, immediately afterwards, discovers a way to unlock the door. (Stereotyping of Catholics is also evident.)

The author's many prejudices permeate the pages of this book.

	ART	WORDS		ART	WORDS			ART	WORDS	N.A.
anti-Racist			non-Racist			Racist	omission	✓	✓	
							commission			
anti-Sexist			non-Sexist	✓		Sexist			✓	
anti-Elitist			non-Elitist	✓	✓	Elitist				
anti-Materialist			non-Materialist	✓		Materialist			✓	
anti-Individualist			non-Individualist	✓	✓	Individualist				
anti-Ageist			non-Ageist	✓		Ageist		✓	✓	
anti-Conformist			non-Conformist	✓	✓	Conformist				
anti-Escapist			non-Escapist	✓		Escapist			✓	

Builds positive image of females/minorities	Builds negative image of females/minorities	✓		Excellent	Good	Fair	Poor
Inspires action vs. oppression	Culturally authentic		Literary quality		✓		
			Art quality		✓		

ICE RIVER
by Phyllis Green
illustrated by Jim Crowell
Addison-Wesley
$5.25, unpaged, grades 3-6

When Dell Carlin's parents get divorced, Dell grudgingly accepts having to live with his mother and stepfather, John Gray. He eagerly awaits his own father's promised Sunday visits, but they never materialize. His mother is now pregnant and stays in bed and "cries a lot."

Dell and friend, Izzy Rito, decide to go ice skating on the river. They have been warned that the spring weather is thinning the ice, but the boys dislike the regular skating rink because "Ugh. Girls go there." They nearly drown, and their rescue involves a helicopter, police, and an ambulance. As a result of the accident, Dell and his stepfather develop a loving relationship and Dell faces up to the reality of his father's behavior.

This book gets a high mark for its depiction of a stepfather who is more concerned about a child than is the natural parent. Mother's miscarriage is another surprising note of realism. But the book's blatant sexism places it squarely in the "no-no" column. Izzy Rito's mother does what all story-book Italian mothers do—she spends all day cooking pasta.

Upon hearing of the unborn baby's death, Dell says, "I always wanted a baby brother." But he is really more concerned about his missing dog who, at that moment is presumed to have drowned in the icy river. Seasoned readers, young and old, will immediately realize that while babies may die and fathers may be too busy for their children, a faithful dog always comes home.

As for the black and white illustrations, they successfully capture the bleak cold of winter.

	ART	WORDS		ART	WORDS			ART	WORDS	N.A.
anti-Racist			non-Racist			Racist omission / commission				✓
anti-Sexist			non-Sexist			Sexist		✓	✓	
anti-Elitist			non-Elitist	✓	✓	Elitist				
anti-Materialist			non-Materialist	✓	✓	Materialist				
anti-Individualist			non-Individualist	✓	✓	Individualist				✓
anti-Ageist			non-Ageist			Ageist				✓
anti-Conformist			non-Conformist	✓		Conformist			✓	
anti-Escapist			non-Escapist	✓	✓	Escapist				
Builds positive image of females/ minorities			Builds negative image of (females)/ minorities		✓		Excellent	Good	Fair	Poor
Inspires action vs. oppression			Culturally authentic			Literary quality			✓	
						Art quality		✓		

THE LUCK OF POKEY BLOOM
by Ellen Conford
illustrated by Bernice Loewenstein
Little, Brown
$4.95, 135 pages, grades 4-6

Charlotte "Pokey" Bloom is a contest freak who dreams of winning fabulous prizes. But meanwhile, she is disturbed by a deteriorating relationship with her older brother Gordon, who constantly rebuffs her while striving to please a new girl in the neighborhood. In the midst of devising new limericks for winning contests, Pokey and her equally dizzy girlfriends conceive a community clean-up project which they hope will result in personal publicity.

The all-consuming desire of a scatterbrained girl to win "big" prizes is the one heavy-handed joke that provides the foundation of this novel. Pokey's mother and other female characters are unstereotypically independent and assertive—a positive feature, but in truth, the only one. Although Pokey and her friends unite to fight off a group of boys who harass them, no positive messages emerge from the encounter. They beat off the boys but then neglect to complete their clean-up project which, in any case, was materialistically motivated.

At the end of this trivial tale, Pokey wins a transistor radio (learning nothing in the process), brother Gordon recovers from his case of puppy love, and yet another author sends out the word that young people are ridiculous and not to be taken seriously. Illustrations can be skipped over, as can the book.

	ART	WORDS		ART	WORDS			ART	WORDS	N.A.
anti-Racist			non-Racist	✓	✓	Racist	omission			
							commission			
anti-Sexist			non-Sexist	✓	✓	Sexist				
anti-Elitist			non-Elitist	✓	✓	Elitist				
anti-Materialist			non-Materialist	✓		Materialist		✓		
anti-Individualist			non-Individualist	✓	✓	Individualist				
anti-Ageist			non-Ageist			Ageist				✓
anti-Conformist			non-Conformist	✓		Conformist		✓		
anti-Escapist			non-Escapist	✓		Escapist			✓	

				Excellent	Good	Fair	Poor
Builds positive image of females/ minorities		Builds negative image of females/ minorities					
Inspires action vs. oppression		Culturally authentic		Literary quality	✓		
				Art quality		✓	

LINDA'S RAINTREE
by Dorothy Hamilton
illustrated by Ivan Moon
Herald Press
$3.50, 118 pages, grades 4-8

Linda's Raintree is a boring, vapid tale centering around a poor Black family whose members are strangely perfect in an imperfect world. Linda, the only girl in the family, is a quiet person who absorbs herself in schoolwork while her contemporaries "run after boys"—a pastime in which Linda has no interest.

Mother is an uneducated woman who takes in ironing from whites to help make ends meet, and who speaks in a totally inauthentic dialect. Father is a determined provider who is always being laid off from various jobs.

The author's elitism is exposed in Linda's encounter in the school library with Amory, a rich white girl. Amory, who is depressed about her father's recent desertion of his family, pours out her sorrow to Linda. Familiar with the desertion problem among Blacks, Linda is suprised to learn that white men also desert their families. "I didn't know rich kids had the same problems," says she. Linda's remarks about her friendship with Amory reek of the author's paternalism. Wondering why Amory had chosen lil' ol' her to confide in, Linda says, "I don't know why you're so good to me, but it's nice."

When Linda is later transferred to another school, Amory becomes her mentor. Fearing that everyone at the new school might be white, Linda thinks "This wouldn't make any difference (to me) but it might to them."

Although Linda's family recognizes the inequality which exists between Blacks and whites, they express no anger or discontentment with the status quo. Not only is this story unbearably monotonous, it is racist, elitist, and encourages Black people to take refuge in fantasy from the realities of oppression. The art work is of the same calibre as the writing.

	ART	WORDS		ART	WORDS			ART	WORDS	N.A.
anti-Racist			non-Racist	✓		Racist	omission			✓
							commission			
anti-Sexist			non-Sexist	✓	✓	Sexist				
anti-Elitist			non-Elitist	✓		Elitist		✓		
anti-Materialist			non-Materialist	✓		Materialist		✓		
anti-Individualist			non-Individualist	✓		Individualist		✓		
anti-Ageist			non-Ageist	✓		Ageist				✓
anti-Conformist			non-Conformist	✓		Conformist		✓		
anti-Escapist			non-Escapist	✓		Escapist		✓		
Builds positive image of females/minorities			Builds negative image of females/minorities		✓		Excellent	Good	Fair	Poor
Inspires action vs. oppression			Culturally authentic			Literary quality			✓	
						Art quality			✓	

COLONISTS FOR SALE
by Clifford Lindsey Alderman
Macmillan
$6.95, 184 pages, grades 5-7

Colonists For Sale tells the story of indentured servants in America, examining how and why the system was developed, where the servants came from, how they were recruited and transported, and the conditions under which they lived. Many of the facts presented are informative and contribute to understanding a virtually forgotten group of working people who were vital to America's colonial development.

The bulk of the book focuses on how the servants fared in different regions and colonies. Although chock full of facts, these chapters are redundant and should have been condensed and supplemented with a more general analysis of how the system affected colonial life. For example, the author implies that the indenture system was not widespread—which is historically inaccurate since at the beginning of the Revolutionary War, at least half of the colonial population (not including Native Americans) consisted of indentured servants or slaves. Without this overview, the magnitude of the indenture system is obscured in a barrage of details.

Behind its facade of historical objectivity, *Colonists For Sale* projects a disturbingly racist and elitist perspective. The author's explanation of landlord greed and the plight of uprooted farm people purports to be social commentary but condonation and rationalization of the profit ethic is implied.

Elitism is manifest in the author's statement that "it was unfair and unproductive to put teachers, scholars and other cultured persons to work in tobacco and rice fields or to do the exhausting labor of cleaning forests and swamps." The concept that certain persons are too good for physical labor, while criminals and poor or working people are not, is repugnant. In addition, his selection of success stories for the "Others Who Made Good" chapter are exclusively professional.

Several statements, although they are factual, are made in such a way as to assume racist overtones. Describing the transition from white servitude to Black slavery, he states that: 1) it was cheaper to buy Blacks for the rest of their lives, and 2) being from Africa, Blacks could better endure summertime work in the fields—the inference being that these factors were justification for Black enslavement. Earlier, he writes that "Indians ran wild in a certain region," perpetuating the "wild Indian" stereotype.

Although *Colonists For Sale* contains valuable information concerning the indenture system, its elitist and racist perspectives make it unacceptable.

	ART	WORDS		ART	WORDS			ART	WORDS	N.A.
anti-Racist			non-Racist			Racist omission / commission			✓	
anti-Sexist			non-Sexist			Sexist		✓		
anti-Elitist			non-Elitist			Elitist		✓		
anti-Materialist			non-Materialist			Materialist		✓		
anti-Individualist			non-Individualist			Individualist		✓		
anti-Ageist			non-Ageist			Ageist				✓
anti-Conformist			non-Conformist	✓		Conformist				
anti-Escapist			non-Escapist	✓		Escapist				
Builds positive image of females/ minorities			Builds negative image of females/ minorities				Excellent	Good	Fair	Poor
Inspires action vs. oppression			Culturally authentic			Literary quality			✓	
						Art quality				

EMMA'S DILEMMA
by Glen LeRoy
Harper & Row
$5.95, 123 pages, grades 5-7

Thirteen-year-old Emma, an only child, lives near New York City's Central Park with her parents and Pearl, her beloved sheepdog. Life is rosy and stable. She goes to school, goes on giggly make-up buying sprees with her best friend Lucy, walks Pearl and baby-sits with next door neighbor Herbie. She does a lot of baby sitting because Herbie's unmarried mother is a whiskey-drinking, man-fixated T-R-A-M-P.

Then one day, everything changes. Grandmother comes to live in Emma's house and immediately discovers that she has a deathly allergy to the dog. Emma sobs hysterically but is helped to rethink her priorities through the thoughtful intervention of little Herbie.

Emma learns that caring about people and trying to help them gives a great deal of satisfaction and meaning to life. Pearl is sent to live with suburban cousins, Grandmother gets well and becomes close to Emma, and Herbie will be helped to read and overcome his many problems by Emma.

This is a neatly tied, worthy-message package, but the contents are just a bit dull.

	ART	WORDS		ART	WORDS			ART	WORDS	N.A.
anti-Racist			non-Racist			Racist	omission			✓
							commission			
anti-Sexist			non-Sexist		✓	Sexist				
anti-Elitist			non-Elitist		✓	Elitist				
anti-Materialist			non-Materialist		✓	Materialist				
anti-Individualist			non-Individualist		✓	Individualist				
anti-Ageist			non-Ageist		✓	Ageist				
anti-Conformist			non-Conformist		✓	Conformist				
anti-Escapist			non-Escapist		✓	Escapist				
Builds positive image of females/ minorities			Builds negative image of females/ minorities				Excellent	Good	Fair	Poor
Inspires action vs. oppression			Culturally authentic			Literary quality			✓	
						Art quality				

SING TO THE DAWN
by Minfong Ho
illustrated by Kwoncjon Ho
Lothrop, Lee & Shepard
$5.95, 160 pages, grades 3-8

Set in a rural Thai village, *Sing to the Dawn* is a moving account of a young girl's struggle to continue her education in the face of oppressive, feudal concepts of women's role. Fourteen-year-old Dawan wins a scholarship to attend high school in the city. Placing a close second, her younger brother Kwai cannot hide his disappointment and hostility. Worst of all, their father unjustly accuses Dawan of "taking her own brother's chance away from him." Like many poor peasants, their father sees an educated son as the family's only hope for a better life. To him, girls can do nothing but marry and bear children.

Dawan is confused and bitter. Her mother fears to become involved, and Dawan's attempts to solicit support prove frustrating. Then she receives unexpected backing from a wise and independent grandmother and from Bao, a young flower girl. Neither of these last two women, both defiant and independent, ever had an opportunity to attend any school. Yet, from Bao, Dawan learns that she must struggle to be free and, like a caged bird, seize any opportunity to fly. From grandmother, she receives the insight of the lotus bud "at first shut up tight, small and afraid, then gradually unfolding, petal by petal, understanding that without these changes, the bud would never blossom." With such wisdom and encouragement reinforcing her own determination, Dawan finally succeeds in soliciting her brother's help and convincing her father to let her go to the city school.

Although brother Kwai professes to oppose injustice he is forced by Dawan to recognize how his own selfish actions actually support the strong against the weak. This conflict between brother and sister is poignantly portrayed, showing the contradiction between their love for each other and their competition for survival. In the end, both justice and principle prevail.

This reviewer has one disagreement with the book. The author's emphasis on education as *the key* to social change has misleading implications. Education, in itself, does not cause social change. The recent history of sweeping change in Asia belies this notion. Mass movements of uneducated peasants have brought great social change which, in turn, has led to more education for the succeeding generation.

Nevertheless, *Sing to the Dawn* is exceptional reading for young people. The author's sensitive understanding of the hopes, fears and struggles of ordinary people is a refreshing change from the patronizing and romantic accounts of Asian peasants by Western writers. The author grew up in Thailand and now lives in Singapore. This book was awarded a first prize in the 1972 contest, for new minority writers, of the Council on Interracial Books for Children. The excellent illustrator, a high school student, is her brother.

	ART	WORDS		ART	WORDS			ART	WORDS	N.A.
anti-Racist	✓	✓	non-Racist			Racist	omission			
							commission			
anti-Sexist	✓	✓	non-Sexist			Sexist				
anti-Elitist	✓	✓	non-Elitist			Elitist				
anti-Materialist	✓	✓	non-Materialist			Materialist				
anti-Individualist	✓	✓	non-Individualist			Individualist				
anti-Ageist	✓	✓	non-Ageist			Ageist				
anti-Conformist	✓	✓	non-Conformist			Conformist				
anti-Escapist	✓	✓	non-Escapist			Escapist				
Builds positive image of females/ minorities		✓	Builds negative image of females/ minorities				Excellent	Good	Fair	Poor
Inspires action vs. oppression		✓	Culturally authentic			Literary quality	✓			
						Art quality		✓		

I KNOW YOU, AL
by Constance C. Greene
illustrated by Byron Barton
Viking Press
$5.95, 126 pages, grades 5-7

The problems of adolescence are here integrated with such timely issues as artificial insemination and premarital sex, and a wide range of ideas and diversity of life styles are presented (unfortunately, in a lily-white context). While the narrator's mother is a housewife who "if she feels like running the vacuum, runs it," Al's mother is a divorcee, who works in a department store and dates a co-worker. Their friend, Polly's mother, is liberal minded on a number of topics, and Polly's older sister, Evelyn, "has been living with boys ever since she was eighteen" with her parents' approval.

The author commendably avoids stereotyping, not only women, but men and the aged—the latter being represented by the narrator's grandfather who is a handsome, debonair gentleman with numerous "dates."

Much of the story focuses on Al's reunion with her father after an eight-year separation, at which time a series of events surrounding her attendance at his second marriage ceremony evoke complicated feelings on both sides. The author's handling of this situation is insightful. A well-illustrated modern story written with perception and wit, *I Know You, Al* is rewarding reading. The illustrations merely divert from, rather than add to, the humor.

	ART	WORDS		ART	WORDS			ART	WORDS	N.A.
anti-Racist			non-Racist			Racist	omission	✓	✓	
							commission			
anti-Sexist		✓	non-Sexist	✓		Sexist				
anti-Elitist			non-Elitist	✓	✓	Elitist				
anti-Materialist			non-Materialist	✓	✓	Materialist				
anti-Individualist			non-Individualist	✓	✓	Individualist				
anti-Ageist	✓	✓	non-Ageist			Ageist				
anti-Conformist		✓	non-Conformist	✓		Conformist				
anti-Escapist			non-Escapist	✓	✓	Escapist				
Builds positive image of (females) minorities		✓	Builds negative image of females/ minorities				Excellent	Good	Fair	Poor
Inspires action vs. oppression			Culturally authentic			Literary quality		✓		
						Art quality				✓

MY FRIEND FISH
by Mamie Hegwood
illustrated by Diane de Groat
Holt, Rinehart & Winston
$4.95, unpaged, grades 3-5

"An inoffensive book" sums this one up.

Attendance at the Soul Day Camp gives Moose, a young Black boy, the chance to pursue his favorite activity—fishing. Pole in hand, he sits all day on the dock, anxiously waiting for that tug on the line. Finally, when everyone else is about to board the bus for home, Moose catches his fish.

Bringing the live fish home, Moose spends most of the day playing with it. But the next day, the fish dies, leaving him wet-eyed and upset. His father's comforting words and the general support of his whole family help him to cope.

Although *My Friend Fish* positively depicts some familiar situations that young people experience, such as enjoying a favorite activity, attending daycamp, and mourning over the death of a pet, the story is basically weak. What do fishing and having a pet mean to Moose? The story never goes beyond the superficial in answering this question.

Moose's attitudes, speech and overall behavior do not distinguish him as a Black person. In fact, the story could be about any little boy. Only the illustrations (besides the name of the camp) indicate that the story has a Black setting. Yet, the black and white drawings, although good in themselves, do not always complement the text or accurately portray an activity described therein. Although Moose's family is warm and loving, the book is bland and boring.

	ART	WORDS		ART	WORDS		ART	WORDS	N.A.
anti-Racist	✓	✓	non-Racist			Racist — omission / commission			
anti-Sexist			non-Sexist	✓	✓	Sexist			
anti-Elitist			non-Elitist	✓	✓	Elitist			
anti-Materialist			non-Materialist	✓	✓	Materialist			
anti-Individualist			non-Individualist	✓	✓	Individualist			
anti-Ageist			non-Ageist			Ageist			✓
anti-Conformist			non-Conformist	✓		Conformist		✓	
anti-Escapist			non-Escapist	✓	✓	Escapist			
Builds positive image of females/minorities		✓	Builds negative image of females/minorities						

	Excellent	Good	Fair	Poor
Literary quality			✓	
Art quality		✓		

(Additional label: Inspires action vs. oppression | Culturally authentic)

THE SECRET SOLDIER
by Ann McGovern
illustrated by Ann Grifalconi
Four Winds Press
$5.95, 62 pages, grades 1-5

The Secret Soldier is Deborah Sampson, a young woman who disguised herself in order to fight in the American Revolutionary army for one-and-one-half years. From a poor family, Deborah experienced the death of her father and separation from her mother (who was too poor and sick to care for her children) at age five. For three years, Deborah lived happily with her cousin Fuller, who taught her to read. Then he died, and for the next ten years, Deborah worked hard as an indentured servant. Gaining her freedom at eighteen, she rejected the idea of marriage because she longed for adventure. She, therefore, decided to assume a male disguise and join the army.

As a soldier, Deborah was brave, uncomplaining and well-liked. But when she caught a serious fever and had to be hospitalized, her secret was discovered. Following her honorable discharge from the army, Deborah married and raised three children. At the age of forty-one, still longing for adventure, she went on a speaking tour to tell people about her army experiences and about the horrors of war.

Ms. McGovern has written a moving and readable biography in a style that effectively intertwines the facts of Deborah's life with historical details. As for Ms. Grifalconi's etchings, they are only fair and ought to have included Black soldiers for historical accuracy.

The author does not pull punches in describing the many obstacles Deborah had to overcome to live her life fully. However, she overemphasizes the adventurous aspect of Deborah's personality and individualizes her struggle to the point that the oppression which was common to all women at that time is negated. In the same vein, the plight of poor people is described without any expression of outrage at indentured servitude. In addition, the phrase, "Most of the country was still wilderness, where Indians live," implies that Indians are wild "things" synonymous with wilderness.

The tricks words can play are clearly exemplified in a description of George Washington as a "brave farmer from Virginia." The reader envisions here a hard working farmer when, in reality, Washington was a rich plantation-owner with many slaves. Such simplistic statements serve to distort historical reality.

As a bicentennial book commemorating two hundred years of American independence, it is interesting that *Secret Soldier* offers a basically pacifist message. Revolutions have never succeeded without violence since those in power always fight to retain their supremacy. Hence, the book's pacifist overtones may negate the revolutionary aspect of our own history and imply contempt for current liberation struggles throughout the world.

	ART	WORDS		ART	WORDS			ART	WORDS	N.A.
anti-Racist			non-Racist	✓		Racist	omission			
							commission		✓	
anti-Sexist	✓	✓	non-Sexist			Sexist				
anti-Elitist			non-Elitist	✓	✓	Elitist				
anti-Materialist			non-Materialist	✓	✓	Materialist				
anti-Individualist			non-Individualist	✓	✓	Individualist				
anti-Ageist			non-Ageist			Ageist				✓
anti-Conformist		✓	non-Conformist	✓		Conformist				
anti-Escapist		✓	non-Escapist	✓		Escapist				
Builds positive image of females/minorities		✓	Builds negative image of females/minorities				Excellent	Good	Fair	Poor
Inspires action vs. oppression			Culturally authentic			Literary quality		✓		
						Art quality		✓		

THE GREAT BRAIN DOES IT AGAIN
by John D. Fitzgerald
illustrated by Mercer Mayer
Dial Press
$5.95, 120 pages, grades 5-7

This is the seventh in a series of books about eleven-year-old Tom Dennis Fitzgerald, a freckled, conniving, self-styled "Great Brain" who lives in a small Utah town at the turn of the century. Cataloged under "humorous stories" by the Library of Congress, it is a vile book in which "humor" is based on cunningly developed tricks played by Tom at the expense of friends and family. What sets the "brain" a-whirring is the possibility of financial profit, but Tom's schemes leave his own brother and every boy in town sadder and poorer, if not wiser, after each foray. Every now and then his larcenous talents are turned to good purpose, but that is accidental, while the profit-motive is fundamental.

Females rarely appear, but when they do sexism reigns. Adult women merit mention only with regard to cooking, baking or sewing. Young girls are necessary for playing "post office" and to have their books carried home—but those things only happen when boys turn "weak" at age thirteen.

But the worst chapter in this worst-of-all-possible books deals with Native Americans. Degradingly racist language is used, including the term "squaw" (originally used by whites to mean whore), the word "band" to describe a large autonomous group of Indians, and phrases like "Indian trouble," "beating on tom-toms," and "young braves began to dance." The Indians are "beating" and "dancing" in honor of Tom, who is now the young white savior of Indians: "Hail to our blood brother! Hail to The Boy Who Wrote The Great White Father A Letter And Saved the Pa-Roos-Its Band." Needless to say, the obligatory "peace-pipe" scene was not left out.

Such is the "humor" in the Native American chapter. Its serious section is of the old-guard, white liberal paternalist variety:

"The Paiutes had been driven from their good hunting and fishing grounds by white men before being put on the reservation. The Mormons tried to make up for this by giving the Chief and his band flour, potatoes, turnips, corn, and other food from the church storehouse. And the Gentile ranchers contributed sheep, hogs, and cattle. The people in town collected old clothing and enough money to buy medicine. The Paiutes came into Adenville to sell beaded buckskin gloves, moccasins, jackets, furs, roasted pine nuts, and other things. Papa had invited Chief Rising Sun to our house for Sunday dinner several times."

So goes the familiar message to young white readers: Yes, some bad things were done to the Indians by some white men. But we kind people give them old clothes, don't let them starve, buy their handicrafts, and even have-an-Indian-to-dinner.

Misguided admiration for Tom's tricky exploits is obviously shared by the author and thousands of young readers who apparently buy the "Great Brain" books in sufficient quantity to merit printing this seventh in the series. No wonder we have Presidents in this country from whom no one would buy a used car and millionaire businessmen who cook up schemes for reducing the incomes of people on welfare.

	ART	WORDS		ART	WORDS		ART	WORDS	N.A.
anti-Racist			non-Racist			Racist — omission / commission	✓	✓	
anti-Sexist			non-Sexist			Sexist	✓	✓	
anti-Elitist			non-Elitist	✓	✓	Elitist			
anti-Materialist			non-Materialist	✓		Materialist		✓	
anti-Individualist			non-Individualist	✓		Individualist		✓	
anti-Ageist			non-Ageist	✓	✓	Ageist			
anti-Conformist			non-Conformist	✓		Conformist		✓	
anti-Escapist			non-Escapist	✓		Escapist		✓	

							Excellent	Good	Fair	Poor
Builds positive image of females/ minorities			Builds negative image of females/ minorities			Literary quality			✓	
Inspires action vs. oppression			Culturally authentic			Art quality		✓		

THE GREY KING
by Susan Cooper
illustrated by Michael Heslop
Atheneum
$6.95, 208 pages, grades 4-9

This volume, part of a five part series ominously titled *The Dark Is Rising*, combines ancient legend, fantasy, symbolism, evocative language and melodramatic adventure to create much sound and fury signifying nothing. The brilliant writing does little other than advocate the concept that "good" equals everything white, Anglo-Saxon, familiar and sexist. "Evil" is strange, mean, dark and scary. Would that so gifted a writer as Susan Cooper address herself to real earthly evils like, say, racism and sexism.

Although significant truths appear to emerge in the story, none of them survives close scrutiny, and all of the story's elements reinforce white/good, dark/evil stereotypes. The bestowal of prestigious awards on such books as *The Dark Is Rising* series makes the task of countering these stereotypes more difficult.

It is not mere coincidence that Roget's Thesaurus lists forty-four favorable meanings for "white," with only ten mildly unfavorable meanings, and sixty unfavorable meanings for "black." Were it not for the reality that ours is a racist society, these color associations would not be harmful. But, given that reality, it behooves us to reflect on the words of Black actor/director, Ossie Davis, who said: "The English language is my enemy. It teaches Black children sixty ways to hate themselves and white children sixty ways to aid and abet them in the crime."

Furthermore, in view of current newspaper headlines, it is entirely likely that young white readers would equate the evil forces in *The Dark Is Rising* with an imagined third world threat to white civilization. Editors, parents, teachers and librarians should be aware of this racist symbolism, however unintended it might be.

Ms. Cooper also succeeds in making it clear to young readers that males are fully in control of destiny—that is, everyone's destiny. Starting with Will, the eleven-year-old "immortal" hero who is "servant of the Light, dedicated to saving the world from domination by the force of evil which calls itself the Dark" (book jacket blurb), all of the "good guys"—Wise Ones, Old Ones, Lords, etc.,—are male, as are the "bad guys." Even heroic dogs are males. Women make only fleeting appearances—to nurse or to feed brave Will. The only exception is a mysterious and beautiful young woman who has "betrayed a trust." It turns out that she is the unfaithful Queen Guinevere, transported through time.

It is, of course, to be expected that the male pronoun is used throughout this book about brave, wise males who tilt with destiny because that is "the price we have to pay for the freedom of *men* on the earth." (emphasis added) All good fellows are saved at book's end, and the Dark is vanquished until the next episode.

Two illustrations appear in this volume which amplify the evil properties of the dark and the unfamiliar, as they are projected in the text. The one human figure who appears in both drawings is not a character in the book, but is an old person dressed in black. She or he is guaranteed to give goose-pimply nightmares to every young reader.

Majestic language need not be devoid of majestic value content. But even without the latter, language *can* be devoid of sexist and racist images.

	ART	WORDS		ART	WORDS			ART	WORDS	N.A.
anti-Racist			non-Racist	✓		Racist	omission			
							commission			✓
anti-Sexist			non-Sexist	✓		Sexist				✓
anti-Elitist			non-Elitist	✓	✓	Elitist				
anti-Materialist			non-Materialist	✓	✓	Materialist				
anti-Individualist	✓		non-Individualist	✓		Individualist				
anti-Ageist	✓		non-Ageist	✓		Ageist				
anti-Conformist			non-Conformist	✓	✓	Conformist				
anti-Escapist			non-Escapist	✓		Escapist				✓
Builds positive image of females/ minorities			Builds negative image of females/ minorities					Excellent	Good	Fair	Poor
Inspires action vs. oppression			Culturally authentic			Literary quality			✓		
						Art quality		✓			

A PRESENT FOR YANYA
by Peggy Mann and Katica Prusina
illustrated by Douglas Gorsline
Random House
$4.95, 119 pages, grades 3-6

The life of a poverty-stricken Yugoslavian girl immediately following the end of World War II is described in this novel for American children. Little Yanya helps her hard-working mother farm, cook, care for baby and sick Papa, and sell eggs and vegetables in the town marketplace. One day, she spots a beautiful doll in a store window, and the balance of the story focuses on her seemingly impossible dream of buying this expensive toy.

Presenting another culture's way of life through the observations and words of a young child is especially difficult when the book is meant for the young readers of an affluent, industrial society. This book might be used by adults who are knowledgeable about World War II events, ethnic conflicts in Yugoslavia and the rigid confines of peasant life, to provoke discussions with children on changing values, lifestyles and living standards.

Not one of the peasants is kind, and only two kind adults are presented—both of them professionals. One is a "plain, skinny" female teacher with very bad breath; the other is a male druggist who sends Yanya to his grandfather, an ancient hermit, who "looked like a devil with his long, scraggly gray beard." But "There was one thing about him . . . that made her certain he was only an old man and not a devil. He smelled. A devil, she felt certain, would not smell so old and dirty."

By buying items at a low price from the old man and reselling them at double, then triple, and finally quadruple the price at the market, Yanya amasses enough money to buy the precious doll. Her purchase fosters the only family togetherness depicted in the entire book:

"They sat on Mama's double bed, and Yanya felt that they had never been so close: Baka (the grandmother), Mama, and herself—all exclaiming over Lulu (the doll). . . . They undressed her. 'Look at the tiny buttons of the petticoat!' said Baka. 'Imagine! these perfect little buttonholes—where no one even can see them.' 'And look at the lace on the panties,' said Mama. 'Real French lace!'"

And on the last page of the book: "'They know how to make things properly in Paris,' Baka agreed. 'Not like this country of Communists and peasants!'"

And so, two women authors present thousands of young readers with an age-old message: Happiness for females is beautiful possessions. When little Yanya grows up, she will probably hum "Diamonds are a girl's best friends."

	ART	WORDS		ART	WORDS			ART	WORDS	N.A.
anti-Racist			non-Racist			Racist omission / commission				✓
anti-Sexist			non-Sexist	✓		Sexist			✓	
anti-Elitist			non-Elitist	✓		Elitist			✓	
anti-Materialist			non-Materialist	✓		Materialist			✓	
anti-Individualist			non-Individualist	✓		Individualist			✓	
anti-Ageist			non-Ageist	✓		Ageist			✓	
anti-Conformist			non-Conformist	✓		Conformist			✓	
anti-Escapist			non-Escapist	✓		Escapist			✓	
Builds positive image of females/minorities			Builds negative image of females/minorities				Excellent	Good	Fair	Poor
Inspires action vs. oppression			Culturally authentic			Literary quality		✓		
						Art quality	✓			

THE ADVENTURES OF YOO-LAH-TEEN
by Ellen Tiffany Pugh
illustrated by Laszlo Kubinyi
Dial Press
$5.95, 83 pages, grades 5-7

This book records the legend of a Wondrous One, a boy born of tears and sand. The tears were those of a mother of the Salish nation who had lost her daughter to a child-eating witch. Yoo-lah-teen grew up very quickly, killed the witch, and rescued the sister he had never seen.

His first adventure led him into many others, including his vision-quest. At the end of it, a great vision came, foretelling his leadership of the nation.

After several other adventures, Yoo-lah-teen became the leader of the nation, a position he held with dignity and honor for many years. At the end of his years he had another vision. Foretelling the coming of white men, it warned of all the dangers they would bring: pollution, diseases, treachery, alcohol, their religion, land-grabbing, and broken treaties. "Be strong!" Yoo-lah-teen warned, "Live in peace. And never let our ancient skills, our arts, and our sacred way of life disappear."

Recorded and translated by a nineteenth-century missionary among the Salish people, this story has a veneer of Europeanism. Concern with witches is basically European; Indian people's bad spirits are of a different character and not so mysteriously capricious or downright cruel as are Europeans' evil ones. Yoo-lah-teen's trip into the spirit world is an Indian thing, but it is told with European values added, which just dilute it.

The end of the story is part of many modern Indian legends and reveals a true Indian thought. It doesn't fit in with the rest of these adventures any more than they fit with most Indian legends, and one wonders how the missionary ever let it stay there.

The drawings in the book are quite frankly European in conception. Resembling the work of Beardsley, they have a never-never-land quality, which fits much better with European myths and legends than Indian ones.

This story will cause children to puzzle and question—which in turn will cause parents and teachers to try to find answers that may not be possible to find. It is too confusing a blend of things Indian and European to be anything other than destructive to children soon to grow up in a world already much too confused about Indian people.

	ART	WORDS		ART	WORDS			ART	WORDS	N.A.
anti-Racist			non-Racist		✓	Racist omission / commission		✓		
anti-Sexist			non-Sexist	✓	✓	Sexist				
anti-Elitist			non-Elitist	✓	✓	Elitist				
anti-Materialist			non-Materialist	✓	✓	Materialist				
anti-Individualist			non-Individualist	✓	✓	Individualist				
anti-Ageist			non-Ageist	✓	✓	Ageist				
anti-Conformist			non-Conformist	✓	✓	Conformist				
anti-Escapist			non-Escapist	✓	✓	Escapist				
Builds positive image of females/minorities			Builds negative image of females/minorities				Excellent	Good	Fair	Poor
Inspires action vs. oppression			Culturally authentic			Literary quality		✓		
						Art quality		✓		

RIDE 'EM COWGIRL
by Lynn Haney
photographs by Peter Burchard
G.P. Putnam's Sons
$6.95, 128 pages, grades 6-8

Ride 'em Cowgirl follows the lives of several young women on the American rodeo circuit, describing in some detail the daily hard work, risks, heartbreaks and excitement. All rodeo events—bull riding, barrel racing, calf and team roping and bucking horses—are described, as is the reason for the recent popularity of all-girl rodeo.

In discussing the sexism that dominates male-female relations in rodeo, the author's perspective emerges. She passively accepts the "separate and unequal" rodeo system in which, she explains:

"As rodeo became more organized and profitable, women's participation decreased. There was pressure against women performers, a reluctance to have them share in the profits, fears that a woman might outshine men."

Girls Rodeo Association was established as a result of this pressure against women, and we are told GRA has "made progress in protecting rights and improving the lot of women in rodeo." Still, the inequity between 3rd prize for bull riding in GRA rodeo $40.40, against $900 for men in a similar event, belies that "progress." The author admits this is unfair, but does not wax indignant. In fact she, herself, reinforces sexist stereotypes by her sexist descriptions of women. *Ride 'em Cowgirl* also reinforces competition to win, over enjoyment for the sake of sport. The cowgirls are not interested in achieving skills, but in elevating their status through winning.

	ART	WORDS		ART	WORDS			ART	WORDS	N.A.
anti-Racist			non-Racist			Racist omission / commission		✓	✓	
anti-Sexist			non-Sexist	✓		Sexist			✓	
anti-Elitist			non-Elitist	✓		Elitist			✓	
anti-Materialist			non-Materialist	✓		Materialist			✓	
anti-Individualist			non-Individualist	✓		Individualist			✓	
anti-Ageist			non-Ageist			Ageist				✓
anti-Conformist		✓	non-Conformist	✓		Conformist				
anti-Escapist			non-Escapist	✓	✓	Escapist				
Builds positive image of females/minorities			Builds negative image of females/minorities				Excellent	Good	Fair	Poor
Inspires action vs. oppression			Culturally authentic			Literary quality			✓	
						Art quality			✓	

NEVA'S PATCHWORK PILLOW
by Dorothy Hamilton
illustrated by Esther Rose Graber
Herald Press
$3.50, 111 pages, grades 4-8

This prolific author seems to have a special gift for writing dull stories about "perfect" people. This one tells of eleven-year-old Neva's deliverance from the squalor of an Appalachian community called Lost Creek by a teacher who visits the area to do research for her thesis. Spiriting Neva away to her own home, teacher Mary introduces the unfortunate waif to middle-class lifestyles and showers her with love and benevolence. Neva adjusts beautifully, makes new friends, and earns enough money babysitting to send fabric home to her mother for making patchwork pillows.

As for the author's depiction of Lost Creek's inhabitants, everyone save

Neva's mother is apathetic, lazy and content with "living off the Government." At no point does she lay responsibility for the subhuman living conditions at society's door; rather, she cites the victims' attitudes and values as the cause. Neva's mother has a different outlook owing to her *non*-Appalachian origins and so consents to Neva's departure from Lost Creek's misery and despair.

Clearly, the singling out of two "special" persons from a group of people who are otherwise regarded with contempt echoes every call to individualism that has ever been sounded in this society and reinforces a host of other negative values.

The competent illustrations are as dull as is the story. There is not a single reason why this book should be included in collections of children's literature.

	ART	WORDS		ART	WORDS		ART	WORDS	N.A.
anti-Racist			non-Racist			Racist omission / commission			✓
anti-Sexist			non-Sexist	✓	✓	Sexist			
anti-Elitist			non-Elitist	✓		Elitist		✓	
anti-Materialist			non-Materialist	✓		Materialist		✓	
anti-Individualist			non-Individualist	✓		Individualist		✓	
anti-Ageist			non-Ageist			Ageist			✓
anti-Conformist			non-Conformist	✓		Conformist		✓	
anti-Escapist			non-Escapist	✓		Escapist		✓	

							Excellent	Good	Fair	Poor
Builds positive image of females/ minorities			Builds negative image of females/ minorities							
Inspires action vs. oppression			Culturally authentic			Literary quality			✓	
						Art quality				✓

THE WAY OF OUR PEOPLE
by Arnold A. Griese
illustrated by Haro Wells
Thomas Y. Crowell
$5.95, 82 pages, grades 2-7

Kano, a young Alaskan Indian boy approaching maturity, has been hunting with his father and has killed his first moose. At the celebration of the event, he is declared ready to become a man and to go hunting alone. Instead of being proud, Kano is ashamed and terrified that a secret he harbors will be discovered—he is afraid of being alone in the woods. The story explains how he overcomes his fear, which, in the way of his people, would bring shame and disgrace.

It is a well-illustrated book and gives a good idea of the way Kano's land and people looked. Done in a not completely realistic style, the drawings catch the essence of the animals, land and people, and they are not derogatory or stereotypical. If the illustrator is not an Indian himself, he understood his subjects well enough to portray them in an objective way.

The text is not so highly recommended, since it has two major flaws. An Indian whose village is in fact part of the woods (or any other type of terrain) is not going to be afraid of that country—it is home where one was brought up from birth. White mentality says that village and woods are separate. Indian mentality makes no separation.

The second flaw concerns the end of the book, in which the village is threatened with a small-pox epidemic. A gentle Russian named Ivan comes to offer inoculations, which the elders refuse, saying their medicine man will take care of them. Kano, who has already taken the shot, is punished. Yet when one woman sickens and dies and Kano sleds through a snow storm to get the vaccine, he is finally allowed to administer it. The village is saved.

This is probably a true story, but the way it is presented is from the white man's point of view. Ivan, who speaks Kano's language perfectly, is the gentle bringer of hope and healing. Yet small-pox did not exist among Indian people before the white men brought it, and there is no explanation of this fact. And the philanthropic individuals who took vaccine to Indian people were not as good as Ivan; they usually didn't speak Indian languages and were not so understanding. The distrust of the medicine they brought, here shown as ignorance or superstition, usually came from greater contact than Kano's people had had with white men, and from well-founded distrust of their motives.

This book enhances white people's image of themselves, as bringers of civilization to ignorant (or just misguided) people. It also reinforces by implication, the false stereotype of Indian people as superstitious savages. For these reasons, this book will not help American children get a true and understanding view of Indian people—100 years ago (the period of the book) or now—and will not help them to grow up with open minds.

	ART	WORDS		ART	WORDS			ART	WORDS	N.A.
anti-Racist			non-Racist	✓		Racist omission / commission			✓	
anti-Sexist			non-Sexist	✓	✓	Sexist				
anti-Elitist			non-Elitist	✓	✓	Elitist				
anti-Materialist			non-Materialist	✓	✓	Materialist				
anti-Individualist			non-Individualist	✓	✓	Individualist				
anti-Ageist			non-Ageist	✓	✓	Ageist				
anti-Conformist			non-Conformist	✓	✓	Conformist				
anti-Escapist			non-Escapist	✓	✓	Escapist				
Builds positive image of females/ minorities			Builds negative image of females/ (minorities)		✓		Excellent	Good	Fair	Poor
Inspires action vs. oppression			Culturally authentic			Literary quality		✓		
						Art quality	✓			

THE THREE WARS OF BILLY JOE TREAT
by Robbie Branscum
McGraw-Hill
$5.95, 90 pages, grades 5-8

Thirteen-year-old Billy Joe Treat does chores on his family's Arkansas farm while his brothers are overseas in World War II, the first war to enter his life. The second war is with his mother who refuses to give him more on his dinner plate than the neck of a chicken. In retaliation Billy Joe refuses to eat at the family table. His third war is the one he conducts against a sadistic schoolteacher who enjoys paddling his students.

The Three Wars of Billy Joe Treat could have been a good story of growing up and gaining important insights about people, including one's parents. The hard life of a poor farmer and the limitations poverty places on the lives of men and women is movingly and wittily portrayed. Humorous dialogue enlivens the tale. "I reckon ye think ye be better than us," says Billy's mother, "wantin' meat betwix yer biscuit and all."

World War II ends with Billy Joe losing a brother and a brother-in-law. The mother-son war has an acceptable ending which is consistent with characters and plot. But Billy Joe's third war totally ruins this book. Implausible and at the same time unnecessary is the author's decision to make the schoolteacher a Nazi spy, who hides secret maps and a radio in the school latrine in this tiny Arkansas farm town. He and his Nazi partner shoot at Billy Joe and wound many of the school children. But Billy Joe, aided by his soldier brother—the brother is really a U.S. secret agent—emerges brave and victorious.

The unrelieved sexism in the book is less offensive than the ludicrous plot.

	ART	WORDS		ART	WORDS			ART	WORDS	N.A.
anti-Racist			non-Racist			Racist omission / commission				✓
anti-Sexist			non-Sexist			Sexist		✓		
anti-Elitist			non-Elitist		✓	Elitist				
anti-Materialist			non-Materialist		✓	Materialist				
anti-Individualist			non-Individualist		✓	Individualist				
anti-Ageist			non-Ageist		✓	Ageist				
anti-Conformist			non-Conformist		✓	Conformist				
anti-Escapist			non-Escapist			Escapist			✓	
Builds positive image of females/minorities			Builds negative image of females/minorities				Excellent	Good	Fair	Poor
Inspires action vs. oppression			Culturally authentic			Literary quality		✓		
						Art quality				

THE CHICHI HOOHOO BOGEYMAN
by Virginia Driving Hawk Sneve
illustrated by Nadema Agard
Holiday House
$5.95, 63 pages, grades 4-9

The European figure of a bogeyman has parallels in North American Native cultures. In traditional Native American societies, silence was often necessary as protection against intruders so the Sioux used the threat of a Chichi, an imaginary figure representing the enemy, to keep children quiet and out of danger, while the Hopis of the Southwest used the Hoohoo kachina doll for the same purpose. All three of these symbols are used by some people today as elements of folklore or to elicit good behavior from children.

Cindy, Lori and Mary Jo are eleven-year-old cousins. With their parents, they are paying a summer visit to their Sioux grandparents. Mary Jo has a white father and has heard stories about bogeymen. Lori is half-Hopi and is fearful of the Hoohoo. Cindy's parents are both Sioux, and she, as well as her cousins, knows about the Chichi.

Shortly after hearing Cindy's father describe a mysterious series of events which may or may not mean that strange spirits are at work, the three girls disobey both parents and grandparents and journey to an island in the river. There they encounter an old deaf-mute Indian man. Fear and guilt combine to create their belief that he is the Chichi Hoohoo Bogeyman. In addition, one of the girls has a nightmare and a second girl runs away from home. All ends well, and the girls are later introduced to the old man, who is known to their grandparents.

Despite the author's depiction of an old person as an object of fear, the book is not ageist. Grandma and Grandpa are useful, productive and wise. It is Grandpa who teaches the girls to use a canoe, prompted by Cindy who reminds him that, "You let Mark (Mary Jo's older brother) do it when he was eleven. We're just as big as he was." Toward the end of the book, Mary Jo explains their disobedience by saying, "I guess we got mad at being treated so different" (than the boys). No wonder the girls are conscious of being treated differently because of their sex. An older brother, Mark, is just as much of a male-chauvinist-pig as are many non-Indian, white older brothers!

Although the book was written at the time of Wounded Knee and other important recent events in the lives of the Sioux nation, only one scene actually touches on current affairs. The three cousins go to a Western movie and are asked to leave because they noisily cheer for the Indians and boo the U.S. cavalry. Remarkably unperturbed by the incident, they go home and entertain one another by acting like "dumb, movie Indians." It would have been helpful if the author had made clear the fact that acting like a "dumb, movie Indian" is a tension-releasing device used by many Indians to avoid blowing up at injustice and/or causing a scene.

Overall, this is an effective book in which readers will meet some young Native Americans who are remarkably similar to themselves, yet who reflect another culture. Both author and illustrator are Native Americans.

	ART	WORDS		ART	WORDS			ART	WORDS	N.A.
anti-Racist	✓	✓	non-Racist			Racist	omission			
							commission			
anti-Sexist			non-Sexist	✓	✓	Sexist				
anti-Elitist			non-Elitist	✓	✓	Elitist				
anti-Materialist			non-Materialist	✓	✓	Materialist				
anti-Individualist			non-Individualist	✓	✓	Individualist				
anti-Ageist		✓	non-Ageist	✓		Ageist				
anti-Conformist			non-Conformist	✓	✓	Conformist				
anti-Escapist			non-Escapist	✓	✓	Escapist				
Builds positive image of females/ minorities			Builds negative image of females/ minorities				Excellent	Good	Fair	Poor
Inspires action vs. oppression			Culturally authentic			Literary quality		✓		
						Art quality		✓		

WHALES TO SEE THE
by Glendon and Kathryn Swarthout
illustrated by Paul Bacon
Doubleday
$5.95, 121 pages, grades 4-8

Whales To See The is a deeply pessimistic, confusing story about ten neurologically impaired sixth graders in San Diego who take a boat trip with their class to observe a whale migration. All of the children in Miss Fish's class are handicapped and cannot function in the public schools. The title of the book is derived from the way one of the children, John, writes about the trip.

In what is seriously meant to be a sympathetic portrait, Miss Fish is described as "a prim and proper spinster of sixty-two" who constantly converses with the Lord when under duress. She asks for and expects "miracles," is a reckless driver even when her Volkswagen bus is loaded with children and insists that a boat Captain proceed with an outing despite small craft and Coast Guard warnings of treacherous weather. Incredibly, this lunatic is described as being the one person who most loves and understands the handicapped youngsters!

John is one of five children of an alcoholic mother on welfare. Because his mother had German measles when she was pregnant with him, John is deaf and also has "dyslexia." The state pays to keep him in private school while Mom drinks away food money (thus, John is always hungry), and all he has to love are two tires left by "one of his fathers," with which he plays endlessly. Should we be grateful that this charming picture of a welfare family presented to young readers features white, rather than third world, characters?

To Miss Fish's dismay, the boat trip includes a class of twenty public school children who are at first curious about, and later insulting to, the ten "specials." When deaf John jumps overboard into a rough sea, one of the "normal" boys jumps in and helps rescue him. The incident brings all of the children closer for awhile and also gives Miss Fish an opportunity to explain brain damage to the other class. She then convinces them to vote in favor of continuing the trip in spite of the dangerous storm that is still raging and the seasickness that has befallen thirty of the youngsters.

Although the children share food and become friends towards the end, the last page of the book makes clear (through an especially cruel analogy) that the "normals" have no intention of ever really being kind and helpful to those they mock as "Re-tards!" In a final paragraph about whales who are "creatures which would guide and protect and care for one another until together, together, all had climbed the ocean to their journey's end," this inhumane and pessimistic conclusion about humans is driven home.

A few more negatives. The author describes, without comment, the endless dosing of the "specials" with pills. It would seem that people undertaking to write a book on such a subject would at least be aware of the controversy surrounding this type of "treatment" and not imply endorsement of these behavior changing drugs. They should also be aware that in a city like San Diego, a class of neurologically disturbed children would not have *one* Black and *one* Chicano among *ten* whites. For reasons having to do with poverty as well as with racism, there would more likely be one or two whites among a majority of third world students.

The treatment, in children's literature, of all types of differences in our society is important. It is hoped that authors, who have faith in human beings as well as in whales, will take up the challenge.

	ART	WORDS		ART	WORDS			ART	WORDS	N.A.
anti-Racist			non-Racist			Racist	omission	✓	✓	
							commission			
anti-Sexist			non-Sexist			Sexist			✓	
anti-Elitist			non-Elitist			Elitist			✓	
anti-Materialist			non-Materialist			Materialist			✓	
anti-Individualist			non-Individualist			Individualist			✓	
anti-Ageist			non-Ageist			Ageist				✓
anti-Conformist			non-Conformist			Conformist		✓		
anti-Escapist			non-Escapist			Escapist			✓	

	ART	WORDS		ART	WORDS		Excellent	Good	Fair	Poor
Builds positive image of females/minorities			Builds negative image of females/minorities			Literary quality		✓		
Inspires action vs. oppression			Culturally authentic			Art quality				

ABU
by Joseph Trigoboff
Lothrop Lee & Shepard
$4.95, 120 pages, grades 5-9

There is a stereotype often used in Western literature which characterizes the Arab child as a "street Arab." The term is defined in the dictionary as "a homeless vagabond, esp. an outcast boy or girl in the streets of a city", (Merriam-Webster). Joseph Trigoboff builds his novel around this stereotype, placing it in the context of Israel and juxtaposing it with the character of a benevolent Israeli soldier.

Abu is described as a cigar smoking, cursing, dishonest street urchin. Motherless and abandoned by his father in a refugee camp, he is befriended by a good-hearted Israeli soldier named Itzhak who tries to find a home for him. The depiction by an Arab writer of a Jewish child who is homeless, dishonest, cigar-smoking, abandoned and aided by an Arab soldier would no doubt prompt cries of "Anti-Jewish" stereotype in the U.S.

Current myths about the middle Eastern situation, in addition to myths about Arabs, provide the foundation of this novel. Only atrocities committed by the Syrians are mentioned, when actually atrocities have been committed on both sides. The soldier, Itzhak, tells how his people struggled to farm the land to make it bloom. Describing that struggle, Itzhak says:

"This time they (Jews) would have to kill the others who were always trying to deprive them of the land that was theirs, always had been theirs, and always would be theirs. They had grown things on the land and had made it live for them as no other group before had done. So Israel must always be theirs."

Actually, Palestinian farmers struggled to make the land bloom for hundreds of years before the state of Israel came into being in 1947.

Various literary devices are used to promote sympathy with the author's Zionist viewpoint. Of course, all authors, consciously or unconsciously, promote their own point of view. But in this case; the reviewers (a Palestinian living in the U.S. and an American Jew) feel the devices serve to misinform young readers. Given that the Zionist viewpoint—Israel must always be Jewish—is one which has generally been supported by the U.S. Government and communications media, to present it to children without including either Jewish or Arab opposing views is a disservice which exacerbates conflict, and which ignores the rights of Arabs and Jews to live together as equals.

At the story's end, the literary technique of irony is employed as a denouement. Having been accepted by Itzhak and become perhaps the first Arab to live in a Kibbutz, Abu is killed by a group of Arab guerrillas. Allegorically, this suggests that the interests of this young Arab were better served by another people than his own!

It is sad that Mr. Trigoboff's considerable gifts as a writer have served here to tremendously distort the Arab-Israeli conflict and, thus, to further confuse children. More importantly, it is sad that the Israeli-Arab conflict has yet to be settled in a way that will protect the interests and rights of both the Hebrew and Arab peoples of the Middle Eastern region.

	ART	WORDS		ART	WORDS			ART	WORDS	N.A.
anti-Racist			non-Racist			Racist omission / commission				✓
anti-Sexist			non-Sexist			Sexist			✓	
anti-Elitist			non-Elitist		✓	Elitist				
anti-Materialist			non-Materialist		✓	Materialist				
anti-Individualist			non-Individualist		✓	Individualist				
anti-Ageist			non-Ageist			Ageist				✓
anti-Conformist			non-Conformist		✓	Conformist				
anti-Escapist			non-Escapist		✓	Escapist				
Builds positive image of females/minorities			Builds negative image of females/minorities		✓			Excellent	Good	Fair	Poor
Inspires action vs. oppression			Culturally authentic			Literary quality			✓		
						Art quality					

CONTRIBUTIONS OF WOMEN: EDUCATION
by Mary W. Burgess
Dillon Press
$6.95, 142 pages, grades 5-9

Emma Hart Willard (born two years before Washington's Inaugural) knew when she was ten years old, as she sat "resentfully punching the needle in and out of homespun linen," that better forms of education for girls had to be found. Hence, she founded an academy where young women were taught to *"Think* not memorize"—the influence of which approach quickly spread to

Europe. The other educators depicted here all demonstrate the same purposeful and sturdy character, each contributing a special vision and a particular focus to the cause of women's education.

Mary McLeod Bethune, the fourteenth child in her slave family and the only one to be born "free" after the Civil War, had visions of "buildings with wide-open doors" while toiling in the cotton fields with her kin. Once she got a chance to go to a Presbyterian church school, there was no stopping her. Arriving in Daytona, Florida, with a nine-month old son and $1.50, she found a two-story "house" near the railroad, for which she paid the $1.50 as down payment. She entered the house and wrote on a cardboard blackboard: "Cease to be a drudge." Thus, was the Daytona School for Girls born, and when the Klan appeared with burning crosses, she stood them down. The last sentence of her will read: "I leave you, finally, a responsibility to our young people. They must never lose their zeal for building a better world."

The book is sympathetically written, with only a lapse or two in taste. The author paints comprehensive portraits of her single-minded, indomitable subjects who used their past to carve out better futures, and who were capable of converting dreams—modest though they sometimes were—into reality.

	ART	WORDS		ART	WORDS			ART	WORDS	N.A.
anti-Racist		✓	non-Racist			Racist	omission			
							commission			
anti-Sexist		✓	non-Sexist			Sexist				
anti-Elitist			non-Elitist		✓	Elitist				
anti-Materialist			non-Materialist		✓	Materialist				
anti-Individualist		✓	non-Individualist			Individualist				
anti-Ageist			non-Ageist		✓	Ageist				
anti-Conformist		✓	non-Conformist			Conformist				
anti-Escapist		✓	non-Escapist			Escapist				
Builds positive image of females/ minorities		✓	Builds negative image of females/ minorities				Excellent	Good	Fair	Poor
Inspires action vs. oppression			Culturally authentic			Literary quality		✓		
						Art quality				

THE DARK DIDN'T CATCH ME
by Crystal Thrasher
Atheneum
$6.50, 182 pages, grades 5-8

Based on the author's experiences during the 1930's Depression, this story aims to reflect the "courage and humor, strength and compassion of people trapped by circumstances beyond their control," but it falls far short of the mark.

Eleven-year-old Seely, who was not "caught by the dark," is the child of a taciturn father and put-upon mother who are both unyielding in their belief that they must ride their children hard in order to prepare them for a cruel life in an unyielding world. Although the author evinces some retrospective understanding and ties up relationships in an enlightened way at the end of her story, the text reads as if the entire Depression were a plot against Seely.

Although a certain period mood is captured, the author's recollections are not tempered with a depth of understanding about her experiences.

The mother's struggles and resentments, expressed mostly in the form of passive resistance—of extra-hard swipes with the mop or the banging of pot lids and spoons—are unsympathetically described. Seely's sister Julie hotly defends her mother, directly confronts her father, helps and sustains the other children and does what needs doing. She is a much more heroic character than is Seely.

In the end, when a brother dies, it is the mother who comforts Seely and explains the futility of family members blaming each other for things "that could not be helped." A needlessly sentimental ending jars this otherwise absorbing story. Better books about the Depression are available.

	ART	WORDS		ART	WORDS			ART	WORDS	N.A.
anti-Racist			non-Racist			Racist	omission / commission			✓
anti-Sexist			non-Sexist		✓	Sexist				
anti-Elitist			non-Elitist			Elitist			✓	
anti-Materialist			non-Materialist		✓	Materialist				
anti-Individualist			non-Individualist			Individualist			✓	
anti-Ageist			non-Ageist			Ageist				✓
anti-Conformist			non-Conformist		✓	Conformist				
anti-Escapist			non-Escapist			Escapist			✓	
Builds positive image of females/minorities			Builds negative image of females/minorities					Excellent	Good	Fair	Poor
inspires action vs. oppression			Culturally authentic			Literary quality				✓	
						Art quality					

RED CLOUD: SIOUX WAR CHIEF
by Virginia F. Voight
illustrated by Victor Mays
Garrard
$3.40, 80 pages, grades 3-5

This book is supposed to be a biography of the great Sioux leader Red Cloud. Instead it is a child's guide to racism in nine easy chapters. There are so many flaws in this book, it is difficult to imagine they can all be enumerated.

The language would be laughable if it were not so insulting. All the old mumbo-jumbo colonialist terminology is trotted out—warpath, brave, and so on—it is all there, written in a maddening, serious manner.

Perhaps the major flaw in the book is that the facts are not correct. It is obvious that the author has not read the 1868 Great Sioux Nation treaty; she got the boundaries of the nation wrong. She also erred in stating that Red Cloud knew he was signing away the Black Hills; *he* thought he was negotiating mineral rights, as almost any Oglala to this day can tell you. Very possibly, she has also not presented the facts of Red Cloud's life straight, either, if these two glaring errors are any indication.

Her presentation of Indian people is atrocious. On the one hand, she attributes American values to them. Example: Poor little Two Arrows—Red Cloud's boyhood name—kills a huge grizzly and is greatly honored for this act of courage, but mourns in a childish way, his horse that died in the fight. Sure, he would mourn, but he would be more proud than sad that his horse had bravely carried him forward in such a way. On the other hand, the author depicts Indians as simple-minded children, especially in their treaty dealings with the wily Indian agents, who really knew better than the Indians on every question. Her conception of the Sioux must be that they are brave, but incredibly stupid.

The author does not emphasize the massive treachery with which the U.S. government treated the Sioux nor the fact that the Sioux fought incredibly hard against great odds. She *mentions* both things, but they are not put in the proper perspective (i.e., that the U.S. government set about *systematically* practicing genocide on the Sioux to get their land, with no regard for any rights the Sioux had—then or now).

The drawings in this book are not as bad as the text, but they are the regularly expected "cowboy-and-Indian" stuff. Still, they have more connection with the way things really looked than the text.

	ART	WORDS		ART	WORDS			ART	WORDS	N.A.
anti-Racist			non-Racist			Racist	omission			
							commission	✓	✓	
anti-Sexist			non-Sexist	✓	✓	Sexist				
anti-Elitist			non-Elitist	✓		Elitist			✓	
anti-Materialist			non-Materialist	✓		Materialist			✓	
anti-Individualist			non-Individualist	✓		Individualist		✓		
anti-Ageist			non-Ageist	✓	✓	Ageist				
anti-Conformist			non-Conformist	✓		Conformist			✓	
anti-Escapist			non-Escapist	✓		Escapist			✓	
Builds positive image of females/minorities			Builds negative image of females/minorities		✓		Excellent	Good	Fair	Poor
Inspires action vs. oppression			Culturally authentic			Literary quality				✓
						Art quality			✓	

RAMONA THE BRAVE
by Beverly Cleary
illustrated by Alan Tiegreen
William Morrow
$5.50, 180 pages, grades 4-6

Ramona The Brave describes the trials and tribulations of a six-year-old girl who wants desperately to grow up, and who seeks her identity through adult approval. Ramona is a very sensitive little girl who lacks a sense of self-worth, and all of her actions are geared to finding that self-worth—her competition with her sister for their parents' love, and her efforts to elicit her teacher's approval. Given the nature of her problem, Ramona's drives are understandably individualistic and materialistic.

The author writes with humor and wit but usually at the expense of Ramona's painful feelings. Her portrayal of Ramona perpetuates the image of little girls as being frightened, unhappy, competitive, bitchy, manipulative and emotional. Furthermore, Ms. Cleary depicts boys/men as strong, responsible figures and suggests that girls/women must rely on them to resolve problems or to achieve an identity. Thus, a boy, Howie is a "great one for thinking things over" and Ramona "gets excited but Howie remains calm."

If *Ramona The Brave* is typical of Ms. Cleary's many books for young readers, this reviewer would recommend avoiding them. Human feelings and needs are mocked in this book, and the sexist, competitive and individualistic values it promotes are not the least bit cute.

	ART	WORDS		ART	WORDS			ART	WORDS	N.A.
anti-Racist			non-Racist			Racist — omission		√	√	
						Racist — commission				
anti-Sexist			non-Sexist	√		Sexist			√	
anti-Elitist			non-Elitist	√	√	Elitist				
anti-Materialist			non-Materialist	√	√	Materialist				
anti-Individualist			non-Individualist	√		Individualist			√	
anti-Ageist			non-Ageist			Ageist				√
anti-Conformist			non-Conformist	√		Conformist			√	
anti-Escapist			non-Escapist	√		Escapist			√	
Builds positive image of females/ minorities			Builds negative image of females/ minorities				Excellent	Good	Fair	Poor
Inspires action vs. oppression			Culturally authentic			Literary quality		√		
						Art quality			√	

SEQUOYAH: THE CHEROKEE WHO CAPTURED WORDS
by Lillie Patterson
illustrated by Herman Vestal
Garrard
$3.40, 80 pages, grades 3-5

This is purported to be a biography of the Cherokee who invented the Cherokee alphabet and system of writing. It begins with a partially inaccurate description of his childhood, wherein all the Cherokees have "adopted the white settlers' way of living." (In fact, the white settlers adopted more Cherokee ways than Cherokees did white ways.) The author also has the young Sequoyah complaining about being only "half-Cherokee," which was not a delineation in those days—*all* Cherokees were complete Cherokee. She also has Sequoyah's grandfather explaining that the word "Cherokee" means "mountain or cave people." That *is* true, but "Cherokee" is not what we call ourselves; it is not even a Cherokee word. Such basic inaccuracies occur throughout the book.

Sequoyah is presented as having learned about writing while in the U.S. Army during the War of 1812. Most Cherokees fought on the British side in that war, but the author has us all on the U.S. side, and she gratuitously gives us a reason: "In addition to fighting the Creeks, they could help the Americans win."

In this book Sequoyah lives an operatic life; he bursts into such songs as "the Song for Thinking," the "Song for Starting New Things," the "Song for Starting Again," and so on until one wonders when he had time to write.

A more important racism in this book is that when Sequoyah finally stops singing long enough to get his syllabary down correctly, all of the other Cherokees resist it with indignation. This concept of one Indian developing something new and all his people rejecting both him and his work has become a stereotype in books about Native Americans.

The book ends with further inaccuracies. The author incorrectly states that Sequoyah believed that all Indian languages are basically dialects of one continental language. (Maybe the author believes that to be true, but Sequoyah, living next to the Creeks and Choctaws, whose languages are not in any way related to Cherokee, would not have made that mistake.) She then offers her fabrication as Sequoyah's reason for traveling to Mexico (to search for a universal Indian language). Sequoyah, and a large group of Cherokees, *did* leave Oklahoma for Mexico in desperation, looking for a place where they could finally live in freedom from U.S. persecution. (They were all killed by the Mexican government.)

The artwork in the book, by contrast with the misleading text, presents an accurate picture of Cherokee dress and lifestyle.

	ART	WORDS		ART	WORDS		ART	WORDS	N.A.
anti-Racist			non-Racist	✓		Racist — omission / commission			✓
anti-Sexist			non-Sexist			Sexist	✓	✓	
anti-Elitist			non-Elitist	✓	✓	Elitist			
anti-Materialist			non-Materialist	✓	✓	Materialist			
anti-Individualist			non-Individualist	✓		Individualist		✓	
anti-Ageist			non-Ageist		✓	Ageist	✓		
anti-Conformist			non-Conformist	✓	✓	Conformist			
anti-Escapist			non-Escapist			Escapist			
Builds positive image of females/minorities			Builds negative image of females/minorities						
Inspires action vs. oppression			Culturally authentic	✓					

	Excellent	Good	Fair	Poor
Literary quality			✓	
Art quality		✓		

FRONTIERS OF DANCE: THE LIFE OF MARTHA GRAHAM
by Walter Terry
photographs
Thomas Y. Crowell
$5.95, 156 pages, grades 5-9

Frontiers Of Dance traces the development of Martha Graham, one of the pioneers of modern dance. We see in Martha's early childhood, spent in an upper-middle-class American setting at the turn of the century, how Catholic rituals, the ceremonial manners of California's Asian Americans, and her psychologist father's view of body movement as honest expression influenced the molding of her artistic philosophy. At seventeen, she saw her first dance concert, given by Ruth St. Denis, and from that moment "her fate was sealed."

Mr. Terry has styled his biography for young dance enthusiasts. His critical analyses of dance styles, techniques, the strengths and weaknesses of different recitals, and the concept of the human body as an expressive tool, reflect his background as a renowned dance critic.

Regardless of Ms. Graham's talents as a dancer, she emerges as a vain, petty, individualistic woman. Mr. Terry constantly reinforces the image of the temperamental artist by condoning her selfishness and tantrums as integral elements of a creative personality. Attempts to combine dance companies' resources and talents failed miserably because of her competitiveness.

As she grew older, Ms. Graham also resented the younger dancers in her company performing her roles. Mr. Terry's uncritical reportage of this backstage in-fighting strengthens the assumption that jealousy is a part of human nature. It promotes the concept that being a star is more important than human relationships. Thus, even our great artists merely reflect the values of society in general.

Mr. Terry makes patronizing, racist statements without batting his ethnocentric eyelashes. "In California, the servants were invariably Orientals . . . with gentle, mystical, beauty-loving characteristics." Ms. Graham is described as having a sense of abandon "rather like a gypsy." Then there is "little Yuriko," one of Graham's star dancers.

Mr. Terry also reveals his basically sexist attitudes in describing female dancers as "really quite sexless." He continually uses the male pronoun ("each of us, sometime in his life"; "the individual is molded by his heritage") and ultimately, even Graham's success is attributed to the influence of men in her life. "Shaw prodded and needled her; Horst whipped her into accomplishment; Hawkins exerted tremendous pressure on her; with Protas at her side, Martha made a spectacular comeback."

Frontiers Of Dance is only recommended for dance novices who are titillated by trivia and name-dropping.

	ART	WORDS		ART	WORDS		ART	WORDS	N.A.
anti-Racist			non-Racist			Racist — omission / commission			✓
anti-Sexist			non-Sexist			Sexist			✓
anti-Elitist			non-Elitist			Elitist		✓	
anti-Materialist			non-Materialist		✓	Materialist			
anti-Individualist			non-Individualist			Individualist		✓	
anti-Ageist			non-Ageist			Ageist			✓
anti-Conformist		✓	non-Conformist			Conformist			
anti-Escapist			non-Escapist		✓	Escapist			

				Excellent	Good	Fair	Poor
Builds positive image of females/minorities		Builds negative image of females/minorities					
Inspires action vs. oppression		Culturally authentic	Literary quality			✓	
			Art quality				

TUCK EVERLASTING
by Natalie Babbitt
Farrar, Straus & Giroux
$5.95, 139 pages, grades 4-8

Not the Fountain of Youth, but the Fountain of Life Everlasting is the theme of this sweet, off-beat, exquisitely written tale.

Eleven-year-old Winnie Foster, an only child, lives in a "Touch-Me-Not" cottage surrounded by a "Move-On-We-Don't-Want-You-Here" iron fence, near the edge of a strange wood. The girl is lonely and overprotected by a fastidious mother and a fussing grandmother. But now she meets the Tucks!

Eighty-seven years previously the poor, illiterate Tuck family had come through the area and had accidentally discovered a small spring. They had drunk from it, as had their horse. None had aged a day in those eighty-seven years.

Fortunately, the Tuck family is the nicest, the most loving, if not-too-clean-or-fastidious folk ever to be met. They suffer considerably from their condition of immortality, and they are determined to keep the world safe from a similar fate by keeping the magic spring a deep secret.

This leads to their kidnapping of Winnie and to other adventures. Winnie's character broadens. At story's end, the spring is destroyed and the Tucks Ever wander.

No deep message other than to extol the virtues of niceness and kindness in this strange little book. But why not enjoy this unusually fine writer and hope she will have more to say the next time around?

	ART	WORDS		ART	WORDS			ART	WORDS	N.A.
anti-Racist			non-Racist			Racist	omission / commission			✓
anti-Sexist			non-Sexist		✓	Sexist				
anti-Elitist		✓	non-Elitist			Elitist				
anti-Materialist		✓	non-Materialist			Materialist				
anti-Individualist		✓	non-Individualist			Individualist				
anti-Ageist			non-Ageist		✓	Ageist				
anti-Conformist			non-Conformist		✓	Conformist				
anti-Escapist			non-Escapist		✓	Escapist				
Builds positive image of females/minorities			Builds negative image of females/minorities				Excellent	Good	Fair	Poor
Inspires action vs. oppression			Culturally authentic			Literary quality	✓			
						Art quality				

ELIZABETH BLACKWELL
by Jean Lee Latham
illustrated by Ethel Gold
Garrard
$3.40, 88 pages, grades 2-5

In a very simple text that is competently illustrated, author Latham has artfully captured the excitement of Elizabeth Blackwell's life as the first woman doctor in the U.S., and of her pioneering efforts to open up the medical profession to women. At the outset, Ms. Latham describes the Blackwell family's early life in England noting Elizabeth's father's advanced thinking on the education of females. Shen then depicts Elizabeth's struggles to be accepted into all-male medical schools in the U.S., her eventual success and internship in Europe and, finally, the establishment both of her own hospital (staffed entirely by women doctors) and of a medical school for women.

Effectively depicted are Elizabeth's love for people, her boundless courage and determination, and her deep concern for rectifying injustices. Deeply interested in women's rights, Elizabeth was also concerned about improving medical treatment for the poor. However, the author totally omits certain other facts that would have enhanced the relevancy of her book: During their early years in America, the Blackwell family was seriously involved in the Abolitionist movement and permitted their home to serve as a "station" for the Underground Railroad. Moreover, Elizabeth herself became active in the Anti-Slavery Society at the age of fifteen. Why were these facts omitted?

	ART	WORDS		ART	WORDS		ART	WORDS	N.A.
anti-Racist			non-Racist	✓		Racist — omission / commission			✓
anti-Sexist	✓	✓	non-Sexist			Sexist			
anti-Elitist			non-Elitist	✓	✓	Elitist			
anti-Materialist			non-Materialist	✓	✓	Materialist			
anti-Individualist		✓	non-Individualist	✓		Individualist			
anti-Ageist			non-Ageist	✓	✓	Ageist			
anti-Conformist	✓	✓	non-Conformist			Conformist			
anti-Escapist	✓	✓	non-Escapist			Escapist			
Builds positive image of (females) minorities		✓	Builds negative image of females/ minorities				Excellent	Good	Fair	Poor
Inspires action vs. oppression		✓	Culturally authentic		✓	Literary quality		✓		
						Art quality		✓		

TURKEYS, PILGRIMS AND INDIAN CORN
by Edna Barth
illustrated by Ursula Arndt
Seabury Press
$6.95, 96 pages, grades 3-7

This book is a perfect example of the insufficiency of good intentions. In a sincere attempt to fairly represent the viewpoints of a minority—Native Americans in this case—Ms. Barth succeeds only in producing one more racist book. The result seems to stem from her failure to recognize *existing* racist stereotypes. By *including* so many of them, the author reinforces them. Given our present society, this cannot be "balanced" by simply including some explanation of the Native American viewpoint. *Pre*-conditioned by racism, readers will automatically be more affected by the racist messages and loaded words than by those words which question white behavior.

Despite some fascinating, myth-shattering background information on the founders of Plymouth and on Thanksgiving symbols, we must reject sections like: A chapter on Pilgrim Children, which speaks of "wild beasts and savage Indians lurking in the woods"; an explanation of the Pilgrims' rejection of Plymouth Rock as a place of residence—"After exploring Cape Cod, the Pilgrims decided that this was not the best place to settle. *There were too many Indians around.* . . . (Emphasis added.) They decided to explore a place to the north, known as Thievish Harbor, so named because an Indian had stolen a harpoon from an English mariner"; a chapter on Indian Neighbors which ever-so-casually cites an Indian head "mounted on the fort by Miles Standish, in the custom of the day, to frighten enemies." (Would the author be so casual about a white mounted head?)

Even the attempts at objectivity are condescending: "(The Pilgrims) tried to be fair and honest, but like other settlers, they took land to which they really had no right. The Indians found selling the land puzzling. They thought it meant the settlers could move in, not that they must move out." (Children will feel the Indians are not too bright.)

"The Pilgrims had done their best to impose their religion on all the Indians they knew. They wanted to 'help' them. But the Indians had their own religion and tribal customs. As is now known, people are better off with their own beliefs and sacred customs. Robbed of these, they lose self-respect and become confused." (This statement attributes good intentions to the Pilgrims, as well as to whites today. Also implied is that Indians have lost their self-respect.)

While the chapter on Pilgrim Fathers discusses at length the piety of Reverend Brewster, the bigot who persecuted Anne Hutchinson, Ms. Hutchinson is not mentioned in the chapter on Pilgrim Mothers.

The book jacket illustration shows three chalk-white Native Americans standing behind a turkey, and greeting the Pilgrims. In this picture, as well as in other poorly executed illustrations throughout the book, an Indian woman is clothed inaccurately.

It is not easy, in our society, for white people to shed their ethnocentric outlook. But it is a worthy goal.

	ART	WORDS		ART	WORDS			ART	WORDS	N.A.
anti-Racist			non-Racist			Racist omission / commission		✓	✓	
anti-Sexist			non-Sexist	✓	✓	Sexist				
anti-Elitist			non-Elitist	✓	✓	Elitist				
anti-Materialist			non-Materialist	✓	✓	Materialist				
anti-Individualist			non-Individualist	✓	✓	Individualist				
anti-Ageist			non-Ageist	✓	✓	Ageist				
anti-Conformist			non-Conformist	✓	✓	Conformist				
anti-Escapist			non-Escapist	✓	✓	Escapist				
Builds positive image of females/ minorities			Builds negative image of females/ minorities	✓	✓		Excellent	Good	Fair	Poor
Inspires action vs. oppression			Culturally authentic			Literary quality		✓		
						Art quality				✓

CONTRIBUTIONS OF WOMEN: SPORTS
by Joan Ryan
Dillon Press
$6.95, 135 pages, grades 5-9

What a shame that there are not more real feminists writing books about women in sports. Joan Ryan attempts to present an account of six women who were "pioneers in this movement for total acceptance of female athletes" yet she is so confused that she is alternately feminist *and* anti-feminist.

The writing is sometimes lively and the photographs sometimes entertaining, but generally the format for each woman is exactly the same—a step-by-step account of their rise to the top, with details of each tournament, meet, race, scores and victories. Anyone but a sports freak who loves memorizing scores and dates would be bored by this. Secondly, the emphasis is misplaced. While the author tries to portray each woman as modest and not grossly competitive, the overall effect of her approach is to stress how great it is to win (something only a few can do), and to play down the exhilaration of sports activity for its own sake (which everyone can experience).

If one is looking for a good all-around book on women in sports, read, instead, *Women Who Win* by Francene Sabin. (Random, 1975)

	ART	WORDS		ART	WORDS			ART	WORDS	N.A.
anti-Racist			non-Racist		✓	Racist	omission / commission			
anti-Sexist			non-Sexist			Sexist			✓	
anti-Elitist			non-Elitist			Elitist			✓	
anti-Materialist			non-Materialist			Materialist			✓	
anti-Individualist			non-Individualist			Individualist			✓	
anti-Ageist			non-Ageist			Ageist				✓
anti-Conformist			non-Conformist		✓	Conformist				
anti-Escapist			non-Escapist		✓	Escapist				
Builds positive image of females/ minorities			Builds negative image of females/ minorities				Excellent	Good	Fair	Poor
Inspires action vs. oppression			Culturally authentic			Literary quality			✓	
						Art quality				

WHITE CAPTIVES
by Evelyn Sibley Lampman
Atheneum
$6.25, 181 pages, grades 3-6

This book is the retelling of an old biographical account of two young white girls "captured" by Apache Indians when their wagon train was attacked. The family of Olive and Mary Oatman was killed. Mary, the youngest, eventually died in the Indian camp, apparently of tuberculosis. Olive was later rescued.

The incident is true; the retelling is fiction. As a phenomenon in the annals of racism the book is interesting and worth reading by *adults* who want to better understand why white Americans think about Native Americans the way they do. Evelyn Sibley Lampman, according to the dust jacket and the author's note, wrote the book with the idea of telling the story objectively, from both sides.

Ms. Lampman takes pains to debunk three myths. She shows that whites did far more scalping than did the Indians, that it was U.S. expansion that caused Indian suffering, and that it was white attacks on Indian villages that provoked Indian attacks on white settlers.

But to understand the serious errors of this retelling, it is necessary to know about the original book. The Oatman family were Mormons, who teach that American Indians are the "Lost Tribes of Israel," and that Indians' dark color is a sign that they are "fallen from grace."

The two Oatman girls accepted that mythology uncritically, and that gives Oatman's account of her captivity a biased slant. The first book about her misadventures was written, not by Olive, but by a Mormon minister who was commissioned to do it by Olive's older brother (who was not killed in the raid).

Ms. Lampman read that book and saw both that the story was interesting and that it was told with considerable prejudice.

But by her own admission, Ms. Lampman has never met an Indian person nor visited an Indian reservation. She has only two ways of portraying Indian people: either they are sullen, inescrutable "savages," or they are just like white people. An example of the latter: the Apache girl Toaquin is resentful towards her mother, and here is how she thinks: "Why were people always criticizing her? Why could she never do anything to please? Sometimes it seemed to her that everyone was against her. In Angry Hawk's whole band, she couldn't name a single friend." That sounds like the musings of an adolescent girl in Centerville Junior High, not a young Apache woman in the year 1850. The author has no real idea of Indian life at the time. Her Indians go out and pick "mesquite berries" (mesquite does not have berries), and dig for "roots" (we are given no hint of what sort of roots these might be—carrots and radishes, maybe? The assumption seems to be that root-digging is an activity of "primitive peoples.") She also has the Mohave Indians building high fences around their individual garden plots because they cannot trust each other. The fences were in fact to keep out deer and other animals.

It is one thing for the character Olive Oatman to speak of the Indians as "savages," but it is racist for Ms. Lampman to refer to them by that term. This book does not belong in the hands of young people, who reading that it is about a true incident, must imagine that the story itself is true, which it is not.

	ART	WORDS		ART	WORDS		ART	WORDS	N.A.
anti-Racist			non-Racist			Racist — omission / commission		✓	
anti-Sexist			non-Sexist		✓	Sexist			
anti-Elitist			non-Elitist		✓	Elitist			
anti-Materialist			non-Materialist	✓		Materialist			
anti-Individualist			non-Individualist			Individualist	✓		
anti-Ageist			non-Ageist		✓	Ageist			
anti-Conformist			non-Conformist			Conformist		✓	
anti-Escapist			non-Escapist		✓	Escapist			
Builds positive image of females/minorities			Builds negative image of females/(minorities)		✓		Excellent	Good	Fair	Poor
Inspires action vs. oppression			Culturally authentic			Literary quality		✓		
						Art quality				

NEW LIFE: NEW ROOM
by June Jordan
illustrated by Ray Cruz
Thomas Y. Crowell
$5.95, 53 pages, grades 3-5

June Jordan has turned a common, realistic problem into a fun story. A Black family with three children is faced with the problem of rearranging their small apartment in a housing project to accommodate a new baby.

Rudy and Tyrone are informed that, henceforth, they must share their bedroom (for "men only") with sister Linda. Uncomfortable with this disruption of their lives, the three children are helped through the transition by a loving and sensitive father who has a great knack for turning adversity into adventure.

On the day their mother goes to the hospital, the children, encouraged by their dad to be independent, self-reliant and considerate of one another, plunge into sorting their toys and setting up their new room.

The reading is fun, too. The furniture is "pushed, pulled, lifted and turned" as it "bumps, slides, rolls, bangs and rocks." The painting project becomes a merriment of "spilling, dabbing, dripping, streaming and splashing." The words give a pulse to the action which matches the exuberant energy of the children in setting up their new life together.

The vibrations in this gem of a book are good and warm, and Ray Cruz's illustrations successfully combine realism and whimsy.

	ART	WORDS		ART	WORDS			ART	WORDS	N.A.
anti-Racist	✓	✓	non-Racist			Racist	omission			
							commission			
anti-Sexist			non-Sexist	✓		Sexist				✓
anti-Elitist			non-Elitist			Elitist				
anti-Materialist	✓	✓	non-Materialist			Materialist				
anti-Individualist	✓	✓	non-Individualist			Individualist				✓
anti-Ageist			non-Ageist			Ageist				✓
anti-Conformist	✓	✓	non-Conformist			Conformist				
anti-Escapist	✓	✓	non-Escapist			Escapist				
Builds positive image of females/minorities	✓	✓	Builds negative image of females/minorities					Excellent	Good	Fair	Poor
Inspires action vs. oppression			Culturally authentic	✓	✓	Literary quality		✓			
						Art quality		✓			

MICHAEL NARANJO: THE STORY OF AN AMERICAN INDIAN
by Mary Carroll Nelson
Dillon Press
$4.95, 66 pages, grades 6-up

Michael Naranjo is a Native American from Santa Clara and Taos Pueblos, New Mexico. In 1967, he was drafted into the army and sent to Viet Nam, where he was permanently blinded. While in the hospital, Michael began to work with clay and, in time, became a talented and famous sculptor working in brass.

The story is engrossing and inspiring. Although it is sketchy at times, this book effectively depicts his feelings about a carefree childhood, restless adolescence, army experiences and maturation as a blind artist. It is a vivid account, not only of a young man's journey through life, but also of his culture and adjustment to different life situations—Indian and non-Indian, sighted and blind, independent and dependent.

The author, a white Eastern-educated woman, is ethnocentric at times. She mentions the 1680 Pueblo revolt, which drove the Spanish back to Mexico for 13 years, but does not mention Pope, leader of the Santa Clara Pueblo. Nor does she explore the reasons why going home for the weekend was frowned upon by authorities at a Bureau of Indian Affairs school. Michael mentions a Sergeant Yazzie whom he had known in the army. Yazzie is a Navajo name, yet the author does not say anything about him or his squad.

Overall, however, this book is honest and compassionate, without being pitying or condescending.

	ART	WORDS		ART	WORDS			ART	WORDS	N.A.
anti-Racist		✓	non-Racist			Racist	omission / commission			
anti-Sexist			non-Sexist		✓	Sexist				
anti-Elitist			non-Elitist		✓	Elitist				
anti-Materialist			non-Materialist		✓	Materialist				
anti-Individualist			non-Individualist		✓	Individualist				
anti-Ageist			non-Ageist		✓	Ageist				
anti-Conformist			non-Conformist		✓	Conformist				
anti-Escapist			non-Escapist		✓	Escapist				
Builds positive image of females/minorities		✓	Builds negative image of females/minorities				Excellent	Good	Fair	Poor
Inspires action vs. oppression			Culturally authentic			Literary quality		✓		
						Art quality				

HIDDEN HEROINES
by Elaine Landau
Julian Messner
$6.64, 91 pages, grades 4-7

Hidden Heroines is well-intended and contains portraits of interesting women. It is filled with valuable historical prints and photographs of women in a variety of roles. This illustrative material of individuals, groups and movements indicates that a good deal of research and thought were invested in the book.

Unfortunately, the book founders badly, as others have done, on the author's penchant for confusing courage with endurance, and on her inability to present information within the context of a sound historical perspective.

Judging from the excellent illustrations, there were feminist "firsts" all over the place in early America. The pioneer women wore neither pretty curls nor crinolines. They were hard-working people with ravaged faces—miners, doctors, soldiers, abolitionists, telegraphers, astronomers.

Elitist romanticism colors the author's selections. She is strangely silent about the lives of slaves and indentured servants who kneaded the flour, cured the meat, milked the cows, planted and plowed. These abused and historically neglected people are not presented as heroines.

Native Americans are appreciated primarily for what they taught Europeans. As for Black women, they are crowded into one inevitable Civil War chapter. Landau's accounts of the Black women who were guides, blew up bridges, helped prisoners escape, served in the Union army, etc., hint that these heroines were perhaps the most "hidden" of all.

	ART	WORDS		ART	WORDS			ART	WORDS	N.A.
anti-Racist			non-Racist		✓	Racist omission / commission				
anti-Sexist		✓	non-Sexist			Sexist				
anti-Elitist			non-Elitist		✓	Elitist				
anti-Materialist			non-Materialist		✓	Materialist				
anti-Individualist			non-Individualist		✓	Individualist				
anti-Ageist			non-Ageist		✓	Ageist				
anti-Conformist			non-Conformist		✓	Conformist				
anti-Escapist			non-Escapist		✓	Escapist				
Builds positive image of females/ minorities		✓	Builds negative image of females/ minorities				Excellent	Good	Fair	Poor
Inspires action vs. oppression			Culturally authentic			Literary quality		✓		
						Art quality				

BLUE TREES, RED SKY
by Norma Klein
illustrated by Pat Grant Porter
Pantheon
$4.95, 57 pages, grades 2-5

Eight-year-old Valerie wants her widowed mother to stay home and give full attention to her. But mother is devoted to her art and "would work even if she had a million dollars." So Mrs. Weiss, an older woman, baby-sits for Valerie and her younger brother Marco. Mrs. Weiss used to be a concert pianist but discontinued her career after she married and had children. Explaining why she had given up what she loved, she says that in her day, "You did not do both."

Set in a white middle-class and very "arty" world, *Blue Trees* is a wryly humorous book whose non-conforming heroine should appeal to many children.

It has several positive features: Readers will learn a few pointers about growing up such as how "sharing" mother can be rewarding and the fact that one can learn from people of all ages. Mrs. Weiss's description of "how things were" and her acceptance of changing mores are useful for helping children understand that values and behavioral standards are not static but evolve. Mother has a lover whom she is not planning to marry (a refreshing new wrinkle to say the least). Heroines who are sports whizzes have almost become a feminist cliché, so it is pleasant to encounter un-athletic Valerie who learns that a mothers' pursuit of what is important to her does not mean she loves her children less.

Klein's style is engaging. However, it is too bad that the tone of the text and the illustrations reflect a totally white, middle-class environment. The book's other drawback is that, through the eyes of the liberated children, the other characters appear to be stupid and shallow. For example, when Marco mentions, during a walk in the park, his plans to become a ballet dancer, an older woman sitting on a bench says, "You can't. You're a boy." "She's not so smart herself" says Valerie because, "She didn't even know there were men dancers. She probably never even went to the ballet." (This is a bit of elitism, too.) On another occasion, Valerie's friend, Leah, responds to a statement by Mrs. Weiss with the comment, "Oh boy, she really is pretty dumb." Although the author deserves praise for portraying children in unstereotypic roles, she must be chided for perpetuating other stereotypes.

	ART	WORDS		ART	WORDS			ART	WORDS	N.A.
anti-Racist			non-Racist		✓	Racist	omission	✓		
							commission			
anti-Sexist		✓	non-Sexist	✓		Sexist				
anti-Elitist			non-Elitist	✓		Elitist			✓	
anti-Materialist			non-Materialist	✓	✓	Materialist				
anti-Individualist			non-Individualist	✓	✓	Individualist				
anti-Ageist			non-Ageist	✓	✓	Ageist				
anti-Conformist	✓	✓	non-Conformist			Conformist				
anti-Escapist			non-Escapist	✓	✓	Escapist				
Builds positive image of females/ minorities		✓	Builds negative image of females/ minorities				Excellent	Good	Fair	Poor
Inspires action vs. oppression			Culturally authentic			Literary quality	✓			
						Art quality		✓		

WINGMAN
by Manus Pinkwater
illustrated by same
Dodd, Mead
$5.50, 64 pages, grades 2-6

This well-written book poignantly depicts the embarrassment often felt, not only by immigrant children, but by all children who are placed in an insensitive environment. Asian American children living in white neighborhoods can especially identify with Wing, a young Chinese American boy who withdraws into a comic book fantasy world.

Wing's salvation comes, ultimately, not from his fantasized Asian super-hero, Wingman, but from his own talents and from the aid of a sympathetic teacher. Predictably, the teacher is white and in this respect, *Wingman* follows the pattern of endless children's books about minority children who are rescued through white benevolence. However, this particular teacher is depicted as an exception among *several* teachers who are described as either racist or incredibly insensitive, unfeeling adults.

The influence of Wing's father is also critical to the boy's emotional growth. He is a laundryman and to that extent he is stereotypical. But this is counteracted by his portrayal as a warm, well-developed character. The father-son relationship is a definite plus, as is a wonderful passage on the significant effects that viewing great paintings can have on young people who are budding artists.

Wing finally adjusts to his school surroundings, mainly because he is an unusually talented child. (He is the best reader in his class and the best artist of his age group in all of New York City!) Since the author fails to suggest any clue as to how less gifted children can deal with racist institutions or dire poverty, the burden of survival and success is (once again) placed on the victim, and society remains uncharged with the responsibility for giving all youngsters an even chance.

One problem with the book is that its depiction of China is dated and will reinforce stereotypes about pagoda roofs, Fu Manchu moustaches and old, traditional-style garb.

Although the author-illustrator's attempt to render a comic book art style is not as successful as his story line, this worthwhile book can still be recommended as superior to most available books about Asian Americans.

	ART	WORDS		ART	WORDS			ART	WORDS	N.A.
anti-Racist	√	√	non-Racist			Racist — omission / commission				
anti-Sexist			non-Sexist	√	√	Sexist				
anti-Elitist			non-Elitist	√	√	Elitist				
anti-Materialist			non-Materialist	√	√	Materialist				
anti-Individualist			non-Individualist	√	√	Individualist				
anti-Ageist			non-Ageist	√	√	Ageist				
anti-Conformist		√	non-Conformist	√		Conformist				
anti-Escapist			non-Escapist	√	√	Escapist				
Builds positive image of females/minorities		√	Builds negative image of females/minorities				Excellent	Good	Fair	Poor
Inspires action vs. oppression			Culturally authentic		√	Literary quality		√		
						Art quality			√	

WILLIAM BELTZ: THE STORY OF A NATIVE AMERICAN
by Ellen Wolfe
photographs
Dillon Press
$4.95, 58 pages, grades 5-9

William Beltz was an Innuit (Eskimo) Alaskan who grew up in the mining towns of northern Alaska. His father was white. During his growing years he witnessed the unjust treatment of Native peoples by whites and resolved to work for change. He managed to get an eighth grade education, unusual for Innuits at that time, and to later become a leader of the Alaskan Carpenters Union.

Widely liked and respected, he entered politics and was the first president of the Alaskan State Senate. He died in 1960 at the early age of forty-eight.

The book gives some details of the passing Innuit culture along with details about Beltz. It is fast-paced and smoothly written by a professional journalist who lets us know, consciously or unconsciously, her own viewpoint about Alaska's relationship to the USA.

We are told that children were cherished and never punished in Innuit society, theft was almost unknown, extended family relationships were loving and strong. People earned respect for what they contributed to the community, rather than for what they kept for themselves. We are told that the coming of the white man brought "For Whites Only" signs and social discrimination. (We are not told of economic exploitation.) The author tells us that discrimination "was not fair, but Will did not become angry or bitter. Instead he tried to show the men he met that people should be judged individually, not by race."

The book presents the territory-versus-statehood debate over Alaska's destiny, leaving out any mention of those native peoples, Indian and Innuit, who wished neither one. We read: "After a ten year struggle, native Alaskans won just compensation for the land the white people had settled. In 1971 Congress passed the Alaska Native Claims Settlement Act, a law that made it possible, at long last, for native Alaskans to become leaders in state, business and politics." The author makes it sound like it was United States largesse to give this "just" settlement and finally allow people to go into business in their own country. Omitted are the initial Innuit compensation demands which were far, far greater than what Congress finally yielded. Omitted is speculation about how the uneducated and poverty-stricken Innuits will launch their careers in any way that will put them on a par with the huge lumber, oil, and other interests exploiting their country. The one billion dollars "given to native groups to administer through twelve regional corporations and a flock of village corporations" cannot possibly solve the problem, but this is never explained.

A young reader will end up feeling—once again—that this nation is benevolent, and that Natives who work hard, get a good education, and stand "above race and personal interest" will succeed.

	ART	WORDS		ART	WORDS		ART	WORDS	N.A.
anti-Racist			non-Racist		✓	Racist omission / commission			
anti-Sexist			non-Sexist			Sexist		✓	
anti-Elitist			non-Elitist	✓		Elitist			
anti-Materialist			non-Materialist	✓		Materialist			
anti-Individualist		✓	non-Individualist			Individualist			
anti-Ageist			non-Ageist	✓		Ageist			
anti-Conformist			non-Conformist	✓		Conformist			
anti-Escapist		✓	non-Escapist			Escapist			
Builds positive image of females/ minorities			Builds negative image of females/ minorities				Excellent	Good	Fair	Poor
Inspires action vs. oppression			Culturally authentic			Literary quality		✓		
						Art quality				

SADDLES AND SABERS: BLACK MEN IN THE OLD WEST
by LaVere Anderson
illustrated by Herman Vestal
Garrard
$3.78, 128 pages, grades 5-10

These short biographies chronicle the lives of a few Black cowboys and soldiers who helped to "settle" the West during 1850 to 1900. Some went West to escape from slavery; others were seeking freedom from the prejudice that pervaded their existence in the South or East. They were generally welcomed if they possessed outstanding physical strength or cowboy skills. And they were especially welcomed if they would participate in fighting or tracking Native Americans.

As indicated by the title of the book, women are virtually absent. The existence of a second sex is acknowledged only in a few sentences such as "The women cooked while the men played cards and talked" or "Isaiah married a Sioux girl." Although describing a sexist culture which glorified male strength and camaraderie and assigned females to sexual or cooking functions, the author could have tried to avoid reinforcing sexism. No such attempt was made.

An attempt was made, however, to include Native American viewpoints in discussing the many battles they fought to defend their homelands. But a mixed message is delivered to readers because many of the Black men are praised for killing Native Americans. Similarly, the author notes, on the one hand, white racism and white broken promises to Native Americans and Blacks but, on the other, supports Blacks and whites against Native Americans!

Certainly it is important for young people to know that the "Wild West" was composed of others besides reds and whites, but it is equally important that books present a historical perspective which will contribute to the liberation of all people.

	ART	WORDS		ART	WORDS		ART	WORDS	N.A.
anti-Racist			non-Racist	✓	✓	Racist — omission / commission			
anti-Sexist			non-Sexist	✓		Sexist		✓	
anti-Elitist			non-Elitist	✓	✓	Elitist			
anti-Materialist			non-Materialist	✓	✓	Materialist			
anti-Individualist			non-Individualist	✓		Individualist		✓	
anti-Ageist			non-Ageist		✓	Ageist			
anti-Conformist			non-Conformist	✓	✓	Conformist			
anti-Escapist			non-Escapist	✓	✓	Escapist			
Builds positive image of females/minorities			Builds negative image of females/minorities				Excellent	Good	Fair	Poor
Inspires action vs. oppression			Culturally authentic			Literary quality			✓	
						Art quality			✓	

THE ANALYSES —3

Into Teen Years

BOY ON THE RUN
by Bianca Bradbury
Seabury Press
$5.95, 126 pages, grades 6-up

Ever since his folks have been divorced, twelve-year-old Nick Fournier's father, a Washington big shot, has had very little time for Nick. His mother is overprotecting him in the extreme—she even refuses to let him play in Central Park (three blocks away) for fear he might get mugged.

One day, out of frustration, Nick throws $5,000 worth of art treasures out of the window; another time, he slashes car tires. Fearing that he has become deranged, his mother takes him to see her psychiatrist. Later, Nick seizes an opportunity to escape to his grandmother's summer house, where he hopes to get a taste of freedom and test his ability to survive on his own. The burning question in his mind is, does he have the guts to break out of his gilded cage and prove his sanity, or is the "shrink" right about him?

The novel follows Nick on his journey, which includes spending lonely nights on the beach, concealing his identity and finding a young dog to love and be responsible for. Alone, Nick begins to sort out his past, and finds himself able to deal with new situations without relying on the pills the psychiatrist had prescribed. By the time he arrives at Grandma's, he is ready to relate to the members of his family in an honest and open fashion.

Prior to his identity-search, Nick had felt odd and out of place in his affluent environment. When he meets average people, like Tom Shaw, in his travels, he discovers how comfortable he can be in unpretentious surroundings. Later, he brings Tom's mother some candy, not to purchase her friendship or approval, but just because he wants to. Throughout his travel experiences, the value of human relationships over material possessions becomes increasingly clear to him.

In discarding his pills, Nick symbolically rejects escapism as a solution to problems. Towards the end of his travels, he learns not to fall apart when confronted with challenges, but to think things out instead.

Although this is an interesting and sensitive story that could serve as a guide to relationships for adults as well as children, the author's portrayal of women is surprisingly sexist. Nick is frightened by beautiful or gracious women like his mother, while the understanding, earthy women with whom he feels comfortable are either old like Grandma, fat or nondescript. The implication is that certain human qualities only come in certain packages. Of all of the women Nick encounters, only the psychiatrist has a non-traditional female role. Yet even her image is undercut by such descriptions and references as "birdlike, small, maybe a witch" and "any shrink with brains in his head. . . ."

Racist stereotyping of Native Americans is also prevalent. At one point, Nick mentions an Indian reservation on which there are no Indians. Later, he imagines Indians sneaking over the turf "to pounce on him."

	ART	WORDS		ART	WORDS			ART	WORDS	N.A.
anti-Racist			non-Racist			Racist	omission			
							commission			✓
anti-Sexist			non-Sexist			Sexist				✓
anti-Elitist		✓	non-Elitist			Elitist				
anti-Materialist		✓	non-Materialist			Materialist				
anti-Individualist			non-Individualist		✓	Individualist				
anti-Ageist		✓	non-Ageist			Ageist				
anti-Conformist		✓	non-Conformist			Conformist				
anti-Escapist		✓	non-Escapist			Escapist				
Builds positive image of females/ minorities			Builds negative image of females/ minorities					Excellent	Good	Fair	Poor
Inspires action vs. oppression			Culturally authentic			Literary quality			✓		
						Art quality					

A MAN AIN'T NOTHIN' BUT A MAN
by John Oliver Killens
Little, Brown
$5.95, 176 pages, grades 7-up

The story of John Henry has been, to most of us, simply an entertaining folktale about a man's peculiar obsession with beating a machine. John Killens' book reveals a larger purpose in the contest—one which adds dimension and clarity to the old tale.

As presented here, John Henry is not ego-tripping; he is making a last-ditch effort to protect the jobs of thousands of men, especially Black men: ". . . you know the first to be laid off gon be our people. Black people!"

John Henry is not really fighting the machine per se. He understands that it is merely a tool of those in control and that by "beating" it he would be able to beat "the Cap'n" and get away with it. As he tells his wife, ". . . who is the enemy? I'm fighting Cap'n Brad this morning. Him and the steam drill the same damn people." An earlier incident had caused John to learn this lesson well. False rumors spread by the Cap'n had succeeded in temporarily severing the friendship between John and a white co-worker. As the two men are about to do battle, their Chinese mutual friend gives John some information which reveals the treacherous way they have been pitted against each other. The three friends then unite and go to challenge the machine.

Unfortunately, the book has sexist overtones. When John Henry dies in his struggle with the machine, his wife, Polly Anne, begins to cry hysterically and grow weak with grief. It is only when she picks up her husband's hammer and feels "the growing strength flow through her body, as if it were transferred to her through John Henry's mighty hammer" that she realizes she must be strong in support of her husband's purpose and for the sake of their expected child. Here, as in some other instances, Polly's worth is mainly a reflection of John Henry's. However, it must be said that Killens' Polly Anne does not lack strength or intelligence: "If she had an opinion she was bound to give it expression, and masculine voices did not intimidate her. The things to do, she told them, was to ignore the captain. 'Show him he can't break up friends so easy.'"

The book also shows the female as accepting of the status quo, while the male is shown struggling against it to maintain his manhood. John's mother tells him: "But just don't talk back to the captain, not even under your breath. . . . A captain is a captain all over this world." His father says: "One man is just as good as another. Sometimes even a whole heap better."

I would also have preferred less reinforcement of the traditional qualities of "a real man," which include attracting women through displays of "vigor and masculinity" and crying silently while the woman is shown as verging on hysteria. But all in all, Killens has provided the young reader with a hero whose life and struggle can clearly be related to the challenges facing today's youth.

	ART	WORDS		ART	WORDS			ART	WORDS	N.A.
anti-Racist		✓	non-Racist			Racist — omission / commission				
anti-Sexist			non-Sexist		✓	Sexist				
anti-Elitist		✓	non-Elitist			Elitist				
anti-Materialist			non-Materialist		✓	Materialist				
anti-Individualist		✓	non-Individualist			Individualist				
anti-Ageist			non-Ageist			Ageist				✓
anti-Conformist		✓	non-Conformist			Conformist				
anti-Escapist		✓	non-Escapist			Escapist				
Builds positive image of females/ minorities		✓	Builds negative image of females/ minorities				Excellent	Good	Fair	Poor
Inspires action vs. oppression		✓	Culturally authentic			Literary quality	✓			
						Art quality				

DUST OF THE EARTH
by Vera and Bill Cleaver
J. B. Lippincott
$6.95, 159 pages, grades 7-up

Dust of the Earth is the story of a mid-western family circa early 1900's, who find a meaningful life together after moving to a new home.

Fourteen-year-old Fern Drawn is the storyteller, and it is through her eyes that we come to know the Drawns. Mama, Papa, two brothers and a sister are alienated from each other, and it is Fern, more than anyone, who feels the coldness and distance in their relationships. Mama and Papa, she finds, are always quarreling—as did their own parents. She, Fern, is forever fighting with her cynical brother, Hobson.

When Fern's mother inherits a house and some property in Chokecherry, South Dakota, the Drawns decide to move. Many physical and economic hardships, as well as sacrifice, mark the family's first year in the new environment. During that year, Fern rejects going to school and decides to tend sheep instead—which later proves to be the family's only source of income.

The hard times in Chokecherry, where survival depends upon cooperation, bring the Drawns closer to one another than ever before. Communications open up, and love emerges.

The strength and charm of this novel lie in the characterization of Fern Drawn, who is a courageous, strong, resourceful young girl, with leadership qualities and a mind of her own.

This is a beautifully written book which young readers will enjoy.

	ART	WORDS		ART	WORDS			ART	WORDS	N.A.
anti-Racist			non-Racist			Racist	omission / commission			✓
anti-Sexist		✓	non-Sexist			Sexist				
anti-Elitist		✓	non-Elitist			Elitist				
anti-Materialist			non-Materialist		✓	Materialist				
anti-Individualist			non-Individualist			Individualist			✓	
anti-Ageist			non-Ageist			Ageist			✓	
anti-Conformist		✓	non-Conformist			Conformist				
anti-Escapist		✓	non-Escapist			Escapist				
Builds positive image of (females) minorities		✓	Builds negative image of females/ minorities					Excellent	Good	Fair	Poor
Inspires action vs. oppression			Culturally authentic			Literary quality			✓		
						Art quality					

THE COUNTRY OF THE HEART
by Barbara Wersba
Atheneum
$5.95, 115 pages, grades 7-up

The Country of the Heart is a romantic novel about an eighteen-year-old man's love affair with a woman of 40, and of his love for writing. The story takes the form of a love letter from Steve to Hadley, written five years after her death from cancer.

Steve had known and admired Hadley's poetry, so when she moved to his town he made every effort to meet her. At first, she resented his intrusion, but later, she responded, finally consenting to read his poetry and tutor him. Their relationship developed into a love affair.

Unknown to Steve, Hadley had cancer and became increasingly cold and distant, easing her pain with pills and alcohol. Steve took her unwillingness to make love as rejection. Arguments ensued and the lovers parted bitterly. Steve's confusion and hurt abated when he learned of the illness. Visiting Hadley in the hospital, he appeared so shocked by her emaciated appearance that she asked him not to return.

The novel's strongest asset is Ms. Wersba's realistic depiction of the hard work involved in writing, which destroys the myth that artists lead glamorous lives of leisure. However, the book is seriously flawed overall.

In a style that is flowery to the point of pretentiousness, readers are fed the concept of the "driven artist." States Hadley: "Artists can't have both life and art." By failing to question the validity of this elitist view of the artist, the book reinforces the notion that art and social commitment are necessarily opposed. The extreme individualism implicit in this view is further supported by Hadley's martyr-like desire to suffer her painful dying in isolation.

Steve's desire to find life's meaning through Hadley, to have their love endure forever, to retreat from the world to the bedroom, reflects attitudes towards love that are escapist and sexist. Steve's love is also possessive, implying that jealousy is a natural component of "True Love." Rather than preparing young people to enter into mature, give-and-take relationships, these old romantic notions encourage unreal expectations.

The male pronoun is used for both sexes. Not until the end of the story, when Hadley is dying, is the age factor dealt with—and then not effectively. Because its good features do not compensate for its extreme reinforcement of negative values in human relationships, this book should be avoided.

	ART	WORDS		ART	WORDS			ART	WORDS	N.A.
anti-Racist			non-Racist			Racist	omission			✓
							commission			
anti-Sexist			non-Sexist			Sexist			✓	
anti-Elitist			non-Elitist			Elitist			✓	
anti-Materialist			non-Materialist		✓	Materialist				
anti-Individualist			non-Individualist			Individualist			✓	
anti-Ageist			non-Ageist			Ageist				✓
anti-Conformist		✓	non-Conformist			Conformist				
anti-Escapist			non-Escapist			Escapist			✓	
Builds positive image of females/ minorities			Builds negative image of females/ minorities					Excellent	Good	Fair	Poor
Inspires action vs. oppression			Culturally authentic			Literary quality				✓	
						Art quality					

MR. DEATH
by Anne Moody
Harper & Row
$5.95, 102 pages, grades 7-up

This collection of four stories examines death—an interesting and unusual theme for children's literature. In each death takes a different form, although it is always unexpected, violent, and tragic.

In a smoothly flowing gothic style, the author relates a great deal about the lives of rural southern Blacks. The men, women and children of these tales live out their hopes, dreams and disappointments in vivid renderings of the Black experience. They ways in which Ms. Moody contrasts Black lives with white and rich lives with poor, illuminate the negative effects of racism, and materialism.

In a foreword to the collection, John Donovan, an author and director of the *Children's Book Council,* warns readers that the stories "will frighten and horrify you," and he suggests reading them "slowly . . . to help us understand the nature of love."

Certainly, adults who enjoy gooseflesh and gore would appreciate the content as well as the magnificent style of these stories. But whether morbidity, horror and the supernatural are essential to depicting death for children is debatable. Pet dogs which rip apart and then devour screaming children, dead children who mysteriously assume the form of cows, plus other assorted horrors, are more likely to give children nightmares than to help them "understand the nature of love."

	ART	WORDS		ART	WORDS			ART	WORDS	N.A.
anti-Racist		✓	non-Racist			Racist omission / commission				
anti-Sexist			non-Sexist		✓	Sexist				
anti-Elitist		✓	non-Elitist			Elitist				
anti-Materialist		✓	non-Materialist			Materialist				
anti-Individualist			non-Individualist		✓	Individualist				
anti-Ageist			non-Ageist		✓	Ageist				
anti-Conformist			non-Conformist		✓	Conformist				
anti-Escapist			non-Escapist			Escapist			✓	
Builds positive image of females/minorities			Builds negative image of females/minorities				Excellent	Good	Fair	Poor
Inspires action vs. oppression			Culturally authentic		✓	Literary quality	✓			
						Art quality				

IS THAT YOU, MISS BLUE?
by M. E. Kerr
Harper & Row
$6.50, 170 pages, grades 8-up

Flanders Brown is sent to an upper crust, Episcopalian boarding school because she gets in the way of her father's sex therapy business and her mother has run off with a younger man. (Despite this 1975 beginning, the school as described, has a 1945 feel.) After a confusing and unexciting year, Flanders learns to appreciate her mother and happily goes to live with her.

If the book sounds pointless, that is because the plot is vague, the message is unclear and the melange of both stock and off-beat characters is poorly delineated. They include: a spoiled, rich and beautiful sorority girl who comes to no good end; a wise-cracking, plain, poor girl with guts—the atheistic daughter of a minister; the big bosomed and mean school mistress, with the usual tiny, sweet and gentle husband.

Also included are: the sex therapist, male-chauvinist-pig of a father; the mother who left in search of her identity; the incredibly beautiful, blonde, deaf-and-dumb girl who rooms next door and continuously punches Flanders black and blue to get her attention; a literally blind, date who is incredibly handsome; and crazy Miss Blue, the teacher who has out-loud dialogues with Jesus.

While the book mocks some of the girls' snobbishness (Southerners are also mocked for their speech and manners), basic materialistic and elitist values remain unquestioned. A little humor here, some good writing there—but nothing comes off terribly well.

	ART	WORDS		ART	WORDS			ART	WORDS	N.A.
anti-Racist			non-Racist			Racist	omission			✓
							commission			
anti-Sexist			non-Sexist		✓	Sexist				
anti-Elitist			non-Elitist			Elitist		✓		
anti-Materialist			non-Materialist		✓	Materialist				
anti-Individualist			non-Individualist		✓	Individualist				
anti-Ageist			non-Ageist		✓	Ageist				
anti-Conformist			non-Conformist		✓	Conformist				
anti-Escapist			non-Escapist		✓	Escapist				
Builds positive image of females/ minorities			Builds negative image of females/ minorities				Excellent	Good	Fair	Poor
Inspires action vs. oppression			Culturally authentic			Literary quality		✓		
						Art quality				

FAST SAM, COOL CLYDE, AND STUFF
by Walter Dean Myers
Viking Press
$6.95, 190 pages, grades 5-up

Here is a touching and moving novel about Black and Puerto Rican close friends who live and mature together in the same community. Filled with un- forgettable characters and memorable scenes, the story describes poignantly the humorous, painful and happy experiences of a group of adolescents who prove to be each other's keepers.

Through the eyes of Stuff, one of the youngest "116th Street Good People" the reader comes to know and understand the other characters: Cool Clyde, who rarely loses his cool; Fast Sam; Gloria, the best friend anyone could have; Maria, who always manages to say what everyone else is thinking; Carnation Charley; Sharon, Stuff's sister, plus a host of others.

The characters come fully alive in some remarkably vivid scenes— a dance contest in which Clyde and Fast Sam team up, with Clyde dressed as a girl; the group's handling of Gloria's grief when her unemployed father leaves home, and the sad moments when Cool Clyde must come to terms with his father's death. The bonds of love, friendship and human understanding are revealed as the tools for these young people's survival in a hostile world.

Even though the boys reflect the sexist culture around them in some of their attitudes and the girls are shown in the usual cheerleading role at a big game, traditional male and female roles are challenged in the story. At one point Sam, Clyde and Stuff cry without feeling uptight because they are males, and the girls participate with the boys in such activities as playing basketball. In addition, they appear to have a sense of themselves that is independent of the males. It is the females who set the young men straight about sex, explaining what it does and does not mean to them as women. Says Gloria: "'Getting some' is done with a guy and a girl. So when we talk about it, let's talk about it as a together thing. If it's natural for you to do it because you're a man and it's not natural for me then who are you going to do it with? It's natural for me, too."

Unfortunately, confrontations with the police and drug pushers which occur in the story are not as fully explained by the author as they might have been, so the reader must possess some knowledge of urban life and racism. Despite this shortcoming, the book is excellent.

	ART	WORDS		ART	WORDS			ART	WORDS	N.A.
anti-Racist		✓	non-Racist			Racist	omission			
							commission			
anti-Sexist			non-Sexist	✓		Sexist				
anti-Elitist		✓	non-Elitist			Elitist				
anti-Materialist			non-Materialist	✓		Materialist				
anti-Individualist		✓	non-Individualist			Individualist				
anti-Ageist			non-Ageist	✓		Ageist				
anti-Conformist		✓	non-Conformist			Conformist				
anti-Escapist		✓	non-Escapist			Escapist				
Builds positive image of females/minorities		✓	Builds negative image of females/minorities					Excellent	Good	Fair	Poor
Inspires action vs. oppression		✓	Culturally authentic		✓	Literary quality	✓			
						Art quality				

THE WATCHERS
by Jane Louise Curry
Atheneum
$6.50, 235 pages, grades 7-up

Thirteen-year-old Ray Siler idolizes his deceased mother and dislikes his stepmother. These feelings, coupled with his constant truancy from school, prompt his father to send him to live with his mother's Uncle Durham and Aunt Star in Withers, West Virginia.

Ray finds his mother's relatives unusual and strange. First of all, he discovers that their last name is not Clark, but Clewarek. Then he learns he has several cousins with last names like Tullo, Yanto, Mattick and Lillico, to which he responds with, "What kind of wacko names are those? Italian?"

Having brought to Withers County a fake urban "sophistication," Ray initially regards his relatives as an ugly, funny-dressing, odd-speaking crew whose lifestyle is outmoded and backward. However, warmed by their reception, he quickly adapts to their ways of doing things.

The plot centers on Ray's involvement with his family's efforts to thwart the evil schemes of Mr. Moar, a grocery store owner who secretly heads a coal mining company claiming rights to land on which Ray's relatives live. After much activity—including the intervention of lawyers, judges, the police, and the bold initiative of Ray's relatives—Mr. Moar is foiled. Traditionally known as the "Watchers" because they had to look out for enemies, Ray's people are then free to live as they always have.

In this elaborately plotted story about families threatened with the loss of their homes and land by corporate interests, the author does not adequately explain the financial motives underlying the conflict. The inference is that Mr. Moar, as well as the Clewareks, Tullos and Matticks, are all acting out some sort of feud inherited from their ancestors. The climate of fate and destiny which thus pervades the story makes it rather escapist reading.

Other problems afflict the novel. The author heavily underscores Ray's feelings of superiority as a way of contrasting him to his relatives, who consequently appear inferior. Whatever the intentions of this literary device, it further reinforces elitist attitudes in young readers. Last but not least, racism surfaces when Ray discovers a diary in which an Indian attack on whites is mentioned. In the absence of any discussion in the diary as to why the Native Americans were hostile, the age-old myth of white settler innocence and "savage" aggression is supported.

	ART	WORDS		ART	WORDS			ART	WORDS	N.A.
anti-Racist			non-Racist			Racist	omission			
							commission		✓	
anti-Sexist			non-Sexist		✓	Sexist				
anti-Elitist			non-Elitist			Elitist		✓		
anti-Materialist			non-Materialist			Materialist			✓	
anti-Individualist			non-Individualist			Individualist			✓	
anti-Ageist			non-Ageist		✓	Ageist				
anti-Conformist			non-Conformist		✓	Conformist				
anti-Escapist			non-Escapist			Escapist			✓	

	ART	WORDS		ART	WORDS		Excellent	Good	Fair	Poor
Builds positive image of females/ minorities			Builds negative image of females/ (minorities)		✓					
Inspires action vs. oppression			Culturally authentic			Literary quality			✓	
						Art quality				

THE SUMMER ENDS TOO SOON
by Mort Grossman
Westminster Press
$6.50, 159 pages, grades 7-up

Diane Elizabeth, a blonde, beautiful, slim and "very feminine" sixteen-year-old "from Cheltenham," reports for work in a Jewish summer camp near Philadelphia. She is the only gentile on staff. "Her neatness was a direct contrast to the way most of the counselors dressed about camp." Izzy, the camp director, is delighted. But Diane's prominent surgeon-father is not. To his complaints, the heroine replies, "I don't think you're an average bigot. You couldn't be an average anything. You're *my* daddy."

But our golden-haired WASP is not the only beautiful female. The description of her "raven haired," "long and aquiline"-nosed bunkmate, Sharon Rothschild, is similar to the "Jewess-Rebecca" in *Ivanhoe*.

Marc Gordon, the seventeen-year-old dramatic counselor, sees these "two dreamy apparitions" and promptly falls for—of course—blonde Diane. "I love you because you're just about the best girl I've ever met, and I've met many. There's a decency and a goodness about you *that is foreign to Camp Ramble Lane.*"—(emphasis added.)

Diane's wealthy, "refined" parents, "a couple who somehow stood out from the usual parents who came to the camp," arrive on visiting day, as do Marc's somewhat less refined, furniture store-owning parents. All parents proceed to mess up the wonderful (though asexual) friendship of Marc and Diane. Sweet Diane is nonplussed to learn of Marc's parents' opposition to her. "Always she had believed that the majority looked down upon the minority. But now! Was it possible that the minority could look down upon the majority as well?"

Camp director Izzy helps smooth things out for a happy ending. On the last page, Izzy says, "When they're small, you've got small problems, and when they're big, you've got big problems. Right?" To which his wife—the proverbial Jewish mother—replies, "Come on, everybody . . . Let's eat."

Should you want to know more about this sexist, elitist, materialistic and anti-Semitic book, the author is—according to the book jacket—a high school teacher who wrote the book "with special understanding and depth of feeling, out of his own experience. He is Jewish and his wife comes from a Christian background." (The book is dedicated to "Reina, my sweet daughter" and "Jeff, my fine son.") The book jacket does not explain how Mr. Grossman developed the self-hatred which caused him to include so many anti-Jewish stereotypes.

	ART	WORDS		ART	WORDS			ART	WORDS	N.A.
anti-Racist			non-Racist			Racist omission			✓	
						commission				
anti-Sexist			non-Sexist			Sexist			✓	
anti-Elitist			non-Elitist			Elitist			✓	
anti-Materialist			non-Materialist			Materialist			✓	
anti-Individualist			non-Individualist	✓		Individualist				
anti-Ageist			non-Ageist			Ageist				✓
anti-Conformist			non-Conformist			Conformist			✓	
anti-Escapist			non-Escapist			Escapist			✓	
Builds positive image of females/ minorities			Builds negative image of females/ minorities				Excellent	Good	Fair	Poor
Inspires action vs. oppression			Culturally authentic			Literary quality				✓
						Art quality				

THE GLAD MAN
by Gloria Gonzalez
Alfred A. Knopf
$4.95, 160 pages, grades 5-9

Here is an absorbing young people's story, full of humor and natural insights, with a good plot and an unusual eleven-year-old heroine whose aim is to "play baseball for the St. Louis Cardinals"—her city's home team.

The book exudes respect for human relationships and honestly attempts to reveal, not distort, lives. It is marred, however, by the startling absence of what could not be absent in a city like St. Louis in 1975—Black people. This omission is a nagging minus throughout what is essentially a positive book.

The story unfolds on several levels, thus conveying a sense of process and change. Nobody is the same at the end of the story—teachers and pupils, parents and children, old and young learn and grow. The teacher, introduced to us by Melissa as someone who would stop to "correct the commas" before she acted on a ransom note, is delightful as she wrestles with a host of classroom problems. In the course of teaching, she learns a great deal—especially outside of the classroom where the children involve her in their lives. The significance of aging, the right to be different, the need for independence and the outrage of hypocrisy and patronage toward old people, are all lessons learned by children and adults in the course of the story.

The author understands and is sympathetic to children, despite her perpetuation of the stereotype that children do not like school. Moreover, the book is generally refreshing and honest in its depiction of a working-class family with a working mother.

One must question the juxtaposition of Melissa's goal to play baseball with a belittling reference to her brother who would be "happy to spend the rest of his life in a library." This type of contrast undercuts the understanding that the women's movement wants to develop. Such downgrading of one set of goals and interests in order to advance acceptance of others is unnecessary.

In addition, the mother is cast somewhat in the mold of a complainer and clinger to tradition. The father is the one who is always ready for a trip, while the mother hesitates ("How will I get all my work done?"). The father understands Melissa's aspirations, while the mother says it is more realistic to marry a St. Louis Cardinal than to try and be one.

There is a bonus in this book that must be mentioned. It does not skirt reality or recent events. When a city official says "You can't change the law to benefit only one person," the answer is that after Nixon it is hard for children to have any illusions about "justice for all." The book ends with the children, assisted by their teacher and parents, daring to "fight City Hall." Off they go into battle in a big, cheerful caravan that makes you wish you were in it.

	ART	WORDS		ART	WORDS			ART	WORDS	N.A.
anti-Racist			non-Racist			Racist	omission		✓	
							commission			
anti-Sexist		✓	non-Sexist			Sexist				
anti-Elitist		✓	non-Elitist			Elitist				
anti-Materialist		✓	non-Materialist			Materialist				
anti-Individualist		✓	non-Individualist			Individualist				
anti-Ageist		✓	non-Ageist			Ageist				
anti-Conformist		✓	non-Conformist			Conformist				
anti-Escapist		✓	non-Escapist			Escapist				
Builds positive image of females/minorities		✓	Builds negative image of females/minorities				Excellent	Good	Fair	Poor
Inspires action vs. oppression			Culturally authentic			Literary quality		✓		
						Art quality				

COMING HOME TO A PLACE
YOU'VE NEVER BEEN BEFORE
by Hanna and Bruce Clements
Farrar, Straus & Giroux
$6.95, 196 pages, grades 5-up

Coming Home to a Place You've Never Been Before is a documentary account of one day in the lives of several young men and women living in Perception House, a rehabilitation center in Willimantic, Connecticut.

Some are there voluntarily, some involuntarily, to discover who they are and what they are doing with their lives. This realistic account of what a rehabilitation center is all about shows the young people struggling together, sharing, supporting one another and working toward group, as well as individual, goals. Rewards and punishments are meted out to each member as a means of developing self-awareness of attitudes and behavior.

Some of the youngsters are third world, and their stories are told as honestly and straightforwardly as the others without overtones of racism. What the book does not depict, however, is by what method these teenagers are taught to deal with the outside world. They do not seem to gain knowledge, through the Perception House program, about the role of societal forces in shaping their lives. Why are so many of them driven to drugs and crime? Why are their home lives so alienated? What kinds of pressures does society place on them? These and other questions are not explored at the center. Thus, problems and solutions become totally individual, and our social system is let off the hook.

The book is also too microscopic, focusing on small details and minor observations which tax attention and provide little significant information.

	ART	WORDS		ART	WORDS			ART	WORDS	N.A.
anti-Racist			non-Racist		✓	Racist	omission / commission			
anti-Sexist			non-Sexist		✓	Sexist				
anti-Elitist			non-Elitist		✓	Elitist				
anti-Materialist			non-Materialist		✓	Materialist				
anti-Individualist		✓	non-Individualist			Individualist				
anti-Ageist			non-Ageist			Ageist				✓
anti-Conformist			non-Conformist		✓	Conformist				
anti-Escapist			non-Escapist			Escapist			✓	
Builds positive image of females/ minorities			Builds negative image of females/ minorities					Excellent	Good	Fair	Poor
Inspires action vs. oppression			Culturally authentic			Literary quality				✓	
						Art quality					

JUDO: A GENTLE BEGINNING
by Jeannette Bruce
illustrated by Don Madden
Thomas Y. Crowell
$5.95, 150 pages, grades 5-up

This potentially fine martial arts book for children (for which there is a great need) is about three-fourths very good and one-fourth awful. It is a comprehensive, yet light and humorous, introduction to judo for children, in the form of an illustrated guide for home practice if no judo school is available. (Careful supervision would be needed for children using this book. Judo can be very dangerous.)

The lively how-to sections include a full set of exercises for stretches and strengthening, as well as falling, throwing and grappling techniques. Though generally accurate, the text and illustrations are sometimes confusing and occasionally incorrect—a person should *never* fall with his/her legs together as depicted in the illustration on page 53. However, the illustrations, which feature as the main characters a white boy, Black boy, white girl, dog and cat, are excellent and very funny. Lo and behold, the girl does everything the boys do and is even chosen to depict the correct way for doing push-ups—a nice anti-sexist gesture. Excellent also is the text's emphasis on judo as the "Gentle Way"—a sport practiced with respect for one's partner and never used consciously to hurt except in self-defense.

The author's decision to include a history of judo, plus a round-up of other martial arts, was unfortunate. These sections are marred by inaccuracies so gross and numerous as to be embarrassing. T'ai Chi is not *like* Kung Fu, it *is* Kung Fu; a Black Belt is definitely not the "mark of an expert" (it may mean only two or three years of training); it is not a principle of karate that weight should always be equally balanced between both feet; Aikido is by no means the "gentlest of all the martial arts," and even if it were, this is no reason for pegging it as "an excellent method of self-defense for girls." Interestingly, the drawings in this part are as grotesque and offensive as they were accurate and cute in the other sections. (For example, Asian adults are pictured with slanted eyes in keeping with that age-old stereotype.)

Also, in an effort to be clever and entertaining, the author and illustrator joke a little too much about these "mysterious" practices, thus reinforcing myths about the martial arts. Case in point: "There was a famous boxer . . . who . . . was so agile that he could put his foot behind his neck. We can only hope he did not do this at the dinner table!" That's funny, but in the context of the book it comes off as racist, vulgar and tacky.

	ART	WORDS		ART	WORDS			ART	WORDS	N.A.
anti-Racist			non-Racist			Racist	omission			
							commission	✓	✓	
anti-Sexist	✓	✓	non-Sexist			Sexist				
anti-Elitist			non-Elitist	✓	✓	Elitist				
anti-Materialist			non-Materialist	✓	✓	Materialist				
anti-Individualist			non-Individualist	✓	✓	Individualist				
anti-Ageist			non-Ageist			Ageist				✓
anti-Conformist	✓	✓	non-Conformist			Conformist				
anti-Escapist			non-Escapist	✓	✓	Escapist				
Builds positive image of females/minorities	✓		Builds negative image of females/minorities	✓	✓					
Inspires action vs. oppression			Culturally authentic							

	Excellent	Good	Fair	Poor
Literary quality		✓		
Art quality			✓	

EVER AFTER
by Janet McNeill
Little, Brown
$5.95, 160 pages, grades 7-up

This rambling, sexist story about a fifteen-year-old English girl named Ruth Ellerby features the heroine's discovery that while marriage has its "ups" and "downs," it's what every girl should aspire to!

When Ruth's practical father and "old-fashioned" mother plan a vacation in Spain, they send Ruth (despite her protests) to stay with her recently married sister, Liz, and Liz's husband, Len.

The next 100 pages, devoted to Ruth's observations on Liz's marriage, are filled with stock situations that are supposed to represent typical marriage problems. Within this framework of domestic ups and downs, a flimsy plot unfolds.

At the end of her stay, Ruth says "and now there were Liz and Len, happy in their flat in Homewood Drive and ready to hand on happiness to their own children when they had them. This was the way it went on. This was what 'ever after' really meant . . . this was much more real than anything the fairy tales promised."

As are most fairy tales, *Ever After* is demeaning to women. Both Ruth's mother and sister, having accepted secondary roles in life, are always bending over backwards to please their husbands, reinforcing the old notion that women should be devoted solely to husband and home. None of the women display any intelligence or the desire to do anything but tend home and hearth. Liz's one-time desire to become a nurse is scoffed at on the grounds that she is too incompetent for such a job.

Materialism creeps in with Liz's and Len's projection that if they had money, everything would be "peaches and cream"—the implication being that money is the stuff of which successful marriages are made. Escapism also taints the book's approach to marriage. The problems Liz and her husband face are extremely superficial and hardly representative of the real conflicts with which married couples, especially young ones, must deal.

In sum, *Ever After* is trash.

	ART	WORDS		ART	WORDS			ART	WORDS	N.A.
anti-Racist			non-Racist			Racist — omission				✓
						Racist — commission				
anti-Sexist			non-Sexist			Sexist		✓		
anti-Elitist			non-Elitist	✓		Elitist				
anti-Materialist			non-Materialist			Materialist		✓		
anti-Individualist			non-Individualist	✓		Individualist				
anti-Ageist			non-Ageist			Ageist		✓		
anti-Conformist			non-Conformist			Conformist		✓		
anti-Escapist			non-Escapist	✓		Escapist				
Builds positive image of females/ minorities			Builds negative image of females/ minorities		✓		Excellent	Good	Fair	Poor
Inspires action vs. oppression			Culturally authentic			Literary quality				✓
						Art quality				

JULIUS NYERERE: TEACHER OF AFRICA
by Shirley Graham
Julian Messner
$5.95, 191 pages, grades 7-up

Here is an outstanding biography which provides readers, young and old, with a comprehensive picture of Africa's historical development. Ms. Graham offers a lucid interpretation of Africa's traditional and colonial past which will assist readers in comprehending both Africa's struggle for independence, and the continuous struggle of her people to build a future based on concepts of *uhuru* (freedom).

The experiences of one of the continent's most important figures reveal Africa's basic systems of family, education, religion and government. We also see "things fall apart" under colonial rule and then rise again through the energy of a determined people.

By avoiding excessive praise of Nyerere and malicious accusation of his opponents, Ms. Graham makes a strong case for the liberation of all oppressed people.

Not only will this biography enlighten readers but, equally important it will give Black children a deep sense of pride and of history.

	ART	WORDS		ART	WORDS			ART	WORDS	N.A.
anti-Racist		✓	non-Racist			Racist	omission			
							commission			
anti-Sexist		✓	non-Sexist			Sexist				
anti-Elitist		✓	non-Elitist			Elitist				
anti-Materialist		✓	non-Materialist			Materialist				
anti-Individualist		✓	non-Individualist			Individualist				
anti-Ageist			non-Ageist	✓		Ageist				
anti-Conformist			non-Conformist	✓		Conformist				
anti-Escapist		✓	non-Escapist			Escapist				
Builds positive image of females/minorities		✓	Builds negative image of females/minorities				Excellent	Good	Fair	Poor
Inspires action vs. oppression		✓	Culturally authentic			Literary quality	✓			
						Art quality				

SHADOW IN THE SUN
by Bernice Grohskopf
Atheneum
$6.95, 182 pages, grades 7-up

Fran Phillips is sent to stay with her Aunt Louise in a Cape Cod resort town for one month during the summer, while her parents are away on a trip. She finds work as the hired companion of a disabled fourteen-year-old girl who is one year her senior. The girl, Wilma Byher, is the daughter of a famous musician and teacher. She is sarcastic, outspoken and moody, but Fran tolerates her behavior out of pity. Sensing this, Wilma enlightens Fran as to what it is like to be constantly pitied.

Fran takes Wilma's cutting remarks in stride when she learns that Wilma feels rejected by her own parents. Wilma's divorced mother does not want the responsibility of caring for her, and her remarried father is ashamed of having a disabled daughter. Wilma turns off everyone who tries to befriend her.

When his new wife is about to deliver a baby, Wilma's father shows such disregard for his daughter's feelings that Wilma explodes, becoming unapproachable and vicious. She attacks Fran by yelling out a rumor that Fran's Aunt Louise is a lesbian, which sends Fran running. Then, suddenly frantic, Wilma wheels herself out of the house, falls, and is taken to the hospital. Upset, Fran tells Wilma's father why Wilma feels rejected and unloved, thus shocking him into recognition of his negligence. Both girls end up having to face painful realities in their lives.

Wilma's wealthy and prestigious family, plus the airs of superiority evinced by the rich young vacationers who populate the resort town, exude elitism and reflect an environment that is far removed from the purview of most readers. Moreover, the young people's talk of money, position, and status reinforce materialistic values.

Regarding the lesbian issue, it seems to have been introduced only as seasoning and is in no way developed. Early in the story, Fran is troubled by the suspicion that her aunt might be a lesbian (the aunt's female roommate wears a man-tailored pantsuit), but her thoughts on the matter are never explored.

Although *Shadow in the Sun* is smoothly written, these negative elements exclude recommendation.

	ART	WORDS		ART	WORDS		ART	WORDS	N.A.
anti-Racist			non-Racist			Racist omission / commission			✓
anti-Sexist			non-Sexist		✓	Sexist			
anti-Elitist			non-Elitist			Elitist		✓	
anti-Materialist			non-Materialist			Materialist		✓	
anti-Individualist			non-Individualist		✓	Individualist			
anti-Ageist			non-Ageist		✓	Ageist			
anti-Conformist			non-Conformist		✓	Conformist			
anti-Escapist			non-Escapist		✓	Escapist			
Builds positive image of females/ minorities			Builds negative image of females/ minorities				Excellent	Good	Fair	Poor
Inspires action vs. oppression			Culturally authentic			Literary quality		✓		
						Art quality				

THE MANY FACES OF SLAVERY
by I.E. Levine
Julian Messner
$5.29, 191 pages, grades 7-up

As an examination of slavery from prehistoric times to the present, *The Many Faces of Slavery* is informative and interesting. A careful reading of the text will assist readers in making a comparative analysis of slavery, and in better understanding the need to work towards its elimination.

When dealing with ancient forms of slavery, the book is historically accurate, and the author's cross references include excellent sources for further research. However, the treatment of modern slavery, i.e., slavery in the last six centuries, must be criticized. A patronizing tone (Abraham Lincoln *was not* anti-slavery and Andrew Johnson *was not* well-meaning, as the author suggests!) and distortions of past and contemporary realities seriously mar his analysis of this period.

In a concluding discussion of slavery's effects on modern American society, one is led to believe that slavery (broadly defined as involuntary servitude), while still existent in other parts of the world, has been eliminated in the U.S. Although the author notes post-emancipation violence against Black people he does not deal with the ever-present realities of economic slavery.

Reality is further distorted by his contradictory terminology. How can a nation—like the U.S.—be "democratic" and still maintain slavery? Curiously, Mr. Levine defines Soviet society as communist—that is, in terms of its economic system. But nations like Colombia or the U.S. are "democratic" rather than capitalist. And while he states that political prisoners are held as "slaves" in the Soviet Union "and other communist countries," he totally ignores the existence of third world political prisoners in the U.S. who are in jail largely due to social conditions caused by racism.

Finally, the author contends that Black people are making great advances in this society, despite available statistical data to the contrary. The majority of Black people still remain on the bottom of the economic ladder (slaves?), Martin Luther King's "dream" remains a nightmare, and the light has yet to appear at the end of the tunnel.

	ART	WORDS		ART	WORDS			ART	WORDS	N.A.
anti-Racist			non-Racist		✓	Racist	omission / commission			
anti-Sexist			non-Sexist		✓	Sexist				
anti-Elitist			non-Elitist		✓	Elitist				
anti-Materialist			non-Materialist		✓	Materialist				
anti-Individualist			non-Individualist		✓	Individualist				
anti-Ageist			non-Ageist			Ageist				✓
anti-Conformist			non-Conformist		✓	Conformist				
anti-Escapist			non-Escapist		✓	Escapist				
Builds positive image of females/minorities			Builds negative image of females/minorities				Excellent	Good	Fair	Poor
Inspires action vs. oppression			Culturally authentic			Literary quality		✓		
						Art quality				

40 MILLION SCHOOLBOOKS CAN'T BE WRONG: MYTHS IN AMERICAN HISTORY
by L. Ethan Ellis
Macmillan
$5.95, 100 pages, grades 6-up

According to the book jacket "L. Ethan Ellis is Professor Emeritus in History at Rutgers University. He taught American history for more than forty years and has written six books on the subject for professional historians. This is his first book for young readers."

Let's hope it will be his last.

Superficial and traditional content, ponderous vocabulary, inadequate explanations, plus assumptions of background knowledge, make this book unappealing for *any* age. Instead of exposing "myths in American history," the author reinforces racist stereotypes, compounds historical distortions and omissions, and generally gives readers that all-too-familiar white male view of this nation's past. Professor Ellis' approach to the Spanish American and Mexican American wars exposes, rather dramatically, the deficiencies of his "myth-shattering" technique.

Consistent with these inanities about a mythical, benevolent Uncle Sam, he feels called upon to offer a "balanced" view of slavery. As do most textbooks, he views slavery through Northern white eyes, balanced with a view of the institution through Southern white eyes. Presumably the oppressed slaves had no views on the matter.

Not surprisingly, the author uses the male pronoun for both sexes and mentions females rarely.

	ART	WORDS		ART	WORDS			ART	WORDS	N.A.
anti-Racist			non-Racist			Racist omission / commission				✓
anti-Sexist			non-Sexist			Sexist			✓	
anti-Elitist			non-Elitist			Elitist			✓	
anti-Materialist			non-Materialist		✓	Materialist				
anti-Individualist			non-Individualist			Individualist			✓	
anti-Ageist			non-Ageist		✓	Ageist				
anti-Conformist			non-Conformist		✓	Conformist				
anti-Escapist			non-Escapist		✓	Escapist				
Builds positive image of females/minorities			Builds negative image of females/minorities		✓		Excellent	Good	Fair	Poor
Inspires action vs. oppression			Culturally authentic			Literary quality				✓
						Art quality				

THE MAN WHO BOUGHT HIMSELF
by Peggy Mann and Vivian W. Siegal
Macmillan
$7.95, 210 pages, grades 7-up

The Man Who Bought Himself is based on the true story of Peter Still, a Black man who, at the age of six, was kidnapped from his home in northern Maryland along with his ten-year-old brother and sold to a Kentucky slaveholder. Three years later, Peter and his brother, Levin, were resold to a brutal man named Nattie Gist, who enjoyed whipping slaves.

In the story as told by authors Mann and Siegal, Peter promises himself that he will someday buy his freedom. When Gist dies in 1818, Peter and Levin are willed to Gist's nephew. As a young man, Peter saves every cent he can. At age thirty-three, he is hired out to a bookseller who allows him to keep most of his earnings, and he later meets two Jewish shopkeepers who also also assist him.

In 1849 at the age of forty-nine, Peter becomes a "free man" for the sum of $500. He leaves his wife and children in Alabama but swears to return with money to free them. Travelling through the northern states, Peter eventually solicits enough funds to free his wife and children (it is now 1854, and he is fifty-four years old).

A good deal of fence-straddling marks the authors' discussion of the slavery issue. Presumably, they were striving for "balance." However, as do most white writers, they succeed only in presenting a variety of slaveholders' viewpoints.

The depictions of individual sadistic acts are so graphic as to be sensational. Indeed, the brutality is so engrossing that its causes—which are inadequately identified—seem extraneous. The book also subtly excuses the slavemasters by always drawing attention to their drunkenness, lust or sudden irrationality.

Peter is invariably submissive after every horrible scene—he never reacts on the spot. Moreover, the reader does not get the impression that he shares a camaraderie with other slaves or fells compassion for *their* plight. His sole interest appears to be buying of his *own* freedom.

A significant question that goes unanswered is what does "freedom" really mean to Peter? Since much of the book is devoted to how he earned the money to buy it and nothing is said about how he coped with life subsequently, the "freedom" becomes meaningless.

	ART	WORDS		ART	WORDS			ART	WORDS	N.A.
anti-Racist			non-Racist			Racist	omission			
							commission			✓
anti-Sexist			non-Sexist		✓	Sexist				
anti-Elitist			non-Elitist		✓	Elitist				
anti-Materialist			non-Materialist			Materialist			✓	
anti-Individualist			non-Individualist			Individualist			✓	
anti-Ageist			non-Ageist		✓	Ageist				
anti-Conformist			non-Conformist			Conformist			✓	
anti-Escapist			non-Escapist			Escapist			✓	
Builds positive image of females/minorities			Builds negative image of females/minorities					Excellent	Good	Fair	Poor
Inspires action vs. oppression			Culturally authentic			Literary quality			✓		
						Art quality					

THE MEAT IN THE SANDWICH
by Alice Bach
Harper & Row
$5.95, 182 pages, grades 6-up

The middle child between an older and younger sister, ten-year-old Mike Lefcourt feels out of it. To compensate for what he regards as a lonely and dull existence, he becomes a collector of soda cans and tee shirts, creating a fantasy world in which he is a superstar.

One day, superjock Kip Statler moves next door and transforms Mike into a winner. Kip is a male chauvinist to the core. He needles Mike for helping out with housework, bullies him to practice harder, indoctrinates him with the play-to-win mentality. Kip even changes Mike's perspective about being in between two sisters: Kip calls Mike the "meat in the sandwich." Finally, Mike feels he is somebody—he is a superjock's friend and a star of the first hockey game.

For awhile, Mike's newly found status goes to his head. At Kip's urging and despite misgivings, he treats his non-jock friends like outcasts and even shuns his old friend Alex, also a hockey star. But when the coach puts Kip and Mike on opposing teams, their friendship suffers from the competition. In the end, with the support of his family and Alex, Mike confronts Kip and emerges the winner.

Here is a moving, realistic and often humorous book about competition and "victory," in and out of the sports arena. Significantly, "Friendship first, competition second" is the author's perspective on sports.

Ms. Bach's portrayals of men and women are warm and diverse. Mike has a liberated family—everyone shares household responsibilities—and the sister is athletic without being "tomboyish." To the author's credit, sexist stereotypes are avoided even in the depiction of Kip's more conventional home. (However, the treatment of Alex, who is fatherless, is questionable in that Ms. Bach seems to pity the one-parent family unnecessarily.) Mike is a multi-dimensional character, with confusions, fears and needs many young readers can relate to.

The resolution of Mike's internal conflicts is commendable: In a moving exchange between Alex and Mike, the boys realize they cannot "just snap their fingers" to change their lives; what they *can* do is offer each other support and empathy. That, they decide, is like "taking a vacation from your own hassles."

	ART	WORDS		ART	WORDS			ART	WORDS	N.A.
anti-Racist			non-Racist			Racist omission / commission				✓
anti-Sexist		✓	non-Sexist			Sexist				
anti-Elitist		✓	non-Elitist			Elitist				
anti-Materialist			non-Materialist		✓	Materialist				
anti-Individualist		✓	non-Individualist			Individualist				
anti-Ageist			non-Ageist			Ageist				✓
anti-Conformist		✓	non-Conformist			Conformist				
anti-Escapist		✓	non-Escapist			Escapist				
Builds positive image of females/ minorities			Builds negative image of females/ minorities				Excellent	Good	Fair	Poor
Inspires action vs. oppression			Culturally authentic			Literary quality		✓		
						Art quality				

HEADSPARKS
by Robert Coles
Little, Brown
$5.95, 88 pages, grades 7-up

This well-written book by a white, male psychiatrist is a prime example of why many feminists advise troubled women to beware of male medical professionals.

Sixteen-year-old Cathy is on the brink of mental collapse because her boyfriend, Rick, is finishing high school and will soon be leaving for college. Cathy has no friends, no close family relationships, no interests. Realizing that she is in trouble, she goes willingly with her mother to visit the family healer, Dr. Strong (no kidding).

The doctor's response: "... you don't quite know where you want to go, or what you want to do.... And apart from Rick, there's your own life facing you. Should you try to become a nurse, as you once mentioned you might want to be, or go to a secretarial school or get a job or try to save money and go to college someday? I don't know how to advise you on all that, though I'm willing to try." Some "helpful" advice!

The next few pages find Cathy in "a reverie." She imagines herself in a nurse's uniform. Then she thinks "what an awful driver" her mother is. But things begin to look up. "She would be seeing Rick and that made her glad even though she'd be in *that boring math class.*" (emphasis added) The last lines of the book sum up its message. "Suddenly it was funny and everything was in focus. Rick was *there.* She saw him coming down the hall and now she stopped all the thinking, the wondering and the figuring out. It would be enough to talk with him, to just be with him. Cathy grinned and almost ran toward him. 'Rick,' she called. 'Hi, Rick.'"

Girls, just get yourself a male saviour and your troubles will melt away.

It is unfortunate that an author reputed to be extremely sensitive on race and class issues, has proven to be stunningly insensitive regarding sexism.

	ART	WORDS		ART	WORDS			ART	WORDS	N.A.
anti-Racist			non-Racist			Racist	omission			✓
							commission			
anti-Sexist			non-Sexist			Sexist			✓	
anti-Elitist			non-Elitist			Elitist			✓	
anti-Materialist			non-Materialist			Materialist			✓	
anti-Individualist			non-Individualist			Individualist			✓	
anti-Ageist			non-Ageist		✓	Ageist				
anti-Conformist			non-Conformist			Conformist			✓	
anti-Escapist			non-Escapist			Escapist			✓	
Builds positive image of females/minorities			Builds negative image of (females)/minorities		✓		Excellent	Good	Fair	Poor
Inspires action vs. oppression			Culturally authentic			Literary quality		✓		
						Art quality				

THE INTEGRATION OF
MARY-LARKIN THORNHILL
by Ann Waldron
E: P. Dutton
$6.95, 137 pages, grades 6-up

Mary-Larkin is a Southern white twelve-year-old about to enter a junior high school which has been ordered to desegregate. The time seems to be the late 1960's, and all of Mary-Larkin's friends either move to neighborhoods that are unaffected by the Court order, enter private schools, or employ some ruse to avoid attending Phyllis Wheatley Jr. High School. Since Mary-Larkin's father is a Presbyterian minister, deeply committed to the "brotherhood of man," these options are not open to her. Along with one white boy, whose Unitarian parents belong to the N.A.A.C.P., she "integrates" the school. Mary-Larkin is not a crusader. She wants to be pretty, popular and a cheerleader. At the end of four months she has been accepted by the Black students, is changing some of her values, and is more discerning about her friends and the townsfolk.

The story is written lightly, with wry humor and fast pacing. In the course of the tale, white racists, unchristian Christians and New York liberals who send their own children to private schools, all receive their comeuppance.

It is gratifying to find a book where whites must prove themselves in order to be accepted by Blacks. Usually, it is the reverse. But closer inspection is in order before one accepts the book's anti-racist message at face value.

Black readers, if not white, will be discomfitted by the author's outrageously stereotypical portrayal of Black young people, most of whom are on welfare. Mary-Larkin's favorite (white) teacher tells her about the Black students' lack of material possessions. She has learned from a social worker friend, says the teacher, that the main reason Black girls who become pregnant out of wedlock want to keep their babies is to have something all of their own. This simplistic treatment of a many-faceted social phenomenon violates the integrity of Black culture and insults the intelligence of young Black women. The sympathy shown by Mary-Larkin and her teacher for ghetto youngsters would be less condescending if some positive Black family strengths or some good relationships between Black children were depicted. But this does not occur. Not one Black parent or Black teacher appears in the book. Young Black men are portrayed as class clowns, goof-offs or rip-off artists—none are serious students.

While it is true that Mary-Larkin's white friends are characterized as obnoxious, each and every one of them is, nevertheless, "straight." Although the Black school, which opens in total disarray, straightens out with some credit being given to a new Black principal whom we never meet, most credit seems to go to a few dedicated white teachers and a new PTA, headed by Mary-Larkin's dynamic mother. Once again, white competence and goodness save the day—and the Blacks.

White elitism and materialism are piously attacked. Yet the belief that a correlation exists between high intellect and class status is reinforced. Mary-Larkin's one good Black friend who reads books is a doctor's daughter—not one of the welfare clients!

One might question the cheerleading activity and mother Thornhill's constant baking. But given the depiction of both mother and daughter as strong and courageous, sexism is absent here.

The book's main problem is its paternalistic racism. Despite the reporting of Black poverty, no note is made of the social system's responsibility for that condition and for racism. Nor is Black resistance to, or action against, oppression described, leaving young readers with the message that things are getting better because there are some good, caring white folks out there who want to help. Young Blacks today do not believe this, and young whites must learn they can be followers—not the leaders—in the Black struggle for freedom.

	ART	WORDS		ART	WORDS			ART	WORDS	N.A.
anti-Racist			non-Racist			Racist	omission / commission		✓	
anti-Sexist			non-Sexist		✓	Sexist			✓	
anti-Elitist			non-Elitist			Elitist			✓	
anti-Materialist			non-Materialist			Materialist			✓	
anti-Individualist		✓	non-Individualist			Individualist				
anti-Ageist			non-Ageist			Ageist				✓
anti-Conformist		✓	non-Conformist			Conformist				
anti-Escapist		✓	non-Escapist			Escapist				
Builds positive image of females/minorities			Builds negative image of females/(minorities)		✓		Excellent	Good	Fair	Poor
Inspires action vs. oppression			Culturally authentic			Literary quality		✓		
						Art quality				

FAMOUS PUERTO RICANS
by Clarke Newlon
Dodd, Mead
$4.95, 162 pages, grades 6-up

Considering the fact that children over twelve can digest quite a bit of information, this collection of short biographies is needlessly superficial in highlighting the accomplishments of three women, ten men and one entire family.

In the foreword—written by Maurice Ferré, nephew of the wealthy industrialist, former governor of Puerto Rico, and Mayor of Miami—some amazing sentiments concerning Native Americans are expressed. But first, note Ferré's use of the words "our" and "we":

> The worst indictment of this collective restriction (of assimilation) was *our* treatment of the American Indian. Worse than Black slavery because, in addition to the removal of their personal freedom by being placed on reservations, *we* took their land. Subjugated by brute force, these original Americans were requested to 'Americanize,' that is, to negate their culture and assume that of the new majority. . . . They have maintained their cultural identity—their nationality—although *they have accepted with pride United States citizenship.* (Italics added.)

This astonishing statement underscores Ferré's values. How strange for a representative of people who—like the Native Americans—suffer U.S. colonial domination, to so closely identify with his dominators. The last sentence is farcical, even ignorant, since an historical analogy between Native Americans and Puerto Rican peoples would prove, beyond a doubt, that neither had a viable alternative to their reluctant acceptance of U.S. citizenship. More than likely, the Anglo author chose Ferré to write the foreword because their viewpoints are so similar.

While some valid points are made about Puerto Rican culture and lifestyles, the biographical selections project individual, rather than group, accomplishment.

Unquestioning acceptance of Puerto Rico's colonial status permeates the book, thus limiting its usefulness in today's classrooms. For example, Operation Bootstrap—funded by the U.S.A. through years of self-congratulatory applause, has long since been discredited by analysts representing most shades of the political spectrum.

Elitism and ethnocentrism are clearly reflected in the author's praise of Puerto Ricans who speak without an accent, and in statements like: "But as the years went on, Muñoz Rivera made impressive friends, men like fellow intellectuals Woodrow Wilson. . . ." He then names several other white Americans, inferring that Muñoz' Puerto Rican friends were not "impressive."

Add to these negatives the use of the male pronoun throughout for both sexes, and one is left with an inferior product.

	ART	WORDS		ART	WORDS			ART	WORDS	N.A.
anti-Racist			non-Racist			Racist omission / commission			✓	
anti-Sexist			non-Sexist			Sexist			✓	
anti-Elitist			non-Elitist			Elitist			✓	
anti-Materialist			non-Materialist		✓	Materialist				
anti-Individualist			non-Individualist			Individualist			✓	
anti-Ageist			non-Ageist		✓	Ageist				
anti-Conformist			non-Conformist		✓	Conformist				
anti-Escapist			non-Escapist		✓	Escapist				
Builds positive image of females/minorities			Builds negative image of females/minorities				Excellent	Good	Fair	Poor
Inspires action vs. oppression			Culturally authentic			Literary quality			✓	
						Art quality				

THE SURVIVORS
by Kristin Hunter
Charles Scribner's Sons
$7.95, 308 pages, grades 7-up

The Survivors describes how the life of a determined but self-hating and reactionary Black woman, Lena Ricks, becomes emotionally intertwined with that of B.J., a poverty-stricken manchild who needs love and physical care. The various experiences of these two individuals afford the reader some insights into the misery of Black life in the U.S. and, at the same time, demonstrate the value of interpersonal relationships and mutual dependency.

Inequalities in hospital care, police officers on the take, abject poverty, loneliness, and dehumanization in the public schools are among the social evils that are exposed in the course of this extremely well-written story. But despite its exciting and culturally authentic texture, *The Survivors* is a dangerous book of the "blame the victim" genre.

Ms. Lena abhors most things Black and, indeed, actively seeks to become part of a white world. She is delighted that the neighborhood in which her shop is located seems to be turning white, and her actions and tastes (ranging from her white carpet and exquisite lounging gowns at home to the French decor of her business establishment) embody her basic belief that "white is right and Black has always been and is always gonna be a drain, drag, strain, ugly, dangerous, loud, lazy, etc." According to Ms. Lena, some people should have their heads examined by the government, and the government should "sterilize all the unfortunate, irresponsible ones."

In the absence of any mention in the novel of the system's role in creating the negative conditions author Hunter so vividly depicts, Ms. Lena's remarks (and thus, the book) reinforce all of the society's most racist/sexist attitudes and stereotypes. Ms. Lena comes off as being a vehicle through which the author is telling readers that the victim of society's evils is the culprit, and that the solution is to annihilate the culprit instead of changing the society. The tone of the story also seems to say, "White folks, we know you think us Black folks are too scared or too lazy to work hard. But we desperately want to move up on the capitalist ladder, and some of us are really willing to make the effort."

If read by young people under the supervision of aware adults who could expand upon its positive qualities and place its negative ones in the proper perspective, this book would be an excellent discussion-stimulation. Otherwise, beware!

P.S. Ms. Lena also despises and mocks women, both Black and white.

	ART	WORDS		ART	WORDS		ART	WORDS	N.A.
anti-Racist			non-Racist			Racist — omission / commission		✓	
anti-Sexist			non-Sexist			Sexist		✓	
anti-Elitist			non-Elitist		✓	Elitist			
anti-Materialist			non-Materialist			Materialist		✓	
anti-Individualist			non-Individualist			Individualist		✓	
anti-Ageist			non-Ageist			Ageist		✓	
anti-Conformist			non-Conformist			Conformist		✓	
anti-Escapist			non-Escapist		✓	Escapist			
Builds positive image of females/minorities			Builds negative image of females/minorities		✓				
Inspires action vs. oppression			Culturally authentic		✓				

	Excellent	Good	Fair	Poor
Literary quality	✓			
Art quality				

WOMEN TODAY: TEN PROFILES
by Greta Walker
Hawthorn Books
$6.95, 174 pages, grades 6-up

Among the women profiled in this journalistically-styled survey are Betty Friedan of *Feminine Mystique* fame who now teaches Women's Studies; Dorothy Pitman Hughes, a pioneer in community day care for working mothers; Marketa Kimbrell, a teacher of acting and theater who works with prison inmates; Eleanor Holmes Norton, attorney and head of the New York City Human Rights Commission; and Eve Queler, symphony conductor. Lola Redford (environmental concerns), Marlene Sanders (TV commentator), Gertrude Schimmel (Police Inspector), Gloria Steinem (*MS Magazine* founder and editor), Marcia Storch (gynecologist) make up the balance.

All of the women live in New York City, and most of them have been written about in similar fashion in newspapers or magazines. Of the ten, two are Black and seven are Jewish. Though the profiles are a bit less superficial than other such respectful accounts published elsewhere, that is largely because the subjects are vital people who are concerned with issues of public significance.

This book might prove useful to career-minded young women.

	ART	WORDS		ART	WORDS		ART	WORDS	N.A.
anti-Racist		✓	non-Racist			Racist omission/commission			
anti-Sexist		✓	non-Sexist			Sexist			
anti-Elitist			non-Elitist		✓	Elitist			
anti-Materialist			non-Materialist		✓	Materialist			
anti-Individualist		✓	non-Individualist			Individualist			
anti-Ageist			non-Ageist			Ageist			✓
anti-Conformist		✓	non-Conformist			Conformist			
anti-Escapist		✓	non-Escapist			Escapist			
Builds positive image of females/minorities		✓	Builds negative image of females/minorities				Excellent	Good	Fair	Poor
Inspires action vs. oppression		✓	Culturally authentic			Literary quality			✓	
						Art quality				

THE TRUTH ABOUT THE MAN BEHIND THE BOOK THAT SPARKED THE WAR BETWEEN THE STATES
by Frances Cavanah
Westminster Press
$6.95, 187 pages, grades 5-up

This is a half-fictionalized biography of Josiah Henson, the ex-slave who served as a prototype for the character Uncle Tom in Harriet Beecher Stowe's novel, *Uncle Tom's Cabin.*

Beginning with Josiah Henson's early years as a slave on a Maryland plantation in the late 1700's, the author traces his rise to the position of over-seer, his travels and exposure to the outside world (as an agent for his master), his preaching, his eventual escape with his family to Canada and his subsequent founding of an ex-slave community called Dawn. The last third of the book describes his activities with the Underground Railroad and the northern abolitionist movement, his meetings with Harriet Beecher Stowe (there's a separate chapter explaining how she came to write *Uncle Tom's Cabin),* his travels abroad as an anti-slavery speaker and fund raiser for Dawn and ends with his death at 93 in the house he had built some 50 years earlier.

In attempting to rid the term "Uncle Tom" of its negative connotations by writing about the real man, Ms. Cavanah has only further stigmatized her subject by showing just how much of a "Tom" Josiah Henson really was.

Henson does not appear as noble as he does tragic, and the fault lies in the author's interpretation of his life. She does not seem to fully understand the psychological destructiveness inherent in slavery and the master-slave relationship. The portrait she gives the reader is that of a passive resister who is all-accepting of his oppressors, even willing to forgive them, ever ready to adopt their values as his own.

This is the kind of book that would make Black children feel very negatively about themselves and Black people in general, and would probably cause anger and resentment in them at what Josiah represents. For although he managed to escape to freedom, Josiah is still depicted as a conformist—always doing the approved things in an approved "white" manner.

The book is also sexist. The author totally skirts the role and importance Mrs. Henson must have played in helping to found the ex-slave community in Canada. And when her husband plots their escape, she is depicted as a terrified weakling: "'We shall be whipped to death,' she sobbed. . . . She begged her husband to remain home. . . ."

Add to this an awful scene in which Harriet Beecher Stowe tells about her ex-slave cook, Eliza, who is portrayed as a guilty, willing concubine of her white slave owner.

Author Cavanah has contributed an abominably racist, escapist, elitist and conformist book to the world of children's literature—a book that is unforgiveably shallow and patronizing and would be misleading and harmful to all young children.

	ART	WORDS		ART	WORDS		ART	WORDS	N.A.
anti-Racist			non-Racist			Racist omission / commission		✓	
anti-Sexist			non-Sexist			Sexist		✓	
anti-Elitist			non-Elitist			Elitist		✓	
anti-Materialist			non-Materialist		✓	Materialist			
anti-Individualist			non-Individualist		✓	Individualist			
anti-Ageist			non-Ageist		✓	Ageist			
anti-Conformist			non-Conformist			Conformist	✓		
anti-Escapist			non-Escapist		✓	Escapist			

					Excellent	Good	Fair	Poor
Builds positive image of females/minorities		Builds negative image of females/minorities		Literary quality			✓	
Inspires action vs. oppression		Culturally authentic		Art quality				

ORPHAN JIM
by Lonnie Coleman
Doubleday
$6.95, 204 pages, grades 5-up

How a sister and brother survive alone during the Great Depression of the

1930's is the subject of this juvenile novel.

Thirteen-year-old Trudy and seven-year-old Jim, who are poor, southern and white, are about to be sent to an orphanage following the death of their mother (their father had deserted the family earlier). Fearing this fate, Trudy decides to take off—first without Jim, but then with him. The children walk and hitchhike their way to Montgomery, Alabama where an uncle, aunt, and two cousins live. This proves to be a mistake—both Trudy and Jim are disliked and treated harshly. When their uncle decides to send them to a "respectable" orphanage, the children take off again.

Running away proves to be more hazardous the second time round: Trudy is raped, and both she and Jim are beaten by Trudy's assailant. They are taken in by a Black woman named Hazel, an ex-whore who is being supported by a white man. With Hazel, the children are fed, cared for and loved. After her white suitor dies, Hazel leaves the children and Alabama. But, by this time, Trudy and Jim are able to make it on their own—never forgetting the Black woman's kindness.

What is most disturbing about this novel is its degrading depiction of Blacks. Admittedly, it is difficult to accurately depict a southern setting during a time when life was harsh and racism was virulent without reinforcing racism. But it is possible. Sadly, author Coleman has not succeeded. Derogatory words like "nigra" and "nigger" are used often without any countering explanation. And although she is portrayed as kind, generous and understanding, Hazel is, nevertheless, a prostitute. In addition, her caring for the two children evokes images of the Black mammy stereotype, and the negative attitudes she expresses regarding all other Black people further sully her image. None of the book's Black role models is positive, and the language is downright offensive.

	ART	WORDS		ART	WORDS			ART	WORDS	N.A.
anti-Racist			non-Racist			Racist omission / commission			✓	
anti-Sexist			non-Sexist	✓		Sexist				
anti-Elitist		✓	non-Elitist			Elitist				
anti-Materialist			non-Materialist	✓		Materialist				
anti-Individualist			non-Individualist	✓		Individualist				
anti-Ageist			non-Ageist	✓		Ageist				
anti-Conformist			non-Conformist	✓		Conformist				
anti-Escapist			non-Escapist	✓		Escapist				
Builds positive image of females/minorities			Builds negative image of females/minorities				Excellent	Good	Fair	Poor
Inspires action vs. oppression			Culturally authentic			Literary quality		✓		
						Art quality				

LIFE IS A LONELY PLACE
by James Fritzhand
M. Evans
$5.95, 204 pages, grades 7-up

Tink is a sensitive fifteen-year-old Maine boy who enjoys collecting beach glass. His schoolmate—crude, cruel Rick Camero—is the *only* character in the book who does not have a proper Anglo-Saxon name. Tink's father—macho, obtuse Willard Rowlandson—is a mill worker who wears a "dingy . . . suit with two wet, half-moons darkening his armpits" and his mother, an ex cheer-leader and beauty queen, is a cipher who barely acts or reacts to anything. Tink's older brother, who is Father Willard's pride and joy, is a beer-swilling jock.

Poor Tink, the lonely outsider, spends many solitary hours on the beach, where he one day meets David, a twenty-seven-year old writer who UN-DERSTANDS. But due to the nasty insinuations of Rick and the Rowlandson family's penchant for believing gossip, a homosexual relationship between Tink and David is suspected. The struggle to clarify this relationship, as well as a relationship with a schoolmate, Margie, leads to heightened self-awareness and maturity for Tink.

In spite of the author's feel for mid-teen emotions and conversation, there are many flaws in this well-meaning book. Why are Tink's father, brother and schoolmate Rick such completely coarse and hopeless characters? And why is proficiency in sports viewed as being synonymous with cloddishness and unintelligence?

Ironically, the author himself offers proof that this is not so in a finely-wrought ice-skating scene involving Tink and Margie. In the course of their encounter, we get a glimpse of how wonderful this world could be for youngsters once they discover how to live outside of themselves. We get a fleeting look at this tranformation in Tink, who turns from corrosive self-pity to an exciting sense of his personhood and purpose—a well-handled, instructive lesson in the book.

Central to Tink's development is Margie, a plump youngster who had an abortion at fourteen and who loses weight to be Tink's "pretty" girlfriend. Margie is depicted as a person who is also learning to respect herself and is helping Tink to do the same. Unfortunately, she seems not to have even one female friend, which makes Tink essential to her salvation. This state of affairs reinforces the notion that girls must depend on masculine approval for achieving their own identity.

In addition to the abortion issue, the author uses homosexuality (or the suggestion of it) as a pivotal element in the story. This is unusual, but most current reviewers of young people's books have probably discerned that homosexuality will be the "in" topic for 1976-77. As an early entry in the trend, this book deserves severe criticism for raising (rather conventionally), and then avoiding, the issue. Like so many children's books which purport to deal with racism and sexism without citing racist/sexist oppression or identifying its perpetrators, *Life Is a Lonely Place* cops out. Tink's classmates and father accuse him of being a "faggot," a "pansy" and so on; his father even goes to beat up the man he believes has corrupted his son. Readers know there has been no sex between Tink and David and that Tink is sexually interested in girls. But readers learn nothing about David's sexual inclinations. All we are told, at the very *end* of the book, is that David was a married man all along—which presumably means he is heterosexual. This is a playing-it-safe approach to the matter, with the ultimate message being that it is okay not to be a dumb, coarse, macho jock—so long as one is not really gay. This reviewer felt compelled to conclude that the author included the topic solely to titillate readers and cash in on a new trend.

	ART	WORDS		ART	WORDS		ART	WORDS	N.A.
anti-Racist			non-Racist			Racist omission / commission			✓
anti-Sexist			non-Sexist			Sexist	✓		
anti-Elitist			non-Elitist			Elitist	✓		
anti-Materialist			non-Materialist		✓	Materialist			
anti-Individualist			non-Individualist		✓	Individualist			
anti-Ageist			non-Ageist			Ageist			✓
anti-Conformist			non-Conformist			Conformist	✓		
anti-Escapist			non-Escapist		✓	Escapist			

Builds positive image of females/ minorities			Builds negative image of females/ minorities				Excellent	Good	Fair	Poor
						Literary quality		✓		
Inspires action vs. oppression			Culturally authentic			Art quality				

A QUESTION OF COURAGE
by Marjorie Darke
Thomas Y. Crowell
$5.95, 208 pages, grades 7-up

A Question of Courage is a lively, exciting novel about the consciousness-raising of Emily Palmer, an eighteen-year-old seamstress from the back streets of Birmingham, England. Emily is portrayed as a very real and sympathetic character whose growth is evident in her decisions regarding involvement in the English women's suffrage movement of the early 1900's.

The anti-sexist and anti-escapist nature of the book is obvious throughout. The story begins with young Emily recognizing her anger at being expected to wait on her father and brothers simply because she is a woman. A bicycle accident leads to Emily's friendship with wealthy Louise and Peter Marshall, as well as her attendance at a women's suffrage meeting. When she spray paints on a golf course in a feminist protest, Emily is fined and loses her job. She then moves to London with a friend, Vera, to take on a new sewing position. Louise is also in London and she encourages Emily to participate in a speak-out despite her fear of public speaking. Even though she is dragged off, Emily escapes and returns to her elderly employer, Mrs. Silver—one of the anti-ageist characters depicted in this book. An independent, sensitive, active businesswoman, Mrs. Silver supports Emily and her cause.

As Emily and Louise, influenced by feminist newsletters, become involved in the more violent protests of Emmeline Pankhurst (another anti-ageist character), rallies and window smashing lead to conviction and imprisonment. There is a vivid description of Emily's hunger strike. The forced-feeding scene makes the reader gain insights into the problems and courage of past women's movements.

The useless death of Emily's friend Vera, added to her own experiences, fills Emily with doubt as to the use of violence. Still, she joins Mrs. Pankhurst's march to present grievances to the king. When a riot occurs, the reader feels the kicks and blows vicariously along with Emily—an experience not many books provide for women. It is also noted that some men are fighting for the cause.

Louise sums up the anti-conformist sentiments of the book with a statement that might prove very helpful to young women: "Do whatever your conscience tells you. There isn't one way only. If peaceful protests are right for you, then that is your path but don't feel alone." The concept of individual freedom and guiltless choice helps Emily understand that she can be courageous without participating in violence.

Materialism is reflected in the frequent references to Louise's expensive car, champagne picnics and lavishly furnished home. Slightly elitist overtones color Louise's portrayal (rich Louise leads, poor Emily follows). But overall the book emphasizes the humanity of rich and poor alike.

	ART	WORDS		ART	WORDS			ART	WORDS	N.A.
anti-Racist			non-Racist			Racist	omission / commission			✓
anti-Sexist		✓	non-Sexist			Sexist				
anti-Elitist			non-Elitist			Elitist		✓		
anti-Materialist			non-Materialist			Materialist		✓		
anti-Individualist		✓	non-Individualist			Individualist				
anti-Ageist		✓	non-Ageist			Ageist				
anti-Conformist		✓	non-Conformist			Conformist				
anti-Escapist		✓	non-Escapist			Escapist				
Builds positive image of females/minorities		✓	Builds negative image of females/minorities				Excellent	Good	Fair	Poor
Inspires action vs. oppression		✓	Culturally authentic			Literary quality		✓		
						Art quality				

THE GIRL WITH SPUNK
by Judith St. George
illustrated by Charles Robinson
G.P. Putnam's Sons
$6.95, 142 pages, grades 6-up

Blending fact with fiction, *The Girl With Spunk* covers forty-eight hours in the life of fourteen-year-old Josie Dexter a few days prior to the first Women's Rights Convention in Seneca Falls, New York in 1848.

Through the plight of Josie, who works as a domestic for 50 cents a week, readers learn about the extremely hard lives endured by poor girls and women in that era. Without legal rights, they were victims of many forms of exploitation by husbands, fathers and employers.

Josie works from sunrise to sunset seven days a week, with one Sunday off each month. All of her pay is taken by her stepfather, who beats his wife and daughter as well. When she is dismissed from her job over a trivial mishap, Josie's indifference to talk of women's rights changes to keen interest. She becomes determined to achieve a meaningful life for herself, rather than be trapped like her mother and other women. An old, maverick woman farmer helps her plot new directions, as does a young friend who believes in the suffrage cause.

Josie's fears and waverings, as she joins the fight against injustice, should strike empathetic chords in most teenagers. The author has created meaningful characters, young and old, and paints a colorful picture of life at that time.

However, despite its realistic portrayal of working conditions in homes and factories, the book includes no references to Black Americans, slave or free. This serious omission weakens the book's impact and is uncalled for since Lucretia Mott, Elizabeth Cady Stanton and other women leaders, who are described as participants in the Women's Rights Convention and are characters in this book, were also actively involved in the anti-slavery struggle. Nevertheless, *The Girl With Spunk* can be recommended as a moving portrait of a young person's maturation through heightened social awareness and determination to act for social justice.

	ART	WORDS		ART	WORDS			ART	WORDS	N.A.
anti-Racist			non-Racist	✓		Racist omission / commission			✓	
anti-Sexist	✓	✓	non-Sexist			Sexist				
anti-Elitist	✓	✓	non-Elitist			Elitist				
anti-Materialist		✓	non-Materialist	✓		Materialist				
anti-Individualist		✓	non-Individualist	✓		Individualist				
anti-Ageist		✓	non-Ageist	✓		Ageist				
anti-Conformist		✓	non-Conformist	✓		Conformist				
anti-Escapist		✓	non-Escapist	✓		Escapist				
Builds positive image of females/ minorities		✓	Builds negative image of females/ minorities				Excellent	Good	Fair	Poor
Inspires action vs. oppression		✓	Culturally authentic			Literary quality		✓		
						Art quality		✓		

MARLY THE KID
by Susan Beth Pfeffer
Doubleday
$5.95, 137 pages, grades 5-up

Fifteen-year-old Marly, who is furious at her mother for yelling at her, reading her mail and constantly comparing her unfavorably to her beautiful older sister Kit, runs away to live with her father and his new wife Sally. In contrast to the stereotyped step-mother of the fairy tales, Sally is understanding, attractive and smart and welcomes Marly warmly.

Although quiet and shy, Marly immediately makes friends at Henderson High and develops a crush on her poetry teacher, Mr. Hughes. All goes well until the history teacher, Mr. Marshall, makes insulting remarks about the suffragettes and about Marly's plainness. In response, she tells him that "teachers shouldn't make uncalled for remarks like the ones you're always making." When she refuses to apologize, she is suspended from school. At a hearing in the principal's office, Marly's integrity is rewarded by the support of twenty-one students, her father, Sally and—surprisingly—her mother, whose sarcastic observation that "anybody who can get Marly to open her mouth must be a remarkable teacher," proves helpful to Marly's defense.

By the end of the hearing, Marly has followed Sally's advice to compromise by apologizing for causing trouble, but not for telling the truth, and the incident is erased from the school records. The book closes with Marly refusing to join a group of students who want to set up a board to review teachers' behavior, but looking forward to becoming the first overweight cheerleader at Henderson High.

One of this book's best features is its contrasting of "sensitive" and "insensitive" male and female figures. The opposition between caring men (Marly's father and Mr. Hughes) and offensive ones (Mr. Marshall), and between shrewish women (Marly's mother) and more rational ones (Sally) breaks down the monolithic image of male and female character traits, as does Marly's decision to live with her father. As Marly comes to recognize, her mother is not all bad. A nurse, she is independent and assertive. As Sally reminds Marly, "You had to get your big mouth from somebody, and I guess you got it from Adele . . . and since you seem to be enjoying it, you should thank her for making you a fighter." The focus of the book is the process through which Marly achieves a balanced personality, learning to assert herself effectively, without being offensive, by integrating the best qualities of two women—her mother and her step-mother.

The story also makes other valuable distinctions: between good education and bad; between true love and "the crush " and between glamor and integrity. One factor, however, remains unclear. Why does Marly shun the student review board (for which she seems so well prepared by experience) and choose, instead, cheerleading—an individual issue—as the arena in which to practice her newly acquired assertiveness? In the end we suspect that Marly may still be motivated by envy of her sister's beauty.

	ART	WORDS		ART	WORDS		ART	WORDS	N.A.
anti-Racist			non-Racist			Racist omission / commission		✓	
anti-Sexist		✓	non-Sexist			Sexist			
anti-Elitist		✓	non-Elitist			Elitist			
anti-Materialist		✓	non-Materialist			Materialist			
anti-Individualist			non-Individualist			Individualist	✓		
anti-Ageist			non-Ageist			Ageist			✓
anti-Conformist		✓	non-Conformist			Conformist			
anti-Escapist		✓	non-Escapist			Escapist			
Builds positive image of females minorities		✓	Builds negative image of females/minorities				Excellent	Good	Fair	Poor
Inspires action vs. oppression			Culturally authentic			Literary quality		✓		
						Art quality				

A SMART KID LIKE YOU
by Stella Pevsner
illustrated by Gail Owens
Seabury Press
$6.95, 216 pages, grades 6-up

Imagine starting a new junior high school and finding that your math teacher is your father's new wife! The book jacket summary for *A Smart Kid Like You* is so suspenseful that youngsters would be sure to take this book home from the library. Happily, the promise of the summary is fulfilled. Short chapters with an abundance of dialogue keep the story moving at a swift pace. In its exploration of bright, eleven-year-old Nina Beckwith's adjustment to the changes that take place during the months following her parents' divorce, this novel is illuminating and instructive. Its focus is particularly welcome since most books on the subject tend to dwell on the trauma of divorce itself.

At first, Nina and her classmates in accelerated math plan to drive their teacher, Dolores Beckwith, up the wall. Departing from the wicked stepmother stereotype, Dolores understands and respects Nina's openly expressed desire to hurt those whom she feels have hurt her. As Nina begins to sense her father's happiness with Dolores and to feel a part of his new family, she encourages her friends to change their plans and become enthusiastic math students.

Nina feels that her mother, Charlotte, a busy cosmetic researcher (thank heaven she is not a helpless divorcee) is not an open person. Following a seance conducted by Merlaine, a college student who is employed to help run Nina's household, Nina communicates her concerns to her mother.

Merlaine, who is interested in veterinary medicine and has decorated her room with jars of roundworms and tadpoles, is a solidly anti-sexist and anti-conformist character. Equally positive is Nina's interest in Tom (her friend Angie's brother), which does not inhibit her from displaying her athletic ability by continuing to make baskets when playing with him. Nina's attitude effectively counters Angie's sexist notion that girls must "let the boy think they're teaching us how to play basketball."

A good balance is struck by the depiction of both working mothers and creative homemakers like Mrs. Rafferty, who enjoys refinishing her antique dolls. Both girls and boys are portrayed as being intelligent and gifted math students, and boys are described making posters for a dance. Boys are also described as wearing braces to improve their appearance. Teachers are depicted, not as authoritarian figures, but as people who have problems and feelings. It is particularly refreshing to see innovative teaching methods presented.

Although materialism is challenged, the author does so at the expense of an older female character—Nina's unsympathetic grandmother who spends her life shopping for unwanted things. Regrettably, no other productive elderly people are shown to counterbalance this. The predominance of professionals and successful business people among the book's characters smacks of elitism, but anti-escapism prevails throughout—summed up in Nina's words of wisdom, "Things aren't bad once you make up your mind to face them."

A rarely discussed minority is dealt with in the book—the intellectually gifted child. Readers are informed about the special needs of this group, and another stereotype is broken with the portrayal of these bright youngsters' childlike qualities. One only wishes that several ethnic groups had been represented in this category.

	ART	WORDS		ART	WORDS			ART	WORDS	N.A.
anti-Racist			non-Racist	✓		Racist	omission	✓		
							commission			
anti-Sexist	✓		non-Sexist	✓		Sexist				
anti-Elitist			non-Elitist	✓		Elitist			✓	
anti-Materialist	✓		non-Materialist	✓		Materialist				
anti-Individualist			non-Individualist	✓	✓	Individualist				✓
anti-Ageist			non-Ageist	✓		Ageist			✓	
anti-Conformist	✓		non-Conformist	✓		Conformist				
anti-Escapist	✓		non-Escapist	✓		Escapist				
Builds positive image of females/minorities		✓	Builds negative image of females/minorities				Excellent	Good	Fair	Poor
Inspires action vs. oppression			Culturally authentic			Literary quality		✓		
						Art quality			✓	

JOHNNY MAY

by Robbie Branscum
illustrated by Charles Bronson
Doubleday
$4.95, 135 pages, grades 7-up

The eleven-year-old child of a widow, Johnny May lives with poor relatives in the Arkansas hills while her mother works in the city. Johnny May's grandparents and two unmarried aunts live off of the land, making barely enough money at berry harvest time to pay their debts and buy a few new clothes.

When Aron McCoy's family moves onto the neighboring farm, Johnny May rejoices in finally having a boy she cannot whip, as she could most others.

Johnny May is a warm, often funny account of life in the hill country. The author's sensitive portrayal of the daily struggles and of the values which bind poor white people together provides insight into their strengths and life styles. Her characters are real people who understand the importance of friendship and of sharing what little they have. Given today's urban individualism the book makes one hanker to taste the simplicity of rural life.

Unfortunately, Ms. Branscum's females leave something to be desired. Domestic functions and giggling consume them, everyone takes pity on "old maids" who "turn into vinegar" if they fail to marry, and Johnny May's healthy, active nature appears countrified and tomboyish by comparison to her town cousin Sue Ella's frilly behavior. Regrettably, as she becomes more aware of sexual differences between boys and girls and acquires the "curse'" (menstruation), Johnny May longs to wear a dress and curl her hair to please Aron. After "winning" him she finds her identity through their relationship.

Despite these tilts toward sexism (which could be dealt with through adult supervision) *Johnny May* is a worthwhile book for young readers. Ms. Branscum's account of hill people is educational, refreshing and sorely needed to counteract the ever-popular "dumb hillbilly" stereotype. The illustrations neither help nor hinder the book.

	ART	WORDS		ART	WORDS			ART	WORDS	N.A.
anti-Racist			non-Racist	✓		Racist omission / commission				✓
anti-Sexist			non-Sexist	✓		Sexist			✓	
anti-Elitist	✓		non-Elitist	✓		Elitist				
anti-Materialist			non-Materialist	✓	✓	Materialist				
anti-Individualist		✓	non-Individualist	✓		Individualist				
anti-Ageist			non-Ageist	✓		Ageist				✓
anti-Conformist			non-Conformist	✓		Conformist			✓	
anti-Escapist		✓	non-Escapist	✓		Escapist				
Builds positive image of females/ minorities			Builds negative image of females/ minorities				Excellent	Good	Fair	Poor
Inspires action vs. oppression			Culturally authentic			Literary quality		✓		
						Art quality			✓	

THE BORROWED HOUSE
by Hilda Van Stockum
Farrar, Straus & Giroux
$6.95, 215 pages, grades 7-up

Happily, the wholesome ingredients in this tale of the Nazi occupation of The Netherlands far outweigh the effects of its ersatz frosting.

Janna, a twelve-year-old member of the Hitler Youth, has been living in the German countryside for two years while her actor parents are traveling to entertain the Nazi troops. When a letter arrives summoning her to Amsterdam where her parents will be working for an extended time, she goes to live with them in a house provided by a wealthy and aristocratic German baron, who is an ardent admirer of Janna's beautiful mother. The house must be shared with another family, whose patriarch is an obnoxious SS troop leader. The wealthy, anti-Nazi Dutch residents, who had been evicted on one hour's notice to make room for the new arrivals, had left a Jewish boy hidden in a secret attic room, as well as loyal kitchen servants and Rembrandts and Van Goghs about the house.

All of the Dutch people with whom Janna comes into contact, including her new tutor, are anti-Nazi. Through interaction with these people, Janna comes to question, and finally reject, all she has been taught in the Hitler Youth movement. She then joins the resistance movement against the Nazis (and, of course, develops a crush on the boy in the attic).

Although the heroine is brave and resourceful, her beauty receives undue emphasis. Added to this touch of sexism is the fact that the boy in the attic is not expected to clean his own space, even though he has been confined there for months. Guess who performs that task?

The story's elitism is also of the old Hollywood variety. The rich baron is *so* much more refined than the gauche SS men. The evicted, wealthy owners of the house are such dedicated resistance fighters and have *such* perfect taste—romantic nonsense, as well as elitist. Romantic too, is the gorgeous, sensitive mother who remains faithful to her common husband while loving the marvelous, sad, baron. But the largest doses of ersatz are reserved for the baron himself: While complaining of the SS's vulgarity, Hitler's mistakes and the excesses agains the Jews, he manages to provide an endless supply of caviar, pheasant, butter and champagne to his love's household, even as the Dutch populace is literally dying of starvation. The ethical implications of this indulgence never seem to trouble either the author or the book's heroine.

Yet the positive picture of a people actively resisting oppression, individually and in organized fashion, makes it all worthwhile. Young people would do well to take note of the grave risks taken by many Dutch people to save Jewish lives and subvert the Nazi occupation. And yes, the suspense, romance and drama do make for exciting reading.

	ART	WORDS		ART	WORDS			ART	WORDS	N.A.
anti-Racist			non-Racist		✓	Racist omission / commission				
anti-Sexist			non-Sexist			Sexist			✓	
anti-Elitist			non-Elitist			Elitist			✓	
anti-Materialist			non-Materialist			Materialist			✓	
anti-Individualist			non-Individualist		✓	Individualist				
anti-Ageist			non-Ageist		✓	Ageist				
anti-Conformist		✓	non-Conformist			Conformist				
anti-Escapist		✓	non-Escapist			Escapist				
Builds positive image of females/minorities			Builds negative image of females/minorities				Excellent	Good	Fair	Poor
Inspires action vs. oppression		✓	Culturally authentic			Literary quality		✓		
						Art quality				

LOVE IS A MISSING PERSON
by M. E. Kerr
Harper & Row
$5.95, 164 pages, grades 7-up

When one learns from the jacket that this book's sophisticated and prolific author lives near an oceanside play area of the very wealthy (Southhampton, L.I.) and near another wealthy oceanside community in which Blacks have become the majority in the local high school (Bridgehampton, L.I.)—then, and only then, do the diverse ingredients of this "now" tale begin to make sense. Get ready.

There are two super-rich sisters, fifteen-year-old Suzy and seventeen-year-old beautiful, wacky Chicago. Their stunning WASP parents are amicably divorced, Daddy keeping his favorite child, Chicago, with him in New York

City. But when dear old Dad marries a dumb, fortune-hunting nineteen-year-old redhead from Brooklyn, Chicago (hurt and upset) returns to Mother and Suzy. Once ensconced in her new residence, she begins to spout radical rhetoric while traversing the countryside on an expensive motorcycle or riding the waves of Long Island Sound in her very own expensive speedboat. She also usurps the Black boyfriend of Suzie's Black girlfriend, Nan. She usurps him and more: She radicalizes this handsome, "black-black, not chocolate-colored like Nan," star athlete AND class valedictorian.

So we start with Ms. Super-Rich-White-and-Gorgeous turning-on Mr. Super-Black to some right-on social convictions. And since this book is Super-Trendy, the Black teenage girls avenge their vanquished soul-sister by shaving off the blonde locks of Ms. Millionairess.

So much for the racism. Now for the sexism. As in an earlier book *(Is That You, Miss Blue)* the author gives us a very eccentric, but sweet, older woman—this time she is a librarian in charge of a valuable pornography collection! Other female characters are silly, self-centered, bitchy or weak. It is not saying much to say that only younger sister, Suzy, emerges as having some semblance of strength and wisdom. Men, it must be noted, are not all that much either. And while possessions, clothes, servants and such are mocked, the author's underlying respect for these appointments of the "good life" shows through.

The book is fast paced, well written, and funny, but with some of the humor being unintentional. The best part: Not only is Roger Coe III "black-black, not chocolate- colored" but "he's got blue eyes, which is not too common."

	ART	WORDS		ART	WORDS			ART	WORDS	N.A.
anti-Racist			non-Racist			Racist — omission / commission			✓	
anti-Sexist			non-Sexist			Sexist			✓	
anti-Elitist			non-Elitist	·		Elitist			✓	
anti-Materialist			non-Materialist			Materialist			✓	
anti-Individualist			non-Individualist			Individualist			✓	
anti-Ageist			non-Ageist		✓	Ageist				
anti-Conformist			non-Conformist		✓	Conformist				
anti-Escapist			non-Escapist		✓	Escapist				
Builds positive image of females/minorities			Builds negative image of females/minorities		✓		Excellent	Good	Fair	Poor
Inspires action vs. oppression			Culturally authentic			Literary quality		✓		
						Art quality				

THE CREOLES OF COLOR OF NEW ORLEANS
by James Haskins
illustrated by Don Miller
Thomas Y. Crowell
$5.95, 128 pages, grades 5-up

This non-fiction work describes the past and present of Louisiana's so-called free men of color, better known as the Creoles—a conglomeration of octoroons, quadroons and mulattoes whose origins date back to the founding of the territory.

Section I traces the origins of this racially mixed group whose members are the descendants of African, French, Spanish, and West Indian peoples.

The slaves who were brought to the French settlement of New Orleans in the early Eighteenth Century were not, according to this study, treated as harshly as were slaves in other parts of the U.S. since their labor was wanted solely for building the city and not for plantation maintenance. (Does that make their status as slaves less onerous?) Although the Code Noir (Black Code), a set of laws formulated by the French to regulate relations between Blacks and whites, forbade interracial marriages, a later revision granted to freed slaves the same rights and privileges as those enjoyed by whites. It was this edict which made possible the emergence of the "free men of color"—a distinct cultural group within U.S. society.

However, it was not until Louisiana came under Spanish rule that the Creoles were able to exercise their rights and privileges. At that time, they began to own property, accumulate wealth, and even acquire slaves. They rejected class or racial identification with Blacks and emulated whites; yet whites lumped them with Blacks and discriminated against them accordingly.

In this first section and throughout the book, the author openly discusses the prejudice and snobbery of the Creoles—their alienation from Blacks and their pride in liaisons with whites—as a point of distinction and pride. Yet, he does not pursue these matters in a context that would help readers place the Creoles' self-hating and elitist values in the proper perspective. Such a framework is necessary to foster understanding of the Creoles' value system as the product of a racist environment.

Instead, the author presents the Creoles' negative opinions and beliefs about Blacks, Native Americans and others with little interpretive commentary, which has the effect of extolling the virtues of the Creoles at the expense of others. The gens de couleur, as they were called, enjoyed their separate status, and took many steps to keep their distance from both whites and the slaves.

Although the mediocre black and white illustrations are compatible with the text, they do not enhance it.

	ART	WORDS		ART	WORDS			ART	WORDS	N.A.
anti-Racist			non-Racist	✓✓		Racist	omission		✓	
							commission			
anti-Sexist			non-Sexist	✓✓	✓	Sexist			✓	
anti-Elitist			non-Elitist	✓		Elitist			✓	
anti-Materialist			non-Materialist	✓	✓	Materialist				
anti-Individualist			non-Individualist	✓	✓	Individualist				
anti-Ageist			non-Ageist	✓		Ageist				✓
anti-Conformist			non-Conformist	✓		Conformist			✓	
anti-Escapist			non-Escapist	✓	✓	Escapist				
Builds positive image of females/ minorities			Builds negative image of females/ minorities		✓		Excellent	Good	Fair	Poor
Inspires action vs. oppression			Culturally authentic			Literary quality				✓
						Art quality			✓	

THAT'S THE WAY IT IS, AMIGO
by Hila Colman
illustrated by Glo Coalson
Thomas Y. Crowell
$5.95, 90 pages, grades 7-up

Following the sudden death of his father, fifteen-year-old David (who is big for his age) runs away from his upper-middle-class home in the East to be free of his demanding mother and takes refuge in the interior of Mexico. In Oaxaca, he meets small Pedro, a fourteen-year-old Mexican from a poor, isolated village who sells bark paintings to help support his extended family. In the course of the two boys' adventures, a crisis develops during which David learns the value of respect, pride, and responsibility.

In challenging myths and stereotypes about Mexicans, the author's intentions appear to be positive. David's ethnocentrism is used as a take-off point for affirming the worth of people who are different, and some information about ancient and modern Mexican civilization is dispensed.

However, *That's the Way It Is, Amigo* is not without flaws. One senses that the writer was trying to compose a morality tale for dissatisfied teenagers, the message being "You don't have it so bad. How would you like to be in Pedro's shoes?" Referring to one culture's characteristics and lifestyle as a means of teaching lessons to youngsters of another culture poses problems. Will white readers be moved by this book to question the values of their own society, or will their stereotypic thinking about Mexicans have been reinforced? It is difficult to say what effect statements like "Pedro's calm acceptance of fate, his father's death, the poverty in his country, made David uncomfortable. . . ." or ". . . he felt better with the Mexican boy than he did with the American kids . . ." will have on readers. Regarding the second statement, the author's misuse of the term American to exclude Mexicans and other Latins, who are also Americans, reinforces the tendency of some Chicanos to reject their cultural ties with people "south of the border." It also reflects North American arrogance.

Another statement reads, "he was twice Pedro's size, and he knew very well he had a far better education. . . ." The implication here is that the U.S. is better than other nations even though the story reveals that Pedro is better *educated* than David who simply has *more schooling*.

Also disturbing is the author's emphasis on the physical differences between David and Pedro which are further accentuated in the illustrations. In virtually every picture, David towers over Pedro, who is furthermore always positioned in the background. In fact, David does not look like a fifteen-year-old. He looks to be about twenty-four, while Pedro looks ten. The mere posing of this issue, as well as its handling, is stereotypical.

Although Pedro helps David improve his Spanish and David in turn tutors Pedro in English, it is stated at one point that "Pedro lapsed into Spanish." David never "lapses" into English. Moreover, Pedro says things like "Me good Catholic."

A youngster's reading of this novel might be a positive experience given the supervision of an adult who is knowledgeable about Mexican culture, and who is capable of identifying the author's "lapses."

	ART	WORDS		ART	WORDS		ART	WORDS	N.A.
anti-Racist			non-Racist			Racist — omission / commission	✓	✓	
anti-Sexist			non-Sexist	✓	✓	Sexist			✓
anti-Elitist			non-Elitist	✓		Elitist		✓	
anti-Materialist			non-Materialist	✓	✓	Materialist			
anti-Individualist			non-Individualist	✓		Individualist			✓
anti-Ageist			non-Ageist	✓	✓	Ageist			
anti-Conformist			non-Conformist	✓	✓	Conformist			
anti-Escapist			non-Escapist	✓	✓	Escapist			
Builds positive image of females/ minorities			Builds negative image of females/ minorities				Excellent	Good	Fair	Poor
Inspires action vs. oppression			Culturally authentic			Literary quality			✓	
						Art quality				✓

RUMBLE FISH
by S.E. Hinton
Delacorte Press
$6.95, 122 pages, grades 7-up

Rusty James comes from the archetypal broken home. Abandoned by his mother when he was two years old, he lives with an alcoholic father and an older brother—Motorcycle Boy—whom he idolizes. Real communication in the family is non-existent.

Rusty James has one ambition in life—to be the toughest hood in town. Already the toughest guy in junior high school, he tries to relive the "good old days" of the street gangs when fighting, drinking and fierce loyalties were the order of the day. Recognizing his younger brother's nostalgia for the gang war era, Motorcycle Boy compares Rusty James' life style to that of the Japanese rumble fish: ". . . they try to kill each other. If you leaned a mirror against their bowl they'd kill themselves fighting their own reflection."

Motorcycle Boy, an intelligent, natural leader, has chosen a lonely self-determined path, and Rusty James' efforts to imitate him fail miserably. He does not have his brother's brains or leadership ability and his brother must continuously bail him out of trouble. When Motorcycle Boy is killed trying to free the rumble fish and other animals from a pet store, Rusty James' life disintegrates. Like the little rumble fish "flipping and dying . . . still too far from the river," Rusty James merely exists—isolated and lonely in the glass bowl of his soul. His friend Steve, on the other hand, moves ahead by adopting the American ethic, "go for yourself, work hard and you'll succeed."

The author's portrayal of men and women is decidedly sexist. The machismo creed is heavily reinforced by Rusty James' refusal to cry, his need to keep up a tough-hood front, his faith that his strong hands are more valuable than a good mind. Girlfriend Patty is jealous and manipulative, turning her tears on and off at will. Girls are classified as "good," cheapies to mess around with, pretty possessions. housewives or runaway mothers.

Behind a colorful and action-packed facade, Ms. Hinton promotes negative images and values.

	ART	WORDS		ART	WORDS			ART	WORDS	N.A.
anti-Racist			non-Racist		✓	Racist	omission			
							commission			
anti-Sexist			non-Sexist			Sexist			✓	
anti-Elitist			non-Elitist		✓	Elitist				
anti-Materialist			non-Materialist		✓	Materialist				
anti-Individualist			non-Individualist			Individualist		✓		✓
anti-Ageist			non-Ageist			Ageist		✓		✓
anti-Conformist			non-Conformist			Conformist		✓		
anti-Escapist			non-Escapist			Escapist			✓	
Builds positive image of females/minorities			Builds negative image of (females) minorities		✓			Excellent	Good	Fair	Poor
Inspires action vs. oppression			Culturally authentic			Literary quality			✓	
						Art quality				

WINTER WHEAT
by Jeanne Williams
G.P. Putnam's Sons
$6.95, 157 pages, grades 7-up

Winter Wheat recounts the hardships faced by a pioneering Mennonite family who settle in Kansas after fleeing religious persecution in Czarist Russia. The dark, bare sod house and treeless Kansas prairie make seventeen-year-old Colbie and her five sisters long for the comfort and beauty of their Russian home. But Colbie has a fighting spirit and is determined to help her family adjust to the new land. In addition to doing the housework and caring for her younger sisters, Colbie tries to compensate for the family's lack of sons by doing as much of the heavy work as possible to help her father. The family is closely knit, with its members drawing strength from one another and from their religion.

One day, while Colbie is caring for her three sisters (her parents and older sister, Rebecca, have gone to town) a neighbor named Stede appears to warn the family of an approaching prairie fire. From that day forward, Colbie admires and respects Stede—an American who speaks both English and her native tongue, German. Stede and his partner Bedad, an old mountain man, provide neighborly assistance with the heavy work in exchange for having their clothes washed and meals occasionally cooked by the girls. The Landers feel fortunate to have such good neighbors who help them adjust, deal with insect pests and wild animals, and learn the new language and customs. When Rebecca goes back to Russia to live, Colbie realizes that her own future lies in America.

Written with warmth and compassion, *Winter Wheat* offers insight into an immigrant family's day-to-day struggle with a new country and a new way of life in an interesting historical context that is defined by information on Mennonite religious persecution. Although Colbie's decision to marry Stede reflects the triumph of the new American values over traditional Mennonite ways, the author does not degrade the latter.

The book partially reinforces the half truth/half myth that America was a haven for the world's "tired, poor and huddled masses." At the same time, the other side of this myth is presented by acknowledgement that the West was "won" at the expense of Native Americans. But despite its honest criticism of the shabby treatment accorded America's original inhabitants, the book still supports racist stereotypes of Indians as "wild."

Taking into account the role expectations for females in the post-Civil War period, Colbie comes off as being a conscientious, thoughtful young woman. Yet the stereotype of beautiful women as weak is reflected in the comment, "Colbie could find only pity for Rebecca, so beautiful, so unfitted to this raw land."

	ART	WORDS		ART	WORDS			ART	WORDS	N.A.
anti-Racist			non-Racist			Racist omission / commission				✓
anti-Sexist			non-Sexist		✓	Sexist				
anti-Elitist		✓	non-Elitist			Elitist				
anti-Materialist		✓	non-Materialist			Materialist				
anti-Individualist			non-Individualist		✓	Individualist				
anti-Ageist			non-Ageist		✓	Ageist				
anti-Conformist		✓	non-Conformist			Conformist				
anti-Escapist		✓	non-Escapist			Escapist				
Builds positive image of females/minorities			Builds negative image of females/minorities		✓		Excellent	Good	Fair	Poor
Inspires action vs. oppression			Culturally authentic			Literary quality		✓		
						Art quality				

THE CIGARETTE SELLERS OF THREE CROSSES SQUARE
by Joseph Ziemian
translated by Janina David
Lerner
$6.95, 166 pages, grades 7-up

A heretofore unavailable record of the children of the Warsaw Ghetto has been provided by Joseph Ziemian in this truly significant piece of literature. At the same time, another contribution to the archives of Jewish literature on the holocaust has been made.

It is not an easy story to read, for the genocide wrought by the fascists is beyond the full comprehension of human sensibility. Nevertheless, it is a story that must be read for a clear understanding of human history. Why was publication of the book in this country so long in coming?

The Cigarette Sellers tells of a group of children who lived, in constant fear of detection by the Nazis, by the wall of the Warsaw Ghetto. The book also tells of the adults—Jewish and non-Jewish Poles—who knew of the children's plight and helped them. It tells of informers who benefitted from their suffering and, most interesting of all, contains actual photographs of the children—as boys and girls struggling to survive in Poland and also as adults, most of whom live in

Israel today. The recurrent questions "Did the Jews fight back?" and "Where was the Polish Underground during the slaughter?" are effectively answered here.

Unfortunately, the book is not well written (or it is poorly translated) and it lacks commentary. In describing some Jews' appearance as though there were such a thing as "Jewish features," rather than "stereotypes of Jewish features" conceived by racists, the book also falters.

These faults notwithstanding, the book should be in every school and library. We owe to all children this chapter from their heritage.

	ART	WORDS		ART	WORDS			ART	WORDS	N.A.
anti-Racist			non-Racist		✓	Racist	omission			
							commission			
anti-Sexist			non-Sexist		✓	Sexist				
anti-Elitist			non-Elitist	✓		Elitist				
anti-Materialist			non-Materialist		✓	Materialist				
anti-Individualist		✓	non-Individualist			Individualist				
anti-Ageist	✓		non-Ageist			Ageist				
anti-Conformist		✓	non-Conformist			Conformist				
anti-Escapist		✓	non-Escapist			Escapist				
Builds positive image of females/ minorities			Builds negative image of females/ minorities				Excellent	Good	Fair	Poor
Inspires action vs. oppression		✓	Culturally authentic		✓	Literary quality				✓
						Art quality		✓		

GAME TIME
by Harvey Hanson
illustrated by Terry Fehr
Franklin Watts
$5.95, 85 pages, grades 6-10

Skip Howard, a talented and smart Black thirteen-year-old growing up in Chicago in the 1950's, refuses to play the many "games" his parents and teachers foist upon him. When asked to prepare a speech on "Why I Am Proud To Be An American" Skip courageously gives his honest response. This does not win him a prize, but does help to resolve his internal conflicts. He gains a new self-confidence and one result is that he fills a void in his life by finding a friend . . . a girlfriend.

The novel honestly portrays a Black family who want their share of what they preceive to be "the good life." Though Skip's sense of self-worth is not defined by material possessions, his parents' values do come through in his speech. After exposing all of the harsh realities of being Black in America, he concludes his talk with "As long as I'm rich and strong nobody will bother me." Since the author does not have Skip say that most Blacks in the USA cannot get rich, this message to readers is fraudulent.

A positive feature of the book is that Skip rejects values he does not believe in and resists many pressures to conform. He refuses to hold a "winning attitude" about ball games. He refuses to look for girls he can "mess" with, despite peer pressure not to be considered a "sissy."

Skip is a positive role model because he resolutely does what he believes is right, no small feat for any thirteen-year-old.

The author reveals, in a non-derogatory or patronizing way, some values and mores to be found in the Black community. Readers are left to decipher for themselves the good, as well as the bad, effects these values have for the hero. Despite shortcomings, *Game Time* is a perceptive, humorous and worth-while book. Simple line cut illustrations are used to highlight episodes in Skip's life.

	ART	WORDS		ART	WORDS			ART	WORDS	N.A.
anti-Racist		✓	non-Racist	✓		Racist	omission / commission			
anti-Sexist			non-Sexist	✓	✓	Sexist				
anti-Elitist			non-Elitist	✓	✓	Elitist				
anti-Materialist			non-Materialist	✓		Materialist			✓	
anti-Individualist			non-Individualist	✓	✓	Individualist				
anti-Ageist			non-Ageist			Ageist				✓
anti-Conformist		✓	non-Conformist	✓		Conformist				
anti-Escapist			non-Escapist	✓	✓	Escapist				
Builds positive image of females/ minorities		✓	Builds negative image of females/ minorities				Excellent	Good	Fair	Poor
Inspires action vs. oppression			Culturally authentic			Literary quality		✓		
						Art quality		✓		

MAKING OUR WAY
by William Loren Katz and Jacqueline Hunt Katz
Dial Press
$6.95, 166 pages, grades 7-up

Making Our Way is a collection of first-person accounts of ordinary working people's daily struggles in turn-of-the-century America. Contrary to the period's popular image of gracious living projected in history books, what emerges is a moving, stark picture of the harsh realities most people had to endure to survive. Inhumane working conditions, child labor, twelve-hour work days, poverty and debt were the rule.

Although the authors do not purport to present a complete picture, the selections are fairly representative of various ethnic groups, races, sexes, ages and occupations (cowboy, meat packer, sweatshop seamstress, miner, sharecropper, etc.). Presented with their original spelling and grammer intact, these narratives have an unpretentious, earthy quality which conveys great emotion and power. In nearly every case, the enduring strength and inner fortitude of these working people comes through.

Although *Making Our Way* provides excellent social commentary, portraying honestly the injustice and hardship people faced (including racism), the authors' introduction fails to squarely point the finger of blame at any source or system which caused such widespread misery and suffering. For example, how were racism and sexism used to divide workers? The issue is not explored. Indeed, except for the bitterness and hopelessness reflected in some of the non-white narratives, most accounts speak of hope for a better life in the future—if not for the subjects themselves, then for their children. In the absence of an analytical overview, these narratives are frozen in time, the authors having forgone the opportunity to link an inglorious past to present deplorable conditions still suffered by many today. *Making Our Way* thus loses much of its potency, indirectly reaffirming the American myth that through perseverance, hard work, sacrifice and education, anyone can make a better life here. "Look how well most people live now compared to how things were then," the book implies. The introduction contains another, but more minor, flaw. "In the North and South," explain the authors, "Blacks found their manhood a farce." A non-sexist term would have been more appropriate.

As social commentary, *Making Our Way* is an excellent book. In a society where the antics and frivolities of the elite are usually passed off as the essential stuff of "history," this book is refreshing and informative.

	ART	WORDS		ART	WORDS			ART	WORDS	N.A.
anti-Racist		✓	non-Racist			Racist	omission			
							commission			
anti-Sexist		✓	non-Sexist			Sexist				
anti-Elitist		✓	non-Elitist			Elitist				
anti-Materialist		✓	non-Materialist			Materialist				
anti-Individualist			non-Individualist	✓		Individualist				
anti-Ageist			non-Ageist	✓		Ageist				
anti-Conformist			non-Conformist	✓		Conformist				
anti-Escapist		✓	non-Escapist			Escapist				
Builds positive image of (females) minorities		✓	Builds negative image of females/minorities					Excellent	Good	Fair	Poor
Inspires action vs. oppression		✓	Culturally authentic			Literary quality	✓			
						Art quality				

WOMEN WHO WIN
by Francene Sabin
Random House
$3.95, 171 pages, grades 7-up

At last, here is a book about women in sports that does not apologize or seek to compensate for women's strength, ability and total dedication to athletic achievement with constant references to their "feminine" appearance and romantic involvements. In her lively, well-written biographical sketches of fourteen top American athletes, Francene Sabin depicts women who are "winners."

True, we do not wish to encourage the heavy competitiveness and drive which "inspire generals in combat, business tycoons in industry," and which the author strangely admires. But it is thrilling to be shown examples of women who are committed to doing something better than it has ever been done before, who have happily sacrificed "traditional girlhood," who have succeeded against terrific odds and are being rewarded for their efforts.

The athletes covered are Billie Jean King (tennis), Janet Lynn (ice skating),

Cheryl Toussaint (track), Jenny Bartz, Lynn Genesko, Nina MacInnis and Sharon Berg (swimming), Paula Sperber (bowling), Cathy Rigby (gymnastics), Marilyn, Barbara and Linda Cochran (skiing), Micki King (diving), and Kathy Whitworth (golf). Unfortunately, most of the sports are individual rather than team oriented—those which have traditionally been most "acceptable" for women, as well as limited to the moneyed, white people of this country. No baseball, basketball, hockey or volleyball stars are presented, and the only non-white woman is Cheryl Toussaint.

	ART	WORDS		ART	WORDS			ART	WORDS	N.A.
anti-Racist			non-Racist		✓	Racist	omission			
							commission			
anti-Sexist	✓		non-Sexist		✓	Sexist				
anti-Elitist			non-Elitist		✓	Elitist				
anti-Materialist			non-Materialist		✓	Materialist				
anti-Individualist			non-Individualist		✓	Individualist				
anti-Ageist			non-Ageist			Ageist				✓
anti-Conformist		✓	non-Conformist			Conformist				
anti-Escapist		✓	non-Escapist			Escapist				
Builds positive image of (females) minorities		✓	Builds negative image of females/ minorities					Excellent	Good	Fair	Poor
Inspires action vs. oppression			Culturally authentic			Literary quality			✓		
						Art quality					

HEART-OF-SNOWBIRD
by Carol Lee Lorenzo
Harper & Row
$5.95, 227 pages, grades 7-up

Laurel Ivy lives in a small southern mountain town. Although she loves the natural wildlife of the red-clay hills around her, Laurel looks forward to the day when she can leave Snowbird Gap for the city where she wants to study dental hygiene.

Presently, a young Native American named Hank Bearfoot and his family come to settle in Snowbird Gap. Much to the disapproval of her father, classmates and the townspeople who resent Indians trying to "integrate" their poor-white community, Laurel Ivy befriends Hank.

Through their friendship, Laurel Ivy becomes increasingly aware of the people in her town—of their prejudices, hates, fears, loves and desires. Struggling to deal with the marital discord between her father and stepmother, Glory (the result of her father's affair with another woman), Laurel Ivy begins to see her father in a new light—as an oppressor of women, including herself. She experiences, too, the joy of her sister's marriage and the pain of Glory's death from a job-related lung disease. With Hank's encouragement, Laurel gradually realizes she has the responsibility to try and change Snowbird Gap.

In the midst of the strained relations between the members of Laurel Ivy's family, there are moving moments of emotion and human warmth that are depicted without sentimentality. And Laurel's friendship with Hank has the positive effect of giving her strength to confront the townspeople's racism.

Unfortunately, in an apparent attempt to redress the ills of racism, the author's portrayal of Hank's family becomes, itself, racist. The Bearfoots are a "model" family—better off financially, better dressed and better educated than most of Snowbird's people. Hank and his father possess infinite wisdom and patience and have a true love of all people. Hank dreams of being a missionary among white men out of his desire to save them with his superior culture. On the other hand, Mrs. Bearfoot is shy and mysterious, never emerging from her dark home—a portrait which compounds racism with sexism.

Although Laurel Ivy is portrayed as an active, intelligent and nature-loving girl, her decision to remain in Snowbird is prompted mainly by Hank's romantic interest in her. Furthermore, all of the women in the book passively accept their dependence upon men for emotional and/or economic support.

Laurel Ivy's individual struggle to challenge the townspeople's racist attitudes is of questionable credibility, due largely to the fact that Laurel Ivy has only one friend other than her pet opossum. Thus, she can be categorized as something of a loner, which undercuts the potential of a struggle against racism.

In its depiction of the lives and struggles of hill people, *Heart-of-Snowbird* has considerable merit. However, the author's regrettable portrayal of the Native American family and other flawed characterizations turn a potentially strong book into a patronizing racist and sexist misadventure.

	ART	WORDS		ART	WORDS			ART	WORDS	N.A.
anti-Racist			non-Racist			Racist	omission			
							commission		✓	
anti-Sexist			non-Sexist			Sexist			✓	
anti-Elitist			non-Elitist	✓		Elitist				
anti-Materialist			non-Materialist	✓		Materialist				
anti-Individualist			non-Individualist	✓		Individualist				
anti-Ageist			non-Ageist			Ageist				✓
anti-Conformist			non-Conformist	✓		Conformist				
anti-Escapist			non-Escapist	✓		Escapist				
Builds positive image of females/minorities			Builds negative image of females/minorities	✓			Excellent	Good	Fair	Poor
Inspires action vs. oppression			Culturally authentic			Literary quality		✓		
						Art quality				

THE EYE IN THE FOREST
by Mary Q. Steele and William O. Steele
E.P. Dutton
$6.95, 144 pages, grades 6-up

The Eye in the Forest is a sad attempt to examine the culture of a Native American tribe. The authors admit to having little knowledge about these people, who existed from about 1,000 B.C., but presume to guess and write about what is sacred to this group. Based on burial excavations, the Steeles have created (in detail) religious ceremonies, sacred grounds and spiritual symbols of a Native American tribe. Why tax their imaginations? Why not ask living Native Americans? Although I am a Native American who, like the authors, knows very little about this particular people, I find in the story the same stereotypes and distortions of Native American life that have proliferated in literature since Columbus.

The Eye in the Forest purports to offer fact in a fictional form. To merely state in an authors' note that the book "has only a most tenuous basis in fact" is a cop-out. Young children will swear to the authenticity of this book. Teachers unfamiliar with Native American history and culture will agree with the jacket blurb and praise it as "an engrossing story that brilliantly evokes the life of Native Americans before Columbus." Native American tales may make exotic reading but are rarely accurate, and worse, are almost always damaging to the perceptions of the reader who is seeking some relevancy from them. *The Eye in the Forest* is relevant to no one.

	ART	WORDS		ART	WORDS		ART	WORDS	N.A.
anti-Racist			non-Racist			Racist omission/commission			✓
anti-Sexist			non-Sexist		✓	Sexist			
anti-Elitist			non-Elitist		✓	Elitist			
anti-Materialist			non-Materialist		✓	Materialist			
anti-Individualist			non-Individualist		✓	Individualist			
anti-Ageist			non-Ageist		✓	Ageist			
anti-Conformist			non-Conformist		✓	Conformist			
anti-Escapist			non-Escapist			Escapist		✓	
Builds positive image of females/minorities			Builds negative image of females/minorities		✓		Excellent	Good	Fair	Poor
Inspires action vs. oppression			Culturally authentic			Literary quality		✓		
						Art quality				

THE TRANSFIGURED HART
by Jane Yolen
illustrated by Donna Diamond
Thomas Y. Crowell
$5.95, 86 pages, grades 5-up

Here is an exquisitely written tale, delicately illustrated, about twelve-year-old Richard Plante, an orphan who has a damaged heart and prefers solitude, and his lively and talkative friend, Heather Fielding. Their deep friendship grows from a shared mission to tame the third leading character, a beautiful albino deer (hart) whom the children believe to be a unicorn. In their efforts to save it at the outset of the hunting season, myth and fantasy come together in a compelling blend.

Heather, who is the brightest in her family of three older brothers, is brave enough to tame a black snake, loves the woods, as well in daytime as nighttime, and enjoys challenge and adventure. Richard's characterization is equally positive: He is neither strong nor courageous but is extremely intelligent and imaginative. The respectful friendship between this boy and girl is a needed image in children's literature. The children and the hart are all capable of kindness and cruelty and possess both strengths and weaknesses. One empathizes with them and shares their experiences. Male hunters, viewed as the enemy, appear stupid in their inability to appreciate the beauty of nature.

The youngsters are both aware of the evils around them and of their inability to change the world, but they act when necessary and succeed in saving the deer (or is it really a unicorn? The question lingers in the end when the creature turns the children's wine-stained napkin white).

When virginity is discussed by the youngsters with regard to the need for a pure maiden to capture the unicorn, one is led to question the sexist nature of myths in which *male* virginity is never an issue.

Overall, the illustrations and writing style combine to make this a memorable book.

	ART	WORDS		ART	WORDS			ART	WORDS	N.A.
anti-Racist			non-Racist			Racist	omission / commission			✓
anti-Sexist		✓	non-Sexist	✓		Sexist				
anti-Elitist			non-Elitist	✓	✓	Elitist				
anti-Materialist		✓	non-Materialist	✓		Materialist				
anti-Individualist			non-Individualist	✓	✓	Individualist				
anti-Ageist			non-Ageist			Ageist				✓
anti-Conformist	✓	✓	non-Conformist			Conformist				
anti-Escapist			non-Escapist	✓	✓	Escapist				
Builds positive image of females/ minorities			Builds negative image of females/ minorities				Excellent	Good	Fair	Poor
Inspires action vs. oppression			Culturally authentic			Literary quality	✓			
						Art quality		✓		

INTRODUCING SHIRLEY BRAVERMAN
by Hilma Wolitzer
Farrar, Straus & Giroux
$5.95, 153 pages, grades 7-up

This nostalgic remembrance-of-things past describes the innocence of life in a Jewish area of Brooklyn during the last year of World War II. Children bring lunches to the movies every Saturday where they sit through two double features, endless serials and shorts. Spelling contests are a big deal, and twelve-year-olds are more interested in new riddles than in sex information. Even a yellow taxi coming down the street signifies a very special event.

The Braverman family consists of Father who works in the garment center, Mother—a happy housewife—and their two daughters and a son. Middle daughter, Shirley, is the sixth grade spelling champ and also the self-appointed protector of little brother Ted. Ted is a sickly, clumsy, fearful, accident-prone stammerer so Shirley and her best friend, Mitzi Bloom, try numerous experiments to make Ted something other than "a sissy." The story's sexism is not offensive since, like the blackouts, air-raid drills and radio shows, it is an authentic feature of the period.

Although many ethnic touches bring back old memories to this Brooklyn-born reviewer, the story might seem namby-pamby and dull to today's readers. To a child who grew up during the last years of the Vietnam war, the patriotism which marked the 1944 period and which this book depicts might be confusing without more adequate explanation.

Yes, the life the author describes (minus a bit of the sugar coating) may have been "the-way-things-were" for some New Yorkers thirty years ago. But the reasons for changes to the way-things-are, are not even hinted at in this tale.

	ART	WORDS		ART	WORDS			ART	WORDS	N.A.
anti-Racist			non-Racist			Racist — omission / commission				✓
anti-Sexist			non-Sexist		✓	Sexist				
anti-Elitist			non-Elitist		✓	Elitist				
anti-Materialist			non-Materialist		✓	Materialist				
anti-Individualist			non-Individualist		✓	Individualist				
anti-Ageist			non-Ageist		✓	Ageist				
anti-Conformist			non-Conformist		✓	Conformist				
anti-Escapist			non-Escapist		✓	Escapist				
Builds positive image of females/minorities			Builds negative image of females/minorities				Excellent	Good	Fair	Poor
Inspires action vs. oppression			Culturally authentic			Literary quality		✓		
						Art quality				

I CRY WHEN THE SUN GOES DOWN: THE STORY OF HERMAN WRICE
by Jean Horton Berg
photographs
Westminster Press
$6.95, 149 pages, grades 6-up

I Cry When the Sun Goes Down is a well-written biography of Herman Wrice, a Philadelphia youth organizer. The story traces Mr. Wrice's life from his early boyhood in Crites, West Virginia, to Philadelphia's Mantua County where he spent his young adult years. The chronicle ends with the dawning of Mr. Wrice's commitment to help the troubled youth of this region.

The struggles of Black people to attain equality in American society are accurately depicted here; however, the author fails to analyze either the underlying causes of racial discrimination or the behavior of Blacks and whites.

Women are portrayed in traditional family roles and seem to have been a dominant force throughout Mr. Wrice's youth. Communication between Herman and the male members of his family circle were minimal. While they provided for their families, the men took a back seat when it came to raising their children. It is a satisfying moment for Mr. Wrice, as well as for the reader, when he finds a male figure whom he can admire and talk to. Young Black women are not portrayed in depth since most of Mr. Wrice's work as a youth organizer has centered on young, Black men. Snapshots of Mr. Wrice's family members at different stages of their lives give the work the warm feeling of a cherished family album.

Few older persons figure in the story, but the ones who do are portrayed as highly motivated, loving individuals.

A minority child should find Mr. Wrice's struggles and triumphs inspiring. His emphasis on careful thought makes the point that material possessions or class standing are not the necessary tools for leading a productive life. His ability to work with others, as well as individually, and his acceptance of the consequences of his actions are instructive facets of this portrait.

I Cry When the Sun Goes Down makes for fascinating reading and is the kind of literature educators and parents should recommend to older children.

	ART	WORDS		ART	WORDS			ART	WORDS	N.A.
anti-Racist		✓	non-Racist			Racist omission / commission				
anti-Sexist			non-Sexist		✓	Sexist				
anti-Elitist		✓	non-Elitist			Elitist				
anti-Materialist		✓	non-Materialist			Materialist				
anti-Individualist		✓	non-Individualist			Individualist				
anti-Ageist		✓	non-Ageist			Ageist				
anti-Conformist		✓	non-Conformist			Conformist				
anti-Escapist		✓	non-Escapist			Escapist				
Builds positive image of females/minorities		✓	Builds negative image of females/minorities				Excellent	Good	Fair	Poor
Inspires action vs. oppression		✓	Culturally authentic		✓	Literary quality		✓		
						Art quality				

THE LIONHEARTED
by Harriet May Savitz
John Day
$5.95, 149 pages, grades 7-up

This is mushy soap opera, circa 1940.

The leading characters in this novel are a disabled girl, her overweight girlfriend and a troubled young man—all of whom face obstacles and challenges in the pursuit of their life goals.

Sixteen-year-old Rennie, who has been paralyzed for two years since a motorcycle accident, wants to live a full life like her other friends. She refuses to go to a school for the disabled, preferring instead to attend Ridge High. Having fully adjusted to her disability in an incredibly Pollyannish manner, Rennie is exasperated with her mother who has not adjusted at all. Mother cannot accept the fact that Rennie will never walk again.

Beautiful Rennie is initially presented as a high spirited and independent person who is undaunted by her handicap. However, just when her independence is about to be demonstrated, the spotlight switches to Lee, a handsome senior at Ridge High with whom Rennie immediately falls in love. The internal conflicts of Lee and his mother (the two have been dependent on one another since the death of Lee's father) now command center stage.

Cut to Bess. Her problem is obesity. Bess's life ultimately intersects with Rennie's when the two meet and become friends, but not before readers are plied with information about Bess's internal conflicts—a third shift in the story's focus.

Eventually, the individual sagas of these characters become one and, in each, the salient issues are resolved: Lee finally admits to loving Rennie, Rennie wins Lee, and Bess loses enough weight to attract the object of her affections—Josh.

For all of the author's good intentions, some serious problems afflict this novel (in addition to the structural one already cited). The characterizations of Rennie and Bess are extremely stereotypical. All of their dreams, goals and actions are focused on gaining the attention of young men, which gives them a one-dimensional and shallow quality. A third and minor female character named Jo is depicted as a mere sex object. And although some useful information is offered about the lack of public facilities for handicapped people (ramps, wide doorways, special buses), the heroine's extraordinary beauty, courage and determination exude such implausible sentimentality that substantial messages are stifled.

	ART	WORDS		ART	WORDS		ART	WORDS	N.A.
anti-Racist			non-Racist			Racist — omission / commission			✓
anti-Sexist			non-Sexist			Sexist		✓	
anti-Elitist			non-Elitist		✓	Elitist			
anti-Materialist			non-Materialist		✓	Materialist			
anti-Individualist			non-Individualist		✓	Individualist			
anti-Ageist			non-Ageist			Ageist			✓
anti-Conformist			non-Conformist		✓	Conformist			
anti-Escapist			non-Escapist		✓	Escapist			
Builds positive image of females/minorities			Builds negative image of females/minorities				Excellent	Good	Fair	Poor
Inspires action vs. oppression			Culturally authentic			Literary quality				✓
						Art quality				

FIRST STEP
by Ann Snyder
Holt, Rinehart & Winston
$5.95, 128 pages, grades 5-10

Teenaged Cindy lives with her younger brother Brett and their divorced mother in suburbia, USA. She has a best friend with whom she samples new shades of eye-shadow, a beautiful, but vicious, classmate with whom she competes for the lead in a class play, and a handsome boy with whom she becomes friends.

Cindy's otherwise lovely life is marred by her mother's alcoholism; but luckily, Handsome Boy has alcoholic parents, too. Circumstances lead to the heroine's introduction to Alateen, an offshoot of Alcoholics Anonymous, through which she learns to deal with her problem mother.

Despite the deplorable literary quality of this tedious book, the "twenty million other kids like us . . . living in alcoholic homes" receive an accurate description of Alateen's approach to the problem of alcoholism. Such organizations have proven helpful to some drinkers and their families, and the book may be useful for teenagers needing help in this area.

If the author has any thoughts on the social causes of alcoholism and other addictions in our society, she keeps them under a tight lid. *First Step* does not inform young readers about the corporate interests involved in the alcohol, cigarette or drug trade nor does it cite the ways in which less profit-oriented social systems are successfully coping with addiction problems.

	ART	WORDS		ART	WORDS		ART	WORDS	N.A.
anti-Racist			non-Racist			Racist omission / commission		✓	
anti-Sexist			non-Sexist			Sexist	✓		
anti-Elitist			non-Elitist		✓	Elitist			
anti-Materialist			non-Materialist		✓	Materialist			
anti-Individualist			non-Individualist	✓		Individualist			
anti-Ageist			non-Ageist			Ageist			✓
anti-Conformist			non-Conformist	✓		Conformist			
anti-Escapist		✓	non-Escapist			Escapist			
Builds positive image of females/ minorities			Builds negative image of females/ minorities				Excellent	Good	Fair	Poor
Inspires action vs. oppression			Culturally authentic			Literary quality			
						Art quality			✓

VARNELL ROBERTS, SUPER-PIGEON
by Genevieve Gray
illustrated by Marvin Friedman
Houghton Mifflin
$5.95, 113 pages, grades 5-up

In this "hip" story, based on an actual behavior modification project recently conducted in a California school, five junior high school students learn to "control" their teacher's behavior through "positive reinforcement." The hero is a very short white boy, Varnell Roberts, who is being forced to steal because he must pay daily "protection" money to three other boys. The three include a white leader, Richard, and a Black supporter, Ernie. The only female in the behavior modification group is a Black girl named Levon. For four of the five trainees, the experiment proves successful, and the students end up changing their own behaviors along with that of their teachers. Children engaged in the scientific manipulation of adults could make an intriguing story.

However, the book presents a white male principal who dumps all "problem" children into a "special ed" class. This comes under the critical scrutiny of a white female teacher who approaches the problem through her "behavior-mod" experiment. Thus, the burden falls on the students, who are really victims of the educational system, to learn the necessary techniques for manipulating that system in their own interests. Neither the morality nor the practical value of this approach is questioned.

Although the illustrations of Blacks are generally vague, one drawing shows Ernie going through Varnell's pockets for money. The text makes it clear that the money is being taken at Richard's behest and is used by Richard. Why, then, does one of the few illustrations in the book show Black hands in white pockets?

Levon is described, in a degradingly racist manner, as being fearfully ugly. But when she learns to comb her hair, wear jewelry and make-up she begins to look "just like Diana Ross" and Ernie begins to carry her books to school each day. On the positive side, Levon eventually helps Varnell overcome his tormentor, Richard.

Despite the fact that Varnell's size is a critical issue in the story, the children's cruelty and lack of sensitivity on the part of the staff in that regard are not commented upon. Rather, the message seems to be that a short boy better grow tall or powerful if he wants to make it in the world. The warm portrayal of the female teacher who leads the experiment and who sees herself as an advocate of the children does not make up for the story's many flaws.

	ART	WORDS		ART	WORDS			ART	WORDS	N.A.
anti-Racist			non-Racist			Racist	omission			
							commission	✓	✓	
anti-Sexist			non-Sexist	✓		Sexist			✓	
anti-Elitist			non-Elitist	✓	✓	Elitist				
anti-Materialist			non-Materialist	✓	✓	Materialist				
anti-Individualist			non-Individualist	✓		Individualist			✓	
anti-Ageist			non-Ageist			Ageist				✓
anti-Conformist			non-Conformist	✓		Conformist			✓	
anti-Escapist			non-Escapist	✓		Escapist			✓	

	ART	WORDS		ART	WORDS		Excellent	Good	Fair	Poor
Builds positive image of females/minorities			Builds negative image of females/minorities							
						Literary quality			✓	
Inspires action vs. oppression			Culturally authentic			Art quality			✓	

THE WHITE SPARROW
by Roy Brown
Seabury Press
$6.95, 158 pages, grades 6-up

The White Sparrow describes the urban wanderings of a threesome; thirteen-year-old orphan lad, Sprog—The Boy, who is nameless, speechless and featureless (his face has been disfigured in a fire)—and a crippled dog. During a harsh London winter, the trio bands together, taking shelter in cattle trucks and abandoned derricks. During the day, Sprog shoplifts or works, but The Boy emerges to steal only at night. Conflict arises when Sprog becomes ill and Connie Angel, a junkman's daughter, offers the boys food and refuge. The Boy abhors being confined (Connie locks them in), and when the junkman offers Sprog a job if he will go to school, The Boy is increasingly isolated.

Opposing material security, family and captivity to poverty, friendship and freedom, this book presents a potpourri of values in which social conformity, individualistic materialism and sexism seem to gain the upper hand. Although Sprog and The Boy have rejected, and been rejected by, society, nothing and no one are held responsible for their hardships. Even the gang which chases The Boy into the Thames is not criticized for punishing his deformity and failure to conform with death. Indeed, Connie, the stereotypical female who drives a wedge between the boys in her anxiety to capture a man, appears as the sole oppressor.

The book's individualist and materialist bias is evidenced in its definitions of friendship as expedience and survival as a "rip-off." When Connie tempts Sprog with gifts from her father's junk-heap, Sprog (although spared the final choice) abandons The Boy to rejoin a despised society in which he is now offered a better deal.

The book's best, and perhaps only, positive feature is the author's spare, poetic and haunting prose.

	ART	WORDS		ART	WORDS		ART	WORDS	N.A.
anti-Racist			non-Racist			Racist omission / commission			✓
anti-Sexist			non-Sexist			Sexist		✓	
anti-Elitist			non-Elitist		✓	Elitist			
anti-Materialist			non-Materialist			Materialist		✓	
anti-Individualist			non-Individualist			Individualist		✓	
anti-Ageist			non-Ageist			Ageist			✓
anti-Conformist			non-Conformist			Conformist		✓	
anti-Escapist			non-Escapist			Escapist		✓	
Builds positive image of females/ minorities			Builds negative image of females/ minorities				Excellent	Good	Fair	Poor
Inspires action vs. oppression			Culturally authentic			Literary quality		✓	
						Art quality			

LAW AND THE NEW WOMAN
by Mary McHugh
Franklin Watts
$5.90, 120 pages, grades 7-up

Part of the "Choosing Life Styles" series, *Law and the New Woman* is a well documented, incredibly detailed, "How-To" book. For any young white woman considering the legal profession as her career, or for parents or friends trying to realistically guide such a young girl in making her choice, this book is worth the price. The author reports on dozens of interviews with women who are lawyers. Perhaps every one interviewed was not white, but, if so, this was not made clear to a reader. The extra obstacles to be overcome when one is not white, as well as not male, were never mentioned.

Many white feminists feel that, by discussing "Women," they automatically are discussing all women. But to omit the special problems of third world women, mainly racism, poverty and inferior education, is to discuss the concerns of whites only. This is a common form of racism by omission.

The interviews, as well as the author's observations, detail the problems and the satisfactions in various types of legal work. The book offers advice on what courses to take in high school and college, how to file for necessary examinations, which colleges are best for particular types of law practice, etc. Quite candidly, it approaches the wide range of earning possibilities of corporate, divorce and "change the world" types of law practice. A student is warned that a law degree requires excellent school grades. The costs of a law education are less clear. Feminist lawyers who believe women will humanize the practice of law are quoted, but the author doesn't take any position. Thus the book never questions the present class structure which prevents most poor and minority women—as well as men—from achieving the grades for, or paying the costs of, a legal education. Nor does the book describe law as one important way for maintaining the status quo, though it does describe the desire of some lawyers to practice law to obtain greater social justice.

Aside from the weaknesses described, this is a forward looking, thoughtful, well researched and well written book.

	ART	WORDS		ART	WORDS			ART	WORDS	N.A.
anti-Racist			non-Racist			Racist omission / commission				✓
anti-Sexist		✓	non-Sexist			Sexist				
anti-Elitist			non-Elitist		✓	Elitist				
anti-Materialist			non-Materialist		✓	Materialist				
anti-Individualist			non-Individualist		✓	Individualist				
anti-Ageist			non-Ageist		✓	Ageist				
anti-Conformist			non-Conformist		✓	Conformist				
anti-Escapist			non-Escapist		✓	Escapist				
Builds positive image of females/minorities		✓	Builds negative image of females/minorities				Excellent	Good	Fair	Poor
Inspires action vs. oppression			Culturally authentic			Literary quality		✓		
						Art quality				

SALAH OF SIERRA LEONE
by Mary Louise Clifford
illustrated by Elzia Moon
Thomas Y. Crowell
$5.95, 184 pages, grades 5-up

Salah, a motherless boy, was raised by his soldier-father in an old-style agricultural village of Mende people in Sierra Leone. The time is mid 1960's and corrupt neo-colonialist Africans rule the country, though England still plays an openly active role in government and education. As the story commences, Salah's father has been transferred to the capital city of Freetown and Salah is enrolled in a new school there. He is immediately befriended by a classmate, Luke, and is torn between allegiance to his own people, the Mendes, and his genuine liking for Luke's upper class, top elite, Creole family.

The conflict becomes overwhelming when, at election time, Salah finds that his father and Luke's father are on opposite sides of the political fence. Salah overhears his father plotting against the more honest opposition and divulges the information to Luke's father, though he had sworn a solemn Mende oath of silence. Subsequently, both men are arrested, and Salah is accused by the Mende secret society of responsibility for his father's imprisonment.

The complex story is weighted with over-long passages of boring narrative interspersed with totally unbelievable dialogue. Fifteen-year-old African boys do not use such terms as, "It all sounds pretty nebulous," and they certainly don't carry on discussions about "the Produce Marketing Board, which had millions in reserve," particularly when one of them is fresh from a traditional village life and secret spirit cults! The boys speak to one another in pure American and British English *without a trace of Africanisms.* There is a moment when Salah "lapsed unconsciously into the Krio dialect." (White authors, in book after book, use the term, "lapse," to infer a slip into what they consider a lower form—such as from English into Spanish. No one ever "lapses" into correct English.)

Ms. Clifford's adult characters are nearly laughable. The African women are dominant, stalwart, and the men, typified by Salah's father, are ne'er-do-wells, "Just chasing shadows. . . . Always thinking he's going to get something for nothing." Hardly a desirable image, Salah's father is pictured in unreasonable tempers, in a drunken rage, and is cast as an uncaring, ignorant parent.

In contrast, Luke's perfect family are the author's obvious stand-ins for "civilized and advanced" white people. True, their skin may be a bit dusky, but they are much lighter than Salah. Luke's father is an attorney. His grandfather was a judge. His mother was a schoolteacher who now bakes scones to serve at tea time and never misses a Sunday at the Christian church. Luke reveres *Albert Schweitzer.* No African heroes or role models for this family!

In between scenes of his father's drunkenness and African riot, Salah and young readers are taught to support white style "democracy" over corrupt home-rule with its inevitable "tribal conflicts," while being spoon-fed the values of individualism, materialism and Christianity.

The drawings are competent, but offer little to catch the eye of a child.

	ART	WORDS		ART	WORDS			ART	WORDS	N.A.
anti-Racist			non-Racist			Racist omission / commission				✓
anti-Sexist			non-Sexist			Sexist				✓
anti-Elitist			non-Elitist			Elitist				✓
anti-Materialist			non-Materialist			Materialist			✓	
anti-Individualist			non-Individualist			Individualist			✓	
anti-Ageist			non-Ageist	✓		Ageist				
anti-Conformist			non-Conformist			Conformist			✓	
anti-Escapist			non-Escapist	✓		Escapist				
Builds positive image of females/minorities			Builds negative image of females/minorities		✓		Excellent	Good	Fair	Poor
Inspires action vs. oppression			Culturally authentic			Literary quality			✓	
						Art quality		✓		

DAISY SUMMERFIELD'S STYLE
by M.B. Goffstein
Delacorte Press
$6.95, 117 pages, grades 7-up

After failing her first year at college, Daisy Summerfield, with her parents' blessing and money, leaves home to attend a New York school of fashion design. On the train, she meets Daphne who wears a peasant blouse and reads *Art and Reality*. Through deceitful maneuvers, Daisy switches suitcases with Daphne and arrives in New York City with a new set of clothes, a new image, and a new desire—to study art on her own.

She uses a block of wood found in Daphne's bags to carve her first piece of sculpture—a "Negro" child—in spite of the fact that "she felt she didn't have the right to, because she didn't even know one."

Daisy spends several months carving, buying art supplies, buying clothes, and counting her money. Suddenly she is a competent artist whose work in clay and wood is good enough to attract the attention of Alan Kodaly, the son of a prestigious art gallery owner. The person who introduces Alan to Daisy is—you guessed it—Daphne. (The two women bump into one another in a museum.) Alan is Daphne's fiancee.

The author succeeds in portraying a spoiled young woman who will go to any end to fulfill her selfish aims. At the same time, the author insults artists by conveying the impression that it is easy to become a successful one.

The book is ridiculous, shallow, and not worth the time it takes to read.

	ART	WORDS		ART	WORDS			ART	WORDS	N.A.
anti-Racist			non-Racist			Racist	omission			✓
							commission			
anti-Sexist			non-Sexist			Sexist			✓	
anti-Elitist			non-Elitist			Elitist			✓	
anti-Materialist			non-Materialist			Materialist			✓	
anti-Individualist			non-Individualist			Individualist			✓	
anti-Ageist			non-Ageist			Ageist				✓
anti-Conformist			non-Conformist		✓	Conformist				
anti-Escapist			non-Escapist			Escapist			✓	
Builds positive image of females/minorities			Builds negative image of females/minorities					Excellent	Good	Fair	Poor
Inspires action vs. oppression			Culturally authentic			Literary quality				✓	
						Art quality					

MAY I CROSS YOUR GOLDEN RIVER?
by Paige Dixon
Atheneum
$7.95, 262 pages, grades 7-up

Jordan Phillips lives in Colorado where he, his three brothers, married sister and mother share a secure and happy existence. When Jordan feels his arm and hand weakening during a tennis match, he sloughs it off as a bad tennis shoulder. Then, at his birthday party, his knee gives way and he collapses. He now suspects something is wrong but has no idea it is as severe as the disease that killed Lou Gehrig. Clinical tests reveal the worst, and Jordan begins to struggle with the reality of his condition. Once an athletic outdoorsman, he is now confined to bed or a wheelchair and is staring death in the face. Refusing to succumb to despair, Jordan helps his entire family cope with his condition. In the process, they find new meaning in their own lives.

In her exploration of this painful subject matter, the author offers no new insights and a few too many platitudes. Moreover, none of the ugly realities of terminal illness are presented—no bedpans, no hospital bills families cannot afford.

Another shortcoming has to do with the materialistic and elitist values that are woven into the story. Firstly, the Phillips are a middle class family in which great emphasis is placed on material possessions; and secondly, Jordan's girlfriend, Susan, is somewhat scorned by his mother because she works as a secretary and does not go to college (Mrs. Phillips is a college instructor). Susan, too, has elitist values. Class conscious, overly concerned about looks and behavior, and selfish, she predictably deserts Jordan in his moment of need.

The author's good intentions notwithstanding, *May I Cross Your Golden River?* is lacking in depth and, thus, shortchanges readers.

	ART	WORDS		ART	WORDS			ART	WORDS	N.A.
anti-Racist			non-Racist			Racist — omission / commission				✓
anti-Sexist			non-Sexist	✓		Sexist				
anti-Elitist			non-Elitist			Elitist			✓	
anti-Materialist			non-Materialist			Materialist			✓	
anti-Individualist			non-Individualist	✓		Individualist				
anti-Ageist			non-Ageist			Ageist				✓
anti-Conformist			non-Conformist	✓		Conformist				
anti-Escapist		✓	non-Escapist			Escapist				
Builds positive image of females/ minorities			Builds negative image of females/ minorities				Excellent	Good	Fair	Poor
Inspires action vs. oppression			Culturally authentic			Literary quality			✓	
						Art quality				

CHICANO ROOTS GO DEEP
by Harold Coy
Dodd, Mead
$5.95, 210 pages, grades 7-up

This is a better-than-average introduction to Chicano history and can be quite helpful to students and teachers who wish to learn about that vast spectrum. The book is easy, interesting reading—fast paced though distractingly organized. Many truths and many insights are interwoven with occasional stereotypes and distortions.

Though the 28 short chapters offer much about Chicanos, Chicanas are generally neglected. When we learn about somebody's great-grandmother, it is for her knowledge of herbs, something all old Mexican women are, traditionally, "supposed" to know. The author throws in a mention of barrio beauty queens and also tells us that "long-suffering and self-sacrificing (are) the qualities most admired in a mother." That sums up Coy's presentation of the Mexican American distaff side.

Many historical and contemporary subjects are competently treated. By covering socio-economic and artistic areas the author helps the reader appreciate the diversity of Chicano culture and life. What is especially valuable is that Chicanos and Mexicans are not viewed as distinct *cultural* units, rather both are connected to provide a broad perspective.

Though Chapter 2 gives a good overview of where Chicanos are today and what Axtlan means to them, Chapter 3 starts with, "A Chicano without a song would be like a duck out of water." (Or a Black without rhythm?) Other stereotypes describe Chicano soloists wearing "Pancho Villa mustaches" and singing long outdated songs.

Both past and present discrimination against Chicanos is woven into stories about the lives of many generations. Employer use of Mexican "wetback" labor as competition to hold Chicano wages to their lowest possible level is described. There are also excellent sections on the history of New Mexico.

Another book for young readers about Chicano history, *Viva La Raza,* by Elizabeth Martinez and Enriqueta Vasquez, while not as broad in scope as this work, does not suffer from the defects spotted throughout *Chicano Roots Go Deep.* But despite some stereotypes, and an approach of "Yes, it's very tough for Chicanos but, if they persevere, some do 'make it,'" the book is packed with useful information.

	ART	WORDS		ART	WORDS		ART	WORDS	N.A.
anti-Racist		✓	non-Racist			Racist — omission / commission			
anti-Sexist			non-Sexist			Sexist		✓	
anti-Elitist			non-Elitist		✓	Elitist			
anti-Materialist			non-Materialist		✓	Materialist			
anti-Individualist			non-Individualist		✓	Individualist			
anti-Ageist			non-Ageist		✓	Ageist			
anti-Conformist			non-Conformist		✓	Conformist			
anti-Escapist			non-Escapist		✓	Escapist			

							Excellent	Good	Fair	Poor
Builds positive image of females/minorities			Builds negative image of females/minorities			Literary quality		✓		
Inspires action vs. oppression			Culturally authentic			Art quality				

CONTRIBUTIONS OF WOMEN: AVIATION
by Ann Genett
Dillon Press
$6.95, 113 pages, grades 7-up

The six women represented in the volume are Amelia Earhart, Anne

Morrow Lindbergh, Jacqueline Cochran, Jerrie Mock, Geraldine Cobb and Emily Howell, the first woman pilot of a scheduled U.S. airline—a full forty years after Ruth Nichols became the first such pilot and was forced to resign when she was banned from joining the all-male Pilot's Union.

All youngsters should respond to the story of Amelia Earhart, dead at the age of 39 after an intrepid career; a strong, independent woman who worked at 28 different jobs to pay for her flying lessons and who later taught others at Purdue University, preparing them not only to fly, but teaching them also to reject the concept of "man's work/woman's work." Few of the six flyers represented could be described as feminists, but Earhart could not be described otherwise. It is somewhat mortifying, for this reason, to see that hundreds of exciting photographs of Earhart were ignored in favor of a photo of her being helped out of the plane by a stolid looking husband.

Another interesting figure, Jacqueline Cochran, the *only woman* in the Aviation Hall of Fame, is one of the few in the book who rose, literally, from a hovel to the stars. An orphan, a cotton-mill worker from Georgia, a nurse and a waitress, she later became a test pilot, the first woman to break the sound barrier, the first woman to fly a jet across the Atlantic and establish perhaps more speed records than any other flyer.

Geraldine Cobb, the first "lady astronaut trainee" as the program called her, trained *and completed* the astronaut training program, proving in the course of the tests that women are better suited to isolation, more stable under stress conditions, have greater resistance to heat, noise and pain, and MOST IMPORTANT, cost less, because it costs $50,000 *per pound* to hurl anyone into orbit! Despite all this, the program to train women astronauts was "cancelled as quietly as it was begun" and Geraldine Cobb now works for the Amazonia Airlift Service (which flies doctors, missionaries and supplies to Indians who would not need doctors, missionaries *or* supplies if the white man had not messed them up in the first place).

This book is written in an easy-to-read style, with interesting details about some of the women. However, there is something "lady-like" about it that turns all the wildness of the women's dreams into neat little scenarios.

	ART	WORDS		ART	WORDS		ART	WORDS	N.A.
anti-Racist			non-Racist		✓	Racist omission / commission			
anti-Sexist		✓	non-Sexist			Sexist			
anti-Elitist			non-Elitist			Elitist		✓	
anti-Materialist			non-Materialist		✓	Materialist			
anti-Individualist			non-Individualist		✓	Individualist			
anti-Ageist			non-Ageist			Ageist			✓
anti-Conformist		✓	non-Conformist			Conformist			
anti-Escapist			non-Escapist		✓	Escapist			
Builds positive image of females/ minorities		✓	Builds negative image of females/ minorities				Excellent	Good	Fair	Poor
Inspires action vs. oppression			Culturally authentic			Literary quality		✓		
						Art quality				

LION YELLOW
by Betty Dinneen
illustrated by Charles Robinson
Henry Z. Walck
$6.95, 169 pages, grades 7-up

Lion Yellow is a beautifully written tale about a British family who are wardens on a game reserve in Kenya, and a lion family living on that reserve. Their stories are intertwined. Soldani, the established head of the lion pride, is threatened when his authority is challenged by Black Prince, a strange, formidable lion that suddenly appears from unknown parts. At the same time, the wardenship of Ben Thorne and his family over Mbuyu Game Park is questioned. A neighboring people claim the game park land as theirs by ancestral birthright. The Kenyan government must decide whether these people shall graze their cattle on the park land or whether the park shall remain a haven for animals and tourists.

Anticipation grows as the family awaits a visit from Mr. Likimani, the government man from Nairobi. Meanwhile, the author heaps adventure upon adventure. The children, Robin and David, meet up with a rampaging rhino, wild dogs, cackling hyenas, scavenger jackals, and lions, keeping a reader in page-turning suspense. Predictably, Soldani defeats the invading lion and we can presume that Mr. Likimani will decide in favor of keeping the game reserve.

The pluses in this book are many. With the importance of wild life conservation as its major statement, the book also seeks to express the validity of the land claim. In this regard, the following statement, made by Ben Thorne to his son, is commendable: "Kenya's African-run now. It's time for the European to move over." Also noteworthy, Ms. Dinneen's portrait of animal personalities and human-animal relationships is sensitive, and the relationship of the children to the environment, equally so. In addition, the finely crafted story is culturally informative about the Masai people.

Unfortunately, *Lion Yellow* is plagued with sexism. Robin and David are gross stereotypes. With Tarzan as his idol, David calls himself "Lion Boy," and is strong, daring and fearless. He is usually occupied rescuing sister Robin or coaxing away her tears.

The African characters, though present, are nearly invisible and are often cast as big playmate or as chauffeur to the children. Only Mr. Likimani achieves some distinction due to his decision making power.

A study in symbolism, the story clearly establishes a parallel between the invading lion and Mr. Likimani. The one is an obvious contender for rule over the park lions; the other could be named a contender for rule over the park land. The one is black-maned, and the other is black-skinned. Both are finally overcome.

A disturbing undertone of elitism and Eurocentrism also mars the story. The Thornes are aristocrats of the bush, protecting it from insensitive "others." The name of the claim-making people is noteworthy on this account. "Wageni" is the Swahili word for "strangers"—a curious label for Africans in Africa. And, while few young readers can translate the frequently used Swahili terms (the author neglected to include a glossary), innumerable references by the European characters to "our land," "our park," "our home," etc., and allusions to the Wageni people as outsiders, occur in precise English phrasing.

Lastly, the bright and rainbow-tinted descriptions of the author were lost to the vision of the artist. His black and white drawings are not only devoid of color, but also detail, and the facelessness of the Africans is racially insensitive and wholly inexcusable.

	ART	WORDS		ART	WORDS			ART	WORDS	N.A.
anti-Racist			non-Racist			Racist	omission	✓	✓	
							commission			
anti-Sexist			non-Sexist	✓		Sexist			✓	
anti-Elitist			non-Elitist	✓		Elitist			✓	
anti-Materialist		✓	non-Materialist	✓		Materialist				
anti-Individualist			non-Individualist	✓	✓	Individualist				
anti-Ageist			non-Ageist			Ageist				✓
anti-Conformist			non-Conformist	✓	✓	Conformist				
anti-Escapist			non-Escapist	✓	✓	Escapist				
Builds positive image of females/minorities			Builds negative image of (females/minorities)		✓		Excellent	Good	Fair	Poor
Inspires action vs. oppression			Culturally authentic			Literary quality		✓		
						Art quality				✓

WOMEN IN SPORTS: TENNIS
by Marion Meade
Harvey House
$4.97, 78 pages, grades 5-up

How could a "well-known feminist" end a chapter on tennis star Chris Evert with Chris's statement, ". . . if I don't get married, what am I going to do when I'm thirty?" and conclude with Margaret Court's disclaimer, ". . . I'm not Women's Lib. I'm just a wife and mother who plays tennis. . . ."

Even when a book on women in sports is part of a supposedly "feminist" series on the subject, the publishing industry seems to find it impossible to produce an unequivocally feminist book. Authors still feel compelled to apologize for success and reaffirm that a woman's place is primarily in the home. It's a shame, for this book of biographies about five ranking tennis stars—the two above plus Billie Jean King, Rosie Casals and Evonne Goolagong Cawley—almost makes it. Parts are very good, with little emphasis placed on the "glamour" and "femininity" of its subjects—an unfortunate feature of many women's sports books.

Written in a fast-paced, lively style, Ms. Meade examines the early lives of these women, their strong dedication to tennis and their courageous struggle for better treatment of women in the tennis world. There is the implication, though, that equality in sports means primarily equal pay, and the author seems to feel that *this* fight, and therefore THE fight, has been won. I would question whether things are all that good and whether the cheesecake, "lace-panties era" is really over, as the author asserts.

Also naive is the assumption that tennis is no longer a "snobbish sport" enjoyed only by the rich. If class were not still a factor, why, we may ask, was it necessary for the aboriginal-descended Evonne Goolagong to be adopted by a wealthy white Australian and given deportment and speech lessons to make her "poised and polished"? Surely such qualities do not help one's serve.

	ART	WORDS		ART	WORDS		ART	WORDS	N.A.
anti-Racist			non-Racist			Racist omission / commission			✓
anti-Sexist			non-Sexist			Sexist		✓	
anti-Elitist			non-Elitist			Elitist		✓	
anti-Materialist			non-Materialist			Materialist		✓	
anti-Individualist			non-Individualist			Individualist		✓	
anti-Ageist			non-Ageist			Ageist			✓
anti-Conformist			non-Conformist		✓	Conformist			
anti-Escapist			non-Escapist		✓	Escapist			
Builds positive image of females/ minorities			Builds negative image of females/ minorities				Excellent	Good	Fair	Poor
Inspires action vs. oppression			Culturally authentic			Literary quality / Art quality		✓	

THE SOONG SISTERS
by Roby Eunson
photographs
Franklin Watts
$5.90, 133 pages, grades 8-up

Eling, Chingling and Mayling Soong were born into a wealthy Shanghai family. Their father, Charlie Jones Soong, believed his daughters should be treated equally with his sons—a very progressive attitude given the feudalistic, tradition-bound thinking which prevailed in turn-of-the-century China. So the sisters were sent to school in the U.S., which exposed them to American values, lifestyles and friends.

Eventually, all three were wed to wealthy and/or influential men—Eling to H.H. Kung, from one of China's richest banking families; Chingling to Dr. Sun Yat-sen, and Mayling to General Chiang Kai-shek. Eling's and Mayling's marriages were motivated by the desire of the families to extend their economic and political power. But Chingling's marriage to the politically active Dr. Sun was motivated by conviction (her family disapproved of the match because Dr. Sun was already married by childhood arrangement).

Regrettably, Ms. Eunson's biography emphasizes the personal lives of the Soongs over their strongly held political beliefs. The differences between Chingling and her sisters symbolized the basic contradictions in Chinese society—between the interests of the wealthy few and the needs of the starving many. Failing to tackle these basic ideological issues, Ms. Eunson has created a vapid book.

The author's sloppy distortions of Chinese history and traditions border on the embarrassing. Also, though the sisters are consistently described as being strong, courageous, determined, etc., sexism prevails. They are constantly identified in terms of the men in their lives—first their father, then their husbands—implying that, alone, they could not have sustained such strong principles. In particular, leftist Chingling is continually described as being naive and idealistic. The author apparently cannot accept that a wealthy woman in her right mind would willingly give up a life of privilege.

Only one valuable lesson can be learned from this chronicle. The story of the Soongs reveals how people can start working for the same goals and end up fighting each other. But the biography fails to delineate the changes that occurred in the Soong sisters' development and, thus, does not help readers understand the dynamics of change.

	ART	WORDS		ART	WORDS		ART	WORDS	N.A.
anti-Racist			non-Racist			Racist omission / commission			✓
anti-Sexist			non-Sexist			Sexist			✓
anti-Elitist			non-Elitist			Elitist			✓
anti-Materialist			non-Materialist			Materialist			✓
anti-Individualist			non-Individualist			Individualist		✓	
anti-Ageist		✓	non-Ageist			Ageist			
anti-Conformist			non-Conformist		✓	Conformist			
anti-Escapist			non-Escapist		✓	Escapist			
Builds positive image of females/minorities			Builds negative image of females/minorities				Excellent	Good	Fair	Poor
Inspires action vs. oppression			Culturally authentic			Literary quality			✓	
						Art quality				

WOMEN IN TELEVISION
by Anita Klever
photographs
Westminster Press
$5.95, 142 pages, grades 7-up

Women in all areas of television work were interviewed and their responses recorded to comprise this shabbily edited book. The women comment on the skills or abilities their work entails, how they landed their jobs, their experiences with sexism, and offer advice to young women readers.

Endless quotations follow, one on top of the other, with inadequate information given as to what type of TV station the person quoted works for. Not knowing whether a station is in a small or large city, or whether it is commercial or public, and unfamiliarity with all of the technical terms that are freely used, set up reader resistance to this onslaught. One egotistical woman after another irritatingly describes how indispensable she is, and reader annoyance is compounded as half a dozen of the women quoted use the male pronoun to signify both sexes. Surely, the writer and/or editor ought to have corrected this offense.

A director advises other women: "You have to *not* scream, not yell, not get emotional. I have watched other girls (sic) here trying to direct. They often don't have a tone of authority. I have found that when I direct, my voice automatically drops in tone. It gets very low, very calm, no matter what happens.'' The anti-female insinuations of this director are seemingly those of the author and of many of the contributors in this how-to compendium (the women who work on the technical side of the TV business seem to have more modesty and less loyalty to the profession).

The most serious drawback of the book is that not *one* woman questions the way the TV industry functions, its commercialism, the mindless garbage which it produces, the pervasive sexism of electronic media messages or the cutthroat competition within the industry. Clearly they, like the author, feel that getting women to do man's work (just as well as, or better than a man) is the essence of feminism.

After the women finish telling us how marvelous they are, the book begins to improve. How they found their jobs and overcame male resistance is interesting, credit being given often to pressure from the government and from the National Organization for Women. Luck is also cited as a factor, but typing skills and the willingness to work for less money than a man emerge as being the usual door openers.

	ART	WORDS		ART	WORDS			ART	WORDS	N.A.
anti-Racist			non-Racist		✓	Racist	omission / commission			
anti-Sexist			non-Sexist			Sexist			✓	
anti-Elitist			non-Elitist			Elitist			✓	
anti-Materialist			non-Materialist			Materialist			✓	
anti-Individualist			non-Individualist			Individualist			✓	
anti-Ageist			non-Ageist		✓	Ageist				
anti-Conformist		✓	non-Conformist			Conformist				
anti-Escapist		✓	non-Escapist			Escapist				
Builds positive image of females/minorities			Builds negative image of females/minorities				Excellent	Good	Fair	Poor
Inspires action vs. oppression			Culturally authentic			Literary quality				✓
						Art quality				

GARDEN OF BROKEN GLASS
by Emily Cheney Neville
Delacorte Press
$5.95, 215 pages, grades 6-up

This is a story of wonderful young people, struggling against heavy odds to avoid being mortally scarred by the sharp edges of a racist and uncaring society.

Brian Moody is a thirteen-year-old white boy living on welfare in a predominantly Black St. Louis neighborhood. Brian lives with an alcoholic mother (his father deserted years before) who takes out her misery on him, and with a younger brother and older sister whom she favors. *Garden* describes how Brian emerges out of numb withdrawal and begins to develop relationships with other children, as well as with his brother and sister.

The shock of his mother's hospitalization contributes to setting the development process in motion, as does the friendly concern of "Fat" Martha, a Black schoolmate and neighbor who cannot comprehend Brian's relatives' lack of concern for him. "'That boy don't know about nothin.' She was so used to her own relatives piling in and out on each other in times of trouble that she couldn't imagine what it would be like to be without cousins."

Dwayne Yale and his vital, spunky girlfriend, Melvita, are two other Black junior high school youngsters whose paths cross Brian's, and whose sagas provide a subplot that is even more intriguing than Brian's story. The three Black characters are also dirt poor, but their families care about them, even though they may not always be sympathetic. Dwayne, trying to make some money to match Melvita's babysitting earnings, joins two older boys in an evening of mugging elderly Blacks. Revolted by the episode, he experiences a severe emotional reaction which results in his doing some reading and thinking. As the book ends, Dwayne is becoming interested in the political ideas of Martha's activist boyfriend.

The oppression of poverty and racism is depicted without evoking sentimental pity for the young characters, who have strengths and are lovable, but who are not idealized. The *Garden of Broken Glass* shows us a spaghetti, Kool-Aid and soda pop world of poverty in which humor, warmth and concern for others are the key to survival and growth.

	ART	WORDS		ART	WORDS			ART	WORDS	N.A.
anti-Racist		✓	non-Racist			Racist	omission			
							commission			
anti-Sexist		✓	non-Sexist			Sexist				
anti-Elitist		✓	non-Elitist			Elitist				
anti-Materialist		✓	non-Materialist			Materialist				
anti-Individualist		✓	non-Individualist			Individualist				
anti-Ageist			non-Ageist	✓		Ageist				
anti-Conformist		✓	non-Conformist			Conformist				
anti-Escapist		✓	non-Escapist			Escapist				
Builds positive image of females/ minorities			Builds negative image of females/ minorities		✓			Excellent	Good	Fair	Poor
Inspires action vs. oppression		✓	Culturally authentic		✓	Literary quality	✓			
						Art quality	✓			

KELLY'S CREEK
by Doris Buchanan Smith
illustrated by Alan Tiegreen
Thomas Y. Crowell
$5.95, 70 pages, grades 6-up

Because of a lack of physical coordination caused by brain damage, nine-year-old Kelly cannot ride a bike, catch a football or write his name. He is in a "special" class for handicapped children and is often the brunt of his schoolmates' laughter. His parents constantly pressure him to "improve" his schoolwork, and his sister Shannon's excellent academic standing is a painful daily reminder of his own ineptitude.

The only place where Kelly feels good about himself is at the marshy creek behind his house. No longer clumsy and tongue tied, he is at his best there, observing the marsh's natural wildlife and talking with Phillip, a college biology student.

The central message of *Kelly's Creek* is that although people may have handicaps, they are not totally different from so-called "normal" people. The author's portrayal of Kelly is refreshingly realistic in its statement that daily struggles and perseverance are necessary for overcoming problems and achieving self-respect. The story reveals how pressures to conform to societal standards of normalcy are unfair and debilitating to handicapped persons who do not wish to be patronized or pitied. But girls fare poorly. Shannon, Kelly's sister, is bossy, competitive, manipulative and a tattletale—and of course, she giggles a lot. Phillip empathizes with Kelly's difficulties since they both "know about sisters." Significantly, the one person who understands Kelly is a male.

The book perpetuates the concept that children and adults are adversaries, as though a silent generational war is natural. In his fight to be understood on his own terms, Kelly notes that "adults could always win." This sense of powerlessness in young people is real enough, but by not depicting a non-combative relationship between Kelly and some adult (still a college student, Phillip is not accorded full adult status), the author has reinforced an unserviceable myth.

Kelly's Creek holds its own as a sensitive book about handicapped children struggling for self-identity and acceptance, despite its flaws.

	ART	WORDS		ART	WORDS			ART	WORDS	N.A.
anti-Racist			non-Racist		✓	Racist	omission	✓		
							commission			
anti-Sexist			non-Sexist	✓		Sexist			✓	
anti-Elitist			non-Elitist	✓		Elitist			✓	
anti-Materialist			non-Materialist	✓	✓	Materialist				
anti-Individualist			non-Individualist	✓		Individualist			✓	
anti-Ageist			non-Ageist			Ageist				✓
anti-Conformist			non-Conformist	✓	✓	Conformist				
anti-Escapist			non-Escapist	✓	✓	Escapist				
Builds positive image of females/minorities			Builds negative image of females/minorities				Excellent	Good	Fair	Poor
Inspires action vs. oppression			Culturally authentic			Literary quality		✓		
						Art quality			✓	

LONG MAN'S SONG
by Joyce Rockwood
Holt, Rinehart & Winston
$6.95, 207 pages, grades 6-up

This book is about a young Cherokee apprentice "medicine man," his family, clan and village. The story takes place as the boy, Soaring Hawk, comes into manhood. He is tested for proficiency at his art by his teacher, goes through trials and plots, heals his sister, finds a woman to love and learns the complexities of life that go with adulthood.

On the whole, it is an excellent book, told with much respect for, and accuracy about, Cherokee life. The author seems to have a special insight into Cherokee humor and human relations.

There are, however, one major and two minor flaws which reinforce racist attitudes. One is a common phenomenon, that of giving the "good guys" names that connote heroism and the "bad guys" names that connote sneakiness or another unacceptable trait. Thus, the central figure is the likeable Soaring Hawk; a certain unlikeable figure is named Scratcher. Why not use untranslated Cherokee names, which are available? A book about the Vietnamese would not translate *their* names into English.

The second minor flaw is that Soaring Hawk complains about the oppressive restrictions placed upon him and his family by the clan system. The Cherokee clan system is complex, but is not tight or oppressive. There are too many fictional Indian heroes who are described as champing at the bit of their "restrictive" cultures.

The major flaw is that Cherokee medicine and doctoring are presented as solely spiritual and magical arts. That is a far too common assumption about all Indian medicine, when in fact most Indian nations, especially the Southeastern peoples, had medical practices which were far advanced over those of Europe and the white settlers of the same period.

Those flaws do not seriously mar the story, and the book is easily the best to come out in a while. It is engaging, instructive and recommended.

	ART	WORDS		ART	WORDS			ART	WORDS	N.A.
anti-Racist		✓	non-Racist			Racist omission / commission				
anti-Sexist			non-Sexist		✓	Sexist				
anti-Elitist		✓	non-Elitist			Elitist				
anti-Materialist		✓	non-Materialist			Materialist				
anti-Individualist		✓	non-Individualist			Individualist				
anti-Ageist		✓	non-Ageist			Ageist				
anti-Conformist		✓	non-Conformist			Conformist				
anti-Escapist			non-Escapist		✓	Escapist				
Builds positive image of females/minorities		✓	Builds negative image of females/minorities					Excellent	Good	Fair	Poor
Inspires action vs. oppression			Culturally authentic		✓	Literary quality			✓		
						Art quality					

HEADMAN
by Kin Platt
Greenwillow
$5.95, 186 pages, grades 7-up

The main character of this horribly hackneyed slice of contemporary urban drama is fifteen-year-old Owen Kirby, the friendless son of an alcoholic mother (his father was killed in a barroom brawl).

We first meet Owen as he is being attacked by three youths brandishing switch blades, chains, and tire irons. The reason for this apparently unprovoked attack is unstated. Owen is stabbed, loses consciousness, is picked up by the police, and ends up with a two-year sentence in a rehabilitation center called Camp Sawyer.

A competitive individualist, Owen secretly aspires to be a gang leader (headman) and learns nothing from his experiences at the camp. Throughout the novel, he remains a shallow character who, like the novel itself, is headed nowhere.

After spending eight months at Camp Sawyer, Owen is allowed to leave due to his mother's illness. Returning home, he is disappointed to find that street life has not changed and is plunged into a new conflict over what to do with himself. He decides to try his hand at working, but his desire to be a part of a gang is stronger than any impetus to go "legit." Hence, he and three buddies form a gang called The Four. Alas, the wish-come-true is short lived. On his first day as a headman, Owen is shot dead by a member of another gang.

And so, as the sun sets in the west, readers are left with a host of unresolved issues. What was Owen really a victim of? What is the significance of his death? In short, what is the point of this story?

In addition to its fatalism, racism, sexism, escapism, conformism, materialism and individualism, this book is badly written. The awkward dialogue mixes out-dated and contemporary slang and is heavily seasoned with profanity and bloody brutality.

	ART	WORDS		ART	WORDS			ART	WORDS	N.A.
anti-Racist			non-Racist			Racist	omission		✓	
							commission			
anti-Sexist			non-Sexist			Sexist			✓	
anti-Elitist			non-Elitist	✓		Elitist				
anti-Materialist			non-Materialist			Materialist			✓	
anti-Individualist			non-Individualist			Individualist			✓	
anti-Ageist			non-Ageist			Ageist				✓
anti-Conformist			non-Conformist			Conformist			✓	
anti-Escapist			non-Escapist			Escapist			✓	
Builds positive image of females/ minorities			Builds negative image of females/ minorities		✓		Excellent	Good	Fair	Poor
Inspires action vs. oppression			Culturally authentic			Literary quality				✓
						Art quality				

ALCOHOLISM
by Dr. Alvin Silverstein and Virginia B. Silverstein
J. B. Lippincott
$2.25, 127 pages, grades 6-up

This informative, fact filled paperback describes alcoholism as a disease and treats excessive drinking as a personal decision. The book gives technical, historical, and current information, and ends with advice to teenagers who may have alcoholic parents or who may themselves be considering if, and how much, to drink. Strangely enough, there is not a single mention of the staggering amounts the liquor and beer industries spend on advertising to encourage *more* drinking.

The book *does* tell us that Chinese Americans "have traditionally been a very family-centered culture, with ties extending to a broader group of relatives. A strong emphasis is placed on the welfare of the group. . . . Heavy drinking is acceptable. . . . But consequences of drinking that might harm the group are strongly disapproved and penalized. As a result, though drinking is common, problem drinking is rare, among Chinese-Americans."

The authors do not tell us that doctors returning from the People's Republic of China report there is no alcohol problem, and that hard drugs—for many years a major problem—are no longer used there. Venereal disease has also been eliminated. Alcohol is freely available, but there is no profit to be made through its sale. And intensive campaigns of public education, public pressure, public penalties, plus retraining of hard-core abusers have been responsible for this dramatic change.

Is China the only country in which this could be accomplished? Are Chinese physically immune from the "disease" of alcoholism? Or can the USA also cure alcoholism *socially*, instead of trying to cure individual alcoholics while the yearly toll keeps claiming more victims?

Young readers should be respected enough to have that basic question posed to them in any book on the subject of drug abuse.

	ART	WORDS		ART	WORDS		ART	WORDS	N.A.
anti-Racist			non-Racist			Racist omission / commission			✓
anti-Sexist			non-Sexist			Sexist			✓
anti-Elitist			non-Elitist	✓		Elitist			
anti-Materialist			non-Materialist	✓		Materialist			
anti-Individualist			non-Individualist			Individualist		✓	
anti-Ageist			non-Ageist			Ageist			✓
anti-Conformist			non-Conformist	✓		Conformist			
anti-Escapist			non-Escapist			Escapist		✓	
Builds positive image of females/minorities			Builds negative image of females/minorities				Excellent	Good	Fair	Poor
Inspires action vs. oppression			Culturally authentic			Literary quality		✓		
						Art quality				

INDIANS OF THE EASTERN WOODLANDS
by Sally Sheppard
photographs
Franklin Watts
$3.90, 88 pages, grades 5-up

This book describes the history and lifestyles of the Native Americans of the Northeastern United States. Social, economic, religious and political organization of the Iroquois and Algonquian peoples are described. History is traced from the supposed migration from Asia to the Indian Power movements of contemporary times.

For all the author's liberal attitudes and intentions (part-royalties of this book will go to two Indian educational organizations), she still retains a few traces of European ethnocentrism. She rather grudgingly grants that the Iroquois "had a relatively advanced democratic form of government," but she does not elaborate on how much of an impact that government had on European political thought of that era, or how it has affected the present world philosophies. Her chapter on Heroes and Leaders raises a question of whose heroes she is talking about; many of the people mentioned (Joseph Brant, Squanto, Massasoit) are considered traitors by their own people. Unearthed bones of Indians are pictured in a dishonorable death-zoo fashion, under the label of archeological excavations.

The book is packed with useful information which is presented logically and intelligently. Many bits of information however, are inaccurate. For examples, the author states few treaties were kept, when in truth *none* were kept. Also, it is stated "Militant leaders took over the town of Wounded Knee" in 1973. It was people of the Pine Ridge Reservation who *re*claimed their land. Books about Indians are best written by those that know: Indians themselves.

	ART	WORDS		ART	WORDS			ART	WORDS	N.A.
anti-Racist			non-Racist	✓	✓	Racist omission / commission				
anti-Sexist			non-Sexist	✓	✓	Sexist				
anti-Elitist			non-Elitist	✓	✓	Elitist				
anti-Materialist			non-Materialist	✓	✓	Materialist				
anti-Individualist		✓	non-Individualist	✓		Individualist				
anti-Ageist			non-Ageist	✓	✓	Ageist				
anti-Conformist			non-Conformist	✓	✓	Conformist				
anti-Escapist		✓	non-Escapist	✓		Escapist				
Builds positive image of females/ minorities		✓	Builds negative image of females/ minorities				Excellent	Good	Fair	Poor
Inspires action vs. oppression			Culturally authentic			Literary quality		✓		
						Art quality				✓

FOUNDING MOTHERS
by Linda Grant De Pauw
Houghton Mifflin
$6.95, 228 pages, grades 7-up

Excellent research and excellent writing make this an important book which successfully unveils some of our nation's concealed revolutionary history. The women described are not presented as isolated cases of individual accomplishment, but as part and parcel of particular times and movements. *Founding Mothers* resurrects the role of ordinary women as well as that of the "greats." It shows that the revolutionary generation was not homogeneous, and that servant-girls, working women, Black women, Native American women, intellectuals and "fine ladies," too, were present "everywhere that men were present, even though they may be invisible in the history books."

Generous quotes from advertisements of the time give a true flavor of the mores of colonial life. The discussion on women doctors, midwives, nurses and barbers shows how seriously women took their responsibility as guardians of the people's health. The sections on children are interesting and should make for lively discussion in classroom or home. The death rate for children was very high; the Puritan ethic was harsh and the "toughening" of children often very backward. Puritan views on discipline, idleness and self-control will call forth strong reactions from young readers.

The chapter on the status of Black women, while extensive, does not fully succeed because it attempts to compare what is essentially not comparable:

"In the 18th century, the approximately 20% of the population that was enslaved was deprived of the right to choose employers freely, to marry without the master's consent, to obey the rules of conduct set down by the master and to be beaten for disobedience. . . . But these restrictions applied to most people in the eighteenth century including wives, indentured servants, apprentices and children."

But to say the foregoing is to *fail* to understand the dehumanizing slave system, or the role of racism in *institutionalizing* for Blacks what was a temporary class phenomenon for poor whites. Nevertheless, there is an attempt to plow through some of the myths and lies that history has piled up about Black and Native American women.

Few individual Native American women are mentioned by name, as most written records were kept by whites who simply took note of those women who were in some way useful to white people. Thus the Indian women who are mentioned—Sacajawea and Nancy Ward—are considered to be traitors to their own people by many Native American activists. Nevertheless the book is useful for rounding out concepts of Native women's life in Revolutionary times. More research needs to be done to fill in huge gaps in our knowledge of Native American women.

Despite some minor flaws, misinterpretations and omissions, this book is highly recommended as an outstanding contribution to our knowledge of women in America's past.

	ART	WORDS		ART	WORDS			ART	WORDS	N.A.
anti-Racist			non-Racist		✓	Racist — omission / commission				
anti-Sexist		✓	non-Sexist			Sexist				
anti-Elitist		✓	non-Elitist			Elitist				
anti-Materialist		✓	non-Materialist			Materialist				
anti-Individualist		✓	non-Individualist		✓	Individualist				
anti-Ageist			non-Ageist		✓	Ageist				
anti-Conformist		✓	non-Conformist			Conformist				
anti-Escapist		✓	non-Escapist			Escapist				
Builds positive image of (females)/ minorities		✓	Builds negative image of females/ minorities				Excellent	Good	Fair	Poor
Inspires action vs. oppression			Culturally authentic			Literary quality	✓			
						Art quality				

WOMEN IN SPORTS: SWIMMING
by Diana C. Gleasner
photographs
Harvey House
$4.97, 63 pages, grades 5-up

This book is billed as an examination "from a feminist viewpoint (of) the lives and careers of five outstanding contemporary women in an individual sport, emphasizing inroads in participation and progress toward recognition." The description is apt. A brief history of competitive swimming is followed by short biographical sketches of Christine Loock, diver; Kathy Heddy, speed swimmer; Gail Johnson Buzonas, synchronized swimmer; Diana Nyad, marathon swimmer; and Shirley Babashoff, also a speed swimmer. All of these young women excel in their particular sport and are in the prime of their athletic careers. Their stories are lively, interesting and highlighted by some good photography.

The book's most distinguishing characteristic is its emphasis on the realities of a competitive swimmer's life—the grueling training and long hours of daily practice, year in and year out. The author talks a great deal, sometimes a little too much, about a subject most sports books ignore—the physical pain involved in speed and marathon swimming. As one swimmer explains it, the difference between a good swimmer and a great one is pain: "Most swimmers back away from it. . . . A champion pushes himself (herself) on into agony."

Surprisingly, the author has a good class and race consciousness and states in her introduction, "American swimming stars have always been white, and almost all came from families with good income." She praises coach Sherman Chavoor who runs an "open" pool—one that is open to all—and who has dedicated himself to the promotion of Jewish (Mark Spitz), as well as Black, swimmers.

What impresses the author most, however, is the determination which has made her five women subjects into champions. "Swimmers have to believe in themselves. They have to say 'I can, I will,' never 'I can't.' If they start with 'can't' they have defeated themselves." Good advice for any and all women.

This is one of the best sports books around.

	ART	WORDS		ART	WORDS			ART	WORDS	N.A.
anti-Racist		✓	non-Racist	✓		Racist	omission / commission			
anti-Sexist		✓	non-Sexist	✓		Sexist				
anti-Elitist		✓	non-Elitist	✓		Elitist				
anti-Materialist			non-Materialist	✓	✓	Materialist				
anti-Individualist			non-Individualist	✓	✓	Individualist				
anti-Ageist		✓	non-Ageist	✓		Ageist				✓
anti-Conformist		✓	non-Conformist	✓		Conformist				
anti-Escapist		✓	non-Escapist	✓		Escapist				
Builds positive image of females/minorities		✓	Builds negative image of females/minorities				Excellent	Good	Fair	Poor
Inspires action vs. oppression			Culturally authentic			Literary quality		✓		
						Art quality			✓	

THE BOOK OF REWI: A UTOPIAN TALE
by David P. O'Neill
Seabury Press
$7.95, 200 pages, grades 7-up

Take three young, handsome, Christian males: One is Joe, a Baptist Afro-American whose grandparents were slaves; second is Rewi, a half-Irish, half-German Catholic; third is Hemi, an Anglican Polynesian Maori. Mix with three lovely young females: Helga, a blonde Lutheran Scandinavian, born in Fiji; Anna, a half-Chinese, half-Samoan Catholic; and one "dusky," spiritual Indian lass named Donna who is, presumably, a Hindu. Add one hurricane shipwreck on a South Pacific isle, and we have this "utopian tale."

Fortunately, the author, a New Zealand Catholic priest, did not add any Moslems or Jews who do not eat pork because the above group is shipwrecked for twenty years, and the pigs they tame and eat are important to their survival. It is also a neat stroke that the two Catholic youngsters fall in love. Other couplings are: Black American with Scandinavian, and Indian with Maori. No Utopia would be complete, of course, without certain essential supplies, and luckily the strandees were able to fill up a dinghy just before the hurricane peaked. Quick thinking led them to include the Bible—in three languages—and a full set of Shakespeare!

Many babies and grandbabies later, an escape route through the surrounding coral barrier reef is discovered. Some of the males leave, discovering, of course, that life is more humane and civilized on their secret isle than in the outside world. And so they return to remain forever.

This story appears to have been written with the purest intentions. Even its pervasive sexism seems well-intentioned. Moreover, the author belongs to that well-meaning coterie, the Color-Blind School—their motto being physical-differences-don't-matter-we're-all-God's-children-under-the-skin.

If those who are purer of heart than this jaded reviewer know any young readers who would be turned on to cooperative living, anti-materialism and love and respect for people of all colors, ages and religions by reading this "utopian tale"—then please buy it for them. The young people I know live too far away from the South Pacific.

	ART	WORDS		ART	WORDS		ART	WORDS	N.A.
anti-Racist			non-Racist		✓	Racist — omission / commission			
anti-Sexist			non-Sexist			Sexist		✓	
anti-Elitist			non-Elitist		✓	Elitist			
anti-Materialist		✓	non-Materialist			Materialist			
anti-Individualist		✓	non-Individualist			Individualist			
anti-Ageist		✓	non-Ageist			Ageist			
anti-Conformist		✓	non-Conformist			Conformist			
anti-Escapist			non-Escapist			Escapist			✓
Builds positive image of females/ minorities			Builds negative image of females/ minorities				Excellent	Good	Fair	Poor
Inspires action vs. oppression			Culturally authentic			Literary quality			✓	
						Art quality				

EL BRONX REMEMBERED
by Nicholasa Mohr
Harper & Row
$5.95, 179 pages, grades 7-up

Can a Puerto Rican be racist? How much sexist and racist ideology have we internalized? How can Puerto Rican writers accurately depict our present and help to create our future at the same time? What do we tell our children about ourselves, and what would we like them to be as adults? Does a Puerto Rican writer automatically possess a more relevant perspective?

El Bronx Remembered consists of eleven short stories and a novella describing the anxieties, fears, loves, hates, pride, despair, nostalgia and hopes of several Puerto Ricans in the barrio, El Bronx, from 1946 to 1956. The subjects of these well-written and descriptive tales want to escape to suburbia, or into the arms of men, or to be accepted and assimilated into a materialistic society which rejects and exploits them. But despite some truths and sharp insights, these are not stories of change, struggle or love. Rather, they are negative stories which reinforce stereotypes.

One incredibly racist story is about Jasmine, a gypsy, who wins the acceptance of her classmates by reading palms and telling stories. The description of Jasmine's appearance reads like a catalog of prejudices and, as in most of the stories in this book, sexism is prevalent as well.

The novella (a sick soap opera) tells of Alice, a pregnant fifteen-year-old who finds temporary comfort and happiness in the home of a mature, understanding homosexual. A conversation between Alice and her mother about the pregnancy reeks of puritanism—"I know you are sorry. I am too, Alice, but it's too late now. Because, now you see, you can be sorry for the rest of your life."—as does Alice's description of her sexual life: "The first time it was painful and she had cried; the second time it was almost as bad, except she had felt numb." To top it off, Alice forgets all the agony of her labor pains as soon as she gazes upon her new-born *son.*

In addition to having internalized myths about females, the novella's characters have also taken to heart certain myths about Puerto Ricans. Herman says of his own people, "Honestly, these people, a bunch of ignorantes, and they just keep making babies and more babies and being more miserable." Alice's mother buys her new clothes to go out with the "respectable" homosexual, so that he will not think their family is a bunch of "jíbaros" (peasants).

Although it is unusual to portray a gay person in a book for young people, no new ground is broken here in developing understanding of sexual differences. Alice marries Herman to escape from her critical mother. For Herman, the marriage serves to pacify his old parents in Puerto Rico who want him to be a husband and father. The characters are neither honest with themselves nor with each other.

Regarding the questions raised at the beginning of this review, *El Bronx Remembered* is evidence that oppressed people (in this case, Puerto Ricans or women) do not necessarily understand the mechanism of oppression. Unless we look critically at our lives, our family relations, our institutions, the positive and negative aspects of our culture, we will not develop the will to resist and to change things. Without that critical approach, our observations are but one small part of the truth and continue to reinforce negative stereotypes about ourselves and reflect the dominant society's negative values.

	ART	WORDS		ART	WORDS			ART	WORDS	N.A.
anti-Racist			non-Racist			Racist — omission / commission				✓
anti-Sexist			non-Sexist			Sexist				✓
anti-Elitist•			non-Elitist			Elitist				✓
anti-Materialist			non-Materialist			Materialist				✓
anti-Individualist			non-Individualist			Individualist				✓
anti-Ageist			non-Ageist	✓		Ageist				
anti-Conformist			non-Conformist			Conformist				✓
anti-Escapist			non-Escapist	✓		Escapist				
Builds positive image of females/minorities			Builds negative image of females/minorities	✓			Excellent	Good	Fair	Poor
Inspires action vs. oppression			Culturally authentic	✓		Literary quality	✓			
						Art quality				

RUFFLES AND DRUMS
by Betty Cavanna
illustrated by Richard Cuffari
William Morrow
$5.95, 223 pages, grades 7-up

Like many other colonists in Concord, sixteen-year-old Sarah Devotion Kent gets caught up in the initial excitement of the war against England. She too wants to be a soldier and curses the fact that she was born a girl. Her neighbor and childhood companion, Tom Fletcher, looks so dashing and handsome marching off to war that Sarah allows herself to become betrothed to him. Then, as the months pass and the glory and adventure of war wears off, harsh realities set in—women must work in the fields, news of the deaths of brothers and lovers comes more often, and schools cannot open for lack of teachers.

On the home front, a romance is brewing between Sarah and a wounded British officer who has been convalescing there. Torn between her ill-considered promise to Tom and her true feelings towards James, Sarah finally decides to follow her heart, realizing that the road ahead will not be easy for a "faithless girl" wed to a turncoat (James has decided to stay in the U.S. instead of returning to England).

Ruffles and Drums is a readable account of the realistic side of war, which books often overlook in favor of its more adventurous aspects. From the viewpoint of the women who are left behind, war is synonymous with uncertainty, waiting, death and daily struggle.

However, the author lapses into sexist stereotyping throughout the book. The curiosity and determination of women like Sarah and her mother are perceived as problems. Mrs. Kent's apolitical, humanistic attitude towards war reinforces the "earth mother" image of women, and James is described as objective and intellectual while Sarah's opinions are dictated by emotion. Ultimately, the only options in Sarah's life relate to her choice of a husband.

Elitist values abound. Sarah's attraction to James is based on his gentlemanly and scholarly background (his family were landed gentry in England) and association with him is perceived by Sarah as elevating her from her simple farmer status. At one point, James chides her for considering marriage with a man (Tom) "who can't even spell."

References to "wild Indians," combined with racism by omission—no Blacks are acknowledged as having participated in the war—seriously detract from the book's social relevance.

As a book commemorating the Bicentennial of the American Revolution, *Ruffles and Drums* is interestingly anti-war and anti-violence in content. A positive interpretation could be that the book is attempting to destroy the "war is glamorous and adventurous" myth. On the other hand, negation of the violence that is necessary to any true revolution may be compatible with this country's current anti-revolutionary policies.

	ART	WORDS		ART	WORDS			ART	WORDS	N.A.
anti-Racist			non-Racist	✓	✓	Racist	omission			✓
							commission			
anti-Sexist			non-Sexist	✓	✓	Sexist				
anti-Elitist			non-Elitist	✓		Elitist				✓
anti-Materialist			non-Materialist	✓	✓	Materialist				
anti-Individualist			non-Individualist	✓		Individualist				✓
anti-Ageist			non-Ageist	✓	✓	Ageist				
anti-Conformist		✓	non-Conformist	✓		Conformist				
anti-Escapist			non-Escapist	✓	✓	Escapist				
Builds positive image of females/minorities			Builds negative image of females/minorities				Excellent	Good	Fair	Poor
Inspires action vs. oppression			Culturally authentic			Literary quality			✓	
						Art quality			✓	

OF LOVE AND DEATH AND OTHER JOURNEYS
by Isabelle Holland
J.B. Lippincott
$5.95, 159 pages, grades 9-up

Of Love And Death And Other Journeys is an outspoken book, in which interesting and offbeat characters are presented. There is fifteen-year-old Meg and her dying mother; Peter, the mother's third husband, and Cotton, a painter, who has often lived with the family as they have moved through Europe (they are now settled in Italy). The story revolves around Meg's developing a relationship with her own father after meeting him for the first time at age fifteen. Also described are the feelings and events Meg experiences as her mother suffers from, and dies of, cancer.

The book contains several anti-sexist characters who break stereotypes. One such character is Meg's mother, who fought for her own freedom and who maintains an open relationship with her daughter, encouraging her to be independent, self-educated and free. Another, Meg's father, provides an example of freedom within his more conventional marriage. A third character is Sylvia, owner and manager of a hotel, who was raised by a naturalist father and is not bothered by scorpions, millipedes or bats. Male characters are depicted as warm, emotional, nurturing persons who respect women.

Anti-conformism is reflected in the characters' free-spirited inclinations and acceptance of one another's differences. And in an outburst of anti-materialism, Meg says with disgust, "Why do all Americans always ask about what people do for a living. Don't they ever think of anything but money?"

Unfortunately, the story's only elderly character is Meg's non-functioning, ailing grandmother who appears in a flashback describing Meg's mother's reunion with her in a nursing home. No other older characters are presented to counter-balance this image.

Though interesting, *Of Love And Death And Other Journeys* contains far too many controversial subjects—cancer, death of a retarded son, adultery, divorce, pornography, free lifestyles, intermarriage (between Meg's priest father and a Jewish woman doctor). Although such subjects have a place in children's literature their overabundance seriously impairs the credibility of the novel's events. Nevertheless, a sophisticated teenage audience would probably be engaged by this unusual story in which touches of beauty and wisdom are to be found amid the painful realities of illness and death.

	ART	WORDS		ART	WORDS			ART	WORDS	N.A.
anti-Racist			non-Racist			Racist omission / commission				✓
anti-Sexist	✓		non-Sexist			Sexist				
anti-Elitist		✓	non-Elitist			Elitist				
anti-Materialist		✓	non-Materialist			Materialist				
anti-Individualist			non-Individualist	✓		Individualist				
anti-Ageist			non-Ageist			Ageist		✓		
anti-Conformist		✓	non-Conformist			Conformist				
anti-Escapist		✓	non-Escapist			Escapist				
Builds positive image of females/minorities		✓	Builds negative image of females/minorities				Excellent	Good	Fair	Poor
Inspires action vs. oppression			Culturally authentic			Literary quality		✓		
						Art quality				

FOX RUNNING
by R.R. Knudson
Harper & Row
$5.95, 182 pages, grades 7-up

Fox Running is the name of a Mescalero Apache girl discovered running in the desert by Sudden Hart, an Olympic runner, and Sudden's coach. Fox Running is more or less abducted for the track team at Uinta University. The Apache girl remains aloof and silent, totally secretive about her past. Gradually, through Sudden's persistent efforts, the two become friends. The mystery of Fox Running is unraveled slowly as Sudden teaches her to run on a regulation track, and Fox teaches Sudden to run outdoors, the Indian way. The suspense builds as the two train to compete in the Olympics.

This book is not really about an Indian. It is about the white girl, Sudden, and her comeback, made possible by Fox. Fox is used as an exotic literary device to add mystery to the story. She is presented as a female Jim Thorpe, a running machine with emotions shown only to Sudden. Ties to her own people have been severed, and she has chosen the company of white running friends. Despite their taunts and ridicule she is "accepted" when she proves she can win races for the team.

The values in this book are misplaced. Fox's achievements are gains for her coach and teammates, not for her people. Fox gains some psychological relief in telling Sudden the painful details of her beloved grandfather's death. But her entire worth as a person centers on her ability to run. She remains a shadowy stick figure character to the end.

The book gives an interesting glimpse into the lives of people who care for nothing in the world except training their bodies to WIN. Not one white character ever speaks, dreams, thinks of anything else. The author, we are told, loves running, and this comes through, vividly and effectively. But the author also seems to totally accept the limited values of her characters. She remains completely uncritical of the vicious competitive drives of coach and runners. Thus she is implying to readers that self-centered, empty-headed, single-track sport life is the *only* path to become a champion. Many of our great athletes have also been great students, or concerned about more issues than crossing a finish line first.

The author also tells us that the University's sport teams are named the Uinta "Indians." She seems to see no more wrong about this than she does about the cruel, racist taunts and "jokes" which she has various characters hurl at the silent, mysterious Fox Running. After all, these sports loving characters learn to respect the Native American girl, once she wins some gold medals, don't they? The white characters emerge as no more believable than the red.

	ART	WORDS		ART	WORDS			ART	WORDS	N.A.
anti-Racist			non-Racist			Racist	omission			✓
							commission			
anti-Sexist		✓	non-Sexist			Sexist				
anti-Elitist			non-Elitist		✓	Elitist				
anti-Materialist			non-Materialist		✓	Materialist				
anti-Individualist			non-Individualist		✓	Individualist				
anti-Ageist		✓	non-Ageist			Ageist				
anti-Conformist			non-Conformist		✓	Conformist				
anti-Escapist			non-Escapist		✓	Escapist				
Builds positive image of females/ minorities			Builds negative image of females/ minorities					Excellent	Good	Fair	Poor
Inspires action vs. oppression			Culturally authentic			Literary quality			✓		
						Art quality					

SANTERIA, BRONX
by Judith Gleason
Atheneum
$7.95, 223 pages, grades 7-up

The opening of this novel finds white teenager Raymond Hunter in his South Bronx, New York, apartment reflecting on his experiences with a cult-religion known as Santería, learned from Concha, his Puerto Rican godmother.

In the course of investigating Santería, a religion that derives from the Yoruba people of West Africa, Raymond encounters two rival Black leaders of the religion. The first leader takes Raymond so completely into his confidence that within minutes he is revealing secrets which only long time initiates are privy to. Raymond then so ingratiates himself with the second leader, the head priest of the Yoruba Temple in Harlem, that the entire Black congregation is kept waiting for half an hour while he and the priest strike up a friendship. Impressed by Raymond's "obvious gifts," the priest sends him to a Puerto Rican priestess to learn more mysteries—that priestess being Concha, who also immediately befriends him.   At story's end, Raymond repays all of the hospitality extended to him by arranging to fulfill Concha's life-long ambition to visit Africa. Better yet, he gets her an ambassadorship!

The images of people and historical details are generally authentic and accurate, and Concha is refreshingly active and imaginative in her confrontations with spirits. Indeed, from a feminist viewpoint, Concha cannot be faulted. Tale after tale of her trials and tribulations with spiritual forces may be fun reading, but their end result is to reinforce the stereotype of Puerto Ricans as superstitious folk who are heavily into supernaturalism. This criticism would not be justified were libraries well-stocked with books about Puerto Ricans that would give young people insights into Puerto Rican culture.

As for the story line, the theme of a thirteen or fourteen-year-old white boy relating to Black adults on the basis of total equality is questionable. When the Black and Puerto Rican adults in this book fall all over themselves to befriend Raymond, the theme becomes doubly questionable. And finally, when the leading adult character's salvation depends on the white boy's intelligence and quick thinking, the theme becomes obnoxious.

	ART	WORDS		ART	WORDS			ART	WORDS	N.A.
anti-Racist			non-Racist			Racist — omission / commission				✓
anti-Sexist		✓	non-Sexist			Sexist				
anti-Elitist			non-Elitist			Elitist			✓	
anti-Materialist			non-Materialist		✓	Materialist				
anti-Individualist			non-Individualist		✓	Individualist				
anti-Ageist			non-Ageist		✓	Ageist				
anti-Conformist			non-Conformist		✓	Conformist				
anti-Escapist			non-Escapist			Escapist				✓
Builds positive image of (females) minorities		✓	Builds negative image of females/ minorities				Excellent	Good	Fair	Poor
Inspires action vs. oppression			Culturally authentic			Literary quality		✓		
						Art quality				

DRAGONWINGS
by Lawrence Yep
Harper & Row
$6.50, 208 pages, grades 7-up

Chinese Americans—like all Asian Americans—have been either "invisible" or seen as one-dimensional laundrymen, Fu Manchus, cooks or Charlie Chans. *Dragonwings* attempts to counter such stereotypes with the story of a talented Chinese immigrant and his son who, in the early 1900's, dream of building a flying-machine and succeed in making their dream come true. Along with the dream they must contend with the realities of the new land—the racism of the "demons," beatings and lynchings, the harshness of life, the sacrifices and the failures. The book tries, and in some ways succeeds, in showing that the Chinese in America were, and are, ordinary as well as extraordinary people.

The story is told in the first person with delightful humor, as young Moonshadow reacts to the strange ways of the white "demons." Through his vision the reader learns many authentic details of life in China, where Moonshadow lived with his mother and grandmother, and of life in San Francisco's early Chinatown where Moonshadow has joined his father. Even the book's unusual combination of mystical belief and scientific brilliance is made believable.

Some of the unpleasant realities of early Chinatown's secret societies, prostitution, and opium dens are depicted, a bit luridly perhaps, but this is offset by warm characterizations of Moonshadow's family and friends. They are not stereotypes and they relate to one another in ways that are culturally distinct from white behaviors.

Windrider and his son meet a white woman and her niece who befriend them and respect their dreams. They are atypical whites and are strongly drawn feminist characters as well. The relationship with the women is important to the father and son, but it is not essential to them in the paternalistically racist way that is common in so many children's books.

The book, though highly recommended, does have a weakness. While oppression and racism are well described, blame is not placed squarely on the economic system which then, as now, used non-whites for maximum profit.

	ART	WORDS		ART	WORDS			ART	WORDS	N.A.
anti-Racist		✓	non-Racist			Racist	omission			
							commission			
anti-Sexist		✓	non-Sexist			Sexist				
anti-Elitist		✓	non-Elitist			Elitist				
anti-Materialist		✓	non-Materialist			Materialist				
anti-Individualist		✓	non-Individualist			Individualist				
anti-Ageist		✓	non-Ageist			Ageist				
anti-Conformist		✓	non-Conformist			Conformist				
anti-Escapist		✓	non-Escapist			Escapist				
Builds positive image of females/minorities		✓	Builds negative image of females/minorities					Excellent	Good	Fair	Poor
Inspires action vs. oppression			Culturally authentic		✓	Literary quality					
						Art quality					

LUDELL
by Brenda Wilkinson
Harper & Row
$5.95, 170 pages, grades 5-up

In this sensitive and powerful novel, the positive and the negative sides of growing up in a rural southern Black community are revealed through the eyes of fifth-grader Ludell. The place is Waycross, Georgia, in the 1950's where Ludell Wilson lives with her grandmother ("Mama"). Next door is the Johnson crew: Mrs. Johnson, sixteen-year-old Mattie and her child, Ruthie Mae (Ludell's best friend), Willie, Hawk and Cathy.

Ludell's keen perceptions expose the harsh underside of life in Waycross—the poverty, the selfishness and unconcern of her teachers in the segregated school she attends, the constant reminders that both Mama and Mrs. Johnson work as maids in white people's homes. Whenever racism and oppression are manifest, it is commented upon and clearly defined.

Each experience, whether humorous or tragic, contributes to Ludell's growing awareness of herself and of others. The reader can sense that one day her aspirations will lead her to seek a life outside of Waycross and to exercise more control over her destiny.

Author Wilkinson effectively captures the subtle nuances of Black southern dialect and draws readers inside the Black experience. In addition she provides a truly positive role model for young Black readers. Ludell has a keen sense of who she is, shares with those less fortunate than herself and is shown overcoming adversities in her life.

	ART	WORDS		ART	WORDS			ART	WORDS	N.A.
anti-Racist		✓	non-Racist			Racist	omission			
							commission			
anti-Sexist			non-Sexist		✓	Sexist				
anti-Elitist		✓	non-Elitist			Elitist				
anti-Materialist			non-Materialist		✓	Materialist				
anti-Individualist		✓	non-Individualist			Individualist				
anti-Ageist			non-Ageist		✓	Ageist				
anti-Conformist			non-Conformist		✓	Conformist				
anti-Escapist		✓	non-Escapist			Escapist				
Builds positive image of females/minorities		✓	Builds negative image of females/minorities				Excellent	Good	Fair	Poor
Inspires action vs. oppression			Culturally authentic		✓	Literary quality	✓			
						Art quality				

WHAT IT'S ALL ABOUT
by Norma Klein
Dial Press
$5.95, 160 pages, grades 5-up

Bernadette's parents are divorced. Her Japanese American father, Fumio, lives in California. Eleven-year-old Bern lives a relatively "normal," middle-class life with her Jewish mom and stepfather, Gabe. Her mother adopts Suzu, a Vietnamese orphan who becomes very attached to Bern. When Gabe loses his job, arguments flare between him and Mom until one day he splits while Bern is away in Boston attending her father's wedding to Peggy.

Torn between living with Fumio and Peggy, a "regular" two-parent family, or staying with Mom and Suzu, Bern finally discovers that a family can be close, strong and loving even though it does not fit the two-parent mold.

Pluses: This is a witty, down-to-earth book about divorce and its effects on children. These modern times, when healthy relationships are difficult to develop and maintain, are appropriately reflected. Women are portrayed as strong and varied. Mom's strong and independent personality is the basis of her conflict with Gabe, who assumes that men should support women but not vice versa. Bern is active, unpretentious, and has an open relationship with a boy, Jonah—"Just because one person is a boy and one person is a girl doesn't mean it's some big romance."

Minuses: Although one of Bern's parents is Asian American, she is portrayed as an all-American girl whose father just happens to be Japanese American. That's hard to swallow in this race conscious society. Moreover, classic stereotypical adjectives are used to describe Fumio—he is "quiet, extremely kind, polite." His image suffers in comparison to Gabe's strong one. Also, what message does the author wish to convey to Asian American girls when she has Fumio marry two white women?

Ms. Klein sinks to the depths of racism when she lumps all Asians together: Bern explains that Mom adopted Suzu "so that we both would have an Oriental heritage." In-laws are stereotyped as being difficult to get along with. Adults consistently dismiss children's questions with such comments as "you're too young to understand" or "it's too complicated to explain" (Bern echoes this condescension when she talks to Suzu). The message seems to be that it is not normal for children to be serious about life. Ms. Klein also assigns rigid age role expectations: Grandma is too old to have a boyfriend.

These criticisms notwithstanding, *What It's All About* has some very humanistic facets.

	ART	WORDS		ART	WORDS			ART	WORDS	N.A.
anti-Racist			non-Racist			Racist	omission / commission			✓
anti-Sexist		✓	non-Sexist			Sexist				
anti-Elitist			non-Elitist		✓	Elitist				
anti-Materialist			non-Materialist		✓	Materialist				
anti-Individualist			non-Individualist		✓	Individualist				
anti-Ageist			non-Ageist			Ageist		✓		
anti-Conformist			non-Conformist		✓	Conformist				
anti-Escapist			non-Escapist		✓	Escapist				
Builds positive image of females/minorities		✓	Builds negative image of females/minorities							
Inspires action vs. oppression			Culturally authentic							

	Excellent	Good	Fair	Poor
Literary quality		✓		
Art quality				

NEW YORK CITY TOO FAR FROM TAMPA BLUES
by T. Ernesto Bethancourt
Holiday House
$6.95, 190 pages, grades 7-up

Twelve-year-old, guitar-playing Tom lives in poverty in Tampa, Florida, with his "Spanish" father, Pancho, his Anglo mother and his three sisters. "Macho" Pancho rules his brood with an iron hand and profane mouth. When Pancho decides (unilaterally, of course) to move the family to Brooklyn, where his relatives have found him a truck-driving job, Tom's adventures begin.

Tough youth gangs, nasty cops and sundry other slum "staples" parade through the pages. Tom survives all of the action, combining his wits and musical talents with those of an Italian shoe-shine boy to earn some money. The undisputed stars of their public school graduation, the boys move onward to a prestigious high school. The future looks rosy at the book's end.

Although Tom's father and numerous relatives were born and raised in Puerto Rico, they never refer to themselves as anything but "Spanish." Pancho dearly loves his only son, holds two jobs, and works very hard. He is also very proud—which means that when he goes on strike, the author describes the strike in two paragraphs and devotes pages to Pancho's resistance to welfare and food stamps.

Stereotypes abound. The three sisters, like Mom, have no personality, cry a lot and seem inept. A virago of a grandmother and an Irish prostitute have hearts of gold. So does a little Italian mother who says, "Girls are a pleasure, next to boys. I always wanted a girl. Instead, I ended up with this bunch of Indians and troublemakers." The author also stereotypes Jews with regard to money and the Irish vis-a-vis liquor, so Native Americans, women and "Spanish" people should not feel they have been discriminated against.

Escapism is evident, as well. Although Tom shares the money he earns from singing with his family, his musical flight from poverty is the stuff of which dreams are made for third world boys and girls in our urban ghettos and *barrios*. The story does have humor and some cultural validity, but overall, it is a negative experience which fails to provide role models and reinforces the worst kinds of stereotypes.

	ART	WORDS		ART	WORDS			ART	WORDS	N.A.
anti-Racist			non-Racist			Racist	omission			
							commission		✓	
anti-Sexist			non-Sexist			Sexist			✓	
anti-Elitist			non-Elitist	✓		Elitist				
anti-Materialist			non-Materialist			Materialist			✓	
anti-Individualist			non-Individualist			Individualist			✓	
anti-Ageist			non-Ageist	✓		Ageist				
anti-Conformist			non-Conformist	✓		Conformist				
anti-Escapist			non-Escapist			Escapist			✓	

	ART	WORDS		ART	WORDS		Excellent	Good	Fair	Poor
Builds positive image of females/ minorities			Builds negative image of females/ (minorities)		✓					
Inspires action vs. oppression			Culturally authentic			Literary quality		✓		
						Art quality				

LET ME BE A FREE MAN: A DOCUMENTARY OF INDIAN RESISTANCE
compiled and edited by Jane B. Katz
Lerner
$6.95, 183 pages, grades 6-up

This anthology of orations by Indian patriots include Sitting Bull, Chief Joseph, Geronimo, Vine Deloria and Dennis Banks. Realistically illustrated with photographs of the patriots, it is a perceptive and incisive history of Native American resistance, amazing in its scope and informative in its well-chosen quotations and examples. The essence of Native American life is fully conveyed in the words of these leaders, and the book is illuminating without being pedantic.

This book would be excellent as supplementary background information for older readers or as an introduction to the history that is omitted in the school books of younger readers. Given the white viewpoint which dominates most historical accounts, the book may disconcert the uninformed.

Ms. Katz's narrative is a fine complement to the eloquent and stirring words of the warriors and chiefs represented. Her transitions display a competent familiarity with the subject and are executed with rare smoothness. Her observations in the book's final pages are astute and demonstrate keen insight into contemporary Native American political movements and current leadership.

	ART	WORDS		ART	WORDS		ART	WORDS	N.A.
anti-Racist		✓	non-Racist			Racist omission / commission			
anti-Sexist			non-Sexist	✓		Sexist			
anti-Elitist		✓	non-Elitist			Elitist			
anti-Materialist		✓	non-Materialist			Materialist			
anti-Individualist		✓	non-Individualist			Individualist	✓		
anti-Ageist			non-Ageist			Ageist	✓		
anti-Conformist		✓	non-Conformist			Conformist			
anti-Escapist		✓	non-Escapist			Escapist			
Builds positive image of females/minorities		✓	Builds negative image of females/minorities				Excellent	Good	Fair	Poor
Inspires action vs. oppression		✓	Culturally authentic			Literary quality		✓		
						Art quality			

TO THE GREEN MOUNTAINS
by Eleanor Cameron
E. P. Dutton
$6.95, 180 pages, grades 7-up

The time: World War I; the place: a small unattractive Ohio town that is too hot in the summer and too cold in the winter. Kath Rule shares a room with her mother, Elizabeth, in a small hotel of which Elizabeth is the manager. The hotel's other help are Black.

Kath dreams of returning to the lush Vermont mountains where she and her mother had once lived. They moved to Ohio to be near Kath's ne'er-do-well and neglectful father, who operates a small, unsuccessful farm. He visits the hotel once a month to sleep with Elizabeth and filch some of her hard-earned money.

The complicated plot embraces Kath's coming of age, Elizabeth's divorce deliberations, interracial problems, a lovesick albino's agonies, and lots more. Although the atmosphere of this intricately woven fabric is often compelling, total success eludes the author. We are never clear about the basis for Kath's Vermont yearnings. Secondly, neither Kath nor Elizabeth seems to have changed significantly during the several years they have spent in Ohio. They arrived as non-conformist individuals, and so they depart, having made little impact on the lives of people around them.

The essence of their involvement with Tiss, a Black-and-beautiful ex-chambermaid, and her headwaiter husband, Grant, is disturbingly vague. While the author would have us believe that Kath and Elizabeth are free of prejudice (unlike the townspeople), a puzzling incident occurs: "One day she [Kath] had taken Grant's hand on one side and her mother's on the other and swung them . . . in a . . . moment of pure happiness. . . . 'If only Grant wasn't married I would like him for a father!' She would never forget how Mama stared at her. 'Don't ever let me hear you say a thing like that again! . . . Never speak of it to anyone, you hear me? . . . Such a thing can so easily be misunderstood no matter how innocently meant. . . .'" Is the author saying that the existence of racist attitudes in society obstructs "what might have been?" We don't know.

Throughout the novel, one must question the use of Black characters as a backdrop for white drama. Moreover, the presentation of white liberal attitudes without any representation of authentic Black viewpoints on racism, contributes to the perpetuation of paternalism.

	ART	WORDS		ART	WORDS			ART	WORDS	N.A.
anti-Racist			non-Racist			Racist	omission			
							commission		✓	
anti-Sexist		✓	non-Sexist			Sexist				
anti-Elitist			non-Elitist		✓	Elitist				
anti-Materialist		✓	non-Materialist			Materialist				
anti-Individualist			non-Individualist		✓	Individualist				
anti-Ageist			non-Ageist		✓	Ageist				
anti-Conformist			non-Conformist		✓	Conformist				
anti-Escapist			non-Escapist		✓	Escapist				
Builds positive image of females/ minorities			Builds negative image of females/ minorities					Excellent	Good	Fair	Poor
Inspires action vs. oppression			Culturally authentic			Literary quality			✓		
						Art quality					

AFTER THE WEDDING
by Hila Colman
William Morrow
$5.95, 189 pages, grades 7-up

Remember those old comic books about teenage romance, in which boys and girls meet, date, fall in love, get married and live happily ever after? *After the Wedding* effectively updates that perennial saga. In a smoothly flowing, down-to-earth style that should engage many teenage readers, Ms. Colman explores basic issues which affect all male/female relationships in our culture, with special consideration being given to the female perspective. Contemporary questions concerning female identity and the changing roles and responsibilities of husband and wife are handled here with sensitivity and realism.

Like so many young people, Katie and Peter are romantically idealistic in their approach to marriage and hold many false assumptions about one another. Both want to escape the hectic pace of city life, but for very different reasons which they fail to thoroughly discuss. Katie, who makes pottery, wants to live a simple country life—perhaps throwing pots for a living. Peter, on the other hand, regards the country as a temporary location where he can gain valuable experience and a reputation as a news reporter before venturing into the bigtime—New York City. These differences are dismissed as minor by the couple, caught up as they are in the excitement of True Love.

As the story progresses, the basic differences in their values become increasingly clear, until a definite conflict emerges. That conflict is intensified when Peter gets the chance to work in New York, and Katie at first chooses to stay in the country. Even the birth of a child fails to bridge the gap. Torn between conventional attitudes about a wife's duties to her husband and the intense need to express her own identity, Katie tries unsuccessfully to adapt to city life with Peter. Eventually, both partners come to accept emotionally what they had realized intellectually months before—that they have grown too far apart for the marriage to work.

The one criticism this reviewer has of an otherwise impressive book is the ending. The discovery of another woman's bathrobe in Peter's apartment frees Katie of any guilt about wanting to live her own life. Ms. Colman cops out here in favor of conventional justifications. Why should Katie feel guilty in the first place?

After the Wedding is an excellent account for teenagers of the contradictions which afflict many relationships between men and women today. The characters are fully drawn, readers are encouraged to evaluate the lifestyles and philosophies presented, and the tragedy which can attend people's failure to communicate on a practical level is well depicted.

	ART	WORDS		ART	WORDS			ART	WORDS	N.A.
anti-Racist			non-Racist			Racist omission				✓
						commission				
anti-Sexist		✓	non-Sexist			Sexist				
anti-Elitist			non-Elitist	✓		Elitist				
anti-Materialist			non-Materialist	✓		Materialist				
anti-Individualist			non-Individualist	✓		Individualist				
anti-Ageist			non-Ageist			Ageist				✓
anti-Conformist		✓	non-Conformist			Conformist				
anti-Escapist		✓	non-Escapist			Escapist				
Builds positive image of females/ minorities		✓	Builds negative image of females/ minorities				Excellent	Good	Fair	Poor
Inspires action vs. oppression			Culturally authentic			Literary quality		✓		
						Art quality				

HIGH 1975 RATINGS

OTHER NOTEWORTHY BOOKS

YOUNGEST BOOKS
Around and Around . . . Love
Hooray for Me

MIDDLE BOOKS
New Life: New Room
Paul Robeson
Sing to the Dawn
Song of the Trees

OLDER BOOKS
Dragonwings
Fast Sam, Cool Clyde, and Stuff
Founding Mothers
Garden of Broken Glass
Let Me Be a Free Man
Long Man's Song
Making Our Way
A Question of Courage

YOUNGEST BOOKS
Amy and the Cloud Basket
Becky and the Bear
The Girl Who Would Rather Climb
    Trees
The Quitting Deal

MIDDLE BOOKS
Arthur Mitchell
Contributions of Women: Education
An Eskimo Birthday
Last Night I Saw Andromeda

OLDER BOOKS
After the Wedding
The Cigarette Sellers of Three
    Crosses Square
Dust of the Earth
The Girl With Spunk
The Glad Man
I Cry When the Sun Goes Down
Julius Nyerere: Teacher of Africa
Ludell
A Man Ain't Nothin' But a Man
The Meat in the Sandwich
Winter Wheat
Women Who Win

FINDINGS

The 235 children's books published in 1975 which are herein analyzed by the Council on Interracial Books for Children are by no means a random sampling. We deliberately selected books on minority, feminist and social-issue themes because we fully believed that such books would reflect a conscious effort towards positive value content. In that respect, our selections were "stacked" to favor positive results. Using our own *Values Rating Checklist,* twenty-four per cent of these "better" books score favorably. (A truly random sampling of all of the 2,292 juvenile titles published in 1975 would show a markedly lower favorable percentage.) Thirty-nine per cent of the 235 titles scored negatively. (Again, in a random sampling, the negative judgments would undoubtedly reach into the ninetieth percentile range.)

In an attempt to determine whether other types of books contain human value messages which could be rated on our checklist, we analyzed and included in this volume one art book, one alphabet book, one math, one mystery, one animal story and one fairy tale. Also included are a few Native American legends, thirty-nine biographies and a handful of informational reports on such subjects as alcohol and oil. The remainder of the reviewed books were (as explained in the opening section of this volume) fiction dealing with minority, feminist or social-issue themes.

Quality

Based on the *Values Rating Checklist* in which literary and artistic quality comprise one part of an overall "score" that considers racism, sexism, ageism, elitism, conformism, individualism and escapism, we found 34 noteworthy books among the 235 examined. (Altogether, 57 of the books sampled received somewhat positive ratings; 85 were in the neutral range, and 93 were decidedly negative.)

Undoubtedly, additional books with positive value content appeared during the year 1975. Many nature, science, and biographical works must be worthwhile. But we are reasonably certain that most of the 2,292 juvenile titles concerning animals, sports, mysteries, adventure, fairy tales, romance and sci-fi would score considerably higher on the negative, than on the positive, side.

few books about working people or books which describe what work really is. We are tired of books that feature mothers, liberated or not, who are "artists." Why not a mother ("wonderful" or not) who types, is a factory worker or a housewife involved in social action? Why not women and men who are active in current controversies, movements for social change? Why not youngsters who are themselves activists, and who are learning that society can be changed for the better: Books on these themes are practically unavailable. We are not prescribing any limitation on themes, but rather suggesting that *any* theme can be explored in such a way as to elicit positive values. For whatever the outlook or actions of the protagonists in new children's books, the author is sending out obvious or subtle value messages on every page.

Conclusion

If we as parents, educators, librarians, writers or editors deliberately select books which contain positive human value messages, we will effectively impact on the quality of children's books and thus, on the quality of our future society.

INDEX

Titles

Illustrators

Books including Blacks or Africans

Books including Asian Americans or Asians

Books including Chicanos or Mexicans

Books including Puerto Ricans

Books including Native Americans

Books including Jewish People

Multicultural Books

Books about Death, Illness or Handicaps

Other publications available from the Council's non-profit Racism and Sexism Resource Center for Educators are:

Racism and Sexism in Children's Books: Ten articles	$2.50
Sexism and Racism in Popular Basal Readers: a feminist group report	$2.50
Racism in Career Education Materials	$2.50
Little Black Sambo: A Closer Look by Phyllis J. Yuill	$2.50
Stereotypes, Distortions and Omissions in U.S. History Textbooks: includes Content Analysis Charts	$7.95
Racism in the English Language: includes lesson plans	$2.00

Also available is an eighteen-minute sound and color filmstrip with cassette or record. It contains a group process curriculum kit suitable for human relations workshops and is called:

From Racism to Pluralism by Dr. Patricia M. Bidol	$32.50

Our regular publication, *The Bulletin,* reviews children's books and other learning materials for human value content.   Individuals $8.00
8 issues yearly   Institutions 15.00

A free catalog listing many more materials is available upon request.

**CIBC Racism and Sexism Resource Center for Educators
1841 Broadway, New York, N.Y. 10023**